D0805423

FIELD METHODS IN CROSS-CULTURAL RESEARCH

CROSS-CULTURAL RESEARCH AND METHODOLOGY SERIES

Series Editors

Walter J. Lonner, *Department of Psychology, Western Washington University (United States)*
John W. Berry, *Department of Psychology, Queen's University, Kingston, Ontario (Canada)*

FIELD
METHODS
IN
CROSS-
CULTURAL
RESEARCH

EDITED BY

WALTER J. LONNER
JOHN W. BERRY

VOLUME 8, CROSS-CULTURAL RESEARCH AND METHODOLOGY SERIES

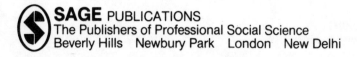

SAGE PUBLICATIONS
The Publishers of Professional Social Science
Beverly Hills   Newbury Park   London   New Delhi

For information address:

SAGE Publications, Inc.
275 South Beverly Drive
Beverly Hills, California 90212

SAGE Publications Inc.   SAGE Publications Ltd.
2111 West Hillcrest Drive  28 Banner Street
Newbury Park   London EC1Y 8QE
California 91320   England

SAGE PUBLICATIONS India Pvt. Ltd.
M-32 Market
Greater Kailash I
New Delhi 110 048 India

Printed in the United States of America

Library of Congress Cataloging-in-Publication Data

Main entry under title:

Field methods in cross-cultural research.

   (Cross-cultural research and methodology series; v. 8)
   Includes index.
   1. Psychology — Cross-cultural studies.   2. Psychology — Field work.   I.
Lonner, Walter J.   II. Berry, John Widdup, 1939-   ; III. Series.
BF76.5.F54   1985   155.8   85-18360
ISBN 0-8039-2549-2 (pbk.)

FIRST PRINTING

Contents

Acknowledgments

There are a number of people who merit special thanks for their roles in helping this book progress from an idea to the printed and bound word. The first to be mentioned are the chapter authors. Excluding ourselves (we were involved with three of the chapters), these people were given specific "marching orders " which were difficult to follow in the limited space that could be given for each chapter. That they did the required job very well is a tribute both to their talent and their patience. The second group of people to thank are the many researchers who participated in our initial survey of what to cover in such a book, and also those who made specific recommendations about coverage during workshops where an assessment of progress on the book was made. Without the kind of guidance provided by so able and interested people, this book would likely be out of balance, if indeed it were even publishable.

We also want to thank our respective universities for the support they provided. Meredith Jacobson of Western Washington University and Audrey Bailey of Queen's both typed two chapters and helped with various other tasks during the past few years. Pat Brown of Queen's University deserves special thanks for the central role she played in seeing to it that indexes were in good and useful shape, and that the integrated reference list was as close to error-free as possible. The editorial work on this book reached a crescendo while the first editor was on leave during the 1984–1985 academic year, associated with the University of the Saar in West Germany. Direct support provided by that university and indirect support provided by the Fulbright Commission and the Deutsche Forschungsgemeinschaft is gratefully acknowledged.

—Walter J. Lonner
—John W. Berry

7

For Marilyn and Joan

About the Series

The Sage Series on Cross-Cultural Research and Methodology was created to present comparative studies on cross-cultural topics and interdisciplinary research. Inaugurated in 1975, the series is designed to satisfy a growing need to integrate research method and theory and to dissect issues from a comparative perspective; a truly international approach to the study of behavioral, social, and cultural variables can be done only within such a methodological framework.

Each volume in the series presents substantive cross-cultural studies and considerations of the strengths, inter-relationships, and weaknesses of its various methodologies, drawing upon work done in anthropology, political science, psychology, and sociology. Both individual researchers knowledgeable in more than one discipline and teams of specialists with differing disciplinary backgrounds have contributed to the series. While each individual volume may represent the integration of only a few disciplines, *the cumulative totality of the series reflects an effort to bridge gaps of methodology and conceptualization across the various disciplines and many cultures.*

This book is the first in the series to be completely devoted to those methodological concerns that are most frequently confronted in cross-cultural research. As explained in more detail in the introduction, the content of the book, as well as the selection of chapter authors, was guided by a survey of seasoned, cross-cultural researchers. Although the book is intended primarily for the cross-cultural *psychological* researcher, the topics and issues are general enough and important enough to be equally useful to the cross-cultural researcher whose allegiance lies with an allied discipline, such as anthropology, sociology, or political science. And, as also noted in the introduction, the book can serve as both a text for upper-division undergraduate students, as well as the researcher who is planning to gather data in the field (or who may be already in the field).

As series coeditors, we take pleasure in adding this book to the series. As coeditors of the book, we are also pleased that it has become part of the series.

—Walter J. Lonner
Western Washington University
—John W. Berry
Queen's University

Preface

The field of cross-cultural psychology is, to a large extent, defined by its methods. Despite this, no current volume is available which brings together recent thinking and research into cross-cultural methods. The first book in the field (Brislin, Lonner, & Thorndike, 1973) is no longer available, while the second (Triandis & Berry, 1980) was cast at a rather high level, suitable more for scholars and graduate students than for field workers.

Our major goals with this book are to meet the needs of the field worker faced with a research question, and the teacher who is talking about research problems and issues in the classroom. The intent, therefore, was to provide field workers — both those actually in the field and those contemplating going into the field — with a handy, comprehensive, practical and up-to-date book which would contain helpful guidelines, background material and even some quite specific "how tos." The intended audience is psychologists and other behavioral scientists who would be sophisticated in many research areas, but not completely conversant with the central problems in cross-cultural research.

Once the decision to go ahead was made, and the length of the book established, we needed to determine content areas and enlist the aid of authors to cover each. There were two ways to go about determining content. One way was to be intuitive: decide by ourselves which topics *should* be in a methods book, and then invite experts in the selected areas to contribute. We opted for a second way, which was more empirical. We developed a list of twenty-eight methodological topics which seemed to us to be of importance to the field worker. We decided to carry out a survey of experienced researchers, asking them to rate the topics on a seven-point scale. The survey was sent to over a hundred active cross-cultural psychologists, and the high response rates and generally enthusiastic comments were helpful and encouraging.

The results of the survey told us that experts considered it very important to have chapters dealing with the underlying rationale for comparative research, the design and analysis of field studies, sampling, translation methods, testing and assessment, various procedures of systematic observation (including unobtrusive methods), and the logistics and problems of fieldwork. The chapters in this book parallel the results of the survey. The authors of each chapter are reasonably consistent with the recommendations provided by the survey respondents, who were also given the opportunity to suggest possible authors, themselves included.

The results of the survey also told us that there is great diversity of opinion regarding what should be included in a methods book oriented toward the cross-cultural field worker. For instance, we received recommendations to include chapters on dozens of topics. A sampling (aside from those already mentioned above): the study of adolescents; attribution of success and failure in different cultures; how to conduct research on substance abuse; principles of studying nonverbal communication; methodology for multigroup analysis; industrial and organizational behavior; studies of ethnic and minority groups in particular societies; physiological measures; nonverbal (pictorial) assessment methods; moral development; sex roles; how to study sexuality and family planning. The list could go on. While it would have been nice to accommodate even the most esoteric recommendation, it would also have been impossible to be so comprehensive. Thus the ten chapters in the book cover most of the important and generic methodological and substantive areas; perhaps to some extent these chapters can be viewed as "common denominators" of methodology. Thus nested within various combinations of chapters will be found important *guidelines* for research, but not a specific list of "how tos."

The development of the book was aided by those who participated in two workshops concerning its progress. These workshops were on the programs of two IACCP conferences:[1] the first in 1982 (Aberdeen) and the second in 1984 (Acapulco). A majority of chapter authors attended both meetings: at the first the overall design of the volume was considered and debated, while at the second authors presented summaries of their coverage and progress, and received helpful comments from those who represent potential users of the book. We thank those who attended these workshops, and we hope that they will see some of their comments reflected in the different chapters. If their ideas or suggestions were not incorporated it is because we could not adequately cover all recommendations.

As work on the book progressed, two factors emerged as stumbling blocks to an expeditious production of a truly useful field methods book. One factor was that many productive and knowledgeable people initially have every intention of completing all the jobs they take on, but apparently tend to overestimate what they can do. Several "deadlines" slipped by, resulting in a delayed publication. The more important factor that emerged relates to the *content* of the book and how useful it may be to the field worker. Looking back at our initial letters inviting people to contribute chapters, we said that we wanted to provide field workers with a "handy, comprehensive, practical, and up-to-date statement on how to conduct cross-cultural research in the field." The operative and contentious word in this statement of plans is "how." To many, this word meant that we intended to produce a cookbook, or a specific guide that would say something like this in various ways: "If you want to study the effects of modernization in Country X, then select samples of sizes Y, give them each Test Z, and analyze the data according to conventional statistical methods." It is clear to us that such a book as that cannot and perhaps should not be written, since it would necessarily be an imposition of a ready-made psychology on the local phenomena to be studied.

What the book does accomplish, we feel, is to give the relatively sophisticated and thoughtful field worker (not only newcomers, fresh from graduate school, but seasoned researchers as well) a reasonably comprehensive statement on epistemological and methodological issues, a review of what has succeeded for many and failed for others, and in general an overview of common concerns and questions that will be asked and that need to be answered during various phases of any cross-cultural research project. We beg the reader's indulgence, and we apologize for not producing the "perfect" field methods book. That remains for others to do after the flaws of the present effort are fully exposed, excised, and replaced by other material that the field worker will find indispensable.

The chapters are not uniform in style, depth of coverage, or use of references. This nonuniformity is attributable to two factors. First, contributors were given a summary statement of what their chapter should *basically* cover. Because experts in any field write best when unconstrained by the stylistic preferences of others we accepted any approach that was consistent with the goals of the book. Second, different topics require differing degrees of abstraction and technicality. For example, the underlying rationale for particular methods, or the psychometric theory behind particular tests, are inherently more difficult than observational methods. What you will read, then, are methodological statements and prescriptions that a panel of experienced researchers consider to be important. Our job as editors involved putting limits on length, seeing to it that the level of treatment was neither too high nor too elementary, cross-referencing, and trying to meet deadlines.

The chapters have been arranged so that broader, more methodological issues are placed first; this includes theoretical issues that are involved in cross-cultural comparison. Then follow some more concrete methods, including chapters on sampling (culture, communities, individuals, and behaviors), carrying out field work, problems of translation, and of using observations in the field. More substantive issues are then addressed, including how to assess abilities and aptitudes, personality and psychopathology, and social behavior. The volume ends with a chapter on acculturation, a necessary topic for two reasons: first, to avoid invalid interpretations of phenomena as due to cultural influences when they may have come about because of intercultural contact, and second, to render the volume as useful for the study of ethnic groups in plural societies as we hope it is for the study of independent cultural groups across nations.

Chapters 1 and 2 are concerned with somewhat complex methodological and theoretical details of cross-cultural research. The authors of these two chapters have done an excellent job of explaining these important matters. However, some readers may prefer to enjoy an appetizer or two before tackling such material. If the reader is not yet familiar with the special technical problems of cross-cultural research, we suggest reading Chapter 3 first, followed perhaps by a perusal of a few of the other more substantive chapters. Because each chapter is more or less an independent unit, this can be done without interrupting the "flow" of the book. Such an approach would probably help one understand the first two chapters much better when one returns to them.

A final introductory statement we wish to make concerns two basic ways in which the book can be used. It can serve as a textbook in classes dealing with considerations of whys and wherefores of cross-cultural psychology. If used in this manner, one of course need not go into the field to derive the benefits of each chapter, for there are as many substantive issues as there are methodological issues in the book; it can therefore be used as a springboard to discussing a wide range of topics in cross-cultural research. The second use of the book, and the main reason it was prepared, concerns its helpfulness as a methodological guide to research. While we would be flattered to think that cross-cultural researchers will take it with them on field trips as a general resource book, it is *essential* that it (or, more likely, it and a number of other books, articles, and other aids) be read long before leaving for the field. The very best cross-cultural research is well-planned from start to finish. This is not a cookbook, but it does cover the major issues and problems of method, and it should serve well as a resource or reference book while in the field. The best research done in cross-cultural psychology demands creativity, scholarship, preparation, and thoughtful reflection of the best way to deal with a specific research question. If this book serves as a stimulus for the satisfaction of these demands, then it will have served its major purpose.

—Walter J. Lonner
—John W. Berry

NOTE

1. International Association for Cross-Cultural Psychology.

1

MAKING INFERENCES FROM CROSS-CULTURAL DATA

YPE H. POORTINGA
ROY S. MALPASS

Cross-cultural psychology is about the explanation of differences — and sometimes similarities — in the behavior of people belonging to different cultures. Usually researchers are not just interested in a description of phenomena. Their purpose is to indicate how the phenomena come about, or what the consequences are. Empirical investigations are intended to have relevance beyond the events which are observed or the questions to which subjects respond. Hence the title of this chapter. We attempt to present a framework for drawing inferences about cross-cultural differences. In terms of the distinction between the "context of discovery" and the "context of justification" we deal almost exclusively with the latter aspect of research. Cross-cultural research would become sterile if our framework were rigidly adhered to. But we think that cross-cultural comparisons will benefit when researchers pay attention to the *kind* of issues we raise, whether they agree or disagree with our particular approach.

In the first section we briefly indicate our own methodological orientation which leans heavily towards a post-positivistic view as described in Cook and Campbell (1979). We make use of a distinction between five metaphysical models suggested by Eckensberger (1979).

Inferences or generalizations about cross-cultural differences in behavior as the consequent effects of sociocultural and ecological

factors[1] are the focus of this chapter. In the second section a
classification of inferences is presented and its rationale developed.
We suggest that inferences can be described as generalizations towards
a "universe."

The third section is concerned with the major difficulty in the
interpretation of cross-cultural differences: the elimination of
alternative explanations of a given set of results. We emphasize that
the onus is on researchers to protect their own interpretation against
plausible alternatives.

Making inferences is an inductive process. *A priori* conceptions
about the nature of cross-cultural differences will affect the choice of
a research topic, the way a study is carried out, and the kind of
inference which is drawn. Some (meta)theoretical notions pertaining
to the conduct of cross-cultural research are discussed in the last
section.

THE CHOICE OF A PARADIGM

The most essential characteristic of scientific investigation and the
one which makes it differ most strongly from nonscientific inquiry is
that scientific statements should lend themselves to empirical
investigation. This we take to mean that the correctness of a
statement can be evaluated against some alternative statement which
explains and predicts a different state of observable affairs. The rules
for evaluation which we think are most fruitful for cross-cultural
psychology are broadly those provided in the neo-Popperian or
neo-positivistic framework (e.g. Lakatos, 1970). Principles for
empirical research generally compatible with this approach can be
found in texts on experimental methods in psychology. We shall
assume that the reader is familiar with the general ideas underlying
experimental research design and also so-called quasi-experimental
research design, as presented in Cook and Campbell (1979).

This orientation may appear self-evident in an Anglo-American-
dominated field of behavior research, but it is not the only one
available. A serious challenge is contained in recent work by
Eckensberger (1979; cf. also Eckensberger & Burgard, 1983). On the
basis of arguments from ecological theory (Brunswik) and action
theory, the status of the experiment is questioned as the *via regia*
(Royal Road) to knowledge about the domain of reality called daily

life. In Eckensberger's opinion, cross-cultural research in particular has shown the limitations of the experimental approach. He argues that theories are not formulated exclusively with reference to objective data, but are based on metaphysical world views about the nature of man, and he maintains that any psychological theory reflects a metaphysical model. He distinguishes five such models.

Eckensberger's Five Metaphysical Models

The first metaphysical model allows only for descriptive relationships between the environment and an individual. The model is associated with the use of statistical tests and relationships, but devoid of substantive psychological theories. With no explicit theory to interpret observed relationships, these cannot be fitted into a cumulative and systematic body of knowledge. This is an important point to note in cross-cultural psychology where a naïve empirical realism is widespread; there is a tendency to interpret differences between cultural groups which are accidentally observed, in terms of variables which are hardly more than impressionistic labels. Since any two cultural groups will differ on a multitude of psychological dimensions, the interpretation of any observed intercultural difference which is not embedded in a fairly extensively validated theory can only be very tentative. As we shall argue in Chapter 2, the probability of finding a difference between any two culturally diverse groups with any psychological measurement procedure is rather high, and the information value of such a result is correspondingly low.

We also have experienced how convincing personal impressions can be, for example about the shyness of children in a certain community, or about their independence. The impression that Bushmen and Eskimo show remarkable adaptations in dealing with their environment is compelling, and one we share. But unless such impressions are substantiated in a properly designed and executed comparative research study, they more than anything else reflect an attitude of paternalism on the part of Western scientists and fall in the same class as nineteenth-century ideas about the intellectual inferiority of savages, which were also based on, to some observers, compelling personal observations. We do not question the value of personal impressions as a source of potential knowledge, but we do recommend circumspicious interpretation. Potential knowledge should not be confused with inferences whose validity has been demonstrated.

In the second metaphysical model distinguished by Eckensberger it is presumed that causal relationships between environmental and behavioral variables can be established. Learning theories are typical of psychological theories consonant with this model. It lends itself to the study of relationships between antecedent sociocultural or ecological factors[1] and consequent behavior, which is the major goal of cross-cultural comparative studies. The scientific paradigm of experimentation — which we have already indicated as our preference — is generally compatible with this metaphysical model. Eckensberger finds serious shortcomings with this metaphysical model as a paradigm for cross-cultural research. First of all, culture is treated as an antecedent of behavior, but there is no scope for the interpretation of culture, and particularly cultural change, as a product of human action and a concomitant of behavioral change.

Culture as a product of human action has not received much attention in cross-cultural psychology and, we think, for good reason. Culture as a human product transcends behavior as studied in psychology. Psychological laws presumably will reflect constraints on the rate of spontaneous cultural change and on the range of possible behavior patterns of individuals belonging to a viable human society. But psychological laws are insufficient to predict developments in cultural products such as fashion and artistic style, or the nature of changes in social norms and social institutions.

A second argument raised by Eckensberger is that concepts like "stimulus" do not refer to the subjects' real world, but to aspects of their environment. In our opinion neither psychology nor any other science deals with a complete real world. The content of science is an abstraction, each discipline taking a different perspective. Again, it is obvious that Eckensberger has opted for a broader view for which the boundaries of psychological science, as they are usually defined in cross-cultural psychology, have to be extended.

This occurs explicitly in the last three metaphysical models which Eckensberger introduces. In his description he mentions teleological elements to explain the development of organisms (which is influenced by but not caused by environmental conditions) and dialectical relationships between environment and individual, to do justice to the self-reflexivity of human beings as emphasized in action theories. To us such theories are acceptable as scientific theories, but only to the extent that they can be empirically tested in the sense described in the first paragraph of this section.[2]

The discussion of Eckensberger's work has led us to make some important distinctions and has enabled us to indicate the perspective from which we intend to approach major methodological issues of comparative cross-cultural research in the remainder of this chapter.

A CLASSIFICATION OF GENERALIZATIONS

Data in themselves are of interest only in purely descriptive studies, and Frijda and Jahoda (1966) made clear that these hardly exist. Generally the body of data gathered in an investigation is used as a basis for (tentative) statements about other events in addition to those observed, or other persons in addition to those who served as subjects. Hence, inferences based on such data can be seen as generalizations. It may seem that we put the cart before the horse by starting with inferences which, after all, are the end product of research. However, the kinds of generalizations researchers want to make determine the research designs they employ and the kind of data they collect.

Interpretations of the results of measurement procedures in cross-cultural psychology mostly refer to psychological characteristics in the behavior of individuals. When, for example, it is argued that the Eskimo are more field-independent than the Temne (Berry, 1966), this implies that an Eskimo is likely to show on more occasions behavior which can be classified as field-independent than a person belonging to Temne culture. It should be noted that there are other kinds of interpretation. For example, in sociology and cultural anthropology generalizations typically refer to social institutions.

In some cases the distinction whether a generalization points to a psychological attribute or to a nonpsychological category becomes rather fuzzy. When it is reported that Dutch secondary school children have less knowledge about physics than their Swedish age-mates, this is meant to reflect a difference in the educational programs of the two countries. But the conclusion can be transformed easily to read that a Dutch youngster is less likely to possess certain knowledge in physics than a matched Swedish counterpart. The lower level of knowledge is now phrased as a psychological characteristic of persons belonging to a certain group.

Another example may further illustrate the multiplicity of generalizations which can be derived from a single set of data. Parents in
developing countries more frequently than in industrialized states
want a large family. This can be interpreted in psychological terms,
stressing parents' needs and motivations such as love and affiliation,
but also in economic terms, emphasizing the economic value of
children for their parents' old age security in regions where societal
provisions such as old-age pensions are lacking (e.g. Kagitcibasi,
1982).

For our further discussion in this section we shall treat any
interpretation of results as a generalization towards a "universe."
Cronbach, Gleser, Nanda, and Rajaratnam (1972, p. 18) stated:

> A behavioral measurement is a sample from the collection of
> measurements that might have been made, and interest attaches to the
> obtained score only because it is representative of the whole collection
> or *universe*....This emphasizes that the investigator is making an
> inference from a sample of observed data, and also that there is more
> than one universe to which he might generalize.

Cronbach and his associates use two terms, *universe* and *population*.
Although in many respects they are interchangeable, *universe* refers
to a set of conditions for observation or items of measurement, while
population is used exclusively for a set of persons. Just as data can be
part of more than one universe, a person can belong to more than one
population, for instance those over thirty years old, the middle class,
the inhabitants of a certain country or region.

A measurement instrument for a particular universe can be
constructed by drawing a (random) sample of elements from that
universe. Such an instrument is of an inventory type. Most
personality questionnaires, attitude questionnaires and cognitive
tests are based on this principle. Typically the measurement scale of
an instrument is formed by the number of elements endorsed or
mastered by the subjects. Sometimes the stimuli or items in a scale
are ordered empirically according to some parameter, such as the
difficulty level of the items in ability tests, or the degree of preference
in Likert type attitude scales.

The approach presupposes that there is a sufficiently precise
description of the universe of interest. Strictly speaking, a precise
operational definition is required to decide which elements belong to

and which do not belong to a particular universe (Cronbach et al., 1972, p. 366 a.f.).

Extending this idea somewhat one can also consider a strictly operationally defined physical dimension, for example length, as a universe. In this example the measurement operation determines unequivocally the way in which elements in the universe are ordered. In psychology an ordered scale can be constructed on the basis of a theory from which a rule can be derived as to how elements should be related to each other. In that case the theory can be tested through investigating the fit of observed data to the theoretically predicted scale (e.g. Coombs, Dawes, & Tversky, 1970). For the remainder of this section it is important to note that both empirically and theoretically derived scales are taken to represent a universe.

Distinctions between Universes

From the point of view that all inferences are about universes of behavior, there are three important distinctions. The first is whether a comparison is made on the basis of a universe which is identical across cultural populations or whether universes are compared which contain different elements. The pitch scale of pure tones is an example of a scale which refers to the same universe (the set of pure tones) everywhere. The sets of words making up different languages constitute different universes.

A second distinction has to do with the sampling of elements which constitute the scale to represent a universe. Occasionally a whole universe is included in a measurement procedure (e.g. all basic color words in a language). We can then speak about comparison at the universe level. But we also do this when a representative sample of elements is selected from a more or less homogeneous universe for the purpose of forming a scale. Presumably it will make little difference for the scores on a psychophysical scale which one of various subsets of stimuli is selected, provided they all have about the same range and stimulus intervals. In other instances the choice of tasks or items to represent a universe can make a considerable difference, for example the choice of visual illusions to assess "illusion susceptibility." We then speak about the comparison of selected elements.[3]

The third distinction is between universes which refer to psychological characteristics such as traits or processes and universes which refer only to behavior outcomes (responses). It is related to the distinction between *attributes* of behavior and the *repertoire* of actions which is at the disposal of a person (Poortinga, 1975). Essential to an attribute-linked universe is a mental process or trait which theoretically is common to the behavior outcomes in terms of which the universe is measured. The term repertoire refers to a universe of responses which is not inferentially linked to internal traits or processes.

An overview of the three distinctions is given in Table 1.1, on the left side. Together they form eight categories which have been labeled A–H. On the right-hand side of Table 1.1 examples are given of studies which fit (more or less) the various categories.

Let us examine in somewhat more detail the comparison categories C and G where selected elements from a universe form an assessment instrument and the generalization is to a domain of manifest behaviors. An example falling in category C is a universe called geographical knowledge. The set of elements in the universe can consist of the names of countries, major cities, and geological features of the world. The score on a sample of items drawn from this universe forms a measure of geographical knowledge. The interpretation of a difference in score distributions between two cultural groups is straightforward when the measure is taken as an achievement test. Zero scores in illiterate societies would accurately reflect a low level of geographical knowledge.

When a universe is defined in terms of manifest behaviors, but the universes are not shared among cultural groups (category G), no comparison is possible. Examples are universes containing local knowledge about local plant and animal life in various regions. These are universes the definition of which is clearly dependent on the location of a population. If the average score on a local flora and fauna test were 70 out of 100 items in one group and 80 out of 100 in some other group, this would be insufficient information to infer — for instance as a sign of adaptation — that the one group has more knowledge of its biological environment. To derive this conclusion one first would have to define a *common scale in terms of which the comparison could be made*. For example, one could ask anthropologists and missionaries to draw up lists of the 100 most important plants and animals for any local region in the world and declare scales based on these lists as adequate comparison scales.[4]

TABLE 1.1
A Classification of Cross-Cultural Universes

Universe of Generalizations	Comparison Category	Example		
		Domain	Measurement Instrument	Interpretation of Cross-Cultural Findings
Identical universe — Representative sample of elements ⟨ repertoire	A	Physical dimension	Mapping color words onto Munsell color scheme	Co-occurrence of basic color terms across languages (Berlin & Kay, 1969)
attribute	B	Physical dimension	Pitch discrimination task	Differences in pitch discrimination ability (Oliver, 1932)
Selected elements ⟨ repertoire	C	Shared educational domain	Geography test	Differences/similarities in educational achievement
attribute	D	Visual illusions	Mueller-Lyer figure	Perceptual strategies (Segall, Campbell, & Herskovits, 1966)
Nonidentical universe — Representative sample of elements ⟨ repertoire	E	Lexicon	Vocabulary test	Differences/similarities in size of vocabulary
attribute	F	Lexicon	Semantic differential technique	Linking locations in EPA space to cultural factors (Osgood, et al., 1975)
Selected elements ⟨ repertoire	G	Nonshared educational domain	Local fauna and flora test	Uninterpretable
attribute	H	Personality traits; abilities/attitudes	Embedded figures test; California Psych. Inventory	Differences/similarities in traits

The *definition* of a comparison scale does not create major problems when there is an identical universe shared by the various cultural groups (categories A–D), because any instrument which is an adequate representation of the universe can serve this purpose. This does not mean that no systematic errors can be made in the interpretation of actual data. Intergroup differences can result from method artifacts, caused by a lack of understanding of the task by members of some group(s), interaction with a foreign experimenter, etc.

As far as nonidentical universes are concerned, a reasonable claim can be made to the effect that a comparison scale can be defined when all the elements in the respective universes are known and either the entire universe (e.g. all adjectives in the lexicon), or a representative sample, are used for its measurement (categories E and F). This rationale seems to be compatible with the work on affective meaning in which a set of adjectives was used and in which by way of the Semantic Differential technique the dimensions of Evaluation, Potency and Activity were identified in a large number of countries (Osgood, May, & Miron, 1975).

These arguments lead to the conclusion that, with the exception of those falling in category A, all intergroup comparisons are — in various degrees — open to erroneous interpretation. We shall further discuss this point in Chapter 2.

Cross-Cultural Comparisons of Hypothetical Constructs

So far we have hardly touched on the last category, H, which is the most common in cross-cultural psychology. To this category belong psychological attributes such as traits and processes, which usually are referred to as "hypothetical constructs." Just as in category G, the set of manifest behaviors covered by a particular concept is unlikely to be the same across cultures. Moreover, the range of behaviors from which "intelligence" or "anxiety" could be inferred in any culture would be very extensive and phenomenally diverse. The rationale for finding a common scale for comparison across cultures may in fact seem quite insurmountable.

However, the idea of hypothetical constructs is not far removed from the idea of universes. According to Carr and Kingsbury (1938, mentioned in Fiske, 1971, p. 32), we first qualify behavior with adverbs (he acted intelligently), then we use adjectives (he is intelligent) and later discuss nouns (he has a lot of intelligence). This appears to indicate that attribute qualities are originally attached to manifest behaviors.

In order to measure a hypothetical construct we usually do not make an effort to draw a representative sample from the relevant universe. Rather we construct a scale based on a small subset of behaviors, which from a theoretical point of view (or intuitively!) capture the essential aspects of a psychological quality. In this way a paper-and-pencil test consisting of items, in which three-dimensional sets of blocks have to be rotated mentally, can be taken as a measure of the hypothetical construct "spatio-visual ability" which is manifest in a far wider range of behaviors than those included in the test.

In cross-cultural studies very frequently comparisons in terms of attribute-linked universals are made despite obvious repertoire differences. The instruments used apparently are assumed to reflect the theoretical universe because they contain allegedly "essential" or "critical" elements of that universe. Other strategies can be followed. On the assumption that important individual differences will become encoded in the language, Goldberg (1981) has recently revived the idea of taking the lexicon as a basis for deriving personality dimensions. However, such alternatives are exceptions so far.

Most cross-cultural comparative studies belonging to category H in Table 1.1, therefore, can be described as follows. The universe of interest is indicated by a hypothetical construct. Any person in any culture presumably has a score value on a hypothetical scale representing the construct. The construct is measured by means of procedures which yield an observed score variable with a score for each subject. In a valid measurement procedure the relationship of the scale of an observed score variable to the hypothetical construct scale is described by a transformation function. This transformation function is usually assumed to be a monotonically increasing function (for more details cf. Poortinga, 1971, 1975a, b). Several possible functions relating an observed score scale to the underlying hypothetical construct scale are presented in Figure 1.1.

We have now arrived at the following situation:

1. There is a hypothetical construct scale which serves as the comparison scale common to the cultural groups of interest. If extended to all cultures, the hypothetical construct scale is a universal.

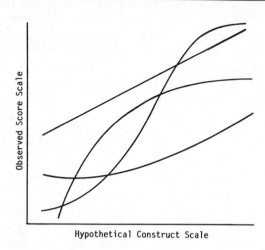

Figure 1.1   **Some Possible Transformation Functions Describing the Relationship between a Hypothetical Construct and an Observed Score Variable**

If extended to all hypothetical constructs and all cultures the assumption can be seen as a psychometric equivalent of the "psychic unity of mankind" idea.

2. There is an observed variable scale in each culture, derived from some measurement procedure applied to subjects. The measurement instrument may consist of the same items or observation categories across cultures, or it may be different from culture to culture.

3. There is a functional relationship between the observed score scale and the hypothetical construct scale. "Bias" or "lack of equivalence" can be defined as an inequality across cultures in any parameter of this relationship.

As both the hypothetical score variable and the transformation of each culture are not known, matters have to be simplified in order to make a cross-cultural comparison. Table 1.2 summarizes various approaches to the category H problem which are present in the cross-cultural literature.

TABLE 1.2
A Summary of Approaches for Interpreting Cross-Cultural Data Reflecting a
Hypothetical Construct

		Hypothetical Variable Scale	*Transformation Function*	*Observed Variable Scale*
H(i)		Identical by definition	Assumed identity	Identical
H(ii)		Identical by definition	Identity checked empirically	Identical
H(iii)		Identical by definition	Identity checked empirically	Different
H(iv)	a)	Identical by definition	Assumed identity	Identical
	b)	Different?	Unspecified	Different
		Different?	Unspecified	Identical
		Different?	Unspecified	Different

H(i): Identity of the hypothetical variable scale in two or more
cultures is assumed and the same or a closely similar instrument is
administered to all subjects. "Lack of equivalence" or "bias" (cf.
Chapter 2) is not analyzed, which means that the transformation
function of the hypothetical score scale to the observed score scale is
also assumed to be identical across cultures. It should be noted that
when comparisons are made in terms of an observed score scale —
and this is most common — it is implicitly assumed that the
transformation function between the hypothetical construct scale and
observed score scale is the same in the cultures which are compared.
In these cases there is not much point, of course, in distinguishing
between a hypothetical scale and the scale of an observed score
variable. Examples of studies in this category are abundant, for
example the work by Berry (1966) referred to earlier, Hofstede's
(1980) comparison of cultures on the basis of questionnaire items,
and studies involving personality variables based on the Human
Relations Area Files. That the scores in the latter case are not
obtained via self-reports of subjects, but indirectly via the rating of
ethnographic reports does not matter in this context. Although for
some of the work in this sub-category statistically sophisticated
methods are used — where, for example, comparisons are made on
the basis of factor scales rather than raw scores — it remains a
shortcoming that the possibility of scale bias cannot be ruled out.

H(ii): Identity of hypothetical constructs is assumed and closely similar instruments are administered across cultures. However, from additional analyses the researcher tries to infer whether or not identity of the transformation function can be reasonably assumed across the cultures to be compared. An early example of this approach is Irvine's (1966) computation of the correlation between item difficulty indices obtained in two cultures. Recent examples include Van der Flier (1982), Lord (1980), and Hui and Triandis (1983).

H(iii): Identity of hypothetical scales is assumed, but the operationalization, i.e. the measurement instrument, may be different from culture to culture. Through a process of construct validation in each culture it is established whether the phenomenally different instruments measure an identical hypothetical construct. This approach is prominent in the writings by Triandis (e.g. 1972). An example is a study by Davidson et al. (1976) in which nonidentical questionnaires were developed in Mexico and the USA to assess intentions concerning fertility behaviors in the two countries. As there is no one-to-one correspondence between the items or observations forming the observed scales in different cultures, the range of techniques for detecting differences in the transformation function is more limited than with the previous approach. However, allowing for formally different manifest behaviors, the range of possible instruments is far broader (Malpass, 1977).

H(iv): Identity of hypothetical attribute scales is assumed for some behavior, marked H(iv)a. There are apparently universal aspects which can be assessed with identical instruments which have identical transformation functions. This is the same as in approach H(i). Other aspects of behavior are seen as culturally specific and unexplainable in terms of common hypothetical constructs. These are indicated as H(iv)b. According to Berry (1972, 1979a) the two kinds of aspects can be separated out in a series of studies. The status of culture-specific hypothetical variables is not clear from Berry's writings, hence the question mark in Table 1.2.

The two other subcategories mentioned in Table 1.2 actually do not belong to category H. They are added to indicate that the idea of identical hypothetical construct variables is not shared by everyone. In fact, the terminology we have employed is not adequate for interpretations of differences based on the phenomenological understanding of behavior. Examples are Culture-and-Personality studies in which differences in behavior organization are concluded to exist on the basis of identical instruments such as the Rorschach or TAT (cf. e.g. Watrous & Hsu, 1972). Ethnographic studies can be mentioned as an example of an approach in which observations in one culture are compared with *a priori* knowledge about some other culture(s). The observed variable scale is clearly not the same in these areas. It should be noted that in most Culture-and-Personality studies the common scale in terms of which comparisons are made is based on subjective notions of the researchers which are not accessible for objective empirical scrutiny. Such studies fall outside the scope of this chapter.

In the following sections we shall elaborate on the implications of various approaches, notably those in category H. Subcategories H(ii) and H(iii), in our opinion the most defensible approaches, will be emphasized.

There is one important aspect in which universes differ that we would like to comment on; namely, that they can be defined at various levels of inclusiveness. A relatively small universe would be the set of arithmetic problems of the type $3 + 5 = 8$. Such a set could be used to assess the achievement of a child after a few months of arithmetic training. The same set of problems could also be used to assess a much larger universe; namely, a child's aptitude to learn arithmetic, although inferences about this much larger domain would probably not be very valid.

In the same sense one finds in cross-cultural psychology explanations of performance differences in terms of rather specific cultural experiences (Serpell, 1979; Serpell & Deregowski, 1980), in terms of trait-like concepts (Vernon, 1979) or even in terms of broad conceptual labels such as innate intelligence or social conformity. A scheme with relationships between cultural conditions and behavior at four levels has been proposed by Berry (1980). A framework with three types of inference about cross-cultural differences (i.e. to domains defined in terms of behavior content, to traits and to psychological mechanisms) has been suggested by Poortinga (1982). A distinction between low and high inference has been mentioned by Irvine (1983b). The level of inclusiveness at which a universe is defined has important implications for research strategy, and particularly for the kind of procedures necessary to support inferences from data to the theoretical universe of interest.

PROTECTING INFERENCES

Empirical researchers assume the task of constructing studies in such a way that the desired inferences can reasonably be attempted. An important part of this burden is the protection of inferences by excluding or evaluating their alternatives. This is a familiar process in psychological research, particularly in laboratory settings. Part of the challenge of experimental research is the attempt to identify and "control for" as many potentially confounding factors as possible. This is not only a matter of procedural control.

At least as important is the confounding of effects which are associated with different theoretical accounts of the responses that form the dependent variable. One need not only think of theories competing with the one held by the investigators; there also may be diverse, empirically established sources of influence such as age or social status that may reasonably be expected to have an effect in a wide range of research domains. Theoretical alternatives to the explanatory hypothesis on which the research is focussed, that are not themselves the object of investigation, should be either excluded or measured in order to make the observations interpretable. In this section we will go a little more explicitly into some of the reasoning behind the various approaches to eliminating plausible rival hypotheses in a cross-cultural investigation. But first we shall introduce some terminological distinctions.

The variables that are of central concern in a particular study we will refer to as the *focal* variables. There are two classes: those which are thought of as theoretically prior we will refer to as *focal antecedents* and those later in time, and theoretically dependent on antecedents we will refer to as *focal consequents*. The propositions which link these variables to each other and to other theoretical entities we will refer to as the *focal theory*.

There are other factors to be considered, from low levels of theoretical development (like order of presentation of stimuli), to high level alternative theoretical accounts of the empirical results obtained. Social desirability is often a competing interpretation where responses to various verbal or written measurement scales are concerned. Intelligence is offered as an alternative to theories about variation in cognitive skills or styles. These we will refer to as *ambient* theories, that is theoretical positions, antecedent variables, or consequences that are not considered within the context of the focal theory, but which can reasonably provide an alternative explanation for observed differences.

The problem in cross-cultural research is not the identification of differences between groups in some focal aspect of behavior (cf. Chapter 2), but rather to protect the scientific value of these differences by making them interpretable (Malpass, 1977b). The line of thinking that lies behind this claim goes as follows:

1. The inference that a consequent focal difference is in some way dependent on some antecedent focal difference requires that ambient differences be excluded as sources of the consequent difference;

2. The greater the number of existing antecedent ambient differences that can plausibly be proposed to account for a potential consequent focal difference, the greater the *a priori* probability of empirically observing the consequent focal difference;

3. The greater the *a priori* probability of observing a consequent focal difference, the more ambiguous is the theoretical meaning of the difference. If a difference can have occurred for a variety of reasons, how are we to say which reason is validated by its occurrence?

4. Reducing the ambiguity of interpreting a difference requires reducing the number of antecedent differences (focal and ambient) that can plausibly be used to account for the observed consequent difference.

5. In principle, one cannot exclude any antecedent factor that has not been brought into the study at some level or another, or whose relationship to the focal consequent difference has not been investigated.

The Identification of Antecedent Variables

In order to protect desired inferences, data collection must be structured so as to isolate the focal antecedent from alternative interpretations of the observed effects on the focal consequent variable. To do this one must first identify these alternatives, and plan for data collection in the two or more cultural locations in a way which allows the isolation of the focal antecedent. As indicated already, we will distinguish between *measurement* issues — issues in the construction and internal structure of data, including their construct validation — and issues in the *design* of a study intended for making comparisons across time or across groups. An illustration is presented in Table 1.3. The example in the right hand column of the table is based on the illusion studies of Segall, Campbell, and Herskovits (1966). They hypothesized that habits of perceptual inference underlie such geometrical illusions as the Mueller-Lyer figure and that these inference habits result from visual experience with one's environment.

They predicted that persons whose visual experience has been exclusively with a material culture in which buildings, furniture and other objects are not carpentered (have few "square" corners), will not have strongly developed the inference habits which contribute to

TABLE 1.3
Some Measurement and Design Issues, with an Example

The General Case	*The Case of Illusion Susceptibility*
A. Measurement Issues	A. Measurement Issues
Equivalence, including effects of: — stimuli or item familiarity — response repertoire — the measurement situation (motivation, social interactions)	Equivalence — simple stimulus format — instructions to improve task comprehension — instruction for experiments in field manual
Validation	Validation — degree to which the Mueller-Lyer results are consistent with those of other rectangular illusions
B. Design Issues	B. Design Issues
Method confounds	Method confounds — distinguishing high susceptibility from a lack of understanding (inclusion of extreme stimuli, balanced presentation order)
Substantive confounds — specific competing theories — general variables (e.g. social desirability, intelligence)	Substantive confounds — degree of retinal pigmentation in respondents' eyes
Focal antecedent [Project-specific]	Focal antecedent — degree of respondents' experience with carpentered environments
C. Unexplained Variation	C. Unexplained Variation

the Mueller-Lyer illusion. On the other hand, those whose visual experience has been with strongly carpentered environments would show high susceptibility to the Mueller-Lyer illusion. They tested this proposition by administering to persons from environments of different degrees of "carpenteredness" an illusion test consisting of a set of Mueller-Lyer figures with different degrees of actual discrepancy between the pairs of line segments.

At the early stages of planning an investigation such as this, one has only a vague idea of what the final measurement of the consequent variable will actually be. Its final form reflects the outcome of decisions about various questions which arise during planning. Consider, for example, that an individual's response to a single illusion item (e.g. choosing which of the two components of the Mueller-Lyer Figure has the longer horizontal bar) is a function of many factors. This response can be taken to reflect the respondent's susceptibility to rectangularity illusions (the class of illusions that Segall et al. reasoned were affected by variations in the world's carpenteredness) only under certain conditions, as follows:

1. The particular illusion figures should be shown to represent the class of illusions known as rectangularity illusions.

2. The stimulus materials and the response task should be constructed so that the groups which are to be compared can be equated with respect to such effects as their familiarity with the stimulus materials, and the social relationships required in the course of the measurement task. Alternatively, these effects can be measured or their presence detected and protocols containing these analyzed separately. By including stimuli with large differences between the two horizontal bars Segall et al. structured their measurement materials so that severe misunderstandings of the materials and tasks could be detected. Various other response strategies were also taken into account. This was done by arranging the order of presentation and by the counterbalancing of the location of the longer of the two segments, so that any systematic preference of figure, position, or simple alternation in response would be detectable in the raw data record. An internally consistent response pattern was visible when the response pattern was reconstructed according to the scale values of the stimulus materials. Through the careful construction of the pattern of the items in data collection Segall et al. were able to render implausible a large set of potential procedural confounds.

3. Alternative substantive explanations for the intergroup differences can be eliminated. This can be clearly illustrated in the case of research on illusion susceptiblity and the carpentered world hypothesis, since in subsequent studies evidence was found that the degree of the respondents' retinal pigmentation was related to illusion susceptibility. Studies designed to allow a choice between retinal pigmentation and the carpentered world hypothesis showed that when pigmentation was held constant, predicted variations in illusion susceptibility were found, associated with environmental variations (for a review cf. Segall, 1981).

This is a simplified presentation of even this fairly straightforward research program. For our purposes, however, it should be noted that before inferences about illusion susceptibility can be drawn on the basis of responses to Mueller-Lyer figures, one must have a means of isolating the illusion susceptibility factor. This was done in the present case by eliminating procedural confounds through design of the materials, focussing selectively on forms of the stimulus materials that appeared to best represent the carpentered world hypothesis, on the basis of *post-hoc* analysis, and examining the competing retinal pigmentation hypothesis in a series of subsequent studies.

We can easily generalize beyond the example. Between the observation of a difference between two or more cultural groups and the inference that the causative factor responsible is some focal antecedent, lies the treacherous problem of anticipating and eliminating alternative plausible rival hypotheses.

The above discussion has omitted the concept of "culture" as an antecedent variable, focal or otherwise. The reasoning behind this is straightforward; as an explanatory or descriptive category, culture cannot be adequately controlled. Because it is so full a category, because its connotations are so rich and varied, by itself it says very little, very specifically. This is not to say that we reject the idea that cultural comparisons are scientifically useful in psychology, or that we reject the idea that there are important issues focussing on the extent and locus of cultural differences and similarities in psychological and social processes. But thinking about "culture" as a singular variable that stands in an antecedent relation to specific response variables is destined to be unproductive. Rather, theoretical categories or dimensions that are contained in or which are part of what is called cultural variation are the entities of interest — the more so when they are explicitly linked, conceptually and empirically, with behavior. This matter is discussed in more detail below.

SOME THEORETICAL NOTIONS CONCERNING METHOD

In cross-cultural psychology we attempt to describe and explain differences and similarities in behavior *in terms of* psychological concepts *with reference to* ecological and sociocultural factors. Notions about the nature of these factors are likely to influence the way research is carried out. In this section we look at some implications of a few selected viewpoints.

We assume that there exists some consistent reality of environmental and behavioral events, and that an important goal of empirical psychology is to construct increasingly useful accounts of that reality. While the methodology is the same for comparative research across cultures as for other areas of empirical psychology, the difficulties, issues and strategies differ in important ways.

Human behavior may well be largely uniform across cultures in the most concrete sense of the term "behavior." The considerable cultural uniformity of concrete physical actions appears to have led Harris (1964) to choose these as the basic level of analysis in his approach to the specification of what he called "cultural things." But Harris's interest immediately went beyond this level of analysis, using uniformities at this level to define higher level units of behavior which were both less universal and more structured as to actor, time, space, and context.

For many social scientists it is at a higher level of analysis at which behavior appears to be diverse. This is the level of social interaction (Barker, 1963; Whiting, Child, & Lambert, 1966) and material culture (objects/artifacts). Variations in customary interpersonal behavior practices, variations in material culture and in the meaning of social interactions give rise to the cross-cultural differences in behavior which are often immediately obvious even to the untrained observer. But these manifest differences may also be thought of as common, mundane, and of themselves trivial. The claims made by cross-cultural researchers are that there exist differences in more super-ordinate categories of behavior associated with cultural variation, or alternatively that despite these manifest differences there exist few really important differences in psychological functioning. Thus, a

major issue of cross-cultural research in psychology becomes
apparent; in the face of manifest differences inferences will be made
about either the presence or the absence of differences in more
abstract categories. To support claims that certain manifest differences are irrelevant while some other differences are important,
requires careful attention to the premises on which investigations and
inferences are based.

The Universalistic Viewpoint

Cross-cultural psychology is seen by some as a method which is
relatively easy to apply, but often has shown haphazard results,
because of the lack of theoretical foundation in much of the empirical
work. Sechrest (1977a, b; cf. also Brown & Sechrest, 1980) has
argued that rigorous and explicit theories are needed for a well-
founded choice of the cultures to be included in a project and the
selection of relevant variables. But Sechrest does not necessarily
want cross-cultural psychologists to construct their own theories.
These should rather be taken from mainstream psychology and be
tested for validity cross-culturally. One can ask whether this
validation is a meaningful exercise. In a paper which has elicited quite
a few comments (Jahoda, 1980; Taft, 1976; Triandis, 1976),
Faucheux (1976, p. 274) argues that a theory by definition is
universal.

> But to the extent that a theory is understandable by researchers from
> other cultures, and assuming that a universal theory of human social
> behavior is possible, it is not immediately clear why a theory aiming at
> formulating universal propositions and being experimentally substan-
> tiated in a given culture should need further testing in other cultures.

Faucheux does admit that it may not be possible to use the same
empirical procedures everywhere in a proper test of the theory, but
he appears to treat this as a minor problem. It is easy to agree with
Faucheux's opinion that any theoretical postulate refers to, or at least
should refer to, universal psychological concepts. However, in
empirical research, the theory may be consistently supported in one
culture and consistently refuted in another, because the conditions
for a proper test were wrongly specified in at least one of the two
cultures. There are two possibilities: either the positive results are
based on some confounding (ambient) factor which falls outside the

specified range of convenience of the theory, or the negative results are caused by some confound. Strictly speaking, the theory should be shelved in both cases until the issue is resolved.

As inconsistent results are found more often than not — at least so it seems to us — universal validity cannot be assumed for psychological theories without empirical testing. To do otherwise places one outside of the scientific enterprise. An almost cynical warning by Finifter (1977, p. 155) underscores this point.

> Failure to reproduce a finding in the *same* culture usually leads the investigator to question the reliability, validity and comparability of the research procedures used in the two studies for possible method artifacts. But failure to corroborate the same finding in a *different* culture often leads to claims of having discovered "cultural" differences.

Universality of theories in Faucheux's sense is an epistemological postulate, which does not mean that a particular theoretical statement has universal validity after attempts to falsify it have not been successful in two or more cultures. Rather, we take it, the postulate is meant to imply that hypothetical constructs as formulated in a particular theory can be represented by identical hypothetical construct scales across all cultures. This corresponds with the approach outlined earlier (cf. Figure 1.1 and related text). Faucheux does not consider the transformation from the hypothetical construct level to the level of observable behavior a serious problem, because "a theory always defines more or less implicitly the conditions to be met for a proper test" (1976, p. 274). In contrast, we believe this transformation should be seen as a major problem, and we agree with Jahoda (1980, p. 122) that theories tend to be formulated in culture-specific operational terms.[5]

The approach to cross-cultural comparison most frequently adopted is the one captured by Strodtbeck (1964) in the dictum "culture as a treatment." It is based on the premise that cultural factors can be seen as independent variables in an experiment. An individual's cultural experiences in respect of any of these factors can be viewed as a treatment condition in the sense of an experiment. Different cultures can then be represented by different values on a scale according to the level of treatment they provide in respect of a specific factor. In other words, each culture may be considered as a stimulus condition in an experimental paradigm. This position, like

Faucheux's appears to disallow, on an *a priori* basis, culturally specific psychological concepts.

If behavior is explained exclusively in terms of universal categories and concepts it is not immediately clear how culture-specific behaviors (i.e. behaviors which are not found everywhere, like material offerings to deceased forefathers) can be integrated meaningfully into a theory. The concept of "adaptability" as introduced by Biesheuvel (1972) can be used to illustrate a way to approach this problem. Central to his argument is that humans have to adapt to various demands and, depending on the circumstances, some behaviors serve better than other behaviors. According to Biesheuvel the concept of intelligence is strongly connected to specific (Western) operationalizations. Adaptability has a more formal meaning and is not so much associated as intelligence with certain kinds of tasks.

However, this approach has a serious problem. The level of abstraction of "adaptability" is so high that it is not obvious whether a particular kind of measure forms an adequate operationalization. Imagine that with some measure of adaptibility (or intelligence for that matter) it was found that people in one or the other culture attain zero scores. Most likely the researcher would reject the instrument as a suitable operationalization of the concept, rather than challenge the scientific status of the concept. Abstract and global concepts are not very open to empirical control, and it can be argued that the cross-cultural validity of such concepts is beyond empirical falsification (Van de Vijver & Poortinga, 1982). Thus, it appears that a universalistic point of view, allowing no culture-specific concepts, can easily lead to untestable global concepts.

The Nonuniversalistic Viewpoint

Cross-cultural psychology can also be seen as a substantive area of psychology, and "culture" as inextricably woven into the psychological making of a person. An implication is that the concept of culture does not only encompass sociological or anthropological distinctions, but also has relevance as a psychological concept. In this perspective a culture is taken as a system with complex interrelationships between variables, rather than as a collection of treatments each one of which can be set apart to serve as an "independent" variable in a study. In the sense outlined earlier, this amounts to stating that there are hypothetical construct scales which are not universal but specific to a particular (set of) cultural population(s). However, when it comes to specifying what in the way of hypothetical constructs is culture-specific and how the culture-specific can be distinguished from the universal, divergent views are found.

One position is that of "radical cultural relativism" (Berry, 1972, 1981). Cultural relativism originally referred to an ethnographer's attempts to describe behavior in another culture without imposing his own ethnocentric evaluations. As Segall et al. (1966, p. 17) state: "he reminds himself that his original culture provides no Olympian vantage from which to view objectively any other culture." Berry (1972, 1981) has extended this point of view to pertain also to hypothetical constructs, taking the position that "for some character-istics of populations it is more appropriate not to assume psycho-logical universals across groups." Mentioning "intelligence" as an example, Berry argues that "any characterization . . . should be relative to the particular adaptive requirements [of the cultural context], rather than to some assumed universal dimension" (1981, p. 397). Triandis (1972, 1980a, b) and Brislin (1980), among others, have taken a less radical position. Triandis is fairly pragmatic about the distinction between the culture-specific and the universal. Data, concepts, and measurement procedures as they are found in a particular culture may be culture-specific, but they may also be found to be appropriate for more than one culture. There appears to be no clear *a priori* criterion by which to distinguish the culture-specific from the universal, or — to use Triandis' terminology — to distinguish the *emic* from the *etic*. At the level of small universes of manifest behaviors differences are obvious. But Triandis (1972, pp. 38–9) argues: "To the extent that the salience of a dimension is different in two cultures it may not be appropriate to make cross-cultural comparisons unless they are made at a higher level of abstraction on which a common dimension can be found." We agree that concepts at a high level of abstraction can easily be perceived as similar across cultures, but have argued above that they are not very open to empirical analysis. Here we shall pursue somewhat further the nonuniversalistic approach.

The idea of culture-specific concepts leads to problems when it comes to explaining actual data in terms of a culture-specific psychological theory. Inasmuch as explanation is specific to a single culture one might expect that the relativistic viewpoint leads to separate explanations, that is to separate psychological theories for different groups. Berry (1981) has argued that *etic* and *emic* aspects of behavior can be separated iteratively in a series of empirical studies. Aspects of behavior which cannot be explained in general psychological terms are labeled as culturally specific as it were *per exclusionem*. Methodologically one can raise the objection that in a comparative study culture-specific aspects and measurement error show a remarkable similarity (Poortinga, 1982).

More serious in our opinion is the objection that also in empirical research the distinction between specific and universal remains unclear. We provide an example, which is, perhaps, the most widely quoted on the *etic–emic* issue. It concerns the concept of *philotimo* which, according to Triandis (1972, 1980b), is prevalent in self-descriptions of Greeks. *Philotimo* has to do with conformity to the norms and values of one's ingroup. Triandis points out that the precise meaning is not easy to define for persons of other cultures, among other things because ingroups are defined in a particular way and the ingroup–outgroup distinction is attributed great importance (compared to the USA). However, a description of *philotimo* is given by Triandis (1972, pp. 308–10) and it appears that none of the essential aspects of the concept defies explanation for readers from another culture. Thus, the explanation of *philotimo* appears to rest on concepts which are not specific to Greek culture. The example in our opinion can be considered as an instance of a general rule, namely that psychological explanations are *always* made in terms of "characteristics" which are not culturally specific, but which are presumably universal.

If we now go back once more to Berry's radical cultural relativism and the example of intelligence, it may be noted that he is not writing about intelligence in the sense of the competence "to solve new problems" or "to deduce new relationships." Apparently Berry is not denying that abstract high-level universes are universal — neither does anyone else for that matter (cf. e.g. Cole et al., 1971, p. 214; Cole & Scribner, 1974) — but the problem seems to be with universes which contain a narrowly defined specific set of manifest behaviors. In the classification of generalizations we proposed earlier on, these would fall in comparison category G of Table 1.1.

In Triandis' approach, the data somehow decide whether universes of category G or category H are being dealt with. If the data by a weak test fit a common model (i.e. if better than chance predictions within the model can be made in each of the groups to be compared, even if the predictions are based on different measurement procedures) the data *post hoc* are taken to belong to category H. It may be noted that in our opinion stricter tests — requiring not only a common model, but also a common scale — are required for quantitative comparisons of data.

When it is accepted that a concept belongs to category G, so-called culture-specific phenomena can be observed. However, for a nonshared universe no comparison scale can be specified. Thus, a concept in category G cannot be operationalized so as to yield equivalent data. In our universalistic view its scientific usage should be abandoned or its meaning changed. Biesheuvel's suggestion to replace intelligence by the adaptability concept is an example of the latter strategy. If one realizes that contemporary psychology is likely to reflect Western conceptions in many theories and concepts and in many operationalizations, extensive reformulations are needed, if psychology is not to fall apart in different sociocultural psychologies.

The relativist position has particularly suffered from scathing attacks by Jahoda (1977, 1980, 1983). He has quite clearly demonstrated inconsistencies in the use of the *etic–emic* distinction and indicated why this pair of terms can be replaced by the contrast culture-specific versus universal. One of the reasons Jahoda mentions which makes the *etic–emic* dichotomy a poor prospect for cross-cultural psychology is that it originally was used by anthropologists in the context of the study of cultural systems. According to Jahoda cross-cultural psychologists do not study systems or parts of systems, but rather relationships between variables within systems. This appears to imply that of the two global approaches to cross-cultural psychology, viz., culture as a composite of treatments in the Strodtbeck sense, and culture as a system, the first one is to be preferred.

Emphasizing Similarities across Cultures

In the arguments considered so far, differences in measurements of behavior as a reflection of differences in larger universes, influenced by antecedent cultural conditions, have been the focus of attention. According to Jahoda (1980, p. 111) "The question of the extent to which basic psychological processes are common to mankind is still

perhaps *the* major one being pursued in cross-cultural psychology."
Emphasis on similarities in human behavior is increasing (cf. Warren,
1980). The search for universals can be seen as a concomitant of this
tendency. In a recent review, Lonner (1980) has mentioned a variety
of concepts from biology, linguistics, anthropology, and psychology
which have been postulated to be relevant for the explanation of
behavior in all cultures. He discusses seven categories of universals,
which have been collected from a variety of perspectives and
viewpoints. The universals mentioned vary considerably in the range
of phenomena which they encompass and the status which can be
attributed to the respective theories on which they are based, if there
is any theory at all in the formal sense.

Lonner writes about a taxonomy of universals, but the organizing
principles for distinguishing between the categories, or for that
matter within the categories, are still vague. So-called universals
appear to differ particularly in the extent to which they are accessible
to objective empirical analysis. Recently an attempt was made to
classify categories of universals according to the degree to which they
lend themselves to this kind of analysis (Poortinga, 1982; Van de
Vijver & Poortinga, 1982). Implicitly attributing universality status to
each theoretical concept, Van de Vijver and Poortinga distinguish
four classes viz: (1) conceptual universals, i.e. theoretical notions at a
high level of abstraction such as adaptability or sensotypes (Wober,
1966); (2) weak universals, i.e. concepts for which construct validity
has been demonstrated in different cultures; (3) strong universals,
i.e. concepts for which an (interval) scale exists so that intracultural
differences between measurements taken on different occasions can
be compared cross-culturally; and (4) strict universals, i.e. concepts
which can be compared across cultures on an identical scale.

Possibly a classification like the one mentioned may lead to a better
distinction of what is common and what is different in behavior across
cultures. After all, similarity and difference are only the two sides of
one coin. Van de Vijver and Poortinga (1982) argue that the
dichotomy between universals and culture specific aspects of behavior should be replaced by a dimension in which the *degree of
invariance* of data between cultural groups can be expressed.

Although we cannot offer much to support this opinion we think
that universality and similarity will gain further importance. Further
advancement of these notions will probably depend to an important
degree on the introduction in cross-cultural comparative psychology

of ideas about similarity and other scaling concepts as found in contemporary mathematical psychology. At the same time it may help cross-cultural psychology to overcome the dilemma between universal and specific as discussed in this section.

Many of the difficulties which we have described in this section appear to reflect unclarity about what, from a psychological perspective, has to be understood under the term "culture." The plea by Jahoda (1980) and others for a more extensive analysis of this concept would seem timely and to the point. However, also on this topic there is disagreement. Segall (1983), in a chapter aptly titled "On the Search for the Independent Variable in Cross-Cultural Research," has argued that culture is not our problem, but rather it is "to identify the various factors in the natural and man-made environments of humans which influence their behaviors in reliable ways." (In passing it can be mentioned that this may not be a bad definition of "culture" as a psychological concept, at least if the term man-made includes social environments.) The attraction of this strategy, mentioned earlier by LeVine (1970), is that researchers start with differences in dependent variables which are considered important and worthy of explanation. To the solution of methodological problems of explanation it does not (and is not meant to) contribute much.

Summarizing this section, we have emphasized that researchers should carefully consider at what level of behavioral complexity they are focussing their study. We have made a distinction between approaches where "culture" is seen as an antecedent condition affecting parameter *values* in theories or measurement instruments and approaches where "culture" is seen as codetermining the very *definition* of the parameters. We found that on the one hand there is a tendency towards the use of universal concepts in explanation, while on the other hand such universals tend to escape proper empirical control. We elaborated on the distinction between universal and culture-specific and suggested that it can be accounted for in the classification of inferences we developed above. Finally, we suggested that the recent trend to emphasize similarities rather than differences in the behavior of people belonging to different groups may well be a worthwhile development, although the status of "culture" in cross-cultural psychology remains unclear.

NOTES

1. Instead of "sociocultural and ecological factors" we shall use the term "cultural factors." Also, we shall use the phrase "comparison between cultures" to refer to "comparison of measurements obtained on groups of subjects belonging to different ecologically, socio-culturally, or racially identifiable groups."

2. We like to emphasize that statistical tests and mathematical relationships can only be formulated at the level of Eckensberger's first metaphysical model, independent of the kind of model underlying the theory being tested. Similarly, the inference of a cause from an observed relationship is only compatible with the second metaphysical model. Although the inference of cause is a matter of debate in the philosophy of science, we shall assume that this is legitimate in a proper experiment (cf. Chapter 2). Functional and dialectical relationships as postulated in the last three metaphysical models can only be empirically investigated in an indirect way. Statements have to be formulated in terms of the second model (cause) or the first model (relationships between observable variables). It may be noted explicitly that these reductionistic views are not shared by Eckensberger. To prevent any misunderstanding, we do not deny the reality of phenomena which Eckensberger wants to encapsulate. We only see the realm of scientific research in psychology as more restricted than he does.

3. It can be argued that this second distinction refers to the universe from which stimuli are sampled rather than to the universe of (response) generalization. This formulation in its consequences does not differ from the one we adhere to. There can be a close correspondence between the stimulus universe and the universe of generalization (representative sampling) or the stimulus universe can only match part(s) of the universe of generalization (selected elements).

4. Offering this as an example does not imply that we would recommend the procedure.

5. Those who consider this distinction between theory and operations a heresy, will probably have to accept culture-specific theories, a point of view to be considered later on.

2

STRATEGIES FOR DESIGN AND ANALYSIS

ROY S. MALPASS
YPE H. POORTINGA

In this chapter we try to deal with some of the consequences of the framework outlined in Chapter 1 for design and analysis in cross-cultural comparative studies. Our choice of topics is to some extent arbitrary. The emphasis is on hypothesis testing rather than on exploratory research and the descriptive interpretation of striking phenomena which a researcher may observe in other cultures. Not all areas of cross-cultural research are equally represented. Much of the literature on the analysis of comparability or equivalence has its origins in the field of ability testing and this is reflected in the text, although we maintain that comparability is a key problem in all cross-cultural studies. Even within our self-imposed boundaries there are notable omissions. For example, developmental studies are rarely mentioned despite the fact that longitudinal data offer several opportunities to protect inferences against alternative explanations. Our excuse is that development and change are methodologically obstinate (Adam, 1978; Roskam, 1976) so their treatment largely falls outside the scope of this book.

A more serious limitation is that we often point out pitfalls without indicating precisely how to avoid them. Here our excuse is that few general rules exist that can point one's way to errorless research design and implementation. Finding creative solutions to evade or overcome methodological problems transcends methodology. In this respect it is the very difficulty of cross-cultural research that makes it so challenging.

In the first part of the chapter we mainly, though not exclusively, deal with problems of design. In the first section we discuss why the traditional approach—in which a null hypothesis is tested stating that no intergroup difference will be found—should be seen as unrealistic in a field where the requirements of the experimental paradigm cannot be met. In the second section we elaborate on this argument, indicating why cross-cultural psychology also does not meet the conditions for quasi-experimental research. Approaches are differentiated with respect to two factors: the kind of control over antecedent variables available to the investigator, and the degree to which subjects are exchangeable between conditions. The third section deals with strategies for reducing the number of alternative interpretations of data, while the fourth section is a discussion of alternative ways to construct the research hypothesis. Briefly discussed are some advantages and disadvantages of a research strategy in which one is looking for similarity in the values of statistics, rather than emphasizing differences. A section on sampling which would have fitted here has been omitted because sampling problems are dealt with in the next chapter.

The last three sections of the present chapter are devoted to problems faced by cross-cultural psychologists after initial data collection; how to rule out effects of measurement "bias" or "lack of equivalence." In the fifth section we briefly describe various meanings of "equivalence," and in the sixth section requirements for equivalence are formulated and some of their implications discussed. A distinction is offered amongst three categories of bias, viz. stimulus bias, method bias, and universe bias. In the final section we attempt a brief overview of various statistical tests to analyze the three forms of bias.

THE SHAKY NULL HYPOTHESIS

The *a priori* probability of rejecting the null hypothesis in cross-cultural comparative research is often so high that a hypothesis of no intercultural difference cannot be considered a meaningful alternative to a research hypothesis which stipulates a difference between certain groups. An implication of this view is that the empirical support for many interpretations of observed cross-cultural differences is far less well established than it appears to be.

To support and clarify this assertion we will briefly examine the rationale for null hypothesis testing. Usually the research hypothesis is accepted when the null hypothesis can be rejected as being improbable to a specified degree. The observed difference to which the hypothesis pertains is then attributed to the effect of some specific factor which was postulated beforehand. This is a reasonable presumption in studies where subjects are randomly allocated to different experimental conditions and the differences between these conditions are restricted to changes which are introduced and more or less completely controlled by the investigator(s). It is normally not a reasonable presumption in cross-cultural research, where the allocation of subjects is determined by their membership in a specific cultural group and the observed differences between cultures follow from antecedent conditions on which the researcher has exercised no influence. Since cultures tend to differ from each other in many respects, it is in principle possible to propose a large number of ambient interpretations for any observed focal difference. Although not all explanations are equally plausible, it remains quite likely that one of the many possible ambient alternatives could be given preference over the focal explanation. This point has been emphasized repeatedly in the cross-cultural literature, notably by Campbell (1964) and by Sechrest (1977a, b; Brown & Sechrest, 1980), and appears to be well recognized. At the same time, the impact of this knowledge on actual research projects seems to have been rather limited. Alternative explanations appear to be treated as possible in principle rather than as plausible in practice.

The Limitations of Replications

When testing the null hypothesis two errors can be made. The first, called Type I error, occurs when the hypothesis is wrongly rejected. The second, the Type II error, is made when the hypothesis is actually false, but not rejected (e.g. Hays, 1973). The *a priori* probability of the two major types of statistical error is exactly known in an ideal experiment. The degree of accuracy can be improved by increasing the number of subjects or by replication studies; that is, the margin of error can be reduced, provided sufficient effort is invested. However, these are strategies for gaining better estimates of a central value concealed in a distribution of error variance. To the extent that the ambient factors are themselves stable across subjects or across assessment procedures, larger samples and replications will serve only to increase the stability of the biased estimation of the population difference, since all the data would have the existing biases in common. Consequently, extensions of projects with larger samples, and replications which are not implemented independently from ambient antecedent factors, will show similar differences as observed originally. In fact, increased sample size contributes to an increased confidence in an erroneous rejection of the null hypothesis. In this way the probability that an observed difference is erroneously attributed to a "real" cultural factor can increase when the body of data is enlarged.

This is illustrated in Figure 2.1, where the probability is depicted that a statistically significant difference between two samples is observed given a certain bias effect. The figure reflects the so-called "power" of the t-test to detect differences between two means. It is

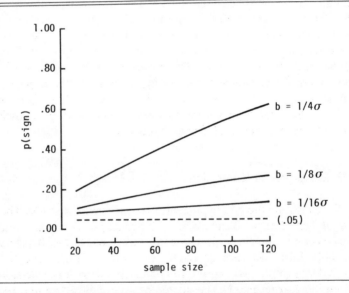

Figure 2.1 The Probability (p sign) that for a Certain Sample Size an Observed Significant Difference ($\alpha \geqslant .05$) will be Found between the Means of Two Samples ($n_1 = n_2$), Given a "Bias" Effect (b)

shown that the probability increases with the size of the bias (b) and with sample size. Of course, when b represents the "real" effect of the cultural factor under investigation the same graphs apply. But the point at issue is that the null hypothesis (stating that no difference on the focal variable exists) becomes a meaningless proposition if the possibility of even a small systematic bias cannot be ruled out. For larger sample sizes the probability of finding a difference exceeds 0.10 (i.e. twice the value of x) even when the bias effect is as small as one sixteenth of a standard deviation unit. With more bias in the data the dice become progressively more loaded towards rejection of the null hypothesis.

Because the notion underlying Figure 2.1 is an essential one, we will summarize the preceding argument. In a proper experiment sources of variance which are not related to the treatment are assumed to be eliminated. If this assumption is met, extensions and replications lead to more accurate estimation. However, "bias"— which serves as a collective label for all unwanted sources of variance differentiating between groups—has a systematic effect that will not disappear when additional data are collected. So long as similar bias effects are operating across extensions and replications, a wrong interpretation will be reinforced.

In a "literal" replication, measurement procedure, sampling, and experimental conditions are held constant as far as possible. In "constructive" replication the method is deliberately changed (cf. Lykken, 1968). In order to make clear what forms a replication in this sense and what does not, sufficiently explicit theoretical notions about the phenomena of interest have to be available. In cross-cultural research one has to realize that some sources of bias have an effect over a wide range of methods. Take for example a comparative study between an illiterate and an educated group in which literacy is not the variable of interest. To find psychological measurements which are not affected by this variable will be extremely difficult if not impossible. These considerations are particularly important in view of the rapid advance of meta-analysis, the approach in which results from a number of similar studies are combined to assess their joint outcome.

With respect to any concrete hypothesis it is difficult actually to demonstrate that the null hypothesis is not viable. To show the validity of such an opinion in a particular instance would require extensive additional research. However, we contend that in view of the high *a priori* probability of ambient factors contributing to observed differences, the likelihood of erroneous inference is so high that in general the results of cross-cultural comparative studies cannot be taken seriously if alternative explanations are not explicitly considered and, preferably, excluded on the basis of empirical evidence. We feel strongly about this point since it can be argued that the high probability of finding differences in the long run will tend to have cumulative effects on our insights about the impact of cultural variation on behavior.

SOME ISSUES IN DESIGNING CROSS-CULTURAL STUDIES

Cross-cultural psychologists appear to believe that their studies meet the requirements of the experimental paradigm, or, at least that cross-cultural research is "quasi-experimental" in the sense of Cook and Campbell (1979). The major problem with this belief arises directly from the complexity of culture as a treatment. It has been argued in Chapter 1 that any focal antecedent variable is rivaled by a number of other variables (ambient antecedents). The effectiveness of any research strategy depends to an important degree on the extent to which controls are used to exclude ambient explanations of dependent variable observations which may compete with the focal antecedent. The concept of control has four meanings in this context:

1. Control over the assignment of treatments to the units of replication, i.e. persons or groups of persons;
2. Control over the treatments themselves, i.e. what form they take;
3. Control over remaining differences (confounds) between experimental units by equating and thus eliminating the differences (e.g. through randomization or balancing), or/and
4. Control by measuring and statistically adjusting for the differences.

Assignment of Subjects

The most effective strategy for eliminating in advance the effect of many alternative antecedent variables is through the use of a proper experimental design, which embodies the first three senses of control noted above. The true experiment, successfully implemented, eliminates rival alternative hypotheses through the random assignment of subjects to treatments. But perhaps more important for its implications for cross-cultural psychology, a proper experiment eliminates many confounding factors without the necessity of investigators knowing about them, and without their effects having become part of the focal theory. With the random assignment of subjects the effects of many confounds are randomly distributed across treatments and thereby canceled out. However, cross-cultural investigators cannot gain control of which persons receive which cultural "treatment," and cannot manipulate "treatments" independently of other antecedent "cultural" variables. Therefore they cannot attain the requirements of a proper experiment. This is important to note. It means that the powerful inferential strategy of the proper experiment is not available for a cross-cultural study unless it meets the requirements of the experimental paradigm. Therefore we can protect the inferences we wish to make from only those threats which we have been able to bring into the theory and have been able to specify operationally.

The Concept of Exchangeability

There are many research settings in which an assessment is needed of the effects of contrasting treatments given to groups which are nonequivalent to begin with. These are called quasi-experiments, and there is a growing body of literature for them (Cook & Campbell, 1979). Samples are not "equated by chance" (Campbell & Stanley, 1966, p.2) when allocation of a subject to a treatment depends on pre-existing group membership (e.g. a school class in a curriculum evaluation study).

The "nonequivalent" groups in a "quasi-experimental" study are usually selected from a population which in terms of pre-treatment differences is homogeneous compared to the range of variation found across cultures. Consider the set of variables in terms of which the subjects in different groups can be distinguished from each other. In a proper experiment a subject is randomly allocated to a particular treatment, which means that he could just as well have been allocated to another treatment. This amounts to perfect exchangeability of subjects between treatments. In a quasi-experiment conducted within a homogeneous population a high degree of exchangeability can be achieved for all but a limited set of imaginable classification criteria. For example, being a pupil in a certain school class implies having a certain teacher, living in a certain neighborhood and maybe belonging to a certain religious denomination. In cross-cultural research the set of variables by which a subject can be identified as belonging to one of two cultures, and not to the other, could include being a member of an extended family, having been raised under the responsibility of a maternal uncle, being illiterate, living in a forest, and attributing an animate existence to major objects in the environment, among other things. Consequently, the exchangeability of subjects is low. The degree to which subjects are exchangeable, and especially the classification criteria which separate existing groups from being highly exchangeable, are important considerations in the design and interpretation of cross-cultural studies.

Control on Treatments

In both experimental and quasi-experimental studies the researcher can provide an operational description of the package of stimuli which contributes a particular treatment. In quasi-experiments the risk of erroneous interpretation tends to be associated with the prevalence of uncontrolled factors exercising an effect on some treatment group(s) in addition to the treatment as presented, rather than with a lack of knowledge about what forms the intended treatment.

The quasi-experimental designs of Cook and Campbell are oriented towards evaluation of specific treatments applied by the researchers to nonequivalent groups. Cross-cultural comparisons are concerned with the presumed behavioral effects of the initial nonequivalence, conceived of as a treatment. Other treatments—introduced differentially within the different cultures—are not generally studied.

Only in some studies are important confounds of the focal dependent variable recognized and taken into consideration. When we attempt to draw inferences about the cause of mean differences observed within what Campbell and Stanley (1966) called the "static group comparison" and Cook and Campbell (1979) called the post-test-only design with nonequivalent groups: "any post-test

TABLE 2.1
Representation of Empirical Studies differing in the Degree of Control on
Treatment Conditions and in the Assignment of Subjects

		Control over Treatment and most Ambient Events	Control over Treatment but over few Ambient Events	"Post hoc" Knowledge of Treatment
CONTROL ON SUBJECT ALLOCATION	Random Assignment of Subjects to Treatments	Experiment in strict sense	Time series experiments	
	Group Membership with Weak Effects on Exchangeability	Quasi-experiment with one data collection session	Quasi-experiment with treatment extending over time	Post-treatment measurement
	Group Membership with Strong Effects on Exchangeability		Differential changes over time	Cross-cultural comparative studies

differences between the groups can be attributed either to a treatment effect or to selection differences between the different groups. The plausibility of selection differences in research with nonequivalent groups usually renders the design uninterpretable" (Cook & Campbell, 1979, pp.98–99). The recommended solutions to this difficulty all have to do with the introduction of one or another pre-test measure (or pre-test surrogate) so that a pre- and post-measure comparison can be examined. But with most "cultural variables" it is not conceptually clear what a pre-test would be. Therefore, we are stuck with the difficult problem of interpreting the effects of treatments we cannot control.

In Table 2.1 we present a scheme with the two dimensions along which control can vary, that is, treatment and subject allocation. Quite arbitrarily we have distinguished three levels on each dimension. Most of the entries will not require further comment. The empty top right-hand cell indicates that it does not make good sense to do research with *a priori* allocation of subjects and only *post hoc* knowledge about treatments. Of more importance in the present context is the empty lower left-hand cell. This reflects that in cross-cultural psychology, where group membership and the holistic nature of cultural treatments are inextricable, an experiment in the strict sense of the word does not appear to be feasible. Either the difference between cultural groups is relevant but the antecedent cultural variable is uncontrolled, or the group difference is not relevant for the variable under investigation. But then we are dealing essentially with the situation represented in the middle cell of the left-hand column, an instance of little cross-cultural interest. If we accept that our knowledge about treatments is largely *post hoc*, the focus of attention falls on the last column of Table 2.1. In the middle cell reference is made to intracultural studies with only post-treatment results. Despite methodological weaknesses the approach is indispensable for psychology.

Controls in Cross-Cultural Research

We are left with the third and fourth control strategies as the ones open to us: "control" by equating, or by eliminating effects through statistical procedures. When we ask about the effects of culture or cultural variables considered as treatments we usually have neither the power of the experiment nor the inferential leverage of the quasi-experiment to help us. The major strategies left for protecting the inferences of interest depend on taking specific procedural steps to eliminate or measure differences aside from the focal antecedent which may be used as alternative interpretations of consequent differences. Not all of these can be anticipated, and ruled out in advance. Segall, Campbell, and Herskovits (1966), for example, did not anticipate the later suggestion that variations in retinal pigmentation could provide an alternative interpretation for their results (Pollack, 1970). New research was designed to test this possibility which showed that there was an effect of "carpenteredness" with pigmentation held constant (Stewart, 1973). Had the investigators been able randomly to assign individuals to develop perceptually in carpentered or noncarpentered environments, retinal pigmentation and many other alternatives to the carpentered world hypothesis would have been taken care of summarily. It will be useful to reflect on the great degree to which cross-cultural research must remain separated from the inferential power of the experimental method, and the degree to which even a simple investigation must be conceived of as a program of research.

Since cross-cultural psychologists in principle have no control over the independent variables, that is, the effects of cultural factors on behavior, they can only make *post hoc* inferences. This does not always mean that convincing evidence is out of reach, only that it may be more difficult to acquire than in areas of psychology where problems can be studied within more homogeneous populations, and with control over antecedent conditions.

STRATEGIES FOR REDUCING ALTERNATIVE INTERPRETATIONS

The overall strategy for improving the quality of evidence amounts to ruling out plausible alternative interpretations which compete with the focal one. There are some general strategies for reducing the number of alternatives that appear viable both with respect to independent and dependent variables. We will touch on these briefly below, taking the dependent variables first.

Mean scores derived for culturally different samples of subjects are vulnerable to the effects of a large set of ambient antecedent differences. To avoid this problem the researcher should ask questions in such a way that the outcome of comparisons is not dependent on the values of sample means. There appear to be two approaches for accomplishing this:

1. to use a comparison scale on which mean differences have no effect, e.g. a scale for *relative differences* (statistical interactions, or difference scores), or
2. to formulate questions in such a way that no actual comparison of data is required.

Before continuing we would like to introduce a distinction between studies in which the same instruments and measurement procedures are used and studies in which different stimuli and responses are applied in separate cultures. The term "same" needs a further qualification. Translated verbal materials which have the same meaning, in our view, are included, provided the original wording is re-established with a high degree of accuracy in a procedure of translation and back-translation by independent translators. For more precise information on translation procedures, the reader is referred to the extensive work of Brislin on the subject (Chapter 5 in this book and Brislin, 1976). It has been shown that equal lexical meaning does not guarantee that bias in the instrument as a representation of some hypothetical construct is necessarily absent (Brislin, 1976).

The advantage of equal instruments is that the results are accessible to a variety of analyses on equivalence, to be discussed later in the chapter. This advantage has to be sacrificed if it is obvious beforehand that insistence on formal equalities of procedures will lead to inequivalent results. However, an investigator who uses different methods in the different cultures in an investigation is obligated to show empirically that whatever cross-cultural differences are uncovered should not be interpreted in terms of these method differences.

Comparison of Inferences

A case in which the comparison is only remotely linked to data is exemplified in Hutchins' (1980) study among the Trobrianders in which he argues that the cultural context determines the incidence of certain cognitive processes. From an analysis of the proceedings of a local court case dealing with a land ownership dispute, he infers that arguments reflecting inductive reasoning are used. Although the evidence is indirect, the analysis is interesting. Reduced to the psychological essentials, however, it only confirms the notion that all human cultures practice inductive reasoning. Hutchins provides only a weak evaluation of an ill-defined theory. Neither cultural conditions that would constitute a quantitative independent variable scale nor a dependent variable beyond a dichotomy are provided.[1]

Stronger comparisons of inferences can be undertaken. One can more rigorously test the "fit" of a theory or model in a society other than that where it was developed by carrying out parallel experiments in the different cultures. Hill's (1964) study of mathematical concept learning in American and Ghanaian children can serve as an illustration. The applicability of the stimulus sampling theory developed by Estes was investigated. A number of hypotheses derived from assumptions underlying the theory were tested in each of the two groups. Hill suggests that the fit of the model is adequate in both cultures.

These findings support the validity of the model under different cultural conditions and at the same time provide evidence that the methods used are appropriate.[2] Also, positive evidence for the construct-validity of the tasks has been found cross-culturally. In the second half of this chapter we shall see that this is a necessary but not a sufficient condition for a meaningful comparison. Hill rightly pointed out that a quantitative comparison of the results of the two groups would be highly invalid, because of differences in experience with the stimulus materials used in the study.[3]

Let us suppose for a moment that Hill found negative results with respect to the fit of the theory. In that case the conclusion might have been that the task performance variables did not reflect identical hypothetical constructs. Whether this should have been attributed to culture-specific aspects of the theory or to method bias would have remained an open question. Nevertheless, Hill's study shows that parallel experimentation can be informative even though it does not enable the researcher to make inferences about quantitative inter-cultural differences.

Relative Differences

There are many quantitative scales on which a cross-cultural comparison can be made. Among them is a scale on which the differences between mean values for the cultures are displayed. There are other scales such as the percentage of variance accounted for by various manipulations, the magnitude of relative differences, or interaction effects, etc. The set of confounding factors which differentially influence the levels of means between cultures is different from the sets of factors which might differentially influence other comparison scales. Where possible, relative differences rather than absolute differences should be studied.

In a relative differences design, group levels are compared on a variable obtained through a combination (difference, or ratio) of two or more measurements rather than on the results of a single measurement. The idea is to use sets of instruments or observations which are similar in all respects (notably the nature of the questions or stimuli and the response procedures), except for a certain critical difference which is intentionally manipulated. In this way the researcher may circumvent the effects of many unwanted sources of variance which might be expected to affect absolute score levels, but not differences or interactions (Poortinga, 1971).

An example is an experiment by Cole, Gay, and Glick (1968) on the identification of conjunctive, disjunctive, and negation concepts by American and Kpelle children. The same stimulus material and the same response procedure were used for the three concepts. The subject was required to select one of two answers in each of a number of trials. Which of the two was correct depended on which concept the experimenter had in mind. The authors concluded that American children learn conjunctive concepts more easily than disjunctive concepts while there is no difference for Kpelle children. It may be noted that this conclusion is based on the interaction between the factors "Type of Concept" and "Culture of Subjects" in an Analysis of Variance design, and does not refer to an overall difference between the two groups (which would be expressed as a main effect of culture in ANOVA terms).

There are other variations possible on the relative differences design. Keating et al. (1981), studying the perception of social dominance from facial expression, used two series of slides, A and B, in each culture. The score of series A observers was the number of times the "lowered brow" model was selected from two contrasting (low brow–raised brow) poses. For observers in series B the score was the number of times the same models were selected but with raised brows, since models reversed poses between series. Any deviation from a 50 percent score in the series A sample which would not be matched by a similar deviation in the opposite direction in the series B sample would have thrown serious doubt on the validity of the measurement procedure. At the same time, the 50 percent score point can be seen as a natural anchor point for the scale.[4] The interpretation of Keating et al. that larger deviations (both being in the expected direction) represent a larger value on the dependent variable, appears to be valid under these circumstances.

For other examples of studies in which relative rather than absolute differences are emphasized we refer the reader to the literature (e.g. Jahoda et al., 1976; Cole, Gay, & Glick, 1968; Poortinga & Foden, 1975; and Poortinga & Spies, 1972).

Assessing the Independent Variable

If researchers expect a cross-cultural difference as the result of some antecedent cultural variable, they should consider it one of their major tasks to demonstrate that the cultures indeed provide the antecedent difference, in Strodtbeck's (1964) sense (cf. also Segall, 1983, 1984). This can be seen as an attempt to validate the independent variable. Sampling of cultures according to known differences occasionally takes place, and Barry (1980) recommends the use of the Human Relations Area Files for this purpose (see Chapter 3). Even then further information on the efficacy of the relevant cultural conditions may be desirable.

An example of this point can again be found in the study of Segall, Campbell, and Herskovits (1966), dealing with the effect of the "carpenteredness" of the environment on the perception of visual illusions. They distributed a questionnaire among the project members in order to assess the independent variable, that is, the degree of carpenteredness of the environment of the various groups of subjects.

A complication arises when objective indices may not adequately represent the subjects' psychological reality which the investigation is after. With an equal amount of income the degree of poverty experienced by people living in an urban area may not be the same as the poverty in a rural area. When a major reason for selecting certain groups of subjects is their availability, additional checks on the independent variable are definitely demanded.[5]

PHRASING THE HYPOTHESIS

The special methodological problem for cross-cultural psychology is the conduct of research on the effects of a focal cultural (antecedent) variable in such a way that other, ambient, cultural differences do not provide more plausible explanations of results observed on the dependent variable(s). This problem is, of course, merely an extension of general problems of research design in psychological research. As we have already discussed, the necessity of protecting inferences across variation in such a powerful, complex, and global "variable" as culture provides some new problems. Strategies for solving them depend in important ways on the way in which one conceptualizes the focus of research. In this section we shall distinguish two approaches to cross-cultural research, which we will refer to as *difference analysis* and the *search for similarities*. We make no strong claims for their independence, but in important ways, they have a different conceptual basis and different implications for the methodology of empirical studies.

In most cross-cultural comparative studies hypotheses are either formulated in terms of expected differences in relationships between variables or as differences in levels of scores. When relationships between variables are studied, the null hypothesis will state that there is no significant difference in some index expressing that relationship. For example, under the null hypothesis equal values for the product–moment correlation between a pair of variables are predicted in two groups. For any kind of statistic there are two possible outcomes. According to some decision criterion, either *different* or *similar* values will be said to result. Consider, then, the following:

(a) *Significantly different values are found.* This means that the null hypothesis has to be rejected. However, the researcher has to consider the possibility that the difference is due to factors other than the focal antecedents. Among these is "bias" in the measurement procedure. There is, for example, a problem of bias in hologeistic studies, in which a large number of populations are involved which differ according to some sociocultural or ecological dimension. A hypothesis tested in such studies typically states that the correlation between an antecedent, or predictor variable, and some psychological index will be equal to zero (Barry, 1980). Bias variables cannot be treated as random error, since they may be correlated with the dependent variable. If, for example, matrilineality versus patrilineality is the independent variable, the level of formal education is likely to exert a systematic effect in a worldwide study of any dependent variable which is also affected by education, since virtually all societies with a high level of schooling are patrilineal. The same argument applies when multivariate correlational analyses incorporating more than two variables show differences, for example in factor structures across groups.

Of course, we do not want to suggest that all differences are to be seen as artifacts, but researchers should protect their interpretations against the alternative of bias. The most obvious way for doing this is to demonstrate that there exists a quantitative intergroup difference with respect to a direct measurement of the construct seen as the determinant of the observed difference in product–moment correlations or in factor structures. We suggest that the cultural variable causing the structural difference be studied as a separate quantifiable scale. In personality research, differences in correlation patterns are often attributed to so-called moderator variables, such as sex, age, or level of education (cf. Saunders, 1956; Wiggins, 1973). In a similar sense "culture" can be seen as moderator variable. However, such an interpretation has virtually no explanatory value, as long as an actual effect has not been demonstrated in terms of a far more specific variable.

(b) *Equal or similar values are found.* The substantive implications of this result are important. It is usually taken to indicate two things simultaneously: that across cultures corresponding aspects of behavior are adequately reflected by the score variable(s) concerned (i.e. no bias in the measurements), and that the cultures occupy the same position on the scale with which the phenomenon is being measured. It may be noted if equal levels of scores are found it is unlikely that there are substantial bias effects.[6]

The most important evidence for accepting that there is no difference between the groups with regard to a certain variable is a large overlap in score distributions. For example, Poortinga and Foden (1975) argued that the level of "curiosity" of black and white South African students was similar. This interpretation was based on six tests which on the average showed a difference of 0.3 standard deviation units between the two samples. There are various statistical techniques which can be seen as variations on the principle of distribution overlap. For example, in an Analysis of Variance design so-called generalizability coefficients (Cronbach et al., 1972) form a convenient kind of statistic.

According to Cook and Campbell (1979, p. 45) no-difference findings are generally interpretable when the expected effect of the difference between treatments can be specified. A researcher may postulate *a priori* the size of the effect which he minimally expects for a particular difference between two cultural treatments. In that case a test on the difference between the postulated and the observed results can be carried out. One of the elegant aspects of the approach is that the size of the samples which are needed to find a difference of a certain size with a certain level probability can be specified in advance. For more information we refer to Cohen (1977). The *a priori* postulate of a minimum difference amounts conceptually to creating a region of values which will be interpreted as evidence in favor of intergroup similarity.

Phrasing the null hypothesis as the hypothesis of interest also has an important conceptual advantage if our earlier argument is correct that present research practices lead to an overemphasis on cultural differences. It provides a methodological underpinning to the search for universals, as mentioned in Chapter 1. When equal values in some statistic are specified *a priori*, a failure to find differences is not a negative but a positive research outcome.

From the previous discussion it may seem that the interpretation of empirical evidence is more straightforward when the null hypothesis cannot be rejected than when the alternative hypothesis is accepted. However, a research design in which the null hypothesis rather than the alternative hypothesis is of primary interest has some important methodological disadvantages. Within the experimental paradigm the null hypothesis cannot be logically proven; we can only act as though it were true (Cook & Campbell, 1979, pp. 44–45). The failure to find a statistically significant difference can mean that the measurement procedures used were too inaccurate and had too large an error in measurement, that the size of the samples was too small, or that a statistical test of insufficient power was used. Moreover, it is possible that the antecedent variable itself does not in fact differentiate between the samples. Laboratory studies in social psychology often include checks on the experimental manipulation precisely to investigate this possibility. As mentioned above, determining the degree to which variation on the antecedent variable(s) actually differentiates between the groups studied gives important opportunities for additional quantitative analysis and checks on inferences.

This line of thinking about alternative interpretations of findings of no-difference leads us back to the relative-differences design discussed briefly above. This design embodies an important idea presented by Campbell (1964). His point was that cultural differences are interpretable only against a background of assumed similarities, and he took as his example the strategies used by Segall et al. (1966) to determine whether or not their subjects understood the task they were asked to perform, through the administration of a number of specially designed "comprehension check" items. Segall et al. were thus able to document that up until the stimulus variations introduced in their study, the subjects were able to perform the judgmental task asked of them as would be expected, and that cultural differences in task comprehension were not great enough to be seen as a serious confound in the study's results.

This kind of research strategy is used in a number of areas of psychological research. Its chief characteristic is the introduction of a variation in procedure which is expected to introduce a change in results. If a pattern of results can be provided showing differences where they are expected on the basis of focal theory, as well as results showing no differences where expected by focal theory, interpretation will have been greatly facilitated, since many alternative interpretations will have been shown to be of unlikely validity.

A study on the effect of tonality in language in various domains of behavior can serve as an illustration.[7] At least two different kinds of stimuli are administered in each domain. One kind of stimulus is supposedly easier for tonal-language speakers. A second kind is expected to lead to no differences, and in some domains there is a third group of stimuli in which the processing of tonal information will supposedly have an inhibitive effect on the performance of tonal-language speakers. In this study a no-difference finding rests on a combination of two or three results, rather than merely on the absence of a single statistically significant finding. The two or three sets of stimuli are part of a single task so that method artifacts are unlikely to occur. A lack of differences, if found, will provide stronger evidence of similarity in information processing between persons with tonal and nontonal background than could be derived with only one kind of stimulus.

By way of conclusion we refer back to the second section of this chapter, where we mentioned that of the four control principles in experimental studies, two are available to cross-cultural researchers. Although control over the independent variable is largely beyond our reach, control on the dependent variable is an important compensation. As the examples given in these last pages show, it is a necessary requirement that the researcher works with theoretical ideas developed well enough to make manipulation of the results a feasible prospect. We would also like to emphasize that the search for no-difference results across divergent cultures may from time to time be a more promising approach than searching for differences. Valuable knowledge can be obtained if researchers take adequate precaution against alternative explanations at the design stage.

BIAS, FAIRNESS AND EQUIVALENCE

Results obtained in different cultures can often be used for two interdependent but mutually exclusive purposes: to evaluate intercultural differences, or to assess whether measurement procedures have yielded equivalent results. In principle a single finding cannot be used for both purposes simultaneously. But from the same set of data different results can be computed, some of which will provide an estimate of a difference between cultural groups, while others are used to check whether the methods (and the resulting data) can be taken as equivalent. There are various meanings of the term "equivalence" in cross-cultural research, with sometimes confusing variations.

Functional Equivalence

This is the most frequently mentioned form of equivalence. Frijda and Jahoda (1966, p. 116) state: "if similar activities have different functions in different societies their parameters cannot be used for comparative purposes." The examples they mention mainly refer to social institutions, for instance, the role of teachers and the position of the church in different societies. This points to the anthropological origin of the concept which is also prominent in other writings (Berry, 1969).

Conceptual Equivalence

Another requirement for meaningful comparison which has been emphasized is that subjects have an equal understanding of the meaning of behavior or of concepts pertaining to behavior. Similarity in meaning is usually identified with the term "conceptual equivalence," following Sears (1961). Concepts can range from the very general or universal—an example is "mother"—to the specific. The idea of bureaucracy, for example, is meaningless in an undifferentiated tribal society (Warwick & Osheron, 1973). Hudson, Barakat, and LaForge (1959) distinguish between stimulus equivalence and response equivalence, arguing that equivalence of meaning is needed for both.

It is noteworthy that conceptual equivalence and functional

equivalence have been taken to be problems of a somewhat different order from the equivalence of instructions or stimulus material (Frijda & Jahoda, 1966), suggesting a contrast between a cultural level and an instrumental (or operational) level of analysis. Less differentiated views can also be found, especially in writings where empirical analyses are advocated. An example is the work on linguistic equivalence. Brislin, Lonner, and Thorndike (1973, pp. 51–55) recommend a procedure of translation and back-translation of instruments and preliminary try-outs with bilingual subjects to attain instruments which allow for valid comparisons of results collected in different cultures (see also Chapter 5).

Discussions about equivalence are by no means limited to psychology. In the anthropological literature the meta-methodological question whether intercultural studies of socio-cultural institutions amount to comparing incomparables has been given considerable attention (cf. Campbell & Naroll, 1972). In sociology and political science, where survey research plays an important role, the problem of equivalence tends to be analyzed in terms of linguistic meaning (Deutscher, 1973). In general, similar ideas are treated as in psychological texts, though the terminology may be different.

Equivalence is often seen as a conceptual rather than a measurement problem. This is probably the reason why authors have provided objective empirical referents in terms of which equivalence can be evaluated.

Metric Equivalence

Metric equivalence is discussed in more recent literature as an additional condition to conceptual or functional equivalence (e.g. Berry & Dasen, 1974; Warwick & Osheron, 1973). This requirement according to Berry (1980, p. 10) is satisfied "when the psychometric properties of two (or more) sets of data from two (or more) cultural groups exhibit essentially the same coherence of structure." It is apparent that a judgment about metric equivalence depends on the outcome of psychometric analyses. However, it is not immediately clear which conditions have to be satisfied for either confirmation or rejection of this essential equality. This point we shall discuss in the next sections.

Rather strongly linked with an empirical analysis of difference are the terms "item bias" and "test fairness." These terms have empirical connotations and are usually seen as characteristics of instruments. The notion of culture-fairness of tests was preceded by the idea of culture-free tests, that is, instruments which were not affected by cultural influences and consequently were suitable for assessing an individual's "genetic capacities" and, by extension, "genetic qualities" of racial groups. This idea is only of historical interest. For a test to be culture-fair, it is "merely" necessary that the influence of cultural factors be common to the populations concerned (Krug, 1966). A test on which every subject's score would be equally affected by cultural factors obviously cannot be used for the evaluation of differences in respect of such factors, and would have little explanatory value in cross-cultural psychology. However, in recent years fairness has acquired a different meaning.

The fairness of a test is currently evaluated in terms of a common criterion, the scores on which have to be predicted for members of different groups within a single society. The criterion forms a common standard—in the sense described in Chapter 1—in terms of which the fairness or unfairness of a test as a predictor can be evaluated.

The most straightforward approach is by means of linear regression techniques. According to Cleary (1968) a test is biased when the criterion score predicted from a common regression line is consistently too high or too low for members of one group compared to another group.

Generally this will be the case when the best-fitting linear regression function is not identical across groups. However, even an equal test-criterion regression line may have less desirable implications as a condition for decisions about fairness. The predicted criterion score of two subjects with an equal test score is not the same when these subjects belong to groups with different test means, since the respective means are used in the regression equation to derive a subject's criterion score. The consequence—for example in a selection situation—can be that of two subjects with equal scores the one is accepted, the other rejected, depending on what population they belong to. The alternative, to use the overall mean of the populations, is unsatisfactory. Subjects with a different expected criterion score, or a different probability of achieving the criterion, are treated alike, just because they happen to have equal test scores.

Several models for fairness were proposed in the early 1970s by Darlington (1971), Thorndike (1971), Einhorn and Bass (1971), and Cole (1973), among others. A review with an incisive discussion of the difficulties with the various models can be found in Peterson and Novick (1976).

Although "bias" is used in a very general sense, the term "item bias" has acquired a rather specific meaning. An item is biased when intergroup differences are not in agreement with expectations based on the response patterns for the other items in the same instrument. The performance on each item is evaluated against that of the other items, which together serve as a common standard. This implies that a cultural bias common to all items cannot be detected. Nevertheless, the analysis of item bias is important for evaluating the equivalence of tests and we shall return to it later.

A conceptually straightforward definition of cross-cultural equivalence follows from Chapter 1. Corresponding sets of data obtained in different populations can be called equivalent when in each population the functional relationship between the scale of the observed scores and the scale of the universe of generalization is identical. That is to say, when the scale of the observed scores is expressed as a function of the scale of the universe scores, the data are equivalent, if all parameters of that function have identical values in the groups compared.

On the one hand this definition refers to scales rather than to score distributions, since the approach via score distributions has created various kinds of ambivalences in the fairness tradition. On the other hand, equivalence in the sense of the definition depends on the generalizations or inferences which a researcher will attempt and is not characteristic of an instrument independent of the generalization context. This contrasts with the item bias approach.

We do not mean to say that our definition is a step towards solving equivalence problems in actual data. The advantage, which we see, is that it helps to bring these problems better into focus. Only thereafter can one determine the best solution to the problems. This is the topic of discussion in the next section.

PSYCHOMETRIC REQUIREMENTS FOR EQUIVALENCE

In this section we shall be concerned with the criteria data sets must meet to be considered equivalent, that is to constitute an identical

TABLE 2.2
Equivalence Issues Associated with Various Categories of Universes

Universe of Generalizations		Comparison Category	Equivalence Issues
Identical universe	Representative sample of elements — repertoire	A	Not applicable
	— attribute	B	Method bias
	Selected elements — repertoire	C	Stimulus sampling bias
	— attribute	D	Method and stimulus sampling bias
Nonidentical universe	Representative sample of elements — repertoire	E	Universe bias
	— attribute	F	Method and universe bias
	Selected elements — repertoire	G	. . . .
	— attribute	H	Stimulus sampling, method, universe bias

scale in the sense of the above definition. To identify these requirements we first must establish in what ways cross-cultural equivalence of data can be threatened. Three issues are mentioned in Table 2.2, namely stimulus bias, method bias and universe bias. We shall associate these three threats to equivalence with certain generalizations.

No Threats to Equivalence

Of course, a psychometric analysis is meaningful only when the equivalence of the data can be questioned. There are no threats to equivalence when a measurement instrument is constructed on the basis of a representative sample of elements from a cross-culturally identical universe of stimuli and when no inference beyond that universe is to be attempted on the basis of results. For example, the chips of the Munsell color scheme used by Berlin and Kay (1969) represent the same universe of colors for all subjects. Basic color terms in different languages were expressed as regions in the Munsell scheme. The finding of Berlin and Kay that the presence of a term within a certain region of the scheme is conditional upon the presence of certain other color terms does not entail a generalization beyond the Munsell system.

Stimulus Bias

When the stimuli in an instrument do not form a representative sample from the universe of generalization, there is reason to question the cross-cultural equivalence of the data. This is the case when there is no precise description of the universe (or listing of its elements), but also when only a small number of items is used to represent a heterogeneous universe, even if this universe is identical across groups. An item asking for the highest peak in the Alps presumably will be answered correctly by many children in Switzerland and a few in Sweden. In a short test of geographical knowledge this would create a noticeable difference in the level of performance in the two countries. Bias attached to the item in question could be detected because of the relatively high scores of the Swiss children, compared to other items. In other words the results would deviate from expectations based on the other items. Therefore it can be stipulated as a psychometric requirement for equivalence that the items meet such expectations. The equivalence of individual items may be evaluated against the test score variable only when the equivalence of this variable is not itself called into question.

Method Bias

The equivalence of data sets is also threatened when there is a possibility of method bias, that is when ambient variables such as interviewer–subject interactions, understanding of the task by the subjects etc., may have led to cross-cultural differences in results. In contrast to stimulus bias, method bias affects all stimuli in an instrument to a similar extent. Oliver (1932), to whose study we referred in Chapter 1, administered the Seashore Measures of Musical Talents to a sample of East Africans and compared their scores with those of American subjects of approximately equal educational standing. The Africans had a higher mean score on three subtests and a lower mean on the other three. Oliver tried to counteract the possible effect of ambient variables by using special administration procedures. In the absence of pertinent data no psychometric analysis is possible which would throw light on the question whether Oliver has succeeded in this respect. The observed intergroup differences in pitch discrimination might have been larger—or smaller for that matter—if the subjects in both groups had been given extensive training on the pitch discrimination task.

On the basis of the six Seashore subtests Oliver made inferences about cross-cultural differences in musical talents.[8] Taking musical talent as a single concept, it is possible to argue that the reported patterning of intergroup differences over subtests is a consequence of bias. In fact, Oliver mentioned that two of the six tasks were correlated with intelligence in the African sample, probably because they were difficult to understand. These two tasks were among the three on which the Africans achieved a lower mean score. A reasonable condition for equivalence is that the extent of inter-cultural differences in scores should be the same for different measurements of the same psychological attribute. Whether or not scores in a certain measurement procedure meet this condition can easily be checked against other variables which reflect the same attribute.

However, if it is assumed that musical talent is a multifaceted construct which may be patterned differently across cultures, it is meaningless to require that similar intergroup differences should be found for the six tests, even if they were all equivalent. This underscores the fact that the analysis of method bias presupposes a sufficiently well-developed theory on the basis of which the researcher can decide whether or not two variables reflect an identical universe. We will come back to this point shortly.

Both method bias and stimulus-sampling bias have to be guarded against in other instances (row D of Table 2.2). For example, susceptibility to visual illusions can be considered as a universe shared by all cultural populations. But illusions form a heterogeneous domain, so that it is of some importance which subset of illusions is included in a study. At the same time bias in the measurement procedures cannot be ruled out *a priori* (Segall et al., 1966). This complicates the analysis, but it does not introduce essentially new problems.

Universe Bias

So far we have dealt with situations where the identity of the domain of generalization is not called into question and bias can be due only to ambient variables related to procedural aspects of measurement or to stimulus selection. However, when the data sets are obtained with measurement instruments constructed on the basis of nonidentical universes, or when the data are to be generalized to nonidentical universes, universe bias (a term selected for lack of a better one) is a serious threat to comparison.

For the sake of clarity we would like to emphasize again that any cross-cultural comparison requires a scale with metric properties which are identical across the groups concerned. If that is not the case there is no logical basis for comparison. As an example we can refer once more to Oliver's study of musical talents. It can be argued that this concept refers to quite different kinds of behavior in Africa and America. The question to be answered is then whether it is possible to construct equivalent scales for "musical talent" which encompass these different domains of behavior. This is a theoretical problem which will not be pursued further here.

For an analysis of universe bias it is important to distinguish between instruments based on known universes, and instruments based on unknown universes. For a known universe all the elements can be obtained by means of some algorithm or they can be exhaustively listed. The lexicon of all the kinship terms in a language is an example. Presumably stimuli for a measurement instrument can be derived by means of a procedure which is equally representative of the universe of each culture (e.g. picking words from a dictionary). This will result in formally different instruments (e.g. lists of words which are not translation-equivalent). Thus checks on item bias are ruled out. For large enough samples (of words) administered in a format which is easy and understandable for all subjects, researchers may assume that the resulting scales are free from method bias. The word "assume" is intentionally used, as there is no empirical evidence on the basis of which either the equivalence or the inequivalence of the instruments can be refuted. By virtue of the assumption that the universe in each culture is adequately represented in the measurement procedure, the problem of universe bias is, rightly or wrongly, eliminated. If the possibility of universe bias is recognized a study of this kind belongs to row E of Table 2.2. If universe bias is assumed not to exist, the study is akin to the top row of our classification scheme. In Table 1.1 of the first chapter, we mentioned the use of a vocabulary test in different groups to assess what proportion subjects know of the total lexicon in their respective languages, as an example . of a study in row E.

Cross-cultural comparisons become particularly tenuous when the universe of generalization is incompletely known, *and* likely to be different across cultures. In Chapter 1 we describe in some detail the line of reasoning underlying comparative studies of hypothetical constructs. It amounts to defining a common universe in terms of some psychological function or trait. On the basis of this definition a measurement procedure can be constructed for application in different cultures. Researchers now have two options. First, they can rely on the validity of the theoretical analysis reflected in the definition of the common universe. A study based on this kind of reasoning, in terms of equivalence problems, is relegated to the top half of Table 2.2, where identical universes are presumed and only method bias and stimulus bias are considered. This option precludes that any psychometric procedure can be formulated for which the definition is correct.

The second option is to consider the definition about identity as tentative. When universe bias is present, analyses for method and item bias are likely to show a lack of psychometric equivalence.

Unfortunately, it is not possible in such instances to decide which kind of bias is responsible for an observed lack of equivalence. The psychometric evidence for the presence of bias will always be circumstantial. It might be argued that the distinctions between various kinds of bias are trivial if their effects cannot be separated. This view has merit for nonidentical universes, but not when instruments have been constructed on the basis of universes which by definition are universal.

If stimulus bias is found for instruments in which bias can only be stimulus-specific, it makes sense to discard the results of the items concerned and make a comparison on the basis of the remaining results. This is an unjustifiable procedure when the universes are nonidentical, since the "biased" stimuli may in fact reflect systematic differences between the universes. The same applies when method bias is found. If this can only be ascribed to ambient variables, one may discard from a larger set of variables those which deviate from the general pattern of results. However, if the possibility of universe bias has to be accounted for, the difference between methods may reflect nonidentity at the universe level. In this situation the researcher will have no justification for disregarding part of the data. Consequently, if only method bias and/or stimulus bias can have affected the results, something can be done (sometimes) to improve the equivalence of data. If universe bias cannot be excluded on *a priori* grounds and data do not meet conditions of equivalence, the possibilities for valid inferences about cross-cultural differences are seriously affected.

In summary, the interpretation of cross-cultural differences requires a number of decisions. The first suggestion to be answered is whether the observed difference is "real" (i.e. present in the universe of generalization) or due to bias. If the latter possibility is accepted the researcher has to decide whether the bias is inherent to the definitions of the universe (which is primarily a theoretical problem) or whether the bias can be explained as due to specific measurement procedures (stimulus bias, or method bias).

THE STATISTICAL ANALYSIS OF EQUIVALENCE

In the previous section we have formulated requirements for equivalence in such a way that they apply regardless of the metric properties of data. The definition given above and the arguments in Chapter 1 refer generally to "functional relationships." In this section we shall briefly review some statistical procedures to analyze equivalence. It can hardly be emphasized enough that such procedures presuppose that the data meet certain scale properties (e.g. measurement at interval scale level) and distributional assumptions (e.g. normal distributions). This implies that statistical tests for the absence of item and method bias cannot be applied indiscriminately to any data set.

If a statistical test is an appropriate one for the data to be compared, there are two possible outcomes. If the data satisfy the formulated condition, the researcher's confidence that the data are equivalent will increase, or—when the postulated condition is not met—it has to be concluded that the data are unsuitable for the intended comparison. However, as we have seen in the previous section, in the latter case one has not necessarily reached the end of the road. Sometimes it is possible to eliminate biased methods or stimuli, and sometimes inspection of the nature and extent of bias can lead to new insights about intercultural differences.

A distinction will be made between procedures testing for stimulus bias and those testing for method bias. Also, an attempt will be made to integrate the two in a single framework.

Tests for Stimulus Bias[9]

Within the so-called classical psychometric model the scale on which the performance level of subjects is expressed is usually the number of items correctly answered. In a group of subjects the contribution of each item to the mean of the raw scores is dependent on its level of difficulty. An intuitively obvious requirement for an unbiased test is that the relative difficulty of items is the same across the groups to be compared.

One approach to analyzing whether this condition is met is to plot the item difficulty levels (p-values) for different groups against each other (Angoff & Ford, 1973). For an unbiased test the points in the plot should be located on a straight line. Points at too large a distance from the line can be taken to represent biased items. As an overall measure the product–moment correlation between p-values can also be computed (Irvine, 1966). However, it is difficult to establish whether an observed value differs significantly from the expected value of $r=1.00$ for an unbiased test (cf. Poortinga & Foden, 1975). There are also some serious difficulties with the p-index itself, especially when items are scored dichotomously, that is, as either right or wrong (Lord, 1977). Nevertheless, Angoff and Ford's approach gives results which are quite similar to those found with psychometrically more adequate procedures (Shepard, Camilli, & Averill, 1981) while it has the important advantage of being easy to carry out.

A related procedure, and one which has similar difficulties,[10] is the use of Analysis of Variance to establish whether there is a significant interaction effect between culture and item difficulty level. For an unbiased test a nonsignificant interaction is expected (Cleary & Hilton, 1968). Through *post hoc* analyses, items contributing substantially to the interaction term can be identified.

In recent years important advancements have been made in the development of analysis models which imply less unrealistic assumptions than the analyses mentioned so far. The application of log-linear models by Mellenbergh (1982, 1983; Van der Flier, Mellenbergh, Ader, & Wijn, 1984) deserves attention. Another important development is the application of item characteristic curve theory or latent trait theory to the analysis of item bias (Lord, 1977; 1980). In latent trait models the performance of subjects is expressed on a so-called latent trait scale. The probability of a correct response forms an item characteristic curve which is a function of the latent trait. For an unbiased item, the item characteristic curve has equal parameter values in the groups to be compared.

For a more detailed introduction to the topic of item bias we can refer to Berk (1982) and Jensen (1980). Of several articles we may note in addition those by Darlington (1971), by Rudner, Getson, and Knight (1980), and by Irvine and Carroll (1980).

So far we have discussed psychometric conditions for bias in studies in which the groups are identified in advance. Even if a test satisfies such conditions at the group level it may be biased in respect of subjects of certain subgroups. On the other hand, if a lack of equivalence is demonstrated for entire groups, this may not apply to certain (subgroups of) subjects. Van der Flier (1982) has developed a method to probe this problem, by looking at variations in item score patterns. The difference between an observed pattern and the expected pattern of scores is expressed in a so-called deviance score. Van der Flier demonstrated that differences in verbal test scores between school pupils from Kenya and Tanzania were related to differences in the command of Kiswahili. Approaches similar to those followed by Van der Flier have elsewhere been labeled "appropriate measurement" (i.e. the test score as an appropriate reflection of a subject's ability, Drasgow, 1982; Levine & Drasgow, 1982), or "aberrant response pattern detection" (Tatsuoka & Tatsuoka, 1982).

Method Bias

A similar bias with regard to all stimuli in a measurement procedure can only be detected by comparing with each other the results of different measurement procedures. So far we have concentrated our discussion on quantitative comparisons: e.g. are people in a carpentered environment more susceptible to the Mueller–Lyer illusion? There are also studies in which qualitative relationships between variables are compared: for example is the relationship between need for achievement and school performance also found outside Western cultures (McClelland, 1961). The terms functional equivalence and scale equivalence have been used for this distinction in earlier publications (Poortinga, 1971, 1975) where scale equivalence (or score equivalence) had the same meaning as equivalence in the present text.

A variable is called functionally equivalent when its scale is linearly related to the universe scale (which by definition is identical across the groups to be compared). It can be shown that if two sets of corresponding data are functionally equivalent, it is a necessary requirement that the product–moment correlation between them is equal in the populations concerned (Poortinga, 1971, pp. 79–80).[11] If the correlation between two variables is not the same across groups, one or both of the variables are lacking in functional equivalence.

The analysis of functional equivalence need not be restricted to the comparison of a single correlation coefficient. Statistical techniques for comparing correlation matrices based on larger sets of variables are available if at the population level normal distributions of scores can be presupposed (cf. Browne, 1978). An extension is possible through the use of factor analysis. For functionally equivalent variables an equal factor structure in each of the cultural groups may be expected, on the basis of the equal correlation matrices.

Differences in factor structures can be interpreted either as differences in behavioral functioning, or as a lack of functional equivalence in (some of) the scales. The choice between the two interpretations is not always obvious and depends on the researcher's confidence in the strength of the theoretical network within which generalizations are made. An explanation in terms of a lack of equivalence is the most conservative as it evades a decision about the existence of "real" cross-cultural differences. On the other hand, if equal structures are found, functional equivalence as well as similarity in a psychological sense follow simultaneously from this finding.

In older studies factor analyses were carried out for the various groups separately, and any differences which might be found were interpreted more or less subjectively. Since about fifteen years ago, techniques for intergroup factor analysis have been developed (e.g. Cattell, 1970; Kaiser, Hunka, & Bianchini, 1971; Buss & Royce, 1975; Tseng, 1977) which provide statistical procedures for the analysis of qualitative differences and similarities of scales.

A score variable is equivalent when it adequately reflects not only qualitative but also quantitative differences in the universe scale. Correlations, and by extension factor analytic scales derived from correlation matrices, do not provide a sufficient procedure for the detection of quantitative method bias, since the value of a correlation coefficient remains the same under any linear transformation.[12]

This objection is considerably less valid for intergroup factor analytic techniques based on variance–covariance matrices rather than correlation matrices. Well known is the confirmatory maximum-likelihood factor analysis developed by Jöreskog (1971). Intergroup comparisons using this technique have been reported by Rock and Werts (1979) and by Rock, Werts, and Grandy (1982). In these studies the notion of equivalence or, as these authors say, "invariant construct validity"[13] is defined as (1) similar patterns of loadings across populations, (2) equal units of measurement across populations, and (3) equal test score precision as defined by the "standard error of measurement" (Rock et al. 1982, p. 7). Different scales with equal units of measurement are identical except for an additive constant, which again, can either reflect a "real" difference (i.e. a difference in the domain of generalization) or method bias. This fact has been recognized by Rock et al. who point out that evaluation against an external criterion or reference scale remains necessary.

The availability of a common standard or criterion variable is the point of departure in the most commonly found approach to the analysis of test score bias which in the previous section was referred to as the test fairness tradition. Closely associated with this approach is the use of linear regression techniques. We have pointed out already that the demand of equal test-criterion regression functions across groups has unsatisfactory implications. A further difficulty arises when of two variables it is not clear which one is the "test" and which one is the "criterion." The demand that both the test-criterion and the criterion-test regression function have to be the same implies that the distributions of test scores and criterion scores have to be equal in the different groups.

Our discussion of method bias started with correlation analyses, but gradually moved to statistical analysis techniques in which quantitative aspects of scale identity are emphasized. In this context it may also be mentioned that method bias can be identified as a culture by treatment interaction when two or more test score variables are analyzed in an Analysis of Variance design. There are close parallels to the use of ANOVA for stimulus bias. However, there is no obvious statistical reason why a main effect for culture should not be attributed to a common bias in all the variables (Van de Vijver & Poortinga, 1982).

Conclusion

It has emerged that most statistical tests for equivalence require identity of some psychometric property of the data across cultural groups. The most stringent conditions are met when identical score distributions are found. This may not be such an unrealistic requirement as it appears. To those holding an egalitarian viewpoint on intelligence, any mean difference between ethnic populations in the distributions of scores on intelligence tests is seen as evidence of bias. On the other hand the meaning of a culture by stimulus interaction is not called into question by personality researchers of the so-called interactionist school (Argyle, Shimoda, & Little, 1978; Magnusson, & Stattin, 1978). Similarly, differences in correlations can be seen as evidence of either "real" differences or bias.

Especially in the case of nonidentical universes, encompassing different behavior repertoires across cultures, a whole string of equivalence conditions can be stipulated. The probability that they all would fail to show some indication of bias is very small, especially when large samples of subjects are involved. Strictly speaking, a single sufficiently consistent indication of bias means that the results of the comparison are erroneous at least to some extent, and that additional information is needed to constrain the range of potential interpretations.

More coherent approaches to the analysis of equivalence are needed. The studies by Rock and Werts (1979) and by Rock et al. (1982) contain such strategies. Another attempt in this direction was recently reported by Van de Vijver and Poortinga (1982). Their procedure is based on the estimation of so-called generalizability coefficients in an Analysis of Variance design and is closely linked to the analysis presented here.

From the point of view of applied research it is important to know how likely it is that data will show a lack of equivalence. Part of the work referred to in this section is on intergroup differences between the major ethnic groups within the United States, and the psychometrically more sophisticated models presume uni-dimensionality of scales. This implies that stimuli are selected from what one might call homogeneous universes. The seriousness of violations of this assumption, and others in comparative studies, is still largely unclear. Many of the investigations in the United States have dealt with the fairness of cognitive ability tests for minority groups. There are indications that bias in most instances is not a serious obstacle for generalization of test results to school achievement and job performance criteria (Jensen, 1980). This implies one of two things; either the major groups in the United States are culturally rather similar, or the criteria against which the fairness of tests is evaluated are psychologically similar to these tests. If the latter possibility is correct the frequently reported intergroup differences, for example between whites and blacks in "intelligence," form a clear example of universe bias.

The cross-cultural psychologist is often interested in a comparison of groups which have a far less similar behavior repertoire than groups of urbanized North Americans, and in cultural factors which are more encompassing than the item content of ability tests. The literature on studies involving populations which are culturally rather dissimilar gives no reasons for optimistic expectations about the equivalence of data. When stringent requirements for equivalence were analyzed a lack of equivalence has been the rule rather than the exception (Irvine & Carroll, 1980; Poortinga & Foden, 1975; Van der Flier, 1982), although it has to be admitted that in older studies inappropriate procedures for analysis may partly be the cause of negative results.

Given the present state of affairs we would submit that it is unwarranted to ignore the problem of equivalence in intercultural studies. After all, comparing inequivalent data gives misleading outcomes about the nature and extent of cross-cultural differences in behavior.

NOTES

Parts of this chapter were written while the second author was a Fellow at the NIAS (Netherlands Institute for Advanced Study in the Humanities and Social Sciences) at Wassenaar.

1. The term "weak" refers to psychometric aspects of Hutchin's study. The relevance of his research vis à vis Lee's (1949) suggestion about the cognitive abilities of the Trobrianders is not the subject of discussion here.

2. Strictly speaking the (in)adequacy of a method should follow directly from the theory (cf. Faucheux, 1976), but this does not seem a realistic requirement in what Meehl (1978) called "soft" psychology.

3. In fact, Hill did make some cross-cultural comparisons on the basis of relative differences between pairs of variables as discussed later in this section, but not in terms of cross-cultural differences in learning rates.

4. The fact that this is not strictly true if series A and series B show some unwanted differences (cf. Keating et al., 1981, p. 618) is of no consequence here.

5. The effort involved in strengthening this aspect of a study *post hoc* may well be greater than choosing more appropriate samples at the start.

6. Of course, one cannot rule out the possibility that the "bias" in a measurement procedure will obscure some real difference, but the probability of this event is fairly low and will not be considered further here.

7. The study is carried out by R.C. Joe at Tilburg University (R.C. Joe, personal communication).

8. Taking Oliver's study as a whole, it would fit better in row H of our table. However, we like to use it for our present argument.

9. In this section we shall use the term bias. The techniques are not restricted to test items, but the terminology reflects that the analysis of item bias has largely been developed in the context of ability testing.

10. For example, the assumption of equal cell variances is violated, because the item variance $(p(1-p))$ is dependent on the value of p for dichotomous items.

11. If there are intergroup differences in the reliabilities of scores, only the correlations between the so-called true score variables are equal.

12. It is a tenacious fallacy that factor invariance across cultures is a sufficient condition for unbiased quantitative intergroup comparison of factor scales (e.g. Buss & Royce, 1975, p. 130). Let us say that a hypothetical scale in two populations is reflected by a score variable X with substantial loadings from a factor F which is considered to be invariant across the two populations. This does not preclude that the factor scores on F of the subjects in the two groups have a different distribution. However, the researcher has no evidence as to whether the difference in factor score distributions are "real" or due to a quantitative method bias effect.

13. In our opinion the two do not have the same meaning. The objective of construct validation is to clarify conceptual issues. Analysis of equivalence is primarily a method for detecting bias. Of course, the two are related, as indicated in this chapter at several places, where we indicate the dependency of psychometric analysis on theoretical insights.

3

SAMPLING AND SURVEYING

WALTER J. LONNER
JOHN W. BERRY

GOALS OF SAMPLING

The nature and purpose of cross-cultural psychology require that the researcher pays particular and special attention to sampling strategies and problems. Comparison of the behavior of individuals from different cultural groups is implicit if not explicit in cross-cultural psychology. Whenever the researcher designs a study involving two or more cultural groups, the problem of drawing equivalent samples will be a major, if not *the* major, methodological obstacle to overcome satisfactorily. Without a defensible sampling strategy, the results of the study may be ambiguous or misleading.

Despite the importance of sampling and surveying, there are no readily available cross-cultural guidebooks which present the ABCs of sampling. In fact, most of what is known about cross-cultural sampling and surveying comes from sociologists and political scientists whose research has involved the use of surveys, polls, questionnaires, or other devices to gauge public opinion, or for various reasons to conduct international comparative research. Basic references include books by Backstrom and Hursh (1963), Rokkan (1968), Holt and Turner (1970), Warwick and Lininger (1975), Sudman (1976), Bulmer and Warwick (1983), and Kalton (1983). These and numerous other sources have served as the principal guides in organizing this chapter.

Random Samples

In all behavioral research, the selection of a sample which is representative of some parent population is of central importance. Samples, of course, are used to make inferences to the population they represent; inferences will be incorrect or misleading to the extent that the sample is incorrectly selected. Complete confidence in making inferences is usually achieved only if a true probability, or random, sample is used; in such a sample each member of the parent population has a known, equal, and nonzero chance of being selected. And each unit in the sample will contribute its proportion, or "share," to the extent to which it is representative of the parent population.

In cross-cultural research, there are certain rules that govern sampling strategies. Rule Number 1 is that drawing a truly representative sample may be possible only when the population is extremely homogeneous and some type of accurate and current list or registry can be used as a sampling framework. As Bulmer (in Bulmer & Warwick, 1983, p. 91) cautions, however, text   on sampling "were not written with the developing countries in mind. There are usually no sampling frames, no central registry of all citizens, no census tracts with home addresses, no comprehensive directories of who's where." Moreover, if documents potentially useful for sampling do exist, they may be inaccurate or outdated. Frey (1970) commented on the likely absence of sampling aids in the developing world that are usually available in most modern societies. Nearly any kind of organized, structured aid, such as maps, aerial photos, and street guides are simply not to be found or are out of date. Frey also notes that secondary data on community size, household size, and so on, are usually lacking as well. Many have faced the realities of poor or nonexistent aids to sampling. For instance, if there are no population estimates within city or town blocks, one would have to choose blocks with equal probability, thereby immediately adding another source of error to the source already implicit with good randomization.

Rule Number 2 is that the best samples in cross-cultural research are those that result from the most careful attempts that the circumstances permit to approximate the kind of sample needed to permit the proper execution of the research. Sechrest (1970, p. 201) remarked that "the only good sampling procedure is the best that is possible under the circumstances and the better an approximation to a representative sample that can be achieved, the greater confidence the research merits." This will usually involve a significant departure from probability samples.

In cross-cultural research, nonrandom samples are much more common than true random samples; perhaps this has been especially true in anthropology (Honigmann, 1970). Hursh-Cesar and Roy (1976), as reported in Bulmer and Warwick (1983), point out that the reliance on nonrandom sampling is due to "indefinite populations, unavailable sampling frames, small budgets, lack of time, inexperienced personnel, pressure for results, and the like."

Types of Nonrandom Samples

A number of terms describing nonrandom sampling procedures are recurrent in the literature. These include the following:

Samples of Convenience: Such samples are defined as groups of individuals who are taken from some convenient collectivity, such as a school, a factory, a railroad station, or a playground. Their accessibility makes them very cost-effective, in terms of both money and time; however, all such samples depart to an unknown degree from true representativeness. And since the flux of time and situation will alter the configuration of such samples, they are not replicable.

Bunch or Grab Samples (also called Fortuitous or Haphazard Samples): As the terms imply, individuals who are included in such samples are grabbed in bunches, probably because they are convenient and fit reasonably well into the research scheme. Concern for representativeness may be secondary to the expeditious completion of the research.

Judgmental Sampling (also variously called Purposive, Deliberate, or Selective Sampling): Here the researcher uses judgment in selecting individuals who will be instrumental in gathering certain kinds of data or in testing certain hypotheses.

Expert Choice Samples: Obviously, the key person in selecting samples of this sort is the "expert," who expresses an informed opinion about the composition of some sample, often without specifying the reasons underlying the selection. Expert choice and judgment samples are obviously very similar.

While none of these sampling procedures needs to be rejected, they do create problems with respect to replicability. For example, if your sample included "the first 25 adult women who entered the local store on Monday morning," there is no guarantee that the composition of a similarly selected sample on Thursday morning would be similar in all respects to Monday's sample, given some definable parent population. Sampling Rule Number 3 is, therefore, as follows: When circumstances warrant departure from random sampling procedures, be as precise as possible in detailing the procedures you used, and make special note of any factor(s) which influenced the present sampling procedures but may not affect future procedures. Giving such deserved care in describing samples serves several purposes (Brislin & Baumgardner, 1971). First, well-described samples allow future researchers to choose their "bunches" with greater certainty of obtaining useful, important results. Second, carefully described procedures will permit others to "follow up another's work with the possibility of combining sets of data into a functional relationship between two variables." Third, carefully described samples "allow the researcher and his subsequent readers to evaluate any plausible rival hypothesis that may threaten a study's validity." Any characteristic of the sample which may affect how the data are interpreted should be described. These include age, sex, educational level, status, income, occupation, special training, and place of residence in relation to other members of the culture.

Which Type of Sampling Strategy?

It should not be assumed that a probability sample is always the best type of sampling strategy to use, or that it is not virtuous to depart from such samples. The purpose, or goal, of the research will dictate whether the sample should be random or some type of nonrandom sample.

Cross-cultural psychologists do research for two general reasons. One reason is to collect data in some systematic manner, covering (ideally) all cultures and all individuals within them so that universal generalizations may be made. It is quite debatable whether a "universal psychology" is possible unless the broad sweep of cultures is considered (Lonner, 1980; Van de Vijver & Poortinga, 1982). Nevertheless, if this sort of grand strategy is desired, representative samples would be necessary. Indeed, a very sophisticated sampling strategy, such as stratified random sampling, would be needed. In addition, the researcher would have to worry about the true independence of each unit in the universe to be sampled, a problem that has plagued holocultural (whole world) hypothesis testers (see below).

The second, and easily the most common, reason for doing cross-cultural *psychological* research is to examine the "systematic co-variation (or cause) between cultural and behavioural variables" (Berry, 1980). In this type of research, the main task facing the investigator is to focus on the range of variation in a variable of interest. In this strategy, "culture" *per se* is *not* important. What *is* important is the "independent variable"—and specifically to find a sufficient range of variation of the independent variable—so that statements about causation can be made. Because this type of strategy constitutes "quasi-manipulation by selection" of the independent variable, the importance of probability samples decreases. Rather, nonrandom samples (for example, judgmental, purposive, or expert choice) of individuals in certain cultures, in which can be found the desired range of the independent variable, are required.

Which *individuals* to choose in this latter type of strategy is another issue, and parallels the issues concerning the selection of cultures. As Berry (1980, p. 15) notes:

> if individuals are to represent their culture (or at other levels, if individuals are to represent their community and, in turn, the community is to represent the culture) then representativeness is definitely required. That is, the sample should mirror the population. On the other hand, if individuals are being selected because they represent some variable of interest, then their representativeness of some population is not important.

The Problem of "Matching"

Because it is often difficult and expensive to draw representative or random samples in culture-comparative studies, nonrandom sampling procedures have frequently been used. In addition to representing their "cultureness" (to some assumed but unknown degree), which is of course the point of the contrast in the first place, these unsystematic samples may also differ and in different ways, on such important more or less static variables as sex, age, marital status, formal education, or other ambient variables (see Chapter 2) that may have been unknowingly or accidentally present at the time the samples were "grabbed" for testing or for interviewing. To control statistically for these irregularities—that is, to "quasi-randomize" and equate people on significant variables—matching has often been used. This procedure has, however, been criticized on methodological and conceptual grounds. This "expedient," as Draguns (1982) calls it, has been acute in epidemiological studies of psychopathology, where researchers have no convenient and acceptable sampling strategy to employ.

Drawing from the work of Campbell and Stanley (1966), Campbell and Erlebacher (1970), and others, Brislin (1977) has cogently converted these methodological cautions for use in culture-comparative research. Draguns (1982, pp. 48–49) has given a very clear example of the problem:

> Whenever individuals from two samples with unequal means are matched, the resulting artificially equated pairs of subjects are susceptible to regression effects upon replication. Suppose that an investigator has succeeded in matching subjects from a nearly universally literate culture with subjects from a culture in which literacy is the exception rather than the rule. This feat has been accomplished by matching illiterate (but, in their own milieu, entirely typical) subjects in one case with highly deviant and atypical subjects in another. Apart from all the other problems that such a procedure entails, this "success" would be unlikely to be repeated upon replication. Unusual arrays of subjects do not usually turn up twice; therefore, the repetition of the study pushes the subjects of the study closer to their population means—they are no longer unable to read or write, although they are still sparsely educated. Such an outcome is almost inevitable in a comparison of two groups when one is at an extreme and the other is typical.

If matching is laden with these multiple and serious defects, what procedures can be recommended to take their place? Brislin and Baumgardner's (1971) proposal is both simple and far-reaching. These researchers suggest that unmatched samples of convenience be left as they are, but their characteristics should be described in scrupulous detail. Once this is done, subsequent investigators can refer the discrepancies in their findings to the specifics of their sample characteristics, and to the data of their predecessors. In the case of abnormal behavior across cultures, such a description should mandatorily include the basis on which the persons' behavior was judged to be abnormal, and the circumstances under which their responses were observed, elicited, or recorded. It is gratuitous to assume that the range of behavior defined as abnormal is constant across cultures or that cultures are identical in their thresholds of acceptability for a variety of acts.

FOUR LEVELS OF SAMPLING

If one were to start "from scratch" in designing a cross-cultural research project, four different levels of sampling would have to be considered. These levels include which *cultures* should be selected, which *communities* should be sampled, which *individuals* within the communities should be chosen, and which *behaviors* should be measured. At all four levels the type of data to be gathered or hypotheses to be tested will be of paramount concern. In short, a sort of overall research guide or manual of procedures would be helpful. Some of these procedures will already have been decided upon (e.g. the selection of cultures, the specific tests to use) before data are gathered in the field. A guide such as this, called the *Ethnocentrism Field Manual*, was developed by LeVine and Campbell (1965), an overview of which was given by Campbell and LeVine (1970) in their discussion of "Field-manual Anthropology." While each separate and different cross-cultural project will require the solution of each level of sampling, some general principles will be common to all. Presented first are major concerns in sampling cultures. In later sections, the sampling of communities, individuals, and behaviors will be discussed.

Sampling Cultures

Unless a research project is completely of an *ad hoc* and spontaneous nature (here I am in Lumbugoo; now what?), the researcher will have decided upon which cultures to study, and why, long before determining if his or her passport is valid. Typically, two (or more) cultures are chosen because each of them represents a different "treatment" of the predictor variable in question. The cultures chosen will usually represent significant contrasts with respect to some independent variable. Or, if one culture or country is selected, the selection is probably based on prior knowledge of groups within it that differ on one or more dimensions which represent different treatments (such as urban–rural, native speakers versus non-native speakers, first versus second generation). This process involves judgment sampling, or expert choice sampling, because the selection of a setting in which to do research is not done with the aid of a table of random numbers. Many cultures which may, on paper, be ideal for the testing of hypotheses, will be inaccessible for financial, political, or other reasons.

It is obvious that the major sampling question to be asked at this level is: To what extent will this culture (or these cultures) be useful in testing the hypotheses in question? Collaborators, colleagues, prior work on the theory or perspective being examined, convenience, accessibility, degree of local acceptance, and similar factors will have helped determine the selection of cultures. In the case of large, ongoing research projects (e.g. Williams & Best, 1982) new groups should be added to the extent that they are expected to add a different dimension to the total research scheme.

The Human Relations Area Files. A major aid in sampling entire cultures, or societies, are the Human Relations Area Files (HRAF). The complete paper files are sponsored by seventeen major universities and libraries, all but four of which are located in the United States. Because of the location of the files and their sheer bulk, they can be used only indirectly during field work. A cross-cultural researcher can make best use of the files either before field work or after. In both cases, but perhaps primarily *before* field work, the more likely uses of the files would be to acquaint the researcher with considerable ethnographic literature concerning the culture or culture area that one anticipates visiting for research purposes, and to help generate or clarify hypotheses about human behavior in the relative comfort of a library before leaving to collect data. In any event, a cross-cultural researcher should become acquainted with the nature, uses, and limitations of the entire HRAF system. This section is primarily concerned with issues and problems in sampling entire cultures, and how the files can and cannot be used in such sampling.

HRAF originated at Yale University in 1937 as the Cross-Cultural Survey, under the general direction of George Peter Murdock. The files essentially are a collection of ethnographic accounts and reports which have accumulated over the years, and which have been assembled according to an alphanumeric coding system. The coding system enables the files to be used as a data archive and a data retrieval system. These ethnographic materials can serve many purposes, including the facilitation of study, teaching, and research. Specific cultures or cultural areas can be the focus of a HRAF-oriented study, or cross-cultural studies (including hypothesis testing) can be facilitated by them.

The files are organized around two principal sourcebooks, or manuals. The first is entitled *Outline of World Cultures* (Murdock, 1975), which inventories and classifies the known cultures of the world. The preliminary, general classification of cultures divides the world into eight major geographical regions, each designated by a single code letter:

A — Asia	N — North America
E — Europe	O — Oceania
F — Africa	R — Russia
M — Middle East	S — South America

Each of these regions is then subdivided into subregions designated by a second letter, and a third level of classification breaks the divisions into "cultures," "societies," "tribes," etc. The files, however, do not contain information on all of these very many culture-bearing units. Rather, it lists more than 320 contemporary and historical cultural units of the world. Inclusion as a Cultural File is based upon the extensiveness and usefulness of the collected material.

The second manual, entitled *Outline of Cultural Materials* (Murdock, 1971) arranges the Cultural Files according to a special subject classification system. This system consists of more than 700 numbered subject categories grouped into 79 major topical sections. Using this system, each page of the source material included in each Cultural File has been analyzed; on the margins of each page are annotations of every subject located on that page. Using as many multiple copies of each page as are necessary, all materials dealing with a particular subject are brought together under a single subject category within each file.

This organizational scheme enables the researcher to select one culture, or a sample of cultures, and compare or contrast them on specific substantive topics. The actual conduct of HRAF-generated or -aided research should be attempted only after complete familiarization with the files and their supporting documents and publications. The main source of information about the files, their supporting materials, and institutional membership is, of course, the Human Relations Area Files, Inc., P.O. Box 2054, Yale Station, New Haven, Connecticut 06520. Descriptions of all these materials are included in free brochures. A letter or telephone call (Area Code 203, followed by 777-2334) will produce a quick response.

An HRAF publication, *Nature and Use of the Human Relations Area Files: A Research and Teaching Guide* (Lagacé, 1974), is the major guide explaining the full scope of these materials. A similar and somewhat briefer account is Herbert Barry's chapter in Volume 2 of the *Handbook of Cross-Cultural Psychology* (Barry, 1980). An earlier description of the files (Moore, 1970), Naroll's (1970) chapter on cross-cultural sampling (of cultures), and related methodological chapters are included in Naroll and Cohen's (1970) *Handbook of Method in Cultural Anthropology*.

Sampling Macroscopic Groups. Whether HRAF or some other source of archival material is used, the basic purpose of sampling from the universe of cultures is the same as in all other social or behavioral research—to make generalizations about some aspect of human behavior. As noted elsewhere in this chapter and probably in any book on research methods, the most useful and statistically sound sampling strategy is the probability sample. When used to its ideal limit, the one cardinal rule in probability sampling is that all members of the entire population (universe) must have an equal chance of being chosen to represent its population or universe. However, Naroll (1970, p. 889) warns that, ". . . it is impossible to use conventional probability sampling methods in cross-cultural surveys because most societies in the universe are not sufficiently well known to study" (and therefore to be included in the sample). Anthropologists and others who have used cross-cultural surveys have typically used judgmental, expert, or quota samples (discussed below), and each of these has large biases.

These sampling techniques may be used in combination. For example, as Naroll (1970) points out, ". . . a quota sample fixes in advance the proportions of units having the stated characteristics. It then uses haphazard or fortuitous sampling to fill its quotas." For instance, it may be decided that one's quota sample must include, in part, one rural Japanese community that has a population of less than

1,000, has no major industry, and is not within 100 kilometers of a city of more than 25,000 inhabitants. Within these stated parameters, the quota sampler now has the license to "grab" any one of many apparently qualified communities.

The Files and Holocultural Research. The HRAF system is frequently used in holocultural (also called hologeistic), or "whole world" research. It is a method for investigating statistically "the relationships between two or more variables theoretically defined and operationalized in a world sample of human societies" (Rohner, Naroll, Barry, Divale, Erickson, Schaeffer, & Sipes, 1978; see also Naroll, Michik, & Naroll, 1976, 1980). As the name of the method implies, the units of study are whole societies or whole cultural patterns.

Hypothesis testing within this method is very broad, and its cost effectiveness is attractive to those who want to test relationships between variables in a sweeping or macroscopic manner. But its major disadvantage is its imprecision, making it particularly vulnerable to error. Because of this, holocultural researchers are vigilant in their efforts to develop methods or guidelines to help in its responsible use. Rohner et al. (1978) have developed a set of guidelines for use in two kinds of holocultural studies—"quick" ones to permit the ready testing of hypotheses, and "safer" strategies which are more persuasive and less subject to criticism by the critics of holocultural research.

With respect to sample selection, Rohner et al. specify that (1) the units must be defined, (2) there must be an adequate geographical distribution of sampling units, (3) probability sampling must be used (this rules out the use of judgmental samples and samples of convenience), (4) explanation of sampling procedures must be given, and (5) the measurement of sampling bias must be included. This last guideline principally involves "Galton's Problem," which merits a brief explanation here (Naroll, 1970, discusses it in detail). Because any cultural characteristic may have been the result of borrowing or migration—that is, by cultural diffusion—Galton's Problem is the problem of how interdependent the units are in a cross-cultural survey or holocultural study. Causal connections between culture and behavior will be inaccurate to the extent that cultures or units in the sample are not historically independent. Potential solutions to Galton's Problem are numerous; Naroll, Michik, and Naroll (1980) discuss several of these approaches.

HRAF Probability Samples. According to Moore (1970), HRAF's aim is not to provide a true probability sample of all the world's cultures. Rather, HRAF provides a limited universe from which the researcher can draw samples. Young says that, ". . . no effort has been made to evaluate the world's supply of cultures and to reproduce a miniature model in the HRAF files of this world of cultures. . . What has been done is to survey the world, area by area, and produce files representative of the range of variation within each area" (p. 644).

This is the idea underlying the HRAF Probability Sample, developed to provide researchers with files designed to deal with a broad range of research topics and problems. This set consists of 50 Cultural Files containing data on a world–wide sample of 60 cultural units that were selected by a stratified random sampling technique. Details of ongoing refinements in drawing HRAF probability samples frequently appear in the HRAF "house" journal, *Behavior Science Research*. The reader is referred to Lagacé (1979) for complete descriptions of how these samples are drawn as well as the specific names of all 60 cultural units spread over the eight major geographical regions.

The following summary will conclude this overview of HRAF as the major means of sampling whole cultures or societies and as a repository of a vast amount of cultural information.

1. As a warehouse of ethnographic information and reports, alphanumerically organized and coded to facilitate research, HRAF is without peer. The files are of central importance in holocultural research, where generally broad hypotheses are tested;

2. Research conducted using only the files is strictly library research; however, the files can be used to acquaint oneself with specific cultures or culture areas, usually of course before field work in the culture or area in question;

3. Sampling strategies used by HRAF are not probabilistic samples simply because not all cultures or societies of the world have an equal chance of being selected. Researchers therefore have to be content with carefully developed probability samples which, in addition to claims of being representative of regions of the world, are sensitive to the requirement that cultures be independent if analyses are to be accurate. This refers to Galton's Problem, which has attracted much attention by hologeistic researchers and others engaged in crosscultural surveys and hypothesis testing.

Sampling Communities

Once a cultural or ethnic group has been defined and selected as a focus for research, it becomes essential to identify communities and individuals who *belong* to it; this is not a simple matter, as we shall see. It is also essential to identify which communities and individuals *represent* the culture or ethnic group in some specified way. These two issues are those of specifying the *population*, and of drawing a *sample*, respectively. Community aspects of these issues are considered in this section, while individual aspects are dealt with in the next.

The selection of communities or groups (sometimes referred to as Primary Sampling Units, or PSUs) to represent the parent culture is guided by judgment and informed, expert advice. The ideal PSU would be a microcosm, or "culture in miniature," of the population it is to represent. In certain classic studies in the United States, for example, places like "Midwest," "Elmtown," and "Orchard Town" have been chosen because they may have satisfied important criteria constituting the essence of "United States-ness," which any one of hundreds of other communities may also have satisfied. However, difficulties in sampling communities or PSUs in heterogeneous populations will be much greater than when dealing with homogeneous populations.

In any research project, the topic being studied or the theory being tested will dictate the type and number of communities or groups needed. Some basic questions to be asked are:

1. What are the key criteria which need to be met in order to test the theory or gather the desired data? Key criteria will include but are not limited to such factors as accessibility, size of community, type and level of education, distinctive features of community, age and sex composition, and political organization.
2. Is this community "typical" or "representative" of the larger group to which inferences will be made?
3. Can the sampling procedures be documented to the extent that someone could replicate the study in another, parallel setting? If this is the only group of its kind, then it should be so stated.

Who belongs? In many field settings it is not possible to say without qualification who belongs to the ethnic or cultural group of interest to the researcher. This is due to a number of factors. One is that there is often a more or less continuous variation in culture and language over broad geographical ranges. In northern Canada, for example,

Algonkian language-family speakers range from Naskapi and Montagnais in Labrador or Quebec, to Cree (Eastern-, Moose-, and Swampy-Cree) around James Bay, to Northern Ojibwe, Oji-Cree, and Saulteaux in Ontario and Manitoba. If the research task were to sample "Cree" people, it would be rather difficult to clearly assign these broad groups of people to either a simple Cree or nonCree category; it would be equally difficult to assign specific communities, and to assign specific individuals. Essentially, we are faced with the problem, well-known to psychologists, of categorizing a continuous variable. In Europe, to take another example, historically across the southern coast of the North Sea, a similar problem existed: who was "Flemish," who was "Dutch," who was "German," and who was "Danish" was not a very easy task to decide until the rise of modern nation states. In other areas, however, very clear-cut distinctions are maintained among the people themselves: who is an Inuit and who is a Cree, and who is a Biaka Pygmy and who is a Bangandu Villager, are not usually difficult decisions to make.

Another problem derives from the phenomenon of shifting alliances and nomadism. Culturally similar (but not identical) groups may co-reside or establish social and political relationships on a temporary or short-term basis. Thus when one researcher visits, the population may be large and somewhat heterogeneous, while at another time for another researcher, it may be smaller and more homogeneous.

A third issue is that of ethnicity, as distinct from culture. If one wants to sample Spanish or French people in the world, one is faced with large ethnic variations within the basic cultural tradition. Are French-Canadian communities to be included in a sample of French people? Are those of Louisiana, Acadia, Manitoba, and Réunion to be sampled as well?

The practical consequence of these issues is that a researcher should be aware of the artificiality of categories, of the temporary presence of some peoples, and of ethnic variation within a cultural tradition, and attempt to guard against including those he does not wish to include. Essentially, the solution boils down to a matter of precise definition of who belongs *for that time and that project*. It cannot be a perfectly valid and permanent definition, but it can be fairly precisely defined, so that the parameters can be understood by others.

Who counts? How can one or a few communities represent a

culture? In most social surveys, as broad a cross-section as possible is sought, while in most anthropological studies, a single (or a very few) communities are studied; in both cases generalizations to the whole population are usually attempted or implied. Given that in general psychology little attention is normally paid to the sample (students will do!), why should cross-cultural psychologists be concerned with the issue at all? The answer is that in field work we have to be guided by the rules of our social science colleagues, and try to attain some representativeness, even without having the resources (or the practical possibility) of carrying out a full social survey.

The most common "solution" in cross-cultural psychology has been to take a single community and assume it to be representative of the culture as a whole. This may be defensible where there is little internal variation, but where there are differences due to acculturation experience, urbanization, economic base, ethnicity, language, or religion, this will not do. With respect to acculturation, one may select one relatively "traditional," one "transitional," and one "acculturated" community (see Chapter 10 for details of assessing variation in acculturation status). This dimension very often co-varies with the urbanization and economic base of the community, and this confound should be monitored.

With respect to ethnicity (including language and religion) in multi-ethnic societies, be they large scale (like France, India, and Nigeria) or smaller scale (like Mauritius, Malaysia, and Fiji), an attempt should be made to represent each group with at least a single community. On the other hand of course, if the concern is with a particular ethnic group rather than the society as a whole, then this need not be an issue, except to the extent that it establishes a broader societal context in which the ethnic group functions.

Once the *kind* of community has been established, the issue of *which one(s)* specifically arises. Here, practical matters may predominate: is there a pre-existing contact, a friendly leader, an appropriate research assistant who originally came from there? Is there availability of accommodation? As long as these practical factors do not bias the community representativeness in some way (e.g. is the community economy specialized in receiving re-searchers!), the choice can to some extent follow these practical considerations.

In sum, communities should be sampled in order to represent the culture, taking into account both the need to include internal diversity, and a variety of practical matters. However, the former should normally take priority over the latter in making a final decision. To the extent that representativeness is achieved, then generalization to the whole culture may be warranted; however, if representativeness is not reached, care should be taken to qualify the generality of the work by referring to the specific community, ethnic group, or region, rather than easily slipping into references to the culture as a whole.

Sampling Individuals

The topic of investigation, research framework, or theory being examined obviously will influence which individuals to include in the sample. Lonner (1980) analyzed the various characteristics of the first 347 articles published in JCCP from 1970–79. One of the dimensions of that analysis concerned the nature of the samples used as a function of the type of research project or topic being studied. For example, in acculturation research adults more frequently than children have served as subjects; perhaps one must first achieve adulthood status before the effects of acculturation can be measured reliably and accurately. On the other hand, children are typically sampled more frequently than adults in cognitive research (largely influenced cross-culturally by the Piagetian, and very child-oriented, framework). College students have generally served as subjects in research on personality, which is more often than not measured in classrooms (samples of convenience) by using paper-and-pencil measures. However, no rules specify that children cannot be used to study the effects of acculturation, that adults are not good candidates for research on cognition, and that personality variables are best examined through college-aged samples. Accessibility, convenience, and tradition appear to be the major factors influencing the selection of individuals to participate in research.

Aside from the directives given by the research topic, sampling of individuals within communities, as Osgood, May, and Miron (1975) point out, poses a dilemma: Does the investigator want representativeness within each country or equivalence across countries? To quote Osgood et al.:

Maximizing representativeness within usually means minimizing equivalence between, and vice versa. A representative sample in India, for example, would involve proportionate numbers of many castes, many religions, and many languages, and it would include many illiterates and people in villages having minimal awareness of the outside world. Such a sample would hardly be comparable with one representative of the Netherlands, using its usual criteria. On the other hand, a sample of Indian college students obviously would be much more highly selected (less representative) than an 'equivalent' sample of Dutch college students. What compromise between these poles is made in an investigator's sampling strategy depends primarily upon the purpose of the research (p. 19).

In Osgood's program dealing with affective, metaphorical meaning, it was required that people were able to read, were relatively homogeneous, were accessible, were interested, and so forth. Therefore, only adolescent males in average high schools were used. It is clear that Osgood et al. chose to maximize equivalence. However, assuring cross-cultural equivalence also increases the homogeneity of the sample and decreases alternative explanations of results. Conversely, maximizing representativeness decreases homogeneity, but at the same time increases the number of variables affecting results.

Unless one is involved with a public opinion poll or some sort of national or community survey, random or representative samples in cross-cultural research are inappropriate except to the extent that randomization can occur after some specialized sub-set of the population is identified. If one is hypothesizing, for instance, that specialized experience or its absence affects cognitive growth, then obviously individuals who do and do not have such specialized experience will be included in the sample.

Once again, at this level of sampling there is no substitute for judgment; probability sampling is somewhat irrelevant. All of the important criteria which each member of the sample should possess should be listed. Then, all individuals who meet these criteria should be identified. Once this has been accomplished, taking a random sample is appropriate. However, listing the criteria necessary for inclusion in a sample (and often the criteria are numerous) often results in the need to use *all* individuals so identified, and therefore makes randomization from a list unnecessary.

Who belongs? The first step in sampling individuals is to define the population; this is as true in field work as in conventional social surveys. Unfortunately, the achievement of a good population description is very difficult in most field settings. Nation states often have national census figures, but for some regions and some groups they may be inaccurate; this is due to a host of problems, ranging from political considerations and dishonesty among census-takers, to simple inaccessibility of individuals. Thus in parts of the world where these problems are likely to exist, national census figures may not be relied upon.

To overcome this problem, the field researcher would do well to attempt population estimates of his own, at least for the communities which have been selected. One may attempt to carry out a census at an initial stage of the work, and this may be a good strategy even if "records" are said to be available for the community. The difficulty is that "records" vary greatly in their reliability and validity. In some jurisdictions, there is detailed information about every individual; for example, Band lists in Amerindian communities in Canada list every person, their age, sex, and whether they reside in or outside the communities. At the other extreme, whole categories of people may be ignored. Band lists exist only for "status" or registered Indians in recognized Bands; those who are "nonstatus" or of mixed ancestry are not listed at all and it is extremely difficult to identify this portion of the native Indian population. In between these two extremes are situations where a person's illegitimacy, forgetfulness or laziness by officials, prejudice against some kinds of people (e.g. lower caste, those pursuing a more traditional lifestyle) all contribute to biased population records.

As part of such an initial census, it is often important to record sex, age (or an age estimation), religion, ethnic self-identity and clan (if appropriate), and location in the community. These may all be useful in either selecting a stratified sample (see below) or in checking the sample representativeness against these demographic criteria.

The determination of age is no simple matter in many field situations. In the absence of birth records, the researcher has to rely upon other information and methods. A "triangulation" has been carried out by van de Koppel (1983) to provide ages of Biaka Pygmy children (in the nine to twelve-year age range). In this work three sources of information were used, and the individual's age was accepted only if all three yielded the same estimate. First, a series of significant local events (e.g. the death of a leader or the killing of a leopard) were documented with precise dates from regional records; parents of prospective children were asked to locate the birth of their child in this time space, a task usually done without difficulty. Second, given that each Biaka camp is associated with a villager family (whose children's birthdates are usually registered), each prospective Biaka child's birthdate was located by the parent in relation to those of similar-aged villagers. And third, dental maturation was taken into account. On the basis of this triangulation procedure, ages of a sufficiently large sample of children of the appropriate age range were determined.

In addition to census records, others may be available in partial form. These include baptismal or other religious records, tax rolls, school class lists, trading post records, and any previous estimates made by researchers.

Who counts? In selecting individuals for a sample, an assumption is made that *some* individuals can represent *all* individuals in the population. From this basic belief of sampling arises the question of *which* individuals. Two basic strategies are usually employed: the *random sample*, and the *stratified sample*. In the former every individual in the population should have an equal chance to appear in the sampling using some randomization procedure. In the latter, on the other hand, the population is first divided into sub-populations or strata (such as males/females, adults/children, urban/rural, traditional/transitional/acculturated) and then randomization is used.

One interesting assumption is made in these procedures: that every individual counts the same as every other individual. This reveals what might be called a "democratic bias," which is that every member displays equally well the culture and behavior of his group. While this may be true for some societies, it is not likely true for all societies. Important cultural information may be restricted in its distribution (e.g. literacy), and certain roles or abilities may be socialized in only a few individuals (e.g. *shaman*, navigator). To the extent that this is true, random procedures may miss important cultural and behavioral features. We are thus faced with the possibility that Western political values of democracy are influencing our research method to the detriment of discovering important phenomena in other cultures.

In part, stratified sampling has been developed to deal with this general issue. Thus males and females might be guaranteed equal proportions in the overall sample or even literates and nonliterates, *shamans* and non*shamans*; but, the subsequent use of randomization to answer the question *which* literates (etc.) betrays a "democratic bias."

Taking the issue a step further anthropologists have tended to avoid the use of random samples in their field work, tending to rely on *key informants*; these are individuals who are considered (by virtue of their central position, reputation, etc.) to be bearers of the culture of their group in ways which are not borne by "just anybody." To illustrate, one hears of an anthropologist from Lapa-Lapa who studied the rules of sport in Western culture using a survey sample technique; one startling finding was that it takes 2.863 strikes and you're out! Cross-cultural psychologists need to be aware of this approach, and to decide whether these random or specific alternative approaches (or some combination) may better suit their purposes.

Randomization may be done in the field in a variety of ways. If a list of individuals is available, they can be numbered, and a table of random numbers (see Table 3.1) may be employed. If a list of families or compounds or clans is available, the random procedure can be carried out in stages, by first randomly selecting the collective unit, then by listing only those individuals in the selected units, then by randomly selecting individuals. Block sampling of defined geographical areas may also be employed in this way if a map (but not a census) is available.

Stratification, by any criterion which may be relevant to the research (e.g. males and females for studies of sex differences, by age groups for developmental studies), is time consuming, but may be essential for these types of studies. Other examples would be schooled versus nonschooled for examining the effects of education, urban versus rural for studying urbanization effects, and similar contrasts.

When drawing up the list of individuals in the sample, some advance estimate should be made of refusals; the list should be larger by the anticipated refusal rate, and then some, to protect against accidents, ill-health, travel, and other reasons for nonavailability. When the final list is drawn up, care must be taken to give every individual the same chance to participate. Reluctance to seek out a particular person by the research assistant, or a series of "missed appointments" should not be accepted easily by the researcher. In one case, a sample of Inuit included the name of a person who could "never be found" (according to an assistant); when it was insisted that we try to locate him, the response was that "he couldn't do the work" that we were asking participants to do. On subsequent testing for spatial abilities, he indeed obtained the lowest score in the sample, and the research assistant provided the information that this person "always got lost" when out hunting! Perhaps psychological tests are unnecessary in the field, where individual differences are so well known to everyone in the community!

In summary, sampling individuals comes up against the same kinds of problems as sampling communities, but many more points of decision need to be made; there are more possible strata, and there are more possible data points (individuals).

Behavior Sampling

The most specific level of sampling concerns the actual behaviors of individuals; it can also be argued that this is the most important level, for it is here that psychologists attempt to quantify matters by assigned test scores, indicating where someone falls on a scale, or counting how frequently certain behaviors occur with or without caretakers present.

A distinction may be made between *maximum* performance (i.e. how well does one perform when presented with a task or test that may measure his or her optimal level of functioning?) and *typical* performance (i.e. what is the nature of an individual's everyday, ongoing behavior?). A measure of maximum performances usually lasts a short period (taking a test for example).

Some test experts (e.g. Cronbach, 1984) use this distinction when categorizing tests. Thus, for instance, tests of ability, skill, aptitude, or intelligence should be designed to sample those kinds of behaviors when they are in fullest flower. On the other hand, when personality or values are being assessed, one would like to measure them under conditions that may be called average, or typical. In either case, a very small segment of a person's life (taken at one or more junctures in time) provides the setting or the vehicle for gathering the data, and the aim of the researcher should be representation.

Whether or not tests or similar devices are used to measure samples of an individual's maximum or typical performance, the systematic observation and recording of behavior is frequently an important activity at the individual level. A good deal has been written about the systematic observation of behaviors in different cultures (see Bochner's chapter, this volume). Longabaugh's (1980) treatment of the topic is the most thorough, and perhaps Whiting and Whiting (1975) is the most well known study in which these techniques played such an important part. Longabaugh distinguishes between the sampling of *settings*, of *behaviors*, and *events*.

Settings, or more accurately behavior settings, is a concept popularized by Roger Barker, a psychologist influenced by Kurt Lewin's field theory (see Chapter 6 for more information on Barker's perspective). Behavior settings are extra-individual, usually fixed, persistent patterns of stimuli that are culturally defined and culturally variable. Settings are phenomenal and ecological, and to a great extent place limits on the range of possible behavior. Barker's concept of "behavior setting claim" is defined as all the forces acting upon individuals in a setting to enter and participate in its operation in particular ways. Thus, settings "claim" (influence, set limits on) all behavior. In sampling behavior settings for culture-comparative purposes, care must be taken to insure the equivalence of settings in terms of the comparability of the behaviors they elicit. For instance, Longabaugh (1980, p. 75) cautions that "While one setting may be physically and culturally equivalent to another, individuals in the setting are likely to perceive and experience the setting differently. Much of the difference may be attributed to the socially defined roles they occupy in the setting." Grocery stores in towns of equal sizes in different countries, even if there are equal numbers of them, may prompt different behavior depending upon socially sanctioned expectations. Sampling behavior that occurs in superficially similar, but functionally different, settings can lead to erroneous comparisons. (Note the similarities between this problem and the problem of matching, discussed earlier.) Perhaps the first task in sampling behavior in settings is to determine which settings are equivalent, or as an alternative in some way control for possible differences. "The main conclusion," writes Longabaugh, "is that behavioral variables have unknown relations to setting variables. Each relationship may be empirically determined. Meanwhile, generalizations regarding findings must be couched carefully to avoid overly inclusive generalizations."

Behaviors. In observing behavior systematically, the issue has been whether the period of observation is to be determined by continuous observation, time sampling, or even recording (Longabaugh, 1980). In *continuous observation*, the entire period of some activity, for example, on the playground, is recorded and then scanned for some criterion behavior. If less than the entire period is to be selected from, then some method of sampling has to be determined, perhaps by using time sampling. In *time sampling*, some ongoing behavior is recorded, and samples of the behavior are determined by three parameters: (a) whether the schedule for sampling is fixed or variable, (b) the duration of the interval of time in which the behavior is observed, and (c) the duration of the interval of time between periods of observation. One might, for example, sample every tenth minute (fixed) or (as a variable schedule) observe and record what happens immediately after some sort of criterion behavior (e.g. child hits another child). The time period may be one minute or one hour, and observations can take place once daily or less frequently.

Event sampling. Many permutations of event sampling are outlined by Longabaugh (1980, pp. 79–82), to which the reader may refer. Essentially, any event will involve people, an environmental setting, behavior, the duration of observation, and the intervals between observation; each of these will be observed/recorded on either a fixed schedule (e.g. a certain target person, or a certain category of behavior) or variable schedule (any setting in which a certain type of behavior occurs, where the behavioral criteria may occur irregularly).

Strategies for sampling behaviors, settings, and events may be decided upon in the field, once the range of possibilities is assessed. However, the researcher will benefit greatly from some fairly detailed and well-reasoned guidelines that he or she would hope to follow. Modifications of these can be implemented, depending upon the demands and constraints of the specific field situation (which itself is a behavior setting which will claim, or evoke, certain types of behavior).

From all this, it should be obvious that the "lamplight" strategy has no place in cross-cultural research; this is where the drunk looks for his car keys under the street light because it's easier there, rather than where they were really dropped. Rather than use our standard kit of handy tests developed to assess Western behaviors, the more appropriate alternative is to try to identify the characteristic behaviors which are developed and displayed in a particular group, and then to sample these behaviors. This indigenous or *emic* approach was first articulated by Goodenough (1936) who argued that the central issue in cross-cultural assessment is to "be sure that

TABLE 3.1
Random Numbers Sample

026	923	974	075	751	680	354	193	562	522
822	801	889	901	045	725	318	749	129	535
246	289	738	836	953	868	110	050	705	920
488	716	221	782	083	783	572	476	163	477
869	035	545	756	255	019	922	985	143	417
551	264	172	776	366	415	275	684	377	156
747	714	503	247	898	962	544	662	348	104
573	158	887	943	753	072	737	938	184	029
378	166	557	128	598	185	436	168	683	549
674	339	945	466	500	574	948	177	511	437
870	592	433	015	736	629	517	644	463	107
169	605	011	119	764	090	647	144	568	601
724	087	042	443	497	584	109	486	589	260
389	534	498	349	462	956	126	857	266	520
286	642	576	981	215	994	441	996	739	245
936	315	585	987	713	788	070	044	608	314
490	524	154	358	813	876	612	655	516	941
501	904	824	872	259	861	888	789	667	364
250	302	543	473	101	637	305	971	209	664
149	865	707	224	131	719	189	899	073	826
735	331	926	424	931	294	089	932	295	611
285	743	594	697	459	054	593	025	448	392
235	280	435	858	508	092	160	242	616	689
201	059	274	398	997	814	866	096	715	617
060	533	192	741	949	835	817	897	711	360

164	968	679	883	723	787	082	954	937	422
730	765	946	145	021	453	241	069	666	346
993	762	341	190	298	502	977	412	918	646
606	095	024	781	351	509	402	388	297	505
777	203	658	182	079	368	081	518	660	867
276	750	519	230	040	136	371	001	345	909
455	610	301	085	352	414	991	106	829	507
588	526	194	005	970	056	895	030	461	219
939	454	278	410	173	431	640	051	310	236
547	792	717	896	602	134	426	428	618	220
118	036	952	217	474	039	020	067	951	047
155	495	894	057	282	322	115	650	238	555
558	957	161	033	340	779	179	434	973	622
122	479	451	855	841	626	009	094	552	112
393	581	362	198	329	074	002	966	123	485
732	539	529	178	891	659	670	712	127	216
615	696	538	105	430	233	308	603	546	763
859	927	014	815	972	472	531	465	758	748
561	720	933	438	700	873	708	571	003	665
446	211	306	309	100	548	591	846	624	816
138	910	311	757	988	157	761	202	681	635
699	639	350	000	580	406	638	068	880	819
290	929	481	613	321	678	213	890	702	900
784	405	239	261	795	530	567	742	226	457
916	959	645	080	595	460	174	328	205	353

the test-items from which the total trait is to be judged are representative and valid samples of the ability in question, as it is displayed within the particular culture with which we are concerned" (p. 5). Or, in Wober's (1969) terms, we should try to assess how well they can do their tricks, not how poorly they do our tricks.

One way to discover what "tricks" a people value and develop, is to do an "ecological analysis" (Berry, 1980) in which day-to-day activities are examined, including subsistence life, social relations, childrearing strategies, etc.; these should reveal some of the more relevant behaviors which can be the basis for a "population" of behaviors from which to draw a "sample" using psychological tests (or other techniques) which are developed for the purpose. All of the theoretical and methodological issues addressed in Chapters 1 and 2 are relevant here, and so will not be repeated. And all of the specific techniques of testing, observation, scaling, etc., covered in Chapters 6, 7, 8, and 9, are also relevant here.

Basically, the argument is that while cross-cultural psychologists have developed awareness for the need to properly sample cultures, communities, and individuals, there appears to have been less concern with properly representing a sample of behaviors in the data-gathering instruments. Until behavior sampling meets these same standards these other sampling methods may have little contribution to make to the overall validity of the research enterprise.

NOTE

1. This table of random numbers was computer-generated by Floyd Rudmin.

4

FIELD WORK IN CROSS-CULTURAL PSYCHOLOGY

ROBERT L. MUNROE
RUTH H. MUNROE

Field work, long associated with anthropology, has come increasingly to be recognized in cross-cultural psychology as a fruitful approach to knowledge. The type of field work practiced by psychologists differs to some extent from the traditional anthropological mode of data gathering, which has been characterized as "an attempt to understand, by close and direct contact, how a living community works and what the beliefs, norms and values by which it lives are" (Firth, 1972, p. 10). One difference is that the primarily descriptive goals of anthropological field work, as reflected in the above statement, are replaced in psychology by more analytically phrased, problem-oriented questions. Another difference is that the issue of "how a community works," that is, how a sociocultural system operates, is subordinated to psychological endeavors revolving around particular variables of interest (Jahoda, 1982; cf. the discussion by Poortinga and Malpass in Chapter 1 of this volume). And third, the "close and direct contact" endorsed and often enthusiastically prescribed by anthropologists[1] would not necessarily be embraced by psychologists. Nevertheless, important similarities remain, and the depiction of field work as the study of a natural population (or a portion of one) with which the investigator maintains day-to-day, personal involvement captures the essence of the undertaking for both disciplines.

Field work is carried on in a great variety of settings, which range from previously unstudied, isolated communities of a few dozen souls[2] to groups resident in large urban centers throughout the world (e.g. Aschenbrenner, 1975; Jacobson, 1973; Lewis, 1966; Seymour, 1980). While this chapter is intended to consider information and issues relevant to every kind of setting, it is oriented less toward plural societies and complex urban groups than toward small-scale, relatively homogeneous settings. We feel that in certain settings, viz. modern cities, the industrial world, and formal schooling sites, field work procedures can partially rely on a minimal "common culture" shared by any investigator and a given culture-group, and that the need to explicate the details of procedures is not so compelling for these instances as for the less familiar settings. We also feel that critical factors about which an investigator in a complex society ought to be knowledgeable in advance—say, concerning personal safety considerations that might affect an Anglo field worker in a Chicago ghetto, or the elaborate social protocol which a field worker should observe in Osaka—can be learned, and typically will be learned, from informed outsiders familiar with the culture-group under consideration. Those interested in discussion of field experiences in complex societies might want to consult Whyte (1984), Spradley and McCurdy (1972), Foster and Kemper (1974), or chapters by Gmelch, Spradley, and Whiteford in Gmelch and Zenner (1980). Spradley and McCurdy (1972) present case studies of such phenomena as fire fighters, an urban jewelry store, hitchhiking, a car theft ring, a second-grade recess, and the kitchen culture in a restaurant.

Field work by its nature is among the least rigorous of methodological strategies. What can it offer cross-cultural psychology, which in any case is said not to meet the most exacting standards of methodology? (Bochner, Brislin, & Lonner, 1975.) For one thing, recent research has demonstrated serious noncorrespondence between laboratory and naturalistic measures of the "same" behavior (Ceci & Bronfenbrenner, 1985; Cole, Hood, & McDermott, 1982; Istomina, 1975), and field work, in promoting naturalistic investigations, can help to illuminate this problem. Further, by enhancing the possibility of observing natural events relevant to the study at hand, it can aid in the formulation of pertinent new measures and techniques. It also enables psychologists to gather data directly from individuals, in contrast to the collective-level archival data from which individual-level inferences have often been made in past cross-cultural psychological research (Whiting, 1968). Even when not used as a basis for systematic data-gathering, field work can provide information that aids in interpretation of results or that enables the investigator to limn the larger sociocultural context in which the data reside (Berry, 1980). Complementing strictly scientific aims, it allows a humanistic *verstehen* that informs the study as a whole (Pelto & Pelto, 1973) and heightens the investigator's awareness of the differences and similarities in acceptable modes of behavior, social interaction, and institutional provisions for human need satisfaction. Finally, field work always holds out as an enticement the serendipitous occurrence, the unexpected insight or finding that comes because one is there and is prepared when it does occur. Such factors as these, and not a potential gain in rigor, justify the use of field work in cross-cultural psychology. Given this understanding, we shall attempt in the present chapter to consider field work in relation to the aims of cross-cultural psychology, concentrating most of our attention on the practical and technical matters that affect the course of research.

PREPARATION FOR THE FIELD

There are two likely possibilities faced by the prospective field worker in cross-cultural psychology. Either a specific research plan has been laid out, with a cultural group chosen, a particular study formulated, and funding and many other practical considerations already thought through and arranged, or an opportunity to reside in a different culture has arisen, but the field work, though being actively projected, has not been planned in any detail.

In the first case, little or nothing may be needed in the way of preparation for the research *per se*, but if the psychologist is not thoroughly familiar with the area to which he/she will be travelling, then advance inquiry is desirable concerning personal matters such as passport and visa requirements, immunizations (cf. "Immunizations," 1983), food, clothing, housing, health, an international driver's license, and local transport, as well as availability and cost of supplies and equipment, for example paper, ink, film, typewriters, cameras, tape recorders, micro-computers, and photocopying and other duplicating facilities.[3] Sometimes climatic conditions dictate special treatment for equipment, for example "tropicalizing" electronic gear to guard against high humidity. Frequently a phone call or correspondence with a colleague who is experienced in the area will yield highly useful information of this sort. Names and addresses of many active cross-cultural psychologists throughout the world can be found in the *Cross-Cultural Psychology Bulletin*, a bi-monthly publication of the International Association for Cross-Cultural Psychology. Culture-area interests of anthropologists can be found in the annual *Guide to Departments of Anthropology* (American Anthropological Association, 1984).

Should the field work represent an unexpected opportunity for which no firm research plans have been drawn, consultation with area specialists is doubly recommended. The research scholar would do well to peruse major sources in order to learn about problems that have engaged psychologists and psychological anthropologists working in the area. See, for instance, Triandis' (1980–81) six-volume *Handbook of Cross-Cultural Psychology*, Hsu's (1972) *Psychological Anthropology* (with chapters on Japan, Africa, North America, and Oceania), and recent issues of cross-culturally oriented journals. Copies of relevant journal articles should be taken to the field because libraries in many countries have scant resources for journal subscriptions.

To increase knowledge of the primary sociocultural configurations characteristic of the area, the psychologist could consult Murdock's (1967, 1975) *Ethnographic Atlas* and *Outline of World Cultures*, and Barry's (1980) "Description and Uses of the Human Relations Area Files" (for a brief description of the files, see Chapter 3 in this volume). A classification and index of the languages of the world has been published (Voegelin & Voegelin, 1977), and descriptions of hundreds of unwritten languages can be found in the *International Journal of American Linguistics*.

The fact that traditional peoples are frequently unfamiliar with social science and its testing techniques renders unworkable many of the measures and laboratory situations or techniques used in modern psychology. It is thus advisable to scan journals not only for articles relevant to one's research interests, but also for measures that may be appropriate in nonliterate populations or in those having little experience with complicated verbal instructions or with instruments that depend on complex technological experience on the part of the subject. Measures that appear promising in this regard, even when not particularly pertinent to one's own specific research interests, can be taken to the field and tried on an exploratory basis.

Sufficient lead time must be given to obtain letters of introduction (if recommended) and research authorization (if this can be achieved at a distance). Embassies and consulates for host countries can often answer questions about the need for national-level research authorization. If there are social scientists in the host country, or university departments of social science, it is recommended that investigators make some preliminary contact with appropriate persons before arrival in the country.

ENTERING THE FIELD[4]

Probably the most critical nonscientific factor affecting cross-cultural research today is the matter of formal authorization, generally required of foreign nationals before any extended residence or study can be undertaken. Understandably, the question of legitimacy, of the investigator and/or of the project, is often carefully scrutinized either in some central government agency or at a regional or local level. Collaborative projects undertaken with professionals in the host country have the greatest chance for approval, and collaboration can sometimes be arranged in advance through correspondence. If, however, there are no clearly relevant in-country professionals or there is no time to make advance arrangements, potential field workers should be aware that there may be some difficulty in obtaining permission. In some nations, research authorization is constantly being opened and closed off in various areas, with sociopolitical conditions influencing the topics that one can or cannot investigate, and lengthy bureaucratic procedures sometimes delaying authorization long enough that research funds and time can be depleted. Compounding the possible difficulty in obtaining authorization are certain moral dilemmas. First, the behavioral scientist may encounter either implied or stated demands for monetary or personal favors in return for rapid consideration or positive decisions. Second, there may be project alterations requested, particularly in developing countries where local professionals are few and where answers to pressing social problems are given priority over basic research which has no immediately discernible payoff. With respect to the first problem, prospective field workers should attempt to avoid being placed in possibly illegal or compromising positions so should, in general, resist all nongovernmental demands. With respect to the second, it is often possible to incorporate some of the problems identified and to provide needed information—with the customary safeguards to individual research participants—in order to try to assist the host nation in the solution of social problems.

Field work is especially susceptible to problems with governmental or agency approval in certain areas of the world, notably in Africa and among indigenous peoples of North America, due to the perception that social scientists have taken much material away and given little of use in return. The best advice on how to proceed in a given setting is in the possession of those who have actually obtained research clearance, and psychologists should attempt to contact such individuals either before setting out or immediately upon arrival in the host country. In general, it may be said that following prescribed procedures and maintaining persistent, polite inquiry about the progress of one's application is likely to result in more expeditious handling. Although research clearance aids in dealing with immigration authorities, official visas often must be secured for the appropriate length of time. Because it is frequently necessary to renew visas after relatively short periods of time, information about the regulations should be obtained before leaving a capital city or other major government center.[5]

Even if there are delays in authorization, one essential aspect of the study frequently can proceed on a casual, unobtrusive basis, and that is reconnoitering in order to locate an appropriate research site. Typically a cultural group will already have been located, and the issue one faces is finding a community which is representative of this culture-group and which, at the same time, meets both research requirements (e.g. has a population adequate to desired size of samples) and personal needs (e.g. has housing available). Considerations of safety, which were once minimal owing to a kind of immunity enjoyed by outsiders, are now an element that must be taken into account. Inquiry among government officials and professionals in the country can often yield the safety information necessary for choice of a study site.

Once a specific community has been chosen (and clearance obtained) for the research, official contact should be initiated at the local level. In some communities there are no superordinate authorities (due to the nature of the social structure), and in some others there is a general amorphousness that makes protocol irrelevant. But in most cases, a visit to high officials (beginning at the

op)—be they mayors, chiefs, parliamentary representatives, or
istrict officers—is *de rigueur*. The point of such a visit is to make
ne's presence and purpose known as well as to show appropriate
cknowledgment of authority and to attempt to enlist assistance or
ooperation. In meeting with local authorities, a broadly phrased
lescription of the research should be offered, with a written
tatement or details supplied if requested. Local authorities should be
pprised of the general procedure one hopes to follow, for example
lassroom testing, home visits, attendance at public gatherings, so
hat the officials may explain one's presence if the occasion arises.
Often, local officials can give the investigator a sense of whether an
pen meeting with community members might prove useful. Many
ocal officials are actively helpful and make suggestions that facilitate
he study, while others tend to let the researcher go his/her way, but
ew—given evidence of formal research clearance—are genuinely
negative or obstructionist.

The choice of living quarters is important. One wishes to be as
close to the community as is feasible, both for effecting rapport with
community members and for maximum exposure to events. Thus
housing within the community itself is preferable to, say, spatially
segregated and/or peripheral housing in a school compound or in a
local tract built primarily for government employees, and these in
turn are preferable to residence in another community. To be
avoided if possible is regular vehicular transportation to the
community, which would emphasize the status of the visitor as an
outsider. The *most* intimate living arrangement would involve the
researcher in sharing the quarters of a family within the community,
but this degree of closeness has its own built-in difficulties revolving
around time and some control over health-maintenance practices.
Even anthropologists, with their reputed penchant for immersion in
the local scene, avail themselves of this option in a decided minority
of instances (see Table 6 in Pelto & Pelto, 1973, p. 263).

Whether or not a general community meeting is held, an early visit
should be made to each potential sample home, primarily to establish
good relations and to dispel possible apprehensive rumors about
one's motives. In addition to attempting to outline the general
character of the research and the ways in which families will be
affected, one should try to gather usable information, such as
household census data, on the initial visit. If data collection will
center around homes, it might be well to avoid setting a pattern in

which the initial visit is defined as a "social" event requiring food, palaver, and disruption of the ongoing routine.

Certain sociocultural features in the chosen community may immediately stand out to the investigator as a result of contrast with the investigator's own experiential background. This saliency will diminish over time due to the phenomenon of "level of adaptation" (Campbell & Naroll, 1972, p. 446). An example of this might be marked segregation of adult male and female household members. Malinowski was cognizant of the initial reaction and of the adaptation, noting that the aspects of many topics "become soon so familiar they escape notice" (cited in Stocking, 1983, p. 100). If complete adaptation takes place, important cultural elements may be overlooked when these become relevant for interpretation. The investigator can avoid the undesirable consequences of the adaptation phenomenon by recording carefully any features that especially attract attention as the field work first gets under way and then at a later point reviewing these early notes for pertinence to the ongoing research.

IN THE FIELD

The Research

Assistants. Ideally, as noted above, cross-cultural psychologists will join forces collaboratively with fellow behavioral scientists who are members of the culture-group under study.[6] One then would have, as Whiting (1970) phrases it, "outsiders to provide objectivity and insiders to provide sensitivity, speaking to one another in 'scientese'" (p. 1). But the production of behavioral scientists from nonWestern areas has been a slow process (Bochner, Brislin, & Lonner, 1975; Triandis, 1980a, b), and it is realistic to assume that for the near term the research team will continue to consist of Western-trained behavioral scientists working with educated and knowledgeable but previously untrained local assistants.

An assistant who is a member of the selected culture-group can provide aid with the indigenous language, research-relevant information concerning the sociocultural system, and personal advice about guidelines for getting along in an unfamiliar setting. If there were no language barrier, one might undertake research without an assistant, but even so, the probability of committing both scientific and personal blunders would be greatly increased. In an earlier time, anthropologists frequently worked on their own, but "the image of the lone fieldworker strolling about the village, casually interviewing informants and watching their daily activities has come less and less to resemble the realities of fieldwork enterprise" (Pelto & Pelto, 1973, p. 277). The use of informants (one or a very few individuals who help the investigator gain information about a particular cultural practice), however, can be extremely useful in providing material for the construction of measures or in providing information that will allow the investigator to interpret results. Although information can first be obtained from an assistant, his/her views should be supplemented by those of other informants, particularly members of the culture whose experience is current and appropriate (e.g. an unmarried male assistant may be aware of the sex-segregation practice but may not know the rules that married females are expected to follow). Though in part acting as an informant, the assistant has a broad range of responsibilities, many of which depend for success on formal education and an intuitive grasp of the value of systematic methods.[7]

We speak of "assistant" in the singular, but the number of assistants employed by the investigator should be determined by the nature of the research and the quality of the individuals available. Under the right circumstances, a team of local individuals can be effectively utilized (cf. Pospisil, 1963).

Often English, French, Spanish, or another language spoken by the investigator will be known to the culture-group under study, and a certain amount of communication will be possible without the aid of an interpreter. Nonetheless, at home and in informal settings, an indigenous, early-learned language is likely to be used much of the time, and here an interpreter is indispensable. Although learning the language oneself is without question a valuable attainment (not least for the acceptance one thereby gains in the community), the process is time-consuming and must be weighed against the inevitable drain on other research activities. Phrases of greeting and common social exchange are relatively easily learned, and can help in simple navigation around the community, but becoming fluent in a completely alien tongue can be difficult even for a talented language-learner. Werner (1984), a native English speaker, relates how he already spoke Spanish and French when he arrived in Brazil and was able to carry on a broken conversation in Portuguese after a couple of weeks, but could not do as well as that with the Amerindian Kayapo language after four to five months of effort in the field. (For guidance in learning a field language, see Burling, 1984.)

Although an assistant should be able to perform adequately in purveying "equivalent meanings" back and forth between the investigator and the people studied, interpreting is to be distinguished from the art of translation, which requires extremely close attention to details of phrasing and expression (see Chapter 5 on language by Brislin in this volume). Without special training, an assistant will be unable to do competent translation work.

Data. Ethnography, that is, comprehensive description of the way of life of the people being studied,[8] is unlikely to be the primary goal of the cross-cultural psychologist. But there are three types of ethnographic information that should prove useful no matter what the study. We shall describe and discuss some of the uses of these three information sets, which we label "basic data," "ethnographic context," and "problem-relevant information."

1. Basic data. Demographic and census material, even when restricted in scope, can be valuable if gathered over a community-wide area or systematically among those members of the community who will comprise a sample. When a complete census is accomplished, not only does one possess information that applies to the community as a whole, but any subjects who subsequently take part in a formal study are then automatically covered in this respect. As noted above, a brief household census can be taken, or begun, on the first visit to a home. On later visits, information could be gathered concerning relevant household arrangements (e.g. eating or household-responsibility patterns), education, languages spoken, religious affiliation, degree of acculturation, occupational histories, socioeconomic status, fertility, and kin relations within and among community households. In most communities, questions about property ownership or other indicators of wealth might be considered unseemly, offensive, or prying. If these data are of import, investigators might do well to secure this information from third parties or through indirect questioning. Such topics should be asked about only if the investigator sees some connection to the thrust of the research, but many involve fundamental questions, and the time and effort required to collect this type of information are fairly

modest. The investigator can add questions to obtain data on any topic for which systematic information is desired.

The use of standard forms is strongly recommended for recording or collecting basic data. Standard forms are not meant to restrict the investigator to collecting only pre-set information or to "fix" prematurely the research questions that may be asked. But standard forms, if not used exclusively, allow checks on completeness of information, facilitation of tabulations, and comparability of data for similar research in other culture-groups. Figures 4.1 and 4.2 offer examples of forms that have been used in field work in East Africa.[9]

Figure 4.1 is essentially a household census form (labeled "Residents of Household") that is designed to contain the following information (the form is filled out with valid data for a Kikuyu household, but with names changed to preserve anonymity):

Head section—background material: name of interviewer, date of interview, name of informant, identification number of informant, identification number of household, field site.

Column 1—I.D.: unique identification numbers (first three digits specify household, fourth-fifth digits specify individual within household). This identification method is particularly useful if data will eventually be analyzed by household.

Column 2—Name: names of individuals in household. In this example, males are designated with upper case letters, females with lower case.

Column 3—Letter Code: unique alphabetical allocation to household members. Assignment of these letter codes is for ease in describing within-household kinship relations (Column 4). Males are assigned upper case letters, females lower case.

Column 4—Relation to Household Head: formal description of relationship between each household member and the head of household. Thus, on the figure, b is related to A, the head of household, by marriage—indicated by an "equal" sign; and c, a female, is the offspring—indicated by a "minus" sign—of the marriage of A and b. (This system of notation was developed by anthropologist A. Kimball Romney of the University of California, Irvine. See Romney, 1965, and Romney and D'Andrade, 1964.)

Column 5—Birthdate: recorded or estimated date of birth of household members.

Column 6—Age Grade: year of formation and label of named age-grouping into which individuals were traditionally placed after

Interviewers JG, Jill Martin

Date mid-'68; corr'd. 4/69

CHILD DEVELOPMENT RESEARCH UNIT

Basic Data Form (2/69)

Residents of Household

Informant's name JEREMIAH NJOROGE   Informant's I.D.No. 60401 and 60402

House No. K604   Field Station Ngeca

I.D.	Names	LETTER CODE	Relation to household head	Birth date	Age Grade	Alternate Residence (Associate member only)	How often home
60401	JEREMIAH NJOROGE	A	Head	c.1912	Ndege 1927	-	-
60402	eunice wanjiru	b	(A=b)	5/6/14	Karara 1930	-	-
60403	mary muguru	c	(A=b)-c	1947	Never	-	-
60404	PAUL KANG'ETHE	D	(A=b)-D	1948	Coka Migundaini 1966	-	-
60405	JOSIAH KAREKO	E	(A=b)-E	1949	Taiti 1968	-	-
60406	elizabeth nyaguthu	f	(A=b)-f	1951	Never	-	-
60407 twin	GEORGE MACHARIA	G	(A=b)-G	1955	-	-	-
twin 60408	esther wairimu	h	(A=b)-h	1955	Never	-	-
60409	JOSEPH KURIA	I	(A=b)-I	1960	-	-	-
60410	margaret nduta	j	(A=b)-j	10/62	Never	-	-

Figure 4.1   An Example of a Household Census Form, with Information Filled in

Date _____   Page No. _____

CHILD DEVELOPMENT RESEARCH UNIT

Basic Data Form (4/69)

Education, Religion, Initiation, and Health

Ego's name _____ Ego's ID No. _____ Ego's sex _____

Informants' names and ID Nos. _____

Household No. _____   _____

Field Station _____   _____

Education: Name of School	Village/location/district	Dates attended	Standard or form completed	Certificates attained

Religion:

Church   denomination _____ frequency _____
now

attending   place _____/_____/_____ office _____
               village   location   district   or role

Baptism: denomination _____ date _____

            place _____/_____/_____ baptismal _____
               village   location   district   name

Trad'l Religion YES/NO   Role in ceremonies _____

Initiation: NOT YET/YES/NEVER   Date _____ Age grade _____

Type: Trad'l   Length of _____ Place _____/_____/_____
                 seclusion   village   location   district

Hospital with   Length of _____ Place _____/_____/_____
ceremony   seclusion   village   location   district

Hospital no   Length of _____ Place _____/_____/_____
ceremony   seclusion   village   location   district

Comments: _____

Health History: serious illnesses and accidents

Description	dates	hospitalization	lasting effects

Figure 4.2   An Example of an Individual Basic-Data Form for Education, Religion, Initiation, and Health

initiation.[10] This category denotes an item that is appropriate to the culture-group being studied, but it would be irrelevant and thus excluded from a similar household-residence form for many culture-groups. It has been retained in the example merely to indicate one type of additional information that could be gathered during the census-taking.

Column 7 and 8—Alternate Residence (associate members only) and How Often Home: former household members—when they left, where they now reside, and how frequently they return for visits. This category is composed primarily of adult, out-married offspring of the head of household, and is recorded as a partial household history.

It can be seen that, excepting in the column on age grades, most information on the form reproduced as Figure 4.1 would be of general interest to an investigator. In contrast, the form reproduced as Figure 4.2 was designed to obtain information primarily useful for certain specific research interests. One of several forms developed for administration to individual household members, it is concerned with a person's experiences regarding education, religion, initiation, and health. Although some of these topics, education for instance, are relevant to a rather wide range of psychological questions, others, such as religion, are problem-specific. They are given as examples only, and investigators can create a series of forms tailored to their own studies.

Another element of basic data is mapping, with information noted that may aid in later descriptions of the community. A generalized house plan can be constructed, and a map of the community may be drawn up. This map should note the location of private buildings (including, eventually, locations of households in the study), public structures, shrines, markets, and other central community resources such as public water sources. Map-making is a useful occupation early in the research because it can be done while preparation for the study itself is still under way, though it should be pointed out that mapping can be a sensitive issue where there are concerns about land (cf. Carter, 1972).

Even in highly cooperative communities, the odds are good that a few families (i.e. heads of families) will refuse to give out information of any sort. To omit such families (or individuals) from the basic data and, ultimately, from any formal study introduces an obvious sampling bias, but for several reasons it is probably best to avoid attempting to cajole. Sometimes an inordinate effort is required to convert these individuals, who after all may change their minds again and decide not to cooperate. And to insist on continuing contact also can turn out to be fruitless or, worse, can backfire, with the rejecting family becoming upset enough to work actively with other members of the community against the investigator.[11]

Should the investigator find that the entire community is openly hostile or uncooperative, or that other major problems have arisen, a decision ought to be made quickly, decisively, and early as to whether the research site needs to be changed. As skilled field workers have learned (cf. Berreman, 1968, p. 345; Williams, 1967, p. 21), community resistance often has nothing to do with offenses or mistakes committed by the investigator. When marked resistance appears, the researcher should have in mind an alternative site to which he/she is prepared to move on short notice.

2. Ethnographic context. For any given culture-group, the basic institutions—techno-economic, social–organizational, and idea-tional—may be well described in the ethnographic literature. If not, an effort to obtain the fundamentals of this material would be worthwhile. Otterbein's (1972) *Comparative Cultural Analysis* and Murdock et al.'s (1971) *Outline of Cultural Materials* indicate the significant topics. The manual *Notes and Queries* (Royal Anthropo-logical Institute, 1951) is a guidebook anthropologists often carry to the field to remind themselves of ethnographic features that should be asked about. Goodenough (1980) covers ethnographic field techniques in his chapter in the *Handbook of Cross-Cultural Psychology*, and Chambers and Bolton (1979) discuss the various systems used by anthropologists to record and organize field notes.[12] The two most common techniques of ethnographic data-gathering, interviewing and observing (the latter, carried on openly by the investigator while events take place in his/her presence, is frequently referred to as "participant observation"), are traditionally done in a relatively informal, nonsystematic style.

Although a solid ethnographic account of the culture-group may be available, the ineluctability of culture change requires that a check be made for currency on the variables of interest (see Chapter 10 on acculturation by Berry, Trimble, & Olmedo in this volume). Other issues involving ethnographic context that should be taken into consideration have to do with intracultural variation (see section on this subject in Chapter 3 by Lonner & Berry in the present volume). There may be, for example, cultural specialists (e.g. in arts and

crafts, or in divination) whom it is necessary to consult for reliable
information concerning their technical or esoteric knowledge. The
social spheres of men and women may differ considerably.[13] And
social categories that exist in the sociocultural system as a whole
(e.g. "beggar" or "female transvestite") may not be present in the
community chosen for study.

A recurrent source of difficulty in ethnographic data gathering is
the existence of defensiveness and distortions that interfere with
objectivity. On the side of the social scientist, Rohner, DeWalt, and
Ness (1973) have demonstrated a "romantic bias" that has persistently afflicted field workers. This tendency to exaggerate the positive
and ignore or downplay the negative characteristics of the people
being studied is mitigated in proportion to the number of cross-
validating methods employed by the investigator (Rohner et al.,
1973). On the side of the culture-group itself, there are likely to be
highly sensitive topics that are not treated in a straightforward way,
especially in response to an outsider's inquiries. For example,
Williams (1967) found among the Borneo Dusun that:

> The members of the community, without regard to their intellectual
> capacities, consistently misled us concerning property, avoided talking
> about aggression while being highly aggressive, openly boasted of
> sexual conquests while actually being conservative in sex activities, but
> gave precise, accurate, and consistently truthful answers to the most
> difficult questions on religious behavior. (p. 27)

Williams discusses ways of overcoming such problems, and also
provides an extensive list of citations concerning interviewing and
means of determining validity of ethnographic data.

3. Problem-relevant information. Naturalistic data pertinent to
specific research variables may be gathered in numerous ways. Owing
to the primary-group character of most small communities, reliable
reputational ratings on members' personal and social attributes can
be made by intelligent, perceptive individuals who are long-time
community residents. For example, Bolton (1973) obtained satisfactory inter-rater reliability on judgments of aggressiveness in a Qolla
Peruvian community, and the ratings were themselves signficantly
correlated with homicide accusations, involvement in litigation, and
levels of hypoglycemia. Event-sampling and time-sampling observations constitute other possible sources of systematic naturalistic data

connected to the research variables. (As Chapter 6 by Bochner in this volume makes clear, systematic observations are of course frequently carried out in order to study naturalistic phenomena for their own sake.) An example of event sampling is Munroe, Munroe, and Whiting's (1973) notation of each observed instance of public inebriation on the part of the members of a sample of Black Carib men. The frequency of such instances was related to informants' Q-sort ratings of sample members' alcohol consumption. An example of time sampling is the study by Nerlove, Roberts, and Klein (1975) of a "natural indicator," the observed frequency of children's participation in self-managed sequences (defined as activities requiring the child to follow an exacting series of steps). Children's degree of participation in these sequences was related to community members' judgments of the children's intelligence.

A loose but highly informative techique was used by Edgerton (1971) in his comparison of eight communities in East Africa. Complementing his test data on personality characteristics, Edgerton supplied a "portrait" of the personality/character type in each community based on his impressions while ensconced there. These impressionistic reports, worked up prior to data analysis, on the whole were in accord with the test findings. Psychological projects dealing with broad characterological or personality variables can employ a complementary approach of this sort, which the holistic nature of field work encourages.

Practical Matters

We mention briefly here a few of the problems that can arise in connection with the scarce resources of time, money, and data. Time is always short in the field because, unlike the ordinary research setting, access to a culture-group—and thus to relevant data of any sort—is limited by the length of one's typically brief stay. Careful planning and apportioning of time are obviously demanded under these circumstances. Even so, the time constraints would probably lead the great majority of field workers to agree with Silverman's (1972) three-month rule: "If I only had three months more ..." (p. 205).

The field worker often will maintain him/herself at a somewhat higher standard of living than the members of the culture-group under study—if not while in the field, then probably on break from the field work, or, almost assuredly, on return to his/her home base. The discrepancy, either present or anticipated, often is accompanied by guilt feelings for which expiation may be attempted via overpayment (to assistants, informants, subjects, landlords, etc.) or perhaps through very generous gifts to community members or "loans" to soliciting individuals. While no one would advise meanness under these circumstances, we have found that "off-scale" remuneration tends to breed escalating expectations and a resentment when such expectations are not met. In addition to current problems, overpayment can create difficulties for future field workers, who may have fewer resources than oneself. A recommended course of action would be to pay well but not extremely well, to make gifts to community (or sample) members on an occasional rather than regular basis, and to be prepared with a reasonable limit and/or excuse if and when personal loans are requested.[14] When long hours are expected of particular community members (e.g. interviews about relations with adult married children) or for designated portions of data collection for all sample members (e.g. a set of questions, a few brief tests), the investigator can set an appropriate payment or gift. The distinction between these particular tasks and other, less demanding requests may not always be apparent to community members, so the investigator should be prepared to defend them in a straightforward way if called upon.

The psychologist should maintain continual alertness to the need for safekeeping of field notes and other data. Always a copy of written material (carbon copy, photocopying, hand-copying if necessary) should be made and stored separately from the originals. If for any reason the authorities might consider information sensitive, copies should be mailed as soon as possible to the investigator's home base. Other materials for which copying might be expensive (e.g. film) or duplication unavailable (e.g. artifacts) should be looked after carefully. Williams (1967), in a section on procedures for recording of cultural data, supplies valuable information on keeping cameras and recording equipment dry, free of dust, and protected against conditions of high humidity (see his Chapter 3).

There are also issues revolving around basic concerns such as food, health, standards of dress, and sex. For example, many anthropologists feel that one can refuse proffered food only at the risk of losing rapport with community members, and that the willingness to eat indigenous food is a key to good relations (Pelto & Pelto, 1973). (Our own experience has been that community members understand the health perils involved if one were immediately to adopt a diet totally different from that to which one is accustomed. Politely declining offers of food has therefore not been taken amiss.) At the same time, boiled water and well-cooked food are advisable under many field conditions, and the field worker in these settings should possess a first-aid kit, a supply of the most frequently needed medicines (e.g., antibiotics and dysentery treatments), and a layman's health guide (e.g., *The Merck Manual*, 1982). All of these can be used in the diagnosis and treatment of illness for the investigator and his/her family and for community members. Investigators living in relatively remote areas are often called upon for medical advice or supplies so ample quantities of aspirin, malarial suppressants (in certain areas), and medications for treating minor surface wounds or infections are often useful.

Community standards of dress are another potential area of difficulty, especially for female investigators. In many societies the dress code stipulates that the adult female body be well covered, and serious offense would be given by various items of garb such as shorts, bathing suits, or skirt lengths above the knee. In other societies pants rather than skirts or long dresses will be looked at askance. And finally, sexual relations with members of the community are apt to commit the investigator to unsought responsibilities and, further, to involve the outsider in a part of community life that is likely to be charged with emotion. For these reasons, field workers have tended to observe a self-imposed sex taboo toward community members.

Although visiting by community members can sometimes be capitalized on for purposes of ethnographic data gathering, the investigator will want to find a way to control the flow of visitors. Chagnon (1983) comments that "privacy is one of our culture's most satisfying achievements, one you never think about until you suddenly have none. It is like not appreciating how good your left thumb feels until someone hits it with a hammer" (p. 15). Implicit in these remarks is the fact that in many small-scale societies the concept of privacy is absent or relatively undeveloped, and this can make difficult the regulating of visits. (Among elites in many societies, and in modern societies generally, highly developed privacy concerns create for a field worker the opposite problem, insufficient access to community members.) For the investigator, the need for privacy arises not only out of work demands (especially organizing and planning) but also, as Chagnon's comment indicates, out of personal requirements. The combination of almost nonstop work and loss of numerous ingrained sources of satisfaction can cause morale problems and sometimes personal crises (Freilich, 1977; Golde, 1970; Spindler, 1970), common responses to which have been alcohol use and long hours of escape-reading. For those to whom intensive field work is trying, planned periodic breaks (e.g. self-declared "days-off" or a short vacation trip) can be renewing.

Ethical Issues

Field work, in confronting the investigator with beliefs and values quite different from his/her own, poses a special ethical problem. Moral absolutism, with its certainties, is indefensible, yet moral relativism, with its predilection to nonjudgmental stances, breeds the dilemma of attempting to reconcile incommensurable systems. There is obviously no fully satisfactory way to resolve this problem, though in practice field workers—as "students" of the culture-group they are investigating—observe a kind of qualified relativism in which they try to avoid negative evaluation of any aspects of the systems they are learning about. The limits of relativism are likely to be seen when the investigator faces a flat violation of one of his/her fundamental ethical principles, for instance that of the sacredness of human life. But problems of this magnitude occur rarely, and we can agree with Rosemary Firth's (1972) pragmatic position asserting that "moral conflicts. . . usually have an inevitable solution dictated by the situation" (p. 28).

Behavioral-science research often involves a degree of deception (Aronson & Carlsmith, 1968), and field work is not exempt from the problem. For ease in communication, the very rationale given for entering the field is commonly a simplification or a partial truth—one has come to "learn the language," or to "find out how children learn," or to "make a record of the customs before they disappear." The real focus of the research, guided by theory or past empirical work, might otherwise appear trivial or irrelevant. If the actual research problem were articulated, in some cases the necessary clearance would not be granted, and in others the study would be vitiated due to the disclosure of information about the key variables. Similar difficulties are present throughout the period of field work; indeed there are times when the exigencies of the situation seem to transform otherwise immoral behavior into appropriate responses, as for example in Werner's (1984) lying to a villager whose honor was thereby preserved, or in Munroe's (1964) invention of a story about himself in order to elicit the truth from subjects who up to that time had been prevaricating about their own experiences. Although behavior should be regulated, as nearly as possible, both by one's own moral codes and by community codes that are more stringent than one's own, the authors feel that compromises with principle are, as in everyday life, unfortunate but comprehensible occurrences (cf. Barnes, 1984; Colson, 1985).

In general, the codes of ethics prescribed by the American Anthropological Association (1973), the American Psychological Association (1982), and the American Sociological Association (1984) can be consulted for guidance. The monthly newsletter of the American Anthropological Association (1985) for the past several years has presented case studies of "ethical dilemmas" arising in field work (and in other anthropological research) together with suggested practical solutions to the dilemmas. And sensitive discussions of ethical issues surrounding field work may be found in Appell (1978), Rynkiewich and Spradley (1976), Tapp, Kelman, Triandis, Wrightsman, and Coelho (1974), and Warwick (1980). Finally, we should point out that some behavioral scientists repudiate any form of deception in field research (Berreman, 1968; Goodenough, 1980; cf. Segall in Chapter 9 of this volume).[15]

Taking Leave

Two factors require careful attention as the investigator prepares to end a field trip. The first is the matter of saying "goodbye" in appropriate fashion. Officials who were instrumental in helping the investigator gain formal clearance or access to the research site should be visited (if possible) and thanked again for their aid. And the members of the culture-group who have acted as subjects or informants should be thanked in some concrete way, either with small individual gifts or a party or feast for community members, or, if appropriate, with a gift to the community (such as a contribution toward a community project or to a community school, church, or recreation center).

The second factor is that the investigator should take steps to insure continuing contact with the community after departure. Even if there are no plans to return, it is desirable to have an assistant or other knowledgeable individual prepared to send a modicum of requested information. While many types of data could not be gathered appropriately by an unsupervised individual, certain kinds of material, such as a specific piece of information, or structured responses to a "factual" question, probably would be reliable. The presence of an on-site assistant can be helpful in situations of this sort.

MAINTAINING CONTACT

In addition to the on-site assistant who may from time to time gather and send information to the investigator, a colleague/ collaborator stationed near the site is of course able to conduct ongoing research. This latter arrangement meshes in a natural way with a recent and desirable trend toward long-term field research (Foster, Scudder, Colson, & Kemper, 1978). With or without local associates, many investigators, cognizant of the advantages of repeated visits, have undertaken field projects that are longitudinal (Gallimore, Boggs, & Jordan, 1974; Wagner, Messick, & Spratt, 1984; Werner & Smith, 1982; B. Whiting, 1977; Whiting, 1970) or that acknowledge the critical need to take sociocultural change into account in their interpretations of psychological phenomena (Berry, 1976; Gewertz, 1981; LeVine, Klein, & Owen, 1967; Seymour, 1980; Spindler, 1978).

The investigator who has maintained contact with colleagues or assistants can solicit their reactions to tentative conclusions and interpretations, a process that has been termed "feedthrough." The supplementary process of "feedback" involves the sending of final written products to key persons or institutions so that they have a record of the outcome of the project. In some cases, agreement to furnish final project reports is part of the set of requirements one must meet for formal research authorization, and failure to adhere to the agreement can result in both difficulties for oneself and potential problems for future investigators in that locality.

There is also a personal side to the continuance of contacts. On returning home, the investigator often will receive written solicitations from one or more field acquaintances who have genuine need. Typically the requests will seek aid in attaining some objective, for instance education, emigration, purchase of a piece of land, and so on. The investigator is likely to feel the guilt alluded to above concerning a disparity in living standards, and the discomfort may well be exacerbated by the knowledge that he/she is financially and otherwise capable of helping the individuals who are asking for aid. Nevertheless, those making the requests are not necessarily the individuals whom the investigator wishes to help, and the further potential problem exists of favorable treatment for a few and nothing for the many. These difficulties admit of no more satisfactory solution than the moral conflicts arising while in the field, and they possess the additional feature of being revived each time the mail brings another importunate letter.

CONCLUSION

We have delineated both imperatives and proscriptions that will affect the course of field work, but it can be seen that the success of the enterprise depends largely upon flexibility, willingness to adapt to the unusual and the unexpected, and the degree to which one genuinely enjoys and appreciates meeting new people and learning about the daily events in their lives. Specific methods and techniques take their place as adjuncts as one primarily lives in the field community and secondarily practices social science. As Cicourel (1964) points out, field work involves the same processes, albeit heightened and intensified, that we experience many times in our personal lives:

> Moving into a new neighborhood, starting work at a new job, applying for a new job, starting school, meeting groups whose customs and language are different from one's own, attempting to befriend someone so as to obtain certain information, trying to sell a customer some merchandise. . . any number of similar and divergent social processes include the same features which are to be found in field research. (p. 68)

Thus each field experience, while pointed toward a definite

scientific goal, broadens one's perspective by enlarging the sum and variety of social processes to which the investigator is exposed. And correspondingly, this enhanced perspective should work to strengthen and inform subsequent projects in the field.

NOTES

The authors are indebted to Charlene Bolton, Ralph Bolton, Donald Brenneis, Susan Seymour, and, in particular, the editors of this volume, Walter Lonner and John Berry, for valuable suggestions. They are obligated as well to Stella Vlastos of Pitzer College for aid in preparation of the manuscript.

1. Early anthropological reports had a certain kinship with an already established genre, the traveler's account of exotic peoples and places. This natural link prompted anthropologists, from the time of men like Frank H. Cushing (1882a, 1882b, 1884–1885) in a North American pueblo and Bronislaw Malinowski (1922, 1929, 1935) in Melanesia, to romanticize the field setting and emphasize its "otherness." And undoubtedly the nature of field work attracted individuals who, more than most, were drawn to this type of research. It was said of one anthropologist with wide experience that he "likes to mention that, besides his field research, he has mushed dogs in Alaska, hunted big game in East Africa, paddled canoes on the Amazon, and ridden horses on the plains of southern Brazil" (Kimball & Watson, 1972, p. xviii). These romantic inclinations, along with the physical and emotional privation attendant upon distant and lengthy field trips (especially the first, initiatory sojourn), have led anthropologists to charge the whole experience with almost mystical overtones. Anthropologist Paul Bohannan claims that being psychoanalyzed, undergoing a religious conversion, and carrying out a field trip constitute three experiences that permit an individual to change the direction of his/her life (personal communication, January 24, 1985). It is only in recent years that "heightened consciousness of the problematic character of the fieldwork process has produced numerous discussions of its epistemological, methodological, psychological, ethical, and political implications" (Stocking, 1983, p. 9).

2. Field work for most behavioral scientists today, in fact, seldom involves either a long-term break with their own way of life or complete absorption in a foreign culture. With modern transportation and communication systems, and research sites that exhibit the effects of significant contact with the modern world, one could hardly undertake classical field research on unchanged traditional culture-groups, aside from isolated pockets in Amazonian South America (Gregor, 1977; Werner, 1984) and highland New Guinea (Lindenbaum, 1979; Schieffelin, 1976).

3. Concerning health, the International Association for Medical Assistance to Travelers (US address: IAMAT, 350 Fifth Ave., Suite 5620, New York, New York 10001, USA) publishes useful information on various topics, for instance climate, malaria-risk areas, and schistosomiasis-risk areas.

Concerning luggage, to ship by surface or by air freight, or to send extra goods as "unaccompanied luggage," can help reduce the steep overweight charges for air travel, as can stuffing oversized, hand-carried travel bags with heavy materials like books and papers (though some airlines weigh hand luggage too). The matter of luggage requires careful consideration, especially since the investigator is likely to be weighted down with data on the return trip. For an extended stay, surface shipment of goods (sent several months in advance) might be advisable although it requires securing an address where one can be notified of receipt. If contacted ahead, banks or other local businesses or institutions will often allow use of their addresses but one will probably need to keep in contact since it is necessary to shepherd such goods through customs.

Concerning money matters, to exchange domestic currency beforehand for a moderate amount of the appropriate paper currency can save time on arrival, but not all nations allow their currency to be purchased internationally. Large sums of money may be deposited in foreign banks upon arrival through the use of travelers' checks or cashier's checks although the latter may involve a delay before being drawn upon.

4. For a set of interesting accounts of entrée into the field, see the brief articles by Langness, Middleton, Uchendu, and VanStone in Naroll and Cohen (1970).

5. In some countries, identity cards or other documents are required for extended visits. Additionally, some countries require filing of certain documents such as tax-clearance forms prior to departure. It is wise to inquire about necessary papers early in the field stay.

6. One of the most ambitious cross-cultural collaborative projects is Williams and Best's (1982) sex-stereotyping work, in which most of the primary data have been gathered by colleagues in 30 nations. Although the project does not involve field work *per se*, its successful completion indicates the promise and potential scope of a collaborative approach. Williams and Best initiated many of the contacts with cross-national colleagues during meetings of the International Association for Cross-Cultural Psychology. Other avenues include publication of a note concerning collaborative possibilities in the IACCP Bulletin or in the newsletter of the Society for Cross-Cultural Research.

7. Few if any individuals with the requisite skills to perform appropriately as assistants might be found in a culture-group having precious little contact with the modern world. But such a situation is now rare to the vanishing point, as Watson (1972) learned on returning to his highland New Guinea site and seeing that the inarticulate villagers of the decade before, "unable to elucidate the obvious because of their inability to realize that what was taken as 'the obvious' might need elucidating" (p. 176), unable to "put together an orderly account of any length or complexity" (p. 179), had completely changed as a result of familiarity with the larger world. "No stranger, I had returned to find I could talk readily with the people, elicit once difficult information with unprecedented ease" (p. 181). And within this village, Watson found a young man who astonished him with a flow of organized, coherent information about male initiation rites. He had discovered an individual who could not have existed in that community ten years earlier, a young man who had the makings of an assistant.

8. Anthropologists, who are of course responsible for the bulk of the ethnographic record, have turned increasingly away from ethnography and toward a more problem-oriented approach. This change has occurred in part because there are decreasing numbers of unacculturated peoples in the world (but see Wolf, 1982, on the issue of "untouched" cultures in the 18th and 19th centuries), in part due to recognition that the major culture-types of the human species have now been described, and, paradoxically, in part due to acknowledgement of the partial and inadequate nature of

even the classic ethnographies (see Harris, 1968, on Franz Boas, and Uberoi, 1962, and Weiner, 1976, on Malinowski).

9. The East African research was carried out by numerous scholars affiliated with the Child Development Research Unit, University of Nairobi. The unit was directed by John W. M. Whiting and Beatrice B. Whiting, and its research activities were financed by the Carnegie Corporation of New York. For some 15 communities in Kenya, basic data were gathered on a wide range of topics through the use of standard forms, two of which are reproduced here. Descriptions of the project can be found in "An Impossible Dream?" (1979) and Whiting (1970).

10. Age-grade sets have fallen into disuse for females, as can be seen by the fact that no female member of the household born after World War II has been assigned to an age grade.

11. In our own research, we have found that shopkeepers are disproportionately likely to be evasive, rude, or hostile. It is an interesting question as to whether this is due more to the unusual personal characteristics possessed by entrepreneurs in quasi-subsistence societies (where resistance to normal kin obligations is necessary for business success) or to the fact that the commercial character of their occupations creates concern in shopkeepers about disclosing information that might affect their tax obligations. But whether shopkeepers or others, the uncooperative few have almost always turned up in our field research.

12. Anthropological methods of data gathering are also discussed in detail in Edgerton and Langness (1974), Pelto and Pelto (1978), and Williams (1967).

13. A recent instance in anthropology was the discovery of Kroeber's neglect of information from a female Yurok informant on menstrual observances and his apparent resulting biased account (Buckley, 1982). Sometimes, too, sexual segregation restricts the field worker's access to information, as, for instance, when male investigators are confronted with the barriers of *purdah*, or when female investigators are unable to observe men's-house activities, male initiation ceremonies, or even informal male gatherings (Diamond, 1970). The obvious way to overcome this difficulty is to ensure that the research team consists of at least one male and one female (e.g. wife/husband, male investigator/female collaborator, female investigator/male assistant).

14. One method for handling the problem of loans is to assent to the first one or two, and then to inform subsequent applicants that nothing more can be lent until the earlier borrowers repay the outstanding amount.

15. Berreman (1968) inadvertently illustrates the difficulty of attaining the complete openness and honesty that he advocates. On the one hand, he tells us that his villagers' lack of hospitality and reticence were proverbial among forestry officers, and that these traits baffled his research assistant (a newcomer to the village) (p. 352); on the other, he tells the villagers that he has chosen them in part because of their hospitality, perspicacity, and reputation for being a "good village" (p. 357).

5

THE WORDING AND TRANSLATION OF RESEARCH INSTRUMENTS

RICHARD W. BRISLIN

The purpose of this chapter is to provide very specific guidelines which will allow researchers:

1. to select or to develop measuring devices which will be readily translatable into other languages;
2. to write items for measuring instruments which will be easily understood by respondents;
3. to insure that the instruments measure concepts which are important in the cultures under study;
4. to insure that there is no imposition of concepts from the researcher's own culture; and
5. to supervise adequate translations of research instruments.

In addition, a few suggestions will be given concerning the administration of research instruments to actual respondents.

Many researchers find that their well-laid research plans must be modified after arrival in another culture. Some opportunities for data collection disappear and others arise; topics originally considered important seem less so upon first-hand examination; political changes make investigations of some topics unacceptable; pre-test data show that changes must be made; and researchers develop new interests given the stimulation of life in another culture. In many cases, then, researchers must start anew but without the benefit of their libraries and technological back-up, which are most often left home. The guidelines to be presented here place few demands on hardware or on extensive library resources, and instead place demands on the researcher's most valuable commodity: careful thought.

APPROACHES TO INSTRUMENTATION

In any research involving the use of questionnaires, interview schedules, or tests, a major decision must be made concerning the relative usefulness of existing instruments, newly designed instruments, or a combination. "Existing instruments" will be a shorthand term to designate measures which were developed and standardized in one culture and which can possibly be used for data gathering in another culture. The advantages of using existing instruments are considerable. There are usually a number of published studies, or at least unpublished but available data, which can be compared with newly acquired data. Such comparisons allow a literature to be built up around a commonly shared set of concepts and operational definitions, an advantage admittedly more difficult to achieve if different researchers use different instruments. Time and expense can often be conserved if existing instruments are used. There is always limited time, energy, and funding for cross-cultural research projects, especially for members of professions who do not yet have a tradition of taking long periods of time away from their home base to do field research in other cultures. Cost/benefit considerations in both economic and scientific matters should become part of the researcher's planning.

Another advantage will be felt more by neophyte than experienced researchers. There is a sense of security when using existing instruments, a sense that if some established researcher has used a certain measure and obtained respectable publications, then it must have merit. In the case of very frequently used instruments such as the Minnesota Multiphasic Personality Inventory (MMPI) or the Internal-External Locus of Control scale, there is often the sense that these edifices cannot possibly be the target of criticism or improvement. Further, to modify the instrument would be like tampering with some sacred writing, rather like trying to improve the King James version of the Bible through additions, deletions, and modifications. A general caution, then, is that one should not be lulled into a false sense of security through choice of a popular existing device.

There are disadvantages, as well, to the use of existing instruments. Researchers run the risk of missing aspects of a phenomenon as viewed by (and seen as important by) people in other cultures. Further, they risk imposing conclusions based on concepts which exist in their own cultures but which are foreign, or at least partially incorrect, when used in another culture. Put another way, existing instruments provide operational definitions of certain concepts. There is no automatic guarantee that those concepts, or those same operational definitions, exist in other cultures.

An important point to keep in mind is that items on existing scales were tried out with people from one culture, most often in a highly industrialized nation such as the United States. Items which "did not work," as shown by low item-to-total correlations, would be discarded. Consequently, items were purified so that they measure a phenomenon as seen by people in the culture-of-standardization. There is *no* reason to suppose that these purified items will also measure the phenomenon as experienced by people in another culture. The clearest example involves tests of intelligence, and no thoughtful researcher gives existing I.Q. tests to people from other cultures and makes conclusions about mental capacities (see Chapter 7 by Irvine, this volume). Questions from such tests, asking for an estimate of the population of the United States or the meaning of the word "esoteric" are obviously culture bound. The fact that psychology's history *does* include cross-cultural use of I.Q. tests to rank cultures on intelligence is a black mark for our discipline. But similar thinking about the contribution of individual test items to a conclusion about psychological processes should be done for any existing tests before its cross-cultural application. Users of the MMPI for cross-cultural studies, for example, should be able to answer a query as to why the item asking about a preference between Presidents Washington and Lincoln should contribute to conclusions about personality traits or syndromes.

Another disadvantage is that the intellectual timidity of researchers can be reinforced if existing tests only are used. Rather than trying to make an original contribution, with its inherent discomfort because of uncertainty regarding the acceptance or rejection of one's work, some researchers busy themselves by using existing tests, reaping the benefits of security already discussed. The exact tests, then, are used not to discover important conclusions but rather to insure that *something* happens during one's research stint in another culture. The unimaginative use of tests should be discouraged.

My recommendation is that existing tests be used only after very careful thought has been given to the meaning of any scores that the test may yield. For example, intelligence tests cannot be used to make conclusions about underlying competencies in other cultures. But if people from other cultures are attending school administered by members of the majority culture for which an I.Q. test was designed, then the test might give valuable information to teachers regarding skills (vocabulary development, reading comprehension) which need more attention. There is a large difference between conclusions about mental capabilities and conclusions about skills which need improvement in a particular school system. As another example, consider use of the MMPI. If a researcher could make a good case for the possible universality of schizophrenic etymology and expression (as discussed by Draguns, 1980, who also reviewed the evidence for culture-specific manifestations), then cross-cultural use of those test items related to schizophrenia might be used in diagnosis. Another *caveat* for such test use is that there is little chance for discovering new insights into the nature of intelligence or schizophrenia.

Another recommendation is that users of existing tests be willing to modify items and to add new ones which should tap additional aspects of a phenomenon *in addition to* those indicated by the original test. In this procedure, researchers use the *emic-etic* distinction to their benefit (Berry, 1969a; Brislin, 1983). Take the example of a two-cultural comparison. The *etic* refers to a phenomenon, or aspects of a phenomenon, which have a common meaning across the cultures under investigation. This can be called the core meaning. For intelligence, such a core meaning might be the ability to give correct answers to problems, the exact form of which has not been seen before by test takers. *Emic* aspects are different in the two cultures, but each *emic* is related to the shared *etic* core. In some African societies, for instance, intelligence includes the ability to get along with kin (Serpell, 1976). In the United States, intelligence includes quickness in problem solving, as shown by the frequent use of timed tests. *Emics* are not necessarily shared: the United States does not share the concern with kin, and there is not a value placed on quickness in the African societies studied by Serpell (1976). A description of the phenomenon for each culture, then, would consist of the *etic* core plus the culture's *emic* aspects. This is a good model for actual research projects and the creation of measuring instruments, and so an example will be reviewed in some detail.

Miller, Slomczynski, and Schoenberg (1981) were interested in the measurement and meaning of authoritarian-conservatism in the

United States and Poland. The researchers had the goal of assessing shared meanings of authoritarian-conservatism, or *etic* aspects, as well as culture-specific aspects necessary for a fuller understanding of the concept. Items from the best known test of authoritarianism, the California F scale, were used, with the addition of other items (based on the ideas of Pearlin, 1962) concerned with submission to authority. The authors felt that these latter items would be useful in more fully documenting the meaning of the concept in the two cultures. The study thus had the benefits of possible comparisons with other data sets through use of the F scale, as well as the opportunity to add new insights through the use of additional items. The researchers also modified the classic F scale items when there were "colloquial expressions" or where there was need for "substitution for situations that do not arise in Poland" (Miller et al., 1981, p. 180).

Factor analysis demonstrated that there was a shared core meaning as well as country-specific aspects of authoritarian-conservatism. The core meaning was measured by the following five items:

1. The most important thing to teach children is absolute obedience to their parents.
2. In this complicated world, the only way to know what to do is to rely on leaders and experts. (This was the wording for the US data collection. The phrase "experts and advisors" was a better wording for the Polish data collections.)
3. It's wrong to do things differently from the way our forefathers did. (This was the US wording. The Polish wording was, "It's wrong to do anything in a different way from past generations.")
4. Any good leader should be strict with people under him in order to gain their respect.
5. No decent man can respect a woman who has had sex relations before marriage.

These items seem to indicate that the core meaning includes deference to respected others (parents, forefathers, leaders, and experts), strict treatment of subordinates, and conventional sexual attitudes. Another advantage of this approach to data collection, analysis, and presentation is that topics for further investigation can be readily identified. Strict treatment of subordinates and conventional sexual attitudes are each measured by only one item, making an in-depth analysis of *these aspects* of authoritarian-conservatism impossible. Further research can investigate these aspects through the development of multi-item scales.

The country-specific meaning for the United States was indicated by four items:

1. Prison is too good for sex criminals; they should be publicly whipped or worse.
2. Young people should not be allowed to read books that are likely to confuse them.
3. There are two kinds of people in the world; the weak and the strong.
4. People who question the old and accepted ways of doing things usually just end up causing trouble.

These items measure two aspects: "the use of stereotypes and the endorsement of public intervention in matters ordinarily addressed elsewhere (e.g., in the family or courts)" (Miller et al., 1981, p. 187).

The country-specific meaning for Poland was indicated by three items:

1. One should always show respect to those in authority.
2. You should obey your superiors whether or not you think they're right.
3. Every legal action is proper or are some actions wrong even if legal? (Respondents chose one of the two positions implied in the question. This item is the English translation from the Polish measuring device, and the item undoubtedly reads more smoothly in the original language.)

These items add detail to the core meaning (above) of deference to respected others. The addition is that the deference is also given to "hierarchical authority which is bureaucratically or legally legitimized" (p. 186).

It is no accident that the labels for the country-specific items are long and convoluted. By definition, since the *emic* aspects are not shared, there will not be a readily available, familiar language with which to describe another country's *emics*. The task for the researcher is much like that of introducing a visitor to one's country to unfamiliar customs. Long explanations are demanded since the visitor has little in his or her background which can be related to the newly encountered custom. Similarly, describing another country's *emics* demands introducing unfamiliar ideas, and this cannot be done with the short, precise, sometimes pithy labels researchers use to communicate the results of factor analysis to like-minded peers.

The work of Miller and her colleagues, then, provides a good example of the approach to cross-cultural questionnaires advocated here. To summarize the steps taken, they used an existing instrument so as to allow comparisons with previous studies, but were willing to modify items when necessary. They added new items to expand the scope of inquiry into the nature of authoritarian-conservatism, and they presented their data in terms of shared meaning and country-specific meaning. Countries can then be compared on the items contributing to the shared or *etic* meaning after the caveats suggested by cross-cultural psychometricians (e.g. Irvine & Carroll, 1980; Poortinga, 1975; this volume) are satisfied. In any interpretation of such comparisons, however, researchers must be mindful that a full understanding of a concept within a culture demands the addition of *emic* results to the shared or *etic* meaning. Various researchers have given practical advice regarding two of these stages, the modification of existing items and the creation of new items, and these "lessons from experience" will now be reviewed.

GUIDELINES USEFUL BOTH FOR WRITING NEW ITEMS AND MODIFYING EXISTING ITEMS

A set of guidelines useful for any sort of item preparation, whether for new items or modification of existing items, has been presented in the cross-cultural literature as "guidelines for writing material which is readily translatable" (Brislin, Lonner, & Thorndike, 1973; Brislin, 1980). The purpose of these guidelines, based on experiences preparing research instruments in over twenty languages, is to assure that translators will:

1. have a clear understanding of the original language item;
2. have a high probability of finding a readily available target language equivalent so that they do not have to use convoluted or unfamiliar terms;
3. be able to produce target language items readily understandable by the eventual set of respondents who are part of the data-gathering stage of the research project.

The guidelines were written with "translatable English" in mind, but they should be of more widespread use since they emphasize clear communication of concepts. While written to help with the methodological step of producing good translations, then, these guidelines should also help in the creation or modification of items which will be readily understandable to respondents. Another benefit is that the items finally produced will be understandable to researchers in other cultures. An important point to keep in mind constantly is that items on a questionnaire or survey instrument constitute the operational definitions of concepts, and clear communication of concepts to colleagues is essential for the growth of knowledge. As more and more research is done by members of cultures who *previously* were only the hosts for visiting research teams, communication among cross-cultural researchers will demand more and more attention. In addition to these general points, there are reasons for specific knowledge about translatable English. English will most likely remain the most frequently used international language of communication in the behavioral and social sciences. The same English easily used by translators may also be helpful for researchers attempting to communicate their findings to widely dispersed colleagues.

This presentation is not being presented as a plea for greater use of English in cross-cultural research. The international use of English (Smith, 1981) is a fact, and some readers will bemoan this state of affairs. But given that communication with a broad, world-wide audience is dependent upon publication in English,[1] knowledge of guidelines for writing readily understandable English may improve cross-cultural communication of research results.

In writing or modifying items, the suggested guidelines and rationales are:

1. Use short simple sentences of less than sixteen words. Use of this guideline leads to items with one dominant idea per sentence. With sentences longer than sixteen words, ideas become difficult to disentangle, with lack of clarity regarding which subordinate clause refers to which idea. This guideline does not have to lead to short *items*. Items can be composed of more than one sentence, each sentence following the suggested sixteen-word limit.

2. Employ the active rather than the passive voice. With the active voice, the translator can more easily identify the subject, verb, object, and can match adjectives and adverbs to the appropriate nouns and verbs. Even though there are languages where a corresponding form of the passive is frequently used (e.g. Tagalog), the active voice is still clearer for translators reading the original English. They may use the passive in their translation, with the comment that what is clearest through use of the active voice in English is communicated best through use of the passive in the target language. Such a difference becomes, then, just one example of the sort of modification necessary for good instrument preparation in other cultures.

3. Repeat nouns instead of using pronouns. With more than one

noun per sentence, use of pronouns leads to the risk of unclear references due to vague noun-pronoun links. In many languages, there are far more pronouns than in English, leading to chances for mistakes (e.g. does "you" refer to one, two, or more people? There are different forms for the three meanings in some languages.)

4. Avoid metaphors and colloquialisms. Such phrases are least likely to have equivalents in the target language. Standardized tests from one country are likely to have many colloquialisms since such terms are very good at communicating *within* a community sharing the same language (e.g. a stitch in time saves nine). Such items survive item purification, as previously discussed. But such terms are very difficult if not impossible to translate for cross-language comparisons. Examples and suggested solutions will be given in a forthcoming section in which cross-cultural use of the MMPI, a colloquialism filled test, is discussed.

5. Avoid the subjunctive, for example verb forms with "could," "would," "should." The rationale here is very pragmatic: other languages rarely have readily available terms for the various forms of the English subjunctive. Researchers who use the subjunctive force the translator to make the best guess or the best approximation. Assuring clear communication is the researcher's job, and it should not be carelessly delegated to translators.

6. Add sentences to provide context for key ideas. Reword key phrases to provide redundancy. This rule suggests that longer items and questions be used in single-country research. There is no contradiction with guideline number 1, above, on sentence length since items can have several sentences. At times, the context is provided to a translator who does not necessarily have to provide target language equivalents for every word, but should have the context as background. For instance, an item asking about "avoiding stepping on cracks in the sidewalk" would talk about the origin of this superstition. For countries in which sidewalks are continous flows of concrete and are not interrupted by cracks, the context would include the reason why this item is on the original test. This information maximizes the probability that a cultural equivalent of avoiding sidewalk cracks can be found. Other contextual information will be demanded by knowledge of the published literature and by pre-test data. Questions asking about whether a gentleman should give up his seat on a bus to a lady might have to be contextualized in Asian countries according to the relative age of the people involved, social

class as shown by dress, degree of acquaintance, and so forth. The fact that most Americans can readily provide a straightforward answer to the inquiry about giving up their seat but that Asians demand additional contextualizing information should not lead to researcher frustration. Rather, such information is often important data, and it provides *emic* coloring to cross-cultural comparisons, as previously discussed. The reason for redundancy is to help translators catch mistakes. If they are unsure of the meaning of an item from one phrase, they may find it in the redundant information found in another phrase. Such items may be marked "wordy" and "repetitive" by high school English teachers, but these people are not the target audience for cross-cultural research instruments.

7. Avoid adverbs and prepositions telling "where" or "when" (e.g. frequently, beyond, upper). Again, the reason for this guideline is pragmatic: there are often inadequate direct equivalents of these words, and so the meaning of an entire sentence can be changed. For instance, how often does an event have to occur for the word "frequently" to be used? Such a term demands knowledge of base rates and subjective reactions to deviations from the base rates, and this information is not always available to researchers. In some cases, cross-cultural analyses have been done of topics which are reflected in adverbs. In analyzing cultural differences in perceptions of time, for instance, Hall (1959) found that concepts summarized by words like "punctually" or "promptly" have very different meanings across cultures. A method for analyzing the connotations of potentially troublesome words and phrases encountered in translation will be reviewed in a subsequent section of this chapter.

8. Avoid possessive forms where possible. Use of possessive forms in English is relatively easy for native speakers since they have a basic understanding of concepts concerning ownership. But to assume that this knowledge will be shared by native speakers of a different language is an example of cultural imposition. The term "his land" may have seemingly adequate linguistic equivalents in another language, but the connotations may be quite different. For instance, the land may be tied to a family or clan, or may be considered "owned" only in the sense that a family is using it at the present time. Another reason for care regarding possessives is that, especially in long sentences, translators may find difficulty in matching exactly what is "possessed" with who is "doing the possessing." Finally, another difficulty is similar to that presented in guideline number

three regarding pronouns. What is presented in one possessive form in English (yours) is presented in one of three forms in many other languages (corresponding to single, dual, and multiple referents).

9. Use specific rather than general terms (e.g. the specific animal such as cows, chickens, or pigs rather than the general term "livestock"). One of the conclusions from the literature on cross-cultural studies of cognition is that people in various language communities do not categorize specific items in the same manner (e.g. Cole & Scribner, 1974). Rather, the items are grouped in different ways across cultures, and consequently any generalized label (when there is one) is likely to refer to collections of items which are not exactly equivalent. Using the above example, for instance, what an English speaker means by "livestock" is unlikely to contain the same specific animals as compared to someone from another language community. Further, people in that other community may not have a general term. For instance, an item asking about good or bad interpersonal relationships with one's brother, while reasonable for speakers of English, would not be appropriate for research in Japan. There, speakers make a distinction between "older brother" and "younger brother," and there is no general term to incorporate both.

A careful literature review prior to research, or good pre-testing, would bring out this fact prior to actual data collection. Upon discovery of this fact, researchers should then ask English-speaking respondents about interpersonal relationships with older and younger brothers. This is an example of decentering (Werner & Campbell, 1970; Brislin, Lonner, & Thorndike, 1973). No one country is the "center" of the research project and consequently no one country is the source of instrument development. Rather, data from both countries are used to design instruments which are sensitive to cultural phenomena. If English speakers do not make major distinctions between relations with older and younger brothers, while Japanese do, this becomes an important finding which can then be related to other facts established in the actual data-collection efforts. But unless the distinction related to age were made, the finding will not be forthcoming from the data. To quote from a wise senior professor during my graduate student era, "If you don't ask, you won't get." Another reason for the recommendation regarding specificity of items is related to progress in attitude measurement. Ajzen and Fishbein (1977, 1981) have concluded that behavior is best predicted, and consequently best understood, when specific rather than general questions are asked about behavior and behavioral intentions. Behavior is very specific: people act in a certain manner, in a certain situation, with other specific actors present or not, and so forth. Using the example of domestic animals again, people do not behave in ways best predicted by responses to inquiries about livestock. Rather, since they behave differently regarding treatment of chickens, cows, sheep, and pigs, behavior is best predicted and understood by inquiries about those specific animals. Another benefit of this concern with specific questions is that researchers have to do great amounts of reading, pre-testing, and listening to people before they are able to formulate specific questions. Such efforts prior to instrument development will surely benefit the growth of cross-cultural research.

10. Avoid words indicating vagueness regarding some event or thing (e.g. probably, maybe, perhaps). This guideline is another reminder of the benefits stemming from specificity in items, discussed above. Even when there are seemingly equivalent terms to words like "probably" or "maybe", the number of times an event has to occur to be labeled "probable" may differ from culture to culture. When doing survey research within one's own country, interviewers can call upon large amounts of shared information and shared experiences with respondents. When a respondent demonstrates a blank stare as a response to a vague inquiry, an interviewer can sometimes break the ice by the phrase, "Oh, you know what I mean!" But his phrase cannot be used when interviewer and respondent are from different cultures. Even if indigenous interviewers are used, often a wise practice, the appeal to shared meaning cannot be used if the interviewer is working from an instrument prepared by the outsider-researcher. The best approach is to specify the referent for the subjective experience of concepts like "probably" through such inquiries as the number of times per hour, day, month, or year, as appropriate.

11. Use wording familiar to the translators. There are a number of benefits to keeping this guideline in mind. One is that if wording is familiar to translators such that they can create a well-worded target language version, then that version will most likely be readily understandable to the eventual set of respondents in the data collection effort. Another benefit is that translators are treated more like colleagues than hired help. Researchers should sit down with

translators and go over the materials to be translated, line by line. When translators point out that such and such a term has no direct equivalent, then the researcher should consider this information as good data. The researcher might then change the original language wording, keeping in mind the philosophy of decentering, previously discussed. Reasons for lack of translation equivalence, such as no single word for "brother" in Japan, can point to a way to fruitful hypotheses. If translators have a difficult time with a phrase or a sentence, the researcher can say, "Well, here is what we are trying to get at." With the underlying purpose of an item in mind, the researcher and translator together can sometimes create a culturally equivalent item.

12. Avoid sentences with two different verbs if the verbs suggest two different actions. If they encounter two verbs in one sentence, translators sometimes have a difficult time attaching the relevant subject to the appropriate verb. The difficulties of translation are extensive enough without burdening research colleagues with problems which can be prevented through good preparation of materials. Another reason for the avoidance of dual verbs in a sentence is that interpretation of respondents' answers is difficult. With dual verbs indicating dual actions, researchers will have difficulty ascertaining why respondents endorsed or rejected a given item. The reason could involve the thought indicated by one of the verbs, the other, or a combination. For instance, here is an item from the California Ethnocentrism (E) Scale which is a *negative model* for materials prepared according to these guidelines. "If there are enough Negroes who want to attend dances at a local dance hall featuring a colored band, a good way to arrange this would be to have one all-Negro night, and then the whites could dance in peace the rest of the time" (used as an example by Ashmore, 1970).

Translators will have a difficult time ascertaining who wants to dance, who is doing the arranging, and who will finally dance in peace. Other violations of the guidelines are that the sentence is far too long, and a few of the phrases are colloquial ("all-Negro night;" "dance in peace"). One of the pieces of incidental learning from cross-cultural research is to discover how many colloquial phrases native speakers of a language use on an everyday basis. Even if there happened to be an adequate translation, the researchers eventually will have a difficult task pinpointing the reasons for item acceptance or rejection. The reason could be the concept of an all-Negro night, the fact that whites can dance without Negroes present, or others. The wisest practice is to have one concept per item so that the respondents' feeling about the concept can be unambiguously measured.

I have found that a good exercise for classes in cross-cultural research methods is to present students with items like that from the California E scale. They are then given the task of rewriting the items using the twelve guidelines. The independent efforts of the students can then be compared and discussed.

Guidelines Useful for Item Modification

To obtain good translations, and thus good terms for data gathering, modifications of existing instruments often have to be made. Butcher (1982; Butcher & Garcia, 1978; Butcher & Clark, 1979) has prepared a very extensive and sophisticated treatment concerning the use of existing instruments for cross-cultural use. He has been actively involved in cross-cultural applications of the MMPI, and many of his examples are drawn from this work. There is no attempt to endorse the MMPI in this treatment (see also Chapter 8 by Guthrie & Lonner, this volume). The fact is that a great deal of sophisticated thinking has been invested in how best to modify the MMPI for cross-cultural use. The resulting suggestions for cross-cultural instrumentation are treated here, not the rationale behind the original development of the MMPI.

The most generally helpful guideline for item modification was formulated by Gough (in Brislin, Lonner, & Thorndike, 1973, p. 26) who drew upon experiences with translators of the test he developed, the California Psychological Inventory (CPI).

Most personality assessment material has some sort of diagnostic rationale which may or may not be apparent from content, and which can be quite different from what content suggests. In translation it is this intent that must be maintained, not the content. Thus, translators must know the infrapsychology of the tools they are converting and they must know the empirical connotations of an item as well as its linguistic and literal referents. The CPI abounds in items of this kind, that is those that need intuitive rather than linguistic conversion. Of course, the person who instructs the translator about the "infra-psychology of the tools" and "empirical connotations" is the researcher in charge of the project.

Gough used the example of a CPI item: "Every family owes it to the city to keep its lawn mowed in summer and sidewalks shoveled in winter." The problem for translation is that people in many countries do not experience harsh winters and consequently the item has no personal relevance. This item is from the socialization scale of the CPI, designed to measure people's integration into their society, their concern with being good citizens, and their acceptance of widespread social norms which contribute to the smooth functioning of everyday life. To design a cultural equivalent, activities are needed which mark the concerned, well-socialized citizen. In Mediterranean countries, the following is a suggested functional equivalent: "The good citizen does not throw his garbage down the stairwell."

Butcher and Garcia (1978, p. 474) use an example from the MMPI which has been referred to earlier: "I think Lincoln was greater than Washington." They argue that "It is necessary to substitute two historical figures who were influential in the historical and cultural development of the target country. The subtle differences between the images of these two historical figures (i.e. one a humanist and the other a militarist or liberator) needs to be maintained."

A more difficult example is provided by Butcher and Clark (1979): "I like poetry." This item is designed to reflect feminine versus masculine interests, but in Japan both men and women enjoy poetry. In addition, there is no general word for poetry: there has to be a distinction made between Japanese poetry and Western-style poetry. The word for the latter was chosen for the translation since Japanese women are thought to enjoy Western poetry more than men do. Again, the important point to keep in mind is the detailed knowledge of the target culture necessary to modify items and to insure good, usable translations.

Another example (Butcher & Garcia, 1978, p. 473) from the MMPI asks about "hobbies." For the Spanish translation, the seeming equivalent of "distracciones" was not used because it had "vague connotations and was thus too imprecise." The solution in this case was to retain the English word "hobbies" since it is a familiar word to the target population and is frequently used by native speakers of Spanish. Another frequently encountered difficulty is that items formulated through negative wording (e.g. "I can read a long time without tiring my eyes") do not read smoothly when translated into other languages. One suggested solution is to rephrase the item and to reverse the scoring key for the item. One such rewording is: "My eyes get tired when I read for a long time."

Eventually, the results from the data-collection efforts with the translated instruments should be subjected to multivariate statistical analyses. Such activities will almost always by done "back home," with the assistance of personnel in computer centers. Conclusions about adequacy of the translated instruments will be made based upon such results as similar factorial structures, item analyses, inclusion of specific items as indicators of specific factors, and so forth (for general discussions see Brislin, Lonner, & Thorndike, 1973; Irvine & Carroll, 1980; Miller et al., 1981; Irvine, this volume). To aid in these complex data analyses, Butcher and Clark (1979) suggest that detailed information concerning translation efforts accompany each item on the final versions of the data-collection instruments. This information is then taken into account during data interpretation. The information would include the following:

1. Indications of which items were difficult to translate, and for what reasons. Reasons can include grammatical problems; problems stemming from seemingly good equivalence, but with the necessity of choosing a lower frequency-of-use word in the target language; good linguistic equivalence, but probable differential experience across cultures with regard to a concept or activity.

2. Indications concerning which items were modified to obtain cultural in contrast to linguistic equivalents, as discussed above with the "shovel snow" and "Lincoln-Washington" items. The reasons for the need for cultural modification should be given, as well as the rationales for the final choices of target-language wording.

3. Indications concerning which items were translated literally, despite careful thought given to the possibility of cultural equivalents. Again, reasons for final choices should be given. In some cases, the reason will be that respondents will be familiar with the meaning of an item even though they do not directly experience the activities indicated in the item. For instance, people in the deep South of the United States can respond to the "shovel snow" item because they are familiar with the activity through pictures in the mass media, stories they read as children, and so forth.

4. Indications concerning which items needed grammatical modification. Often the tense of original language items must be modified. As previously discussed, many languages do not have good equivalents of the English subjunctive.

5. Indications concerning which items contained idioms in the original language version which were rendered into standard,

nonidiomatic phrases in the target language. "Feeling blue" from an English language test might best be translated as the more direct "depressed," especially when the word for the latter is used frequently in everyday conversations. Since many readers of such explanations will be from nonEnglish-speaking countries, researchers should also explain the meaning of the original language version. Such explanations are especially important since the meaning of items, and the diagnostic inference from item endorsements, changes over time. The MMPI item involving a choice concerning whether or not to label oneself as a personal representative of God may be far less diagnostic of bizarre thinking in the 1980s given the widely disseminated phrases used by devout (sometimes called "born again") Christians.

6. Indications concerning which items were changed from negative to positive wording, or vice-versa, necessitating changes in the scoring key.

7. Indications concerning which items were easily translated, with no need for modification, but about which researchers have doubts. The doubts could be due to relevance of the concepts or activities designated in the items, the relative frequency or infrequency of activities across cultures (e.g. people may have little time for "hobbies" in subsistence-level societies), possible inappropriateness due to trampling upon cultural taboos, and so forth.

As more and more such information is made available about translation procedures with existing tests, future efforts to develop new translations should be far easier and more psychometrically sound. It is hard to imagine a translation effort of an existing test not benefiting from Butcher's (1982; Butcher & Clark, 1979) analyses of cross-cultural investigations using the MMPI.

Guidelines for Developing New Items

If researchers choose to use existing tests *and* to add to these tests for the purpose of investigating *emic* aspects of a concept in other cultures, then they must concern themselves with developing new items. There are very definitely two schools of thought on new item development: some researchers point to its ease, and others point to its difficulty. Burisch (1984, p. 219) presents arguments from the standpoint of economics, an important consideration given the time needed for, and expense of, cross-cultural studies.

> Not too much need be said about economy in the sense of *construction* economy. Some of the better known inventories, like the MMPI or the Sixteen Personality Factor Questionnaire (16PF), have taken years to build, not to speak of the funds spent and the man-and-woman power consumed in the process. In contrast, it cost me two hours and a bottle of wine to write an aggression and a depression scale that turned out to be of equal or superior validity, compared to much more sophisticated instruments [Burisch, 1984, Table 3]. As I learned later, even weeks of discussion over item formulations did not lead to scales that were appreciably better than that.

Another proponent of the idea that item development is a straightforward task undemanding of massive resources is Campbell (1968, p. 255). Given Campbell's visibility in cross-cultural research, and the provocative nature of these ideas, his position has been surprisingly undercited.

> [Researchers should not] feel that tests are well constructed just because they have been expensively conceived or are much used. The methodology in test construction is in such flux that any well trained graduate student today can construct a better test (for cross-cultural or intracultural purposes) than the Manifest Anxiety Scale, the MMPI, the F-scale measure of authoritarianism, etc. For the applied practitioner it may be well to use a test rigidly in its original format as a magical bundle of rituals of which he does not dare disturb any part. But [this] is not science, and one does not then know what aspect of the test is producing its correlates. For the scientist's test of intersubjective communicability, loyalty is required only to the theoretically relevant aspects of the tests—all the rest of the vehicular specifics should be free to vary.

On the other hand, Gorsuch (1984, p. 235) is of the opinion that the development of new measuring devices is very difficult. His analysis is specifically concerned with the measurement of religious phenomena:

> Even a single, simple scale requires a considerable amount of time and empirical analysis to have any possibility of competing on psychometric grounds with previously existing scales. This means that scale development in the psychology of religion has progressed sufficiently

so that it should generally be left to those with advanced training in the psychology of religion, in scale development, and in related topics such as factor analysis. Certainly, it is not a task for the average master's level project.

As with all quotes taken from longer articles, the authors' thoughts are contextualized. Campbell (1968) distinguishes between diagnosing or demonstrating the presence of a phenomenon and understanding it, and his argument is that new scales are necessary for theory development to incorporate data gathered in other cultures. Burisch (1984) argues the merits of the deductive approach to scale development in which item generation follows after very careful definitions of explanations of a phenomenon. To use his examples, the straightforward creation of items could take place only after very careful definitions of depression and aggression were written. Such definition, when written about concepts in other cultures of which researchers are not members, is undoubtedly a difficult but not insurmountable step. Jackson (1975) has shown that educated members of a culture, in his research college students untrained in psychometrics, can write usable items as long as they are provided with good definitions of the researchers' concepts under study. Gorsuch (1984) argues that many good scales exist for the study of various well-defined religious phenomena and the researchers must make a case that there is a need for new ones. The resources needed for the development of new scales, which are extensive in his opinion, could go into more data gathering with existing instuments so as to obtain the benefits discussed previously.

Even understanding the context of these positions concerning scale development, disagreements will exist among researchers for many years to come. Such disagreement is part of the "flux" to which Campbell refers. For readers who decide to take up the call for new scale development, or *emic* additions to *etic* scales, the following guidelines are offered. These suggestions are meant to help answer these queries:

> I am in another culture working on a research project, but had to leave my library behind. I have identified an indigenous concept which I would like to operationalize by means of a measuring device. In another case, I found an existing test useful, but there seemed to be aspects of the concept as exists in this culture which are not picked up

by the existing test. What are some hints for writing new items for these two types of problems?

One guideline is to have previously followed the Boy Scout motto, "Be prepared." Prior to field work, there should be a careful literature review, not just of the psychological literature but also the writings of anthropologists, sociologists, political scientists, missionaries, governmental officials, and so forth. Fortunately, much of the relevant materials have been efficiently catalogued by the developers of the Human Relations Area Files (HRAF: see Barry, 1980, and Chapter 3 of this volume for descriptions concerning its use), a resource available either in printed form or on microfilm in many large university libraries. Cataloguing has been done not only by culture, author of materials, and the author's disciplinary background, but also according to concepts covered. Use of HRAF is mandatory since it is one of the few places where researchers can obtain excellent but out-of-print materials on various cultures. One use of the HRAF would be to designate the research topic (e.g. mental illness), examine the materials with potentially applicable *etic* concepts in mind (e.g. the nature of intervention by outsiders), and to search for *emic* colorings to the *etic*. One difficulty with HRAF is that coverage reflects the interests of the people who lived in the cultures. There is more information of use to anthropologists than to psychologists. Still, for many topics which are the focus of research in several disciplines (e.g. alcohol use, the family, sex role distinctions), much valuable information will be found. Another benefit, in my experience, is that if researchers are familiar with the written ethnographic materials about a culture, they are respected by indigenous people. If researchers show that they have a good knowledge of local customs, as learned through their library study, then indigenous hosts are quicker to cooperate in the researcher's own investigation.

If a number of perplexing problems can be overcome, collaboration with colleagues from other cultures can yield tremendous benefits (Brislin, 1979; various chapters in Bulmer & Warwick, 1983). Difficulties stem from decisions regarding the relative status levels of research team members, the dangers of imposition by the best-funded members, decisions concerning publication credit and order of names on the final book or journal article, as well as the typical personality clashes which exist in any team effort. If such problems can be overcome, one way to benefit from the varied cultural backgrounds of team members is to ask each person to be a spokesperson from his or her culture. They could examine a concept, such as depression, and ask themselves, "How would a person from my culture manifest this psychological state? What might they say about themselves, and why?" Those statements might then be good items which the eventual target population can endorse or not. Another approach might be to examine items on established tests and to ask, "which of these might people in my culture endorse if they are depressed? Do these established items remind me of other things depressed people might say about themselves, or about things they would deny? Do any of the established items demand modifications before they are usable?"

Pre-test work with bilingual and bicultural people can also yield good items (Wesley & Karr, 1966). Such people have lived in two or more cultures, perhaps as a function of extensive study abroad, traveling with their parents as a result of their job assignments, or a personal history of immigration (Brislin, 1981). These people can be asked to think about a concept, and then asked to reflect upon it from the viewpoint of one culture, then the other. Researchers should be careful about the potential imposition of *etics* by starting with *emic* concepts and then working up and down through various levels of abstraction (e.g. a culture's broad labels as well as very specific behaviors through which a concept is manifested).

Another approach is to take advantage of the research literature concerned with bilingual individuals. Ervin-Tripp (1964) showed that people are able to tell quite different stories when asked to reflect upon pictures from the Thematic Apperception Test (TAT), depending upon which language they use. Similarly, researchers can present bilinguals with a variety of stimuli (pictures, items, stories, experimental situations) and ask them to comment, first in one language, then the other. Controls could be added, such as counterbalancing for order of language; and use of one language only for a percentage of the stimuli to guard against simple repetition of what was already said. Responses could then be analyzed in terms of what is common across all the bilinguals' verbalization, and what is specific to each language.

Researchers can also use the Human Relations Area Files in innovative ways. A commonly shared goal in item generation methods under discussion here is that researchers want people to be verbal so that their responses can later be content analyzed. The key, then, is to find approaches which bring out large amounts of verbal output. Some questions put to respondents bring blank stares, such as "Tell me about your culture." Such a question is too broad and has too little focus to help the respondent know what is desired. But if the question is specific, or if the respondents are asked to comment about specific stimuli, then there is a much greater chance of helpful replies. Brislin and Holwill (1977) found that 105 educated respondents from 24 different countries, or distinct cultural groups within a political entity, had no trouble reading and commenting upon written materials about their cultures drawn from the Human Relations Area Files. They were able to label certain points as correct or incorrect; suggest corrections; make expansions on certain points; bring other points up to date; and make recommendations for better research methodology. Brislin and Holwill found that the respondents enjoyed their task, finding the concept of insiders commenting on the work of outsiders provocative. In most cases, the insider-respondents knew that certain anthropologists had done work in their cultures, but few of the 105 respondents had read the materials prior to participation in this research project.

If researchers find that respondents are skilful at giving answers to questions which demand that they fill in blank spaces, or complete sentence stems (e.g. Phillips, 1960), or place marks on semantic differential scales, then the antecedent-consequent method can be used (Triandis, 1977). Using this approach, researchers phrase questions in the following form to obtain perception of what is necessary for a phenomenon to occur (the antecedents), and what happens once the phenomenon does occur (consequences). Using the example of depression again, the questions would take the form:

(Antecedents)

If you have _____ , then you have depression.

If _____ happens, then you are depressed.

If _____ happens, others will know that I am depressed.

(Consequences)

If I am depressed, then I _____ .

If others think that I am depressed, then _____ .

If I am depressed, I then try_____ .

Like the debate concerning the straightforwardness versus difficulty of generating new scales, these and similar approaches which ask respondents to complete sentences or to make check marks on scales divide researchers into various camps. Anthropologists, especially, are wary of questionnaire approaches, fearing imposition of concepts and preferring long-term participant observation. There may be more disagreement among neophytes, however, than among experienced researchers. Often, judgments about another discipline's methods seem based on the worst examples, not those studies which have made important contributions. Once researchers become secure in their identity and do not have to establish their credentials by criticizing other disciplines, they often draw from a variety of approaches in their actual research endeavors (e.g. Howard, 1974, trained in anthropology but sophisticated in questionnaire development). Irvine (1968, p. 3), trained in psychology, has pointed to the benefits of participant observation: "to collect valid data the psychologist needs adequate and sympathetic training in understanding a society system that is alien, complex, and conceptually different. Participant observer research will acquire greater scientific status, it seems, as a result."

TRANSLATION: A RECOMMENDED PROCEDURE

A close relation exists between the modification of existing instruments, and the creation of new items, and subsequent translation into other languages. If materials are prepared according to the suggested guidelines, they are more likely to be translatable than if the guidelines were ignored. Further, much information can be gained about desirable wording in both the target *and original* languages through examinations of the translators' efforts.

The recommended procedure is back-translation, and its close relative, decentering (Werner & Campbell, 1969; Brislin, 1970; Brislin, Lonner, & Thorndike, 1973). In back-translation, one bilingual translates from the source to the target language, and another blindly translates back to the source. The procedure can be repeated for several rounds, as different bilinguals work with the efforts of their predecessors. The work of the team of bilinguals, each working independently on a different step, can be depicted as follows:

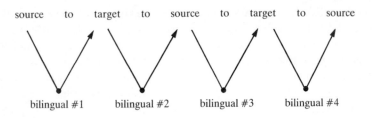

source   to   target   to   source   to   target   to   source

bilingual #1   bilingual #2   bilingual #3   bilingual #4

Moving back and forth between languages in this way is the basis of decentering, since no one language is the "center" of attention. The procedure can be repeated for several more rounds. The researcher then compares the last back-translated version with the original version. If a concept "survives" the decentering procedure, it is assumed to be *etic* since there must be readily available words and phrases in the two languages which the translators could use. If a concept is not in the final back-translated version, the reason could be that it is *emic*. That is, the concept might be readily expressible in only one of the languages. At this point, there should be extensive discussions with the bilinguals who can indicate reasons why materials were and were not translatable. For instance, Phillips (1960, p. 302) found it very difficult to have this sentence stem translated into the Thai language: "Sometimes a good quarrel is necessary because ..." He wrote, "After much discussion the translators decided that although it was conceivable that an American might enjoy a quarrel for its cathartic effect, the notion would be incomprehensible to a Thai." To use the terms already introduced, "having a good quarrel" is not an *etic*. Rather, the translation procedure has pointed up a very important difference which can be built into cross-cultural investigations of interpersonal relationships.

Another benefit to this procedure is that it guides final decisions about the wording of the original language version which will eventually be used in actual data collection. That version will often be the final back-translation. The reasoning for this suggestion is that the final back-translation is most likely to be equivalent to a target language version, probably the version immediately preceding the final step in the decentering process (see diagram). For instance, Brislin (1970) wanted the following item from the Crowne and Marlowe social desirability inventory (1964) to be translated into Chamorro, the language of Guam and the Marianas Islands. "I have never intensely disliked anyone." The final back-translated version was "I have never really disliked someone." Discussions with translators yielded the facts that it was difficult to translate "intensely" (translators often have difficulty with adverbs), and the equivalent of "someone" was more readily available than for "anyone." It was this back-translated version which was later used in data-gathering with English-speaking respondents. The position defended by Campbell (1968) cited previously was taken very seriously. The topic of investigation was the need for approval, and it is measured by a set of statements which allow people to present themselves in a positive light. If changes from "intensely" to "really," and from "someone" to "anyone," change the meaning so much that there will be a differential response, then the underlying concept is weak. Still, changes in stimuli cause discomfort since Campbell's position is not universally accepted. If researchers are worried that these sorts of changes can lead to noncomparability with previous studies which have used the original version, they can gather data using both versions. English-language respondents can see versions which contain one-half original items, and one-half revised based on decentering efforts. Basic controls can be added to counterbalance the order of original and revised items. Data analysis can then indicate whether or not different conclusions should be made about respondents based on their reactions to original versus revised items. Brislin (1970), for example, found no differences and concluded that the items on the Marlowe-Crowne scale are robust enough to allow modifications based on what is easily expressible in other languages. This conclusion seems similar to that of Butcher (1982), who has written most extensively about cross-cultural use of the MMPI.

Like any single method or approach, back translation is no panacea. All materials should be pre-tested with respondents similar to those in the proposed main sample since there will always be items which simply do not work well in actual use. The major advantage of back-translation is that it gives researchers some control over the instrument development stage since they can examine original and back-translated versions and make inferences about the quality of the translation. Researchers rarely know the target language well enough to do their own translations. Even researchers who are native speakers, because of the large number of years they have devoted to their formal education, may use phrases which are unfamiliar to the sample of respondents. At times, they can prepare first drafts and then ask *monolinguals* similar to the respondents to rewrite the material so that it will be clear to native speakers. In such a case, the sequence would be:

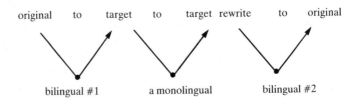

This sequence can also be used if the researcher is concerned that the back-translation is better than the target-language version. This problem can occasionally arise if a highly-skilled bilingual can make sense out of a mangled target version. Just as all readers of this chapter can make sense out of broken English when interacting with visitors from other countries, back-translators can sometimes take very rough materials and polish them so much that they appear as "diamonds" in the final version. Adding the target rewrite step minimizes this possibility, but even here pre-testing is necessary.

I have frequently given this advice regarding pre-testing, but have been met with this complaint: "It took me a great deal of effort to receive permission to do research in such-and-such an organization in another country. I have limited time there, and have no facilities to duplicate a revised instrument in any case. How can I pre-test?" The answer is that pre-testing in the other country may not be possible on any large scale, but work with approximately ten respondents is still wise to determine what questions *they* will have and what items need oral explanation in the instructions-to-respondents step. I once advised a researcher who was about to work in a Malaysian factory, but who would have no opportunity for extensive pre-testing, to do the pre-test work in his own country using the back-translated English items. He listed key aspects of his eventual sample in Malaysia: limited education, not familiar with filling out question-naires, not much experience with researchers, limited reading skills in their native language, and so forth. He then sought out a factory in his own country which employed similar people. He administered the English-language version there, identifying a number of places where there were communication difficulties with respondents. He then made changes, incorporating them into the Malaysian version. He reported to me that he had no problems in the actual data gathering in Malaysia.

ADMINISTRATION OF RESEARCH INSTRUMENTS

Although space limitations prevent an extensive discussion, a few guidelines can be suggested for the administration of measuring instruments. Usually, administration will be in the form of interviews, questionnaires, or formal tests. Various biases in instrument administration have been given names (e.g. Pareek and Rao, 1980). The rudeness bias occurs when researchers forget that they are requesting the valuable time of people in other cultures and plunge ahead with their questions without knowledge of local norms. The sucker bias occurs when respondents give nonsensical answers in the spirit of fun, to see how much of their silliness the researcher is willing to record. The "I-can-answer-any-question-bias," more prevalent in some parts of the world than others, refers to the deep-seated belief among respondents that no question should go unanswered. People thus have answers, however poorly formulated, on topics ranging from the most appropriate age at which children should start writing, to fighting inflation through the planned introduction of an economic recession.

The courtesy bias occurs when respondents try to discover what the questioner wants, and then direct their answers accordingly. The hidden premises bias occurs, more frequently than many researchers believe, when respondents try to discover who the researcher *really* represents and what the researcher is *really* trying to learn. Often, researchers are judged based on the source of funding for their studies, and any government-funded investigation is seen as an attempt to have that government's influence permeate the local culture.

There is no single magic solution to dealing with these potential biases. As with any interaction in another culture, sensitivity to the host point of view and to the time they invest in a study is extremely important. Thorough preparation, including extensive reading of the ethnographies written about the culture, results in an ability to see through the sucker bias. Researchers may want to strive for the goal of good lawyers: never ask a question of a witness unless the answer is already known. While impossible to achieve in all cases, the goal is a good one to keep in mind. Researchers should have a good understanding of the potential range of answers to their questions or else they will be unable to make distinctions between honest attempts to answer questions and error of various kinds.

A specific technique for dealing with potential biases has been suggested by Schuman (1966). Called the "random probe," researchers select a random sample of items from their instruments for a probing follow-up question. The sample of respondents which receives the probe for a given item is also randomly selected. The probe might be, "What do you mean?", or "Could you tell me more about that?" The answer to the probe from any one person should make sense, especially when compared to the answers provided by other respondents. Further, the quality of answers can be judged according to whether or not answers make sense given the answers to other probing questions. Answers to all the probes should provide excellent contextualizing information which will make interpretation of the original measuring instrument more precise and will allow distinctions to be made between biased and valid answers.

NOTE

1. Some readers will undoubtedly argue that French and/or Spanish could be added here. Some of the guidelines to be presented are also applicable to materials prepared in these languages. Even proponents of research carried out from the beginning stages in indigenous languages, to study indigenous phenomena more precisely and to avoid *imposed etics* (e.g. Enriquez and Marcelino, 1984, in the Philippines) recognize the need for eventual publication in a language of world-wide use.

6

OBSERVATIONAL METHODS

STEPHEN BOCHNER

INTRODUCTION AND OVERVIEW

The topic is the use of observational methods in cross-cultural research. Rather than offering a formal definition of an observational method, I shall develop a picture of this process by describing the kinds of procedures investigators using this approach have employed. A great deal has been written about observational methods, including several books and major chapters in edited volumes (e.g. Bickman & Henchy, 1972; Bochner, 1979, 1980; Brandt, 1972; Longabaugh, 1980; Sechrest, 1979; Webb, Campbell, Schwartz, & Sechrest, 1966). It is not possible or desirable to go over much of this ground. In this chapter I want to restrict myself to the basic, practical issues. Thus a viable research project must deal with the problem of subject reactance, the interaction between context or situation and behavior, the level of abstraction being employed, the sampling problem in its various guises, the choice of a suitable control group, and the special problems of incorporating a cross-cultural dimension in the project.

In trying to limit my exposition to manageable proportions, I have put myself in the shoes of a person about to embark on a cross-cultural research project, and list the questions such a person should be asking. The rest of the chapter consists of an attempt to provide answers to some of these questions, which include the following:

(a) How does one choose between different psychological methods? Why adopt this rather than that procedure? In the present context, why choose an observational method over something else, like an interview?

(b) Having decided on an observational approach, how does one choose between the various observational methods that are available? Indeed, what are the various categories of such methods?

(c) How does one decide between the various categories of dependent variables? What does one measure? Whom does one measure? How often? Where?

(d) How does one interpret observational data? What do they mean? Do they say anything about the "inner person"? What are the limitations and special advantages of observation in comparison to some of the other standard methods?

It is outside the scope of this chapter to provide a detailed, nuts-and-bolts account of how to collect specific empirical data. Rather, I shall list the principles of conducting such research, and identify one or two studies that illustrate the method in question. Readers may then go to these references for more detailed practical guidance. From the preceding discussion it should be clear that I regard the process of designing a research project as a series of decisions about what and whom should be studied how and when. This chapter is essentially about the rules that govern such decisions, about the principles that need to be followed to ensure that the procedures that have been selected do the intended job. The purpose, or the "why" of a particular research project, ties all the other considerations together, and provides the structure within which questions about who, what, when, and where can be framed.

There is a vast literature dealing with within-culture observational methods and issues. These studies will only be mentioned if they make some point that is not covered by the cross-cultural literature. Where possible, the examples and instances will all be derived from investigations that have a cross-cultural component.

ISSUES AND PROBLEMS

The emphasis on empirical data has been psychology's major strength, but also the source of many of its problems and controversies. In the final analysis, most of the arguments in psychology relate to methodological issues, such as whether the results of a particular study mean what the investigators attribute to the outcome, whether the data were validly collected, properly analyzed, correctly interpreted, and so on. Outsiders, that is nonpsychologists, often get impatient with this process. "Why don't you tell us what are the effects, say, of marijuana smoking on driving behavior, instead of humming and hawing and hedging your bets with all sorts of arcane and confusing qualifications?" When the psychologist insists that it depends on sampling considerations, observer bias, subject react-ance, choice of dependent variables, context effects, or other factors, the average lay person turns away perplexed. Such a person may even go so far as to write off the social sciences, deeming them to be irrelevant, as largely a game being played by and for the benefit of remote, ivory tower academics (e.g. Shaffer, 1977).

It is difficult to measure complex human behavior, and Hull's (1951) noble failure to develop precise "laws" attests to this. Psychology can, and of course does, use sophisticated methods and instruments to measure phenomena. But because a human being is the subject of observation and measurement by another human being, this complicates matters. These complications include the following:

Reactance

When human beings become aware that they are being watched, they react. The behavior observed usually changes simply as a function of being studied, sometimes making it quite different from its "natural" state, that is when the subject is unaware of being under scrutiny. Often the only practical solution is to observe the subject unobtrusively, which raises many ethical issues.

Contextual Effects

The behavior of human beings is very much a function of where they are located, of the behavior setting that provides the physical and psychological stage for the action (Barker, 1963, 1968, 1978). For instance, children will respond differently depending on whether they are being observed in their school playground, their homes, or in the psychological laboratory. The usual distinction in methodology texts is to contrast field "naturalistic" settings on the one hand, with laboratory studies on the other, but that distinction obscures the more basic point that human behavior is almost always a complex product of the actor's personality, interacting with the situation in which it occurs (Argyle, Furnham, & Graham, 1981). What is not usually mentioned is that the differences between various "natural" settings may be as large as the differences between a particular field setting and a particular laboratory environment. One "solution" is to study the subjects in their various behavior settings, which in turn creates enormous practical problems. Most people participate in a large number of behavior settings, and it is often not possible to sample all of them adequately. For instance, does one observe a child with its mother, its father, both its parents, in the class room, in the playground, in a dentist's office, or what? And which of these pictures will reflect the "real" person?

Distorting the "Natural" Stream of Behavior

One response to the above problem has been to employ time- and event-sampling techniques, so as to be able to observe standardized and representative instances of behavior in a variety of settings. This approach attracted the criticism that by imposing pre-determined observational categories on phenomena, the investigator is interfering with the natural sequence of behavior and as a consequence may miss recording some acts altogether, or get a biased picture of their frequency and intensity. This approach in turn has been criticized on the grounds that merely recording everything that occurs in a free-floating way leads to a mass of unrelated, unmanageable data that are difficult to quantify and interpret, and which are highly prone to observer bias. I shall look at this issue in more detail later in this chapter.

The Internal/External Distinction

In psychology we tend to make a distinction between overt, observable behavior (speech acts, gestures, facial expressions, problem-solving behavior); underlying "mental" processes (motives, feelings, emotions, cognitions); and underlying physiological processes (brain waves, endocrine functions). Some of these underlying processes are inferred, hypothetical constructs whereas others can be directly observed. For instance, brain activity can be measured with a EEG machine. Poor industrial morale, on the other hand, cannot be directly measured, but must be inferred from what people say and what they do, such as a high frequency of complaints and absenteeism.

A "physical" model is sometimes used in psychology, in the sense of implying that physiological processes are somehow primary and "cause" mental and behavioral phenomena to occur. This is a mistaken view, since there is considerable evidence to indicate that all of the three components mentioned earlier—behavior, cognition/emotion, and physiological/endocrine processes can and do influence each other. This has implications for decisions regarding the level at which a phenomenon should be studied, and the interpretations that can be placed on the results. I shall return to this issue later, also.

The Base Line Problem

In the physical sciences, many measurements can be reduced to some quasi-absolute value, or at least related to some invariable effect, thus providing an anchoring point for the measurements. The speed of light is the ultimate bench mark of the physical sciences, all other velocities are related to it, and the entire universe can be reduced to Einstein's law of relativity. At a less esoteric level, one nautical mile is equal to one minute of latitude on the earth's surface, or 6,080 feet. Such absolutism is rare in psychology, where most conclusions are relative, meaning that they are based on a comparison between two or more comparable individuals, groups, or behaviors. For instance, if a newly married couple has sexual intercourse fifteen times a week, is this a high or a low frequency? We cannot say, unless we know how often other newly married couples make love, what the average frequency is, whether the frequency declines with length of marriage, and so forth. This means that to be able to draw conclusions in psychology about quantities or amounts, we have to either make more than one set of observations, or relate our findings to a suitable comparison group whose relevant characteristics are known. The particular contribution of the cross-cultural method is to extend the base line beyond the confines of one society. Many otherwise potentially interesting studies in psychology are rendered worthless due to the lack of a suitable control condition in the design.

The Relationship Between Variables over Time

Many research questions in psychology are concerned with how two variables are related over time. For instance, does performance on intellectual tasks increase linearly with age? Does worker satisfaction increase with levels of pay? The usual approach to this issue is to take several measurements over time, either longitudinally or cross-sectionally. Thus, to establish the relationship, say, between age and performance, an investigator may test various groups of children differing in age. The problem is that the shape of the curve may depend on how many measurements are taken, and at what point in the life cycle of the subjects. For instance, if only two groups were included, say children aged ten and children aged fifteen, the result would almost certainly be a linear curve. But if a further group of twenty-five-year-olds was added, the curve would probably plateau. Then, if one added a group of seventy-year-olds, it is quite likely that a curvilinear pattern would emerge. Researchers wishing to draw conclusions about how two or more variables co-vary must ensure that they include sufficient measurement points to their design and that these points are suitably spaced, or if that is not possible, that they limit their interpretations accordingly.

Here too, the cross-cultural method had made a special contribution. For instance, developmental psychologists have been interested in the relationship between onset of weaning and personality development. In Western societies the range is typically somewhere between one and six months, but there are cultures where it may be several years before a child is weaned (for a review, see Jahoda, 1982), providing a much greater range of the independent variable and hence more measurement points. Indeed most of the variables in the socialization process (e.g. harsh versus permissive, early versus late toilet training, single versus multiple caretakers) can be "stretched" by employing a cross-cultural design.

Individual Differences

In the natural sciences the problem of variance either does not exist or is relatively minor. For instance, in physics, a particular substance will have the same atomic structure, irrespective of whether the element was found in Australia or Guatemala. Even in medicine, certain drugs have more or less the same effect on most patients, although exceptions are by no means unusual because we are now getting into the realm of human responses. In psychology, by contrast, there are vast individual differences in the way in which various people respond to theoretically identical stimuli, depending on the subjects' age, sex, socioeconomic background, culture, and so forth. This creates two kinds of research problems. The first is to uncover how these differences systematically interact with the stimulus of interest, both as a research object in its own right, as well as a means of controlling in future studies what then become known effects. The second is to treat these individual differences as extraneous variables, concentrate on eliciting the "pure" effect of the stimulus or independent variable, and reduce the "noise" due to individual differences by sampling procedures, large Ns, randomizing subjects to conditions, statistical juggling, and so forth. But here again, the task can be immense. For instance, if one is interested in how children respond to a particular style of playground supervision, does one sample different ages, socioeconomic levels, ethnic backgrounds, urban–rural differences? Where do you stop? I shall return to this problem, too.

Cross-Cultural Differences

The problem of individual differences becomes greatly magnified when we take into account differences between cultural or ethnic groups. Whereas Australian and Saudi Arabian crude oil has fairly similar properties, Australian and Saudi Arabian children differ in all sorts of fundamental respects. Does this mean that if we want to make some universal statement about the behavior of children, we need to sample all of the cultures in the world before we can say anything sensible? Clearly this too is not a practical proposition, although there exist a few studies (e.g. Osgood, May, & Miron, 1975; Rohner, 1975) that contain samples from most parts of the globe, but casting such a wide net is beyond the means of most investigators.

CHOOSING A RESEARCH STRATEGY

Doing effective research depends on the investigator having a clear idea about the purpose of the investigation (see especially Chapters 1 and 2). Many research projects are vague in their aims, lack a clear structure, and therefore produce incomplete or unsatisfactory results. Different research purposes may require different strategies, so it is important first to pinpoint goals. In general, the aim of psychological research can be classified on a continuum that has the *purpose of exploration* at one end, and the *confirmation of hypotheses* at the other. However, whatever the overall purpose, in my view the investigator should approach the problem with a fairly specific research question. It is insufficient to say: "I am interested in how children in playgrounds behave." Such statements are not scientific questions but vague musings. "What makes children in playgrounds aggressive?" is a little better but still not a proper basis for a scientific investigation. The researcher must have some particular idea that can be tested, such as for instance that the size of the playground could affect aggression, or that children in mixed ethnic settings could be more aggressive on warm than on cold days. Once the problem is stated in the form of a hypothesis, a study can then be designed that should be able to produce an unequivocal result that either confirms or does not confirm the hypothesis. However, sometimes we may know the problem but have no clear idea of the hypotheses that might arise in connection with it, of the questions that we should be asking. In this case, we must first do an exploratory study.

Exploratory Studies

Exploratory studies should not be vague excursions into the field to see what might or might not be there, although many of them are exactly that, and consequently largely a waste of time and resources. I am aware that the ethnographers (see later in this chapter) would strongly disagree with this statement, arguing that the only way to achieve a real understanding of a particular situation is to approach it without any preconceived notions about what to observe, how and when. I shall look at this issue later in this chapter. The useful exploratory study will have a particular set of objectives which the competent investigator sets up before embarking on the project. To illustrate, let us consider the steps in designing a hypothetical experiment which includes an exploratory study.

Let us imagine that complaints have been received by the ministry of education about increased violence in school playgrounds, and they want us to find out what the determinants of aggression in the school yard are, so that they can take measures to counter this trend. Let us assume that it is a virgin field (which it is not), i.e. that it has not been studied before, and that therefore we cannot go to other people or to written documents for advice on how to proceed. What should we do? One solution is to set up a series of exploratory studies that will give us the information we need *subsequently* to tackle the actual problem.

For the purpose of the present exposition, we know practically nothing about the problem other than that it is alleged to exist. The first step would be to visit a school, talk to the teachers and get their impressions, keeping an open mind about what we learn since their view of the matter could be incomplete, biased, or wrong. The next step would be to install ourselves in an inconspicuous corner of the playground, and as unobtrusively as possible begin to observe the action. But remember that we have come here to study aggression. We would therefore concentrate on those acts that relate to the aim of the investigation, rather than just observe a seething mass of children. Thus our observations would be filtered so as to select instances of behavior relevant to our purpose. However, our overall goal, to study aggression, in turn has several subsidiary aims embedded in it, related to various aspects of the research design. Thus we would need a perceptual "filter" for each of the following categories of behavior, in order to gain the essential minimum amount of information required to subsequently design the study proper.

Identifying the Target Behavior. In order to proceed at all, we must be able to identify and agree on what constitutes the target behavior, aggressive acts. There is probably little doubt that a punch in the nose qualifies, but is a shove in the ribs a mark of hostility or of playful endearment? Is a wrestling match a game or an act of aggression? Is a particular form of verbal abuse an expression of respect or of contempt? It may take many hours of systematic observations to come up with a set of categories that are unequivocally instances of aggression, in the sense that several observers independently agree on their classification to some acceptable criterion of correspondence.

Quantifying the Target Behaviors. Once the categories have been established, the next step is to see if they can be ordered in some way. The simplest measurement consists of determining whether a particular behavior is present or absent. But that is a fairly crude procedure which loses a lot of information, and has assumptions that are awkward for some statistical analyses. It is desirable to devise a dependent variable measure that can be scaled in some way. In the present context, the investigators may try to assign different weights to different categories of behaviors. For example, they might wish to develop a five-point scale of aggressive acts, with five being assigned to a black eye and one to a "playful" shove. Again, developing such a scale may take a great many observations to accomplish. In any case, Chapter 9 in this book should be helpful in this regard.

Sampling the Subjects and the Time Periods. Let us say that there are thirty children in the playground, and the recess lasts for thirty minutes. All the children cannot be watched all the time owing to lack of resources, and because even if the resources were available the army of researchers would contaminate the field and alter the "natural" behavior of the children. So, do we randomly select five children, watch them for the first five minutes, then switch our attention to five different children and watch them for the next five minutes, and so forth? This may sound fine in theory, but experience may indicate that such a procedure could be misleading. For instance, our exploratory observations may show that most of the aggression occurs in the last ten minutes of the recess, so that those children randomly allocated to the latter half of the study would score systematically higher than those in the first half, hence distorting the results. If this is the case, perhaps it might be better to make observations only in the last ten minutes, and try to include everyone in the trial or some other solution may suggest itself after further observations are made.

Forming Hypotheses. We now have a reliable, valid, quantifiable, representative dependent variable, but what we lack is an independent variable. No amount of systematic observation of aggressive behavior will tell us what leads to it unless we can relate the patterns in our observations to some antecedent set of conditions. That is the next and final step in our exploratory study. We must now cast our mind beyond the target behavior to any regular occurrences that appear to be connected with it. Is there more aggression before or after lunch? Is there more aggression after a particular class, in the presence of a particular teacher, at certain times of the year (such as before examinations), on hot days? In addition we may need to visit a variety of different playgrounds and see whether school size, the ethnic composition of the pupils, the religious affiliation of the parents, the proximity to heavy traffic, or whatever, has an apparent effect. Putting all these clues and hunches together, we may then design a study in which we systematically vary some of the conditions and deliberately control others, as a means of testing specific hypotheses about what produces or increases aggressive behavior in children. A couple of years after receiving the call from the ministry of education we may be in a position to call them back with some tentative conclusions.

Confirmatory Studies

The bulk of research in contemporary psychology consists of studies aimed at confirming or disconfirming particular hypotheses, that is experiments.

Types of Confirmatory Investigations and Their Dimensions. Confirmatory investigations can be classified according to three principal dimensions. The first continuum relates to the extent to which a study is an experiment, technically meaning the extent to which the conditions constituting the independent variable have been manipulated or created by the experimenter. The second dimension relates

TABLE 6.1
The Principal Dimensions of Confirmatory Research

	SETTING			
	Laboratory		Field	
	Verisimilitude		Verisimilitude	
	Artificial	Real	Artificial	Real
Manipulated	1	2	5	7
Naturally Occurring	3	4	6	8

Distinctions that cut across the three principal dimensions:

The derivation of the hypothesis:	Theoretical vs Pragmatic
Aim of the experiment:	Pure vs Applied
Nature of dependent variable:	"Verbal" vs Behavioral
Time frame of study:	Longitudinal vs Cross-sectional
Participants:	"Real" People vs Subjects

to the amount of realism that a study can capture or simulate. The third distinction is between studies that are conducted in the laboratory and studies that are conducted in a nonlaboratory, field, or "natural" setting. For the purpose of the present exposition, the three dimensions are being treated as independent of each other, resulting in a 2 × 2 × 2 matrix as represented in the top portion of Table 6.1. However, in practice some of the conditions tend to be correlated; thus most laboratory studies will probably have an independent variable that is introduced or varied by the investigator. But the opposite is not true with respect to field studies, some of which contain a high degree of experimental manipulation whereas others rely on contrasts between naturally occurring events only minimally under the control of the investigator.

Several other distinctions cut across the three principal dimensions, and these are listed in the lower portion of Table 6.1. They include whether the hypothesis was derived theoretically or pragmatically; whether the purpose was "pure" (i.e. to test a theory) or applied; whether the dependent variable is primarily "verbal" or behavioral in nature; whether the time frame of the study takes a developmental perspective or is only concerned with the here and now; and whether the participants are "real" people or subjects knowingly recruited for the study. The investigator is thus confronted by several choices: Should the study be done in the laboratory or the field? Should the independent variable be manipulated or should naturally occurring variations be exploited to serve as the independent variable? How realistic should the experimental situation be, that is should it be a relatively abstract but tightly controlled event as far as the subject is concerned, or should the subject be involved in a more or less real-life encounter that may be more difficult to control? Each alternative has advantages and disadvantages which need to be carefully considered, not just in general but also in relation to the specific topic being investigated, since not all methods are equally appropriate to all topics.

Laboratory Studies and Verisimilitude. Let us suppose that the investigator is interested in the similarity-attraction hypothesis, that is the idea that people prefer others who are similar to themselves over persons who are different, and has decided to test it in a laboratory experiment. Such studies vary in the extent to which the conditions mimic the real world outside. At one end of the continuum there are the so-called "paper-and-pencil" studies. A good example, illustrating Cell 1 in Table 6.1 is the "anonymous stranger" technique (Byrne and Nelson, 1965) where subjects are given written descriptions of strangers who are either similar to or different from themselves, and are asked to indicate on some scale how much they liked or would enjoy working with these hypothetical individuals. The advantages of this method include: (a) it is economical because a great many subjects can be tested in a short period of time; and (b) the investigator can achieve good control over the experimental situation. Thus the independent variable (the description of the anonymous stranger) is fully controlled, as is its administration. The conditions under which the testing occurs can be standardized and easily replicated, so that in theory all subjects in a particular experimental condition are treated equally. Plans can be made for the reliable measurement of the subjects' responses. And once the basic paradigm is de-bugged, it can be extended in all sorts of ways. For instance, the similarity dimension can be exhaustively explored by running different experiments that vary only in how the anonymous stranger is or is not similar, on such variables as age, sex, ethnic background, political affiliation, and so forth.

There is no doubt that such studies are very efficient. However, they have been criticized as being rather remote from real-life encounters, and hence the results may not generalize beyond the conditions obtaining in the laboratory. For instance, when people meet real strangers rather than receive simple descriptions of them, they may respond differently. The other problem, common to most laboratory situations, is that the participants know that they are taking part in a psychological experiment, which has all kinds of unintended consequences that will be discussed later in a section devoted to this specific issue.

To counter the problem of artificiality, some investigators have tried to make the laboratory resemble more closely the real world. In effect this means arranging for the subjects to interact with other people under controlled conditions. Out of this has been born the idea of the experimental confederate, often abbreviated C, an actor who under the direction of the experimenter is programmed to behave in a specific, pre-determined way (e.g. Rokeach & Mezei, 1966).

Studies such as these are certainly less artificial than the paper and pencil variety, and it is easier to disguise their intent, thus reducing some of the problems associated with reactance. However, this occurs at the expense of diminished control, since the performance of the Cs is likely to vary from trial to trial and hence affect the results. It is also a fairly labor-intensive process, since each trial requires the presence of an actor and in order to build up credibility the interaction must be spread over a reasonable length of time. To overcome both the loss of control and the costs in using live actors, some experimenters employ a tape recording or a video tape of the interaction they wish to simulate, but in doing this they sacrifice realism (e.g. Callan, Gallois, & Forbes, 1983).

Systematic observation as such does not play a large role in most laboratory experiments, the reason being that in such studies the dependent variable is usually "verbal" in the sense that subjects are asked a question which they then have to answer in terms of some predetermined set of categories. For instance, Ss might respond to a seven-point scale regarding how warm the other person appears to them, or how much they like that individual, or which are the other persons with whom they would prefer to spend further time. The experimenter's task is to record the marks the Ss make on a piece of paper or a computer screen, or record what the Ss say. These essentially verbal responses are then coded and quantified in some way. Systematic observation, as the term is commonly understood, is more complicated than that. It usually makes greater demands on the experimenter, because what is being recorded is some aspect of the S's total behavior (which may include the person's verbal responses), but where the interest lies in quantifying or categorizing ongoing, more complex response units, not all of them reducible to verbal self reports.

There are topics which lend themselves particularly well to behavior measures, and hence there are some (but relatively few) laboratory studies that can be said to employ systematic observation in their data collecting. An example is the study by Argyle and Dean (1965), in which subjects were told that they were participating in an experiment on perception. They were instructed to "stand as close as comfortable to see well" either a book, plaster head, cut-out life size photograph of Michael Argyle with his eyes closed, or a photograph of Argyle with his eyes open. The dependent variable was the distance from the stimulus at which Ss placed themselves in the various conditions, a behavioral measure that had to be systematically observed before it could be recorded. The laboratory study of proxemics is one area which depends considerably on systematic observational techniques.

Field Studies and Verisimilitude. If the purpose of a study is to demonstrate simply that the derivation of a particular principle can be empirically supported, it does not greatly matter how artificial or abstruse the actual demonstration is, as long as the rules of the game have been carefully observed. Many of the early dissonance experiments are good examples of this genre, and although they were castigated as being essentially "fun and games" rather than serious research (McGuire, 1967; Ring, 1967), the critics missed the point. The point is that as long as a hypothesis is validly derived from a theory, and the experimental conditions provide a valid test of the hypothesis, then the rules of the game have been observed, no matter how bizarre or unusual the actual circumstances of the investigation might be.

However, if one is interested in the intrinsic aspects of a particular phenomenon and not just its location in some theoretical or mathematical space, then the question of generalizability becomes all important. For instance, our brief may be to account for and then try to reduce racial prejudice in a multi-ethnic housing development. It is an open question whether the results of a particular laboratory study, even one with a reasonable degree of verisimilitude, will generalize to a particular real-life social setting (although the findings of such an experiment may suggest how one should go about designing a field study. It should also be noted in passing that it is an open question whether the findings of a particular field study will generalize to other, similar field settings).

On both intuitive and empirical grounds, there is a number of reasons why certain types of laboratory-derived data do not generalize all that successfully to outside social settings. We shall discuss these shortly. Thus, if a researcher has a pragmatic as well as a theoretical interest in a particular social phenomenon, the investigator would be well advised to get as close to the topic as possible. In practice this means studying the process in its natural setting, represented by Cells 7 and 8 in Table 6.1. It also means studying the behavior in the raw, as it were, that is directly rather than via self reports or self ratings. That way, by maximizing verisimilitude, at least the problems associated with generalizability can be reduced to an acceptable level. There are several other issues, though, which cut across the verisimilitude dimension, the most crucial being the problem of the intrusiveness of the experimenter, the often observed inconsistency between attitudes and behavior, and social desirability effects.

Attitude–Behavior Consistency. There is now a great deal of evidence (e.g. Bochner, 1980; Liska, 1974; Wicker, 1969) that under certain conditions the stated intentions of people do not correspond with their behavior. This does not necessarily mean that individuals will deliberately lie to an investigator about their actual or intended activities. It merely means that sometimes people may not be able or willing to make veridical statements or predictions about their actions. Probably the major contributing factor to the lack of correspondence between attitudes and behavior is social desirability.

Social Desirability. Under certain circumstances, people (not just subjects in psychological experiments) may be inhibited from being open and frank with an interlocutor, particularly when considerations of social desirability intrude. The social desirability effect comes into play whenever there is a "socially correct answer" to a particular question.

The main implication is that if the investigator wants to study and predict actual behavior, particularly behavior in natural settings, and more particularly still behavior about which there exist powerful cultural "oughts," then this purpose is best served by directly measuring these acts. In practice this means conducting studies that would fit into Cells 7 and 8 in Table 6.1, with "real" people as subjects, and with the dependent variable couched in behavior terms. Thus the collecting of the data would largely depend on the technique of systematic observation.

THE UNOBTRUSIVE METHOD

The unobtrusive method (Webb et al., 1966) was developed to combat the effect on the subjects of being aware that they are participating in a psychological experiment. There is an extensive literature, summarized in Bochner (1980), about how the behavior of individuals may be distorted simply through the knowledge that they are serving as experimental subjects. Psychological measurement is almost always reactive, that is, the very act of measurement tends to change the process being scrutinized. This problem is not confined to the behavioral sciences. For example, testing the tensile strength of a wire alters its nature irretrievably, and carbon dating tends to destroy the particular sample involved.

Sechrest (1975) has distinguished between two forms of reactivity. One occurs when the act of measurement so changes the phenomenon that it cannot be remeasured. For example, publicly asking subjects to state their opinions on a topic may have the effect of committing them to that particular position even if they had no firm view on it previously, and so the act of assessment will have formed as well as measured the attitude. The second type of reactivity refers to the tendency for human and other sentient beings to behave differently when under observation than when not under scrutiny.

The consequences of subjects being aware that they are under surveillance fall into two broad categories: (a) a constant error which appears uniformly in the scores of all or most subjects; and (b) a variable effect which alters the responses of different individuals in different ways. An example of a constant error is the tendency of most subjects to give answers that will make them appear in as favorable a light as possible, thereby uniformly inflating the scores of all of the participants in a particular experiment. A much more serious problem stems from the tendency of subjects to arrive at their own idiosyncratic interpretation of the circumstances of the experiment. Subjects may view the study as an intrusion into their privacy, or resent the deception, or on the other hand welcome the opportunity to make a contribution to science. Some subjects may feel coerced into participating, or regard their participation as a duty, or in the case of paid subjects as a job. In turn, these interpretations may lead subjects to behave in a hostile, ingratiating, perfunctory, suspicious, or routine manner. It follows that the data produced by subjects in psychological experiments always contain at least two ingredients — their reaction to the independent variable, and their reaction to the process of being observed and studied. Since the conclusions of experiments are based on how subjects respond to the independent variable, it is vital that the data mix does not contain an unacceptably high proportion of reactive ingredients, or more precisely that the reactive components in the data do not drown out, override, or change beyond recognition the effect due to the experimental manipulation.

The paper-and-pencil, realistic laboratory, and intrusive field experimental methods all have to contend with the reactivity problem, since in all of these procedures the participants are explicitly recruited to play the role of subjects. The unobtrusive method circumvents this problem, because the subjects are unaware that they are serving in an experiment, and usually do not even realize that their behavior is being observed by another person. This does not mean, however, that the preferred technique for studying social psychological processes is the unobtrusive method.

Unobtrusive research has its own inherent shortcomings, which have to be balanced against its advantages. The main limitations of the unobtrusive method are: (a) The problem of achieving adequate control, since unobtrusive studies are usually conducted in complex public settings; (b) difficulty in collecting psychodynamic data (how subjects *feel* as distinct from what they *do*), since the typical dependent variable of an unobtrusive study is some piece of overt behavior, and subjects are seldom interviewed or asked the reason for their responses; (c) difficulty in following up subjects, since the typical and indeed desirable pattern is for subjects to depart from the scene as soon as their behavior has been recorded; and (d) the ethics of studying people without first obtaining their informed consent or debriefing them afterwards.

Thus, when an investigator opts to use an unobtrusive procedure rather than one of the other methods available, the decision will have been a deliberate one, and will have taken into account the technical as well as the ethical implications of selecting an unobtrusive design. Such a decision is always a compromise, since it entails choosing the most suitable (or least unsuitable) technique for the job. The research aim always precedes and dictates the choice of a method; it is only after the investigator has established the purpose of the study that a decision can be made about which method to use. Investigators employing an unobtrusive method are obliged to exert as much ingenuity in solving the ethical problems generated by their experiment as they expend on the technical aspects of their design. The end seldom justifies the means; if the ethical problem remains intractable, the experiment ought to be abandoned until a solution is found.

Nevertheless, the unobtrusive method is particularly well suited for pragmatic cross-cultural research into socially sensitive topics, because it is in those areas that subjects are least likely to provide truthful verbal responses, due to the effect of social desirability, the tendency to present oneself in as favorable a light as possible, and the legal and other constraints that prevent people from being totally frank in their responses. In such studies the dependent variable will often be a behavioral category, and recording the data will usually depend heavily on the technique of systematic observation.

The Within-Skin, Between-Skin Issue

One final consideration may enter into choosing a research strategy, namely whether the investigator is philosophically inclined to locate the explanation of behavior inside the individual, or in the person's social setting. Psychologists can be categorized according to where they stand on this continuum. At one end are those who favor the view that behavior is determined largely by internal, personal attributes, whether physiological or dispositional. Their account will rely on constructs such as genes, personality traits, enduring dispositions, habits, and other similar within-skin constructs. Consequently the target of their research, reflected in their research designs, will be the focal person or some aspects of that person (e.g. their perceptual style, locus of control, etc.). Contextual aspects will receive only incidental attention.

At the other end of the continuum are those psychologists who incline towards a situational explanation of behavior, that is who recognize that the responses of individuals are affected by the situation, by the behavior setting or stage on which the action is taking place. Between-skin psychologists argue that individuals must be studied in their social context, because the situation has a marked effect on what the person brings to that setting. This assumption is reflected in studies that explicitly include aspects of the behavior setting in their research designs (Barker, 1968), that is where the target is not merely the individual, but the individual in a particular social situation. Furthermore, the dependent variables are usually also interpersonal in character, and include such phenomena as helping behavior, obedience, aggression, nurturance, and other processes that occur between individuals.

Because of their emphasis on situational effects, between-skin psychologists are likely to favor naturalistic field studies so as to capture the ongoing stream of behavior. Hence they will try to use "real" people as subjects, tend towards a longitudinal time frame in their studies, and rely on the systematic observation of ongoing behavior for collecting their data. By contrast, within-skin psychologists are more likely to favor the laboratory, use experimental subjects and measure discrete dependent variables, usually by means of recording the verbal or written responses of their subjects to a particular stimulus.

In many respects cross-cultural psychology can be said to have a between-skin, situational orientation, in that differences between cultures are usually assumed to depend on differences in their social arrangements rather than any genetic or dispositional differences between their peoples.

Methods, Techniques, Research Traditions

Having covered the "why" of selecting an observational technique, I now turn more closely to the actual process of research, to the "how" aspects of conducting studies employing systematic observation. In this section we will review the main techniques and list their problems, strengths and weaknesses. The material will be organized by describing particular traditions, either collectively as in the case of the unobtrusive method, or by referring to the work of a particular research team, such as the groups led by Barker, the Whitings, the Munroes, and other persons prominent in the field. This approach will enable me to illustrate how various people have overcome the basic problems inherent in the method, listed earlier and summarized by the question: whom does one measure when, where, and how, and what does it all mean?

Unobtrusive Cross-Cultural Research: Principles and Guidelines

Once the research aim has been identified, the next step is to find a suitable setting in which to conduct the study. Then, the investigator must select a method for recruiting the subjects, determine how the dependent variables will be defined and quantified, devise a procedure for processing the subjects through the experiment at an efficient rate, and record their responses without either the subjects or the public becoming aware that there is an experiment in progress.

The Research Setting. Research settings can vary according to how open they are, in the sense that there may or may not exist restrictions on what sorts of subjects will be observed, a variable that has implications for the generalizability of the results. Bochner (1979) has classified research settings according to two principal dimensions:

their size, and the extent to which the subjects are homogeneous or heterogeneous.

SUBJECTS	SETTINGS	
	Large	Small
Heterogeneous	1	3
Homogeneous	2	4

Studies that fit into Type 1 are those in which, theoretically, practically any member of the public could appear as a subject. Type 2 studies are also conducted in large public areas, but the settings are chosen because they provide a subject population that is homogeneous in some respect, perhaps because the design requires it.

There are also many experiments that have been carried out in narrower settings which are less public, more institutionalized, and where the subjects are linked together by some common attribute. These studies are instances of Types 3 and 4, depending on the homogeneity of their subject populations.

Although the bulk of the unobtrusive literature does not deal with cross-cultural topics and issues, cross-cultural studies that have used the various types of research settings do exist. (For a review of this literature, together with examples illustrating the various types of studies, see Bochner, 1979, 1980.)

Recruiting Subjects for Unobtrusive Experiments. The strategies that are used to recruit subjects fall into two broad categories. The investigator can stage a public incident to which any passer-by is exposed, and which the witness can either ignore or actively react to in some way. Bochner (1980) called this the "street-theater" strategy. Or the researcher can select specific members of the public to serve as subjects, and explicitly deliver the independent variable to these persons. This method has been called the "accosting" strategy.

The main problem with the street-theater strategy is to make the event sufficiently salient so that everyone in the surrounding area will notice it, and yet that it should not be so intrusive as to injure, alarm, or affront members of the public. For example, in a study by Piliavin, Rodin, and Piliavin (1969), the incident was a person collapsing in a subway car, hardly an event to escape notice.

The principle of the accosting strategy is to select a specific subject, who then becomes the target for the experimental intervention. The main problem is to make the intervention plausible, and to ensure that the person who was chosen to serve as the subject makes the response without any prompting or help from anyone else. It is therefore necessary to avoid bizarre requests, and to somehow single out the subject from the crowd. For instance, in Thayer's (1973) study of helping behavior, the investigator simultaneously varied the race and sex of both the person in need and the potential helper. A black male, black female, white male, or white female experimenter, each conspicuously wearing a hearing aid, approached ten black and ten white male, and ten black and ten white female subjects, in New York's Grand Central Station. The experimenter held out a dime to the subject, and a notebook opened at a page which had written on it: "I am deaf. Could you please help me? Dial (phone number) and just ask if Harold will pick me up at school. Thank you." The phone was being monitored by an assistant, and the dependent variable was the frequency of calls in each of the sixteen experimental conditions.

It should be noted that all "accosting" studies actually involve interacting with a subject. What is crucial is that a particular subject is pre-selected for observation. Indeed, the "subject" need not even be a human being. For instance, in an unobtrusive, cross-cultural investigation of the pace of life, Levine and Bartlett (1984) employed three dependent variables: the accuracy of clocks in public places; the walking speed of pedestrians in the central business areas of cities; and the average speed with which a postal worker completed a standard request. The study was conducted in Japan, England, the United States, Taiwan, Italy, and Indonesia. It was hypothesized that tempo, as measured by these indices, would be positively associated with economic development. Clock accuracy was checked by observing fifteen clocks in each city in randomly selected banks. Walking speed was measured over a distance of 100 feet, and randomly selected pedestrians, walking alone, served as subjects. The setting was the downtown business district in twelve cities in locations that were flat, unobstructed and sufficiently uncrowded so as not to interfere with walking speed. Finally, work pace was measured by approaching postal clerks at randomly selected post offices, who were handed a note in the native language requesting one stamp for a commonly used small denomination, together with a bank note that required change in both coins and paper. The dependent measure was the time required to complete the transaction. Only in the case of the postal clerks were the subjects literally accosted. The clocks and pedestrians were selected for observation rather than approached to elicit a particular response. The hypothesis was confirmed in all three cases, with Japan having the highest and Indonesia the lowest tempo.

Measuring the Dependent Variable. The two strategies for recruiting subjects have important consequences for the manner in which the dependent variable is quantified. In the *street-theater paradigm*, the measure is the number of subjects in each condition who emit the required response, or the relative proportion of responders to nonresponders in the various experimental conditions. For example, in Bryan and Test's (1967) Salvation Army kettle study, the measure was the number of people who donated when either a black or a white woman attended the kettle, expressed as a percentage of passers-by making a contribution (2.22 percent and 3.89 percent in the black and white conditions respectively).

The effectiveness of comparing ratios of responders to non-responders across experimental conditions depends on meeting three requirements: (1) the number of potential subjects or responders should be identical in each condition (or known, so that appropriate ratios of responders to nonresponders can be calculated if the two populations are not the same size); (2) the make-up of the population should remain constant over the duration of the experiment; and (3) the duration of each data-collecting sequence should be kept identical for each of the experimental conditions. For example, Bryan and Test (1967) placed two kettles at two different but comparable store exits, each disgorging a similar mix of people. The two experimenters were rotated between the two kettles, the study was run on two days over 28 observational periods each lasting 25 minutes, and Bryan and Test counted all the people who went past the kettles (a total of 3,703) so as to be able to work out the exact proportion of responders to nonresponders in each condition. A desirable aspect is that each subject is tested only once, so that none of the scores is contaminated by prior exposure to an experimental intervention. The analysis therefore consists of comparing the responses of different but comparable subjects to different experimental manipulations, with each subject encountering only one treatment.

In the *accosting paradigm*, specific subjects are selected from a larger population. Then, two alternative strategies can be employed.

The subjects' behavior can be observed, quantified, and then compared across cultural or other conditions, as in the Levine and Bartlett (1984) study. Or, the independent variable is delivered directly to the subjects, and their response to the experimental intervention constitutes the dependent variable. Usually these responses are cast into a "Yes–No" form, and analyzed by comparing the proportion of "Yes–Nos" across the various experimental conditions. For example, in Gaertner and Bickman's (1971) "wrong-number" study, the measure was the proportion of subjects in each condition who rang "Ralph's Garage" (white subjects – white victim 65/251, black victim 53/236; black subjects – white victim 67/247, black victim 60/239).

The main requirement of the "accosting" strategy is adequate sampling. The experimenter must predetermine rigid criteria for the following contingencies: (1) How is the *population* going to be defined, that is, who is to be excluded and who is included (for example, all passers-by qualify who are between the ages of twenty and sixty, and who are unaccompanied); (2) Who is to be *selected* from the population (for example, every fifth passer-by who satisfies the inclusion criterion); and (3) Who is to be *assigned* to the respective experimental conditions. This latter problem arises where different experimental conditions are run in some kind of sequence. An ingenious solution was the jelly-bean method devised by Ellsworth, Carlsmith, and Henson (1972). The experimental manipulation consisted of staring at selected pedestrians waiting at an intersection. The prediction, which was confirmed, was that stared-at subjects would cross the street faster then non-stared-at controls. Each experimenter had to attend to sixteen subjects, eight who were to be stared at, and eight who were to serve as controls. The experimenter was supplied with sixteen jelly-beans, eight of one particular color signifying the stare condition, and eight of a different color signifying the control no-stare condition. When a potential subject would arrive at the crossing, the experimenter would pull a jelly-bean out of his pocket, note its color, eat it, and then adminster the appropriate treatment to the subject.

The Flow Sequence of Subjects. Ideally, subjects should enter the experimental sector from outside its boundaries, remain in the setting only long enough to be exposed to the experimental treatment and produce a score, and then depart the scene for good. An experiment can be seriously compromised if subjects remain in the vicinity of the experiment after being tested and observe other subjects being treated, because they may strike up a conversation (or an argument) with the experimental team, or offer advice to the other subjects. Another problem occurs if subjects return to the experimental scene and are tested again unbeknown to the experimenter, because if a respondent appears more than once in an experiment of this type, the assumptions of the statistical procedures used to analyze the results are violated. Finally, experiments become impractical if the investigator has to wait a long time for each subject to leave the scene, as not enough trials can be run in a reasonable period.

The Response Rate. Not only must the subjects pass through the procedure at a steady rate, but each subject should emit the required response soon after entering the experiment. In principle, therefore, the behavior that constitutes the dependent variable should have a high probability of occurring spontaneously, or at least be capable of having its rate increased experimentally.

Generally, naturalistic and representative (i.e. "ordinary") behaviors will have a higher spontaneous rate of occurrence than exotic or esoteric acts; they will also be easier to evoke, their evocation will arouse less suspicion, and they have the added advantage of greater generalizability.

The Observation of Subjects. Unobtrusive studies not surprisingly require that the experimenter remain unobtrusive, but it is often forgotten that the subject is not the only person who must be kept in the dark. For obvious reasons, it is vital not to attract the attention of curious bystanders, specially official persons such as police, park attendants, train guards, beach inspectors, and similar authorities, who may feel that it is their professional duty to intervene. Unfortunately, staying out of the limelight is easier said than done, since an experiment may last for several hours, the procedure may be repeated many times in the same location, and the recording of the data may require difficult-to-conceal items such as clip boards. The setting up of an observation post requires careful thought and pre-testing, and ideally should blend naturally into the environment. Incidentally, it is paramount that the experimental procedures are not in violation of the law or endanger the public, because apart from the ethical implications of irresponsible research, nothing will bring the authorities to the scene more quickly than illegal or dangerous behavior.

SYSTEMATIC OBSERVATION IN
NATURALISTIC SETTINGS

As we have seen, the main features of unobtrusive field experiments are that they generally have a confirmatory, hypothesis testing aim; the independent variables are manipulated; the dependent variables tend to be couched in behavioral terms; subjects are recruited in a systematic way and observed in a highly standardized manner; and the subjects are unaware that they are participating in a psychological investigation. Thus unobtrusive experiments tend to employ the laboratory paradigm in the "real" world, with systematic observation as the main means of gathering the data.

There is another category of research that also employs systematic observation in naturalistic settings, but whose intellectual origins, traditions, and aims are quite different. The primary aim of these investigations is to classify, describe, and provide an "account of" (Harré, 1977) the phenomena they are dealing with. These studies have a much greater affinity with zoology and anthropology than they do with experimental psychology, although they tend to use psychological techniques. Because of their orientation, the research is often only incidentally interested in confirming hypotheses; the selection of subjects and their observations tend to be less standardized; and there is less concern with quantification and statistical analysis. To the extent that theory does inform these studies, it often has a psychoanalytic or psycho-biological flavor to it.

The main method is participant observation, which of course is "obtrusive" (Berry, 1979b), and the visibility of the investigators tends to increase if they and their subjects come from different cultures. Another problem is that because of the way that the data are collected, the conclusions that are drawn depend to some extent on the subjective interpretations of the investigators, particularly when there are cross-cultural differences between the observer and the observed. Nevertheless, a great deal of useful material has been gathered in this way. The literature can be classified according to the extent that various authors regard it as desirable to standardize their procedures and observations. In practice this ranges from those who employ minimum controls and restrictions, because they regard any interference with the natural sequence of behavior as counterproductive; to those who carefully pre-determine the behavioral categories that will be attended to, set up elaborate sampling techniques, and establish *a priori* how the data will be recorded, coded, and quantified. Associated with this divergence in attention to control is the extent to which there is a concern with testing theory-derived hypotheses, with those imposing more order also having a greater interest in confirmatory research.

Ethology and Systematic Observation

Ethologists study the behavior of the total organism and its relationship with its environment. They assume that all behavior has a cause and is functional in the sense of contributing to the preservation of that particular species. Once the function is known (e.g. why does a particular species of bird sing in this and not that way) they ask how the repertoire developed.

Ethology emerged out of zoology, through the work of Lorenz (1966) and Tinbergen (1951), and concentrates on those behaviors that are relatively uninfluenced by learning and experience, on those behavior patterns deemed to be innate. The systematic observation of animals and humans in their natural environments is central to ethology, and is based on the view that science begins with the description and categorization of the phenomena it studies. The goal of each ethological investigation is the ethogram, the precise catalog of all the behavior patterns of an animal. To build up this catalog one selects functional units of behavior which are neither too small nor too large (e.g. the mating sequence, territorial defense, and so forth). Their preferred method is to film these behavior patterns and analyze them at leisure, including inspecting the films under slow and fast motion.

Although the bulk of the work of the ethologists has been with animals, the method has been extended to studies of human behavior, in order to establish which human responses, if any, might be pre-programmed in the same way as those of other species (for a review, see Eibl-Eibesfeldt, 1970). Human responses which have been studied include fixed action patterns and their releasers (e.g. rhythmic searching movements for the nipple during the first days after birth; the grasping reflex in young infants; swimming, walking, and crawling behavior); facial expressions (e.g. smiling, laughing, foot stomping, flirting, threatening); territorial behavior, and so forth. Since the argument for the biological basis of these behaviors is strengthened if the responses can be shown to be universal or pancultural, the ethologists have employed cross-cultural comparisons to test some of their hypotheses. Thus, for instance, Eibl-Eibesfeldt (1970) has filmed naturally occurring expressive responses in more than twenty different cultures and claims to have found a great deal of uniformity in how human beings everywhere display emotions, and interpret those displays. It is outside the scope of this chapter to comment on the substantive findings of this line of research except to note that cross-cultural comparisons of systematically recorded functional units of behavior need not be restricted to testing hypotheses about the biological bases of behavior. In other words, the method that the ethologists have developed can be put to use in studies that have quite a different theoretical orientation.

Two such areas are the cross-cultural study of gestures, and cross-cultural comparisons of greetings. For instance, Desmond Morris and his colleagues (Collett, 1982; Morris et al., 1979) have systematically recorded gestures in various cultures, usually on film or video tape. Their research indicates that some gestures are universal, others are used in one culture and not in others, and that the same gesture can have different or even opposite meanings depending on where it occurs. For instance, in the United States a raised thumb is used as a signal of approval (the "thumbs up" signal) whereas in Greece it is employed as an insult, often being associated with the expression "katsa pano" or "sit on this." Findings such as these have implications for the effectiveness of cross-cultural communication, and can also be used in designing cultural-training programmes (Bochner, in press).

Greetings, according to Argyle (1975), also have both a biological and a cultural component. Some forms of greeting occur in most cultures, and are also used by chimpanzees (e.g. touching hands, embracing). Other forms are culture-specific, such as clicking the heels, the deep bow, the gallant hand kiss, kissing beards, and so forth.

Barker's Ecological Psychology

Roger Barker (e.g. 1963, 1968, 1978) established the Midwest Psychological Field Station in Kansas, which operated from 1947 until 1972, its aim being "to describe in concrete detail the conditions of life and behavior of all the children of a community ... although we know a great deal about how children behave under relatively controlled, standardized conditions ... we know little about the nature of the situations that actually confront children in their daily lives and how they react to them" (Barker, 1978, pp. x–xi). Barker and his colleagues soon discovered that to achieve this ambitious aim they faced some major methodological and conceptual problems which had to be solved before they could proceed. Barker also realized the value of making systematic cross-cultural comparisons, because although the bulk of his data came from Oskaloosa, Kansas, he replicated some of his studies in a comparable town in Yorkshire in England. Only the main concepts, issues, and techniques can be briefly mentioned here. Any reader intending to embark on a program of systematic observation would be well rewarded by a perusal of the original literature.

Barker's main theoretical contribution is the notion of the behavior setting. My own distillation of this idea, which may not do full justice to Barker's original conception, is that when places have people in them, they become situations or behavior settings. Behavior does not occur in a physical vacuum, but in a built environment. These places evoke, facilitate, or hinder certain activities, partly because of the way they and their contents are arranged physically, and partly because of the rules, norms, expectations, and prohibitions that are perceived to pertain to them by the actors. Behavior settings are therefore the socio-physical stage on which people enact their various parts. For instance, a kitchen may be thought of primarily as a place for preparing food. However, in some homes it is also the center of social activity, where people discuss their day, do their homework, drink, make phone calls, and generally carry on. The modern "efficient" kitchenette does not readily support such nonproductive behavior, so that other settings must be found for it (or the behaviors abandoned or modified). Thus the observation of behavior must also take into account and describe its physical and social milieu. In practice this means specifying the places, such as the garages, banks, stores, beauty parlors, telephone booths, and the hundreds of other settings where the behaviors were observed; noting the physical and psychological characteristics of these places; and their effect on the responses of those being observed.

The second major contribution of Barker's work is the notion of the stream of behavior and how to deal with it empirically. Whereas in experimental psychology both the behavior and the environment are arranged in discrete segments (e.g. interviews, personality tests, experimental manipulations), in natural settings the action marches relentlessly on from sunrise to sunrise, with no gaps whatsoever. This problem led Barker to make a most important distinction between behavior that occurs independently of the investigator and behavior that occurs in response to something the investigator does. Barker called the two types of responses *behavior units* and *behavior tesserae*, respectively: "Behavior units enter psychology when investigators function as transducers, observing and recording behavior with techniques that do not influence its course" (Barker, 1978, p. 4), for example when a child is observed to hit a ball with a cricket bat. *Behavior tesserae* are fragments of behavior which are created or selected by the investigator in accordance with the scientific aims of the investigation. When an investigator says "Tell me what you see on the card" or "Judge which of these weights is the heavier," the natural units of the behavior stream are destroyed and replaced by *behavior tesserae* (pieces of glass or marble used in mosaic work, selected by the mosaic makers in accordance with their artistic aims). *Behavior tesserae* are produced by tests, questionnaires, interviews, by all methods that require the subject to undertake actions at the behest of the investigator. They are also produced by research methods that divide the behavior continuum into predetermined time periods or number-of-occurrence segments. Thus according to Barker, for example when the occurrence of aggressive behavior in a child is tallied in a sample of one-minute observations, the investigator has disregarded the intrinsic structure of the behavior stream because the beginning and end points of the selected parts are established by the technical requirements of the investigation and may not coincide with the inherent units of the behavior continuum.

Although there would be general agreement with Barker about the advantages of non*tesserae* oriented psychological research, and in the importance of observing behavior in a nonreactive manner, in practice most investigators do use some form of time and event sampling, techniques which will be reviewed in the next section. My own response to Barker is that he has insufficient faith in sampling theory: if enough events and time segments are sampled, the results should provide an adequate representation of what would have emerged if the investigator had adopted what I have referred to as the bird-watching technique (Bochner, 1980). And since even bird watchers have to sleep sometimes, the hours during which they are on duty might as well be systematically arranged rather than left to chance.

The Six Cultures Study

Prominent among the psychologists are the Whitings (for a review of their work, see Whiting & Whiting, 1978), best known for their comparative research on the socialization of children. This work was carried out simultaneously in six different societies (Whiting & Whiting, 1975), each culture chosen for its theoretical relevance to the hypotheses being tested. It is outside the scope of this chapter to comment on their psycho-cultural model of child rearing, nor is it possible to summarize the results. What is notable in the present context is that their dependent variable was the social behavior of the children rather than more commonly employed personality or projective tests. Furthermore, because of the difficulty of contriving an experimental setting that would be comparable across all of their six cultures, they decided to observe the children's behavior as it occurred in natural settings. To make the task manageable and for theoretical reasons, they restricted their observations to the children's interactions with other children and adults. These behaviors in turn were analyzed within a framework consisting of nine predetermined behavior systems. Thus all of the behaviors were recorded and coded in terms of what they called "interacts" — exchanges between individuals which could be classified as either helping, being responsible, hurting, roughhousing, seeking help, seeking physical contact, seeking competition, seeking dominance, or seeking friendly interaction. The full method is described in a field manual that was specially written as a guide for the research team (Whiting, Child, and Lambert, 1966). This manual provides a wealth of information on how to plan, carry out, and analyze standardized, systematic cross-cultural observations in natural settings. Only the main points can be briefly mentioned here.

Because reliability has been shown to decrease with fatigue, the unit of observation was a five minute behavior sample. No more than one observation per day was made on any particular child, and each child was observed a minimum of fourteen times over several months. The nine categories — nurturance, succorance, sociability, achievement, dominance, submission, aggression, responsibility, and self-reliance — were chosen on the grounds that they described social interactions that occurred naturally in all six cultures (although to different degrees and extents) and indeed were likely to be universally applicable.

In addition to time sampling, settings were also sampled and included places such as the house, garden, courtyard, school, and school playground. Various activities were also sampled, and included play, work, learning, and casual social interaction. Size of the groups was also taken into account, the number of persons in the settings varying from two upwards.

The coding of the behaviors was a very complex task and cannot be described fully here. The final analysis yielded twelve response types, and a frequency distribution of these twelve acts for each culture was calculated. This enabled cross-cultural comparisons to be made, which in turn made it possible to test some of the hypotheses that guided this research. For instance, the act "offer help" occurred 280 times in the Tarong sample and only 60 times in the Khalapur one, and since equal numbers of subjects were used throughout, certain conclusions could be drawn from these differences. The work of the Whitings and their team provides an excellent model for this form of research, and is required reading for anyone contemplating a program of systematic observations in natural settings, particularly if these observations are to be made in more than one culture.

Time Sampling: "Spot Observations"

The spot observation technique has been developed by the Munroes as a form of controlled naturalistic observation, which allows investigators to obtain standardized information without unduly disrupting the behaviors being observed. Orthodox time sampling involves recording pre-determined categories of behavior for a pre-determined number of observations during a pre-determined segment of time (e.g. one observation per minute lasting ten seconds during a fifteen minute period while visiting the home of a selected respondent). In their study of infant care among the Logoli people of Kenya, Munroe and Munroe (1971) found the traditional time sampling technique to be reactive in the sense that the interest expressed by the investigators led to a "display" of the child; when the observers arrived at the home, the infant was picked up, readied for observation, and then brought forward and shown to the investigators. The Munroes felt that although this indicated that the Logoli mothers were highly cooperative, their observed behavior was unlikely to be representative of their usual caretaking practices. Consequently, the investigators had to make themselves more unobtrusive, which they achieved by quietly approaching the research setting (in this case the house) unannounced, and recording information about the people and the activites surrounding the infant on a standard observation form before greeting or questioning the people in the house. Data less subject to reactance, such as the identity of the caretaker or the location of the mother, were recorded after contact with the household had been made. In the study that first employed the spot observation technique, fourteen such brief samplings were made, seven in the morning and seven in the afternoon, with no two observations being made during the same morning or afternoon. In order to approximate the usual balance of caretakers, half of the observations were made on weekends or during school vacations, and half during school hours. The observations included information on the location of the infant (e.g. in the house or yard), whether the infant was being held and by whom, the location, activity, proximity, and identity of persons within ten feet of the infant, the cleanliness of the child, and the identity of the caretaker.

In the intervening years the spot observation technique has been used successfully with a variety of subjects and in a variety of contexts (Munroe & Munroe, 1978, 1980; Munroe et al., 1983; Munroe, Munroe, & Shimmin, 1984; Nerlove, Munroe, & Munroe, 1971). Variations on the method include noting the information mentally and only recording it after leaving the immediate scene if it is deemed inadvisable to make written notes in the presence of the respondents. In the United States where houses are designed to preserve privacy, the investigators obtained the permission of the families to enter their homes without notice, or by having the mothers tell their children not to answer the door bell. Telephone "observations" were also conducted. Thus the investigators would ring the mothers at unarranged times and ask them the same questions that appeared on the observation forms, regarding the child's behavior at the time when the phone had started ringing.

Event Sampling

The Munroes have also extensively used the method of event sampling, again mainly in their observation of infant behavior in a variety of different cultures. In several of their studies they were interested in the incidence, frequency, and duration of infant crying, and in the responses of caretakers to that crying. Thus, for instance, an infant was observed for a total of four hours, two in the morning and two in the afternoon. Using a pre-determined record form, observers noted the onset of each cry, its duration until the caretaker responded to the infant, the identity of the person who responded, and the character of the response, and the time from when the caretaker made the response to the cessation of the cry. An attempt was also made to judge the cause of each cry.

Both time and event sampling techniques lend themselves to the observation of a wide range of behaviors, and are particularly useful in cross-cultural comparisons, since there is a good opportunity to achieve equivalence (see Chapter 2) between the two sets of observations. A major problem is the effect of the observer's presence on the behaviors being observed, an effect that tends to be magnified if the observer comes from a culture that is markedly different from that of the respondents. Hence any method or device that renders these observations more unobtrusive will increase the validity of these procedures.

CONCLUSION

In psychology, methodological issues are often treated in the abstract, as an area that can be regarded in its own right. However, method, theoretical issues, and to some extent substantive concerns are all inextricably intertwined. Thus investigators employing systematic observation are likely to be interested in relatively molar, naturally occurring behavior rather than in relatively narrow reflexive, verbal, or projective expressions of hypothetical constructs such as drives or personality traits. Within that broad orientation I can discern two distinct streams, both concerned with bridging the disciplines of psychology and anthropology, but in different ways and from different starting points (for a comprehensive account of the relationship between psychology and anthropology, see Jahoda, 1982; Spindler, 1978). On the one hand there are those investigators, who are primarily psychologists but who wish to broaden their approach by applying some of the perspectives and techniques of anthropology to their work. These might be called the anthropological psychologists. At the other end of the continuum there are investigators who, irrespective of how they have labeled themselves, are primarily anthropologists but also employ methods that are commonly in use in mainstream psychology. This distinction can be used to summarize the material reviewed in this chapter.

Anthropological Psychologists

Many psychologists have become disillusioned with the psychological laboratory, because of its artificiality, lack of ecological validity, reliance on verbal responses of doubtful utility, and the demand characteristics and reactivity of intrusive measurement. The remedy has been to transfer the laboratory technique into the real world, apply it as unobtrusively as possible, concentrate on behavioral rather than verbal dependent variables, and employ theoretical frameworks that are fairly tough-minded about intrapsychic hypothetical constructs. Most of the studies are manipulated, theory based, hypothesis testing experiments in which the dependent variable is a relatively molecular, segmented response of relatively short duration, which is observed, recorded, and then quantified and subjected to conventional statistical analyses. Sometimes the response is narrowly elicited, as in the accosting method, sometimes it is more broadly evoked, as when passers-by are exposed to a street-theater scene, but essentially the production of the response and its timing is at the behest of the investigator. Where this approach departs from traditional experimental psychology is that the environment in which the response is being observed is far more natural than even the most realistic of psychological laboratories, and the subjects are unaware that they are participating in a psychological experiment. Often, too, the behavior constituting the dependent variable — although molecular in a general sense — is far more molar than that usually measured in the laboratory, and also often has an interpersonal connotation, such as being an indication of attitude, liking, helping, and so forth.

Psychological Anthropology

Some investigators have argued that the traditional psychological approach, even when it is translated into the field, still is limited because it either destroys or alters the very phenomena it sets out to study, or misses the essential aspects that characterize the behavior. This is not just due to the reactivity of measurement, but more importantly to the way in which the phenomena are selected and sliced up prior to being measured. What these workers are after is spontaneous, complex, molar, unsegmented, unsolicited "streamed" behavior, and the sociocultural and physical context in which it occurs. This is essentially the method of anthropology, the model for which was set at the turn of the century by Western investigators who would spend a year or two in some remote village or island, immerse themselves as participant observers in the local culture, and then produce an ethnography of that society. The primary aim was to provide an account of what it is like to be a member of that culture rather than to test particular hypotheses, and when statistics were employed they were descriptive. Since this approach depends almost entirely on the subjective interpretations of the participant observer, it has limitations similar to those of psychoanalysis. The recent controversy about the validity of Margaret Mead's findings in Samoa (Freeman, 1983) is a case in point.

Where the psychological anthropologists depart from traditional anthropology is in trying to overcome some of the limitations of a free-floating participant observation. They do this by introducing time and event sampling, segmenting the stream of behavior, creating distance between the observer and the observed, reducing the intrusiveness of the observer, selecting particular behaviors and their settings on theoretical grounds rather than attempting to observe everything everywhere, in some cases further restricting their observational targets by testing particular hypotheses that require particular behaviors to be observed, and they may employ inferential statistics so as to be able to draw certain conclusions.

Each approach has its strengths and weaknesses. Conducting experiments in natural settings may impose some *tesserae* on the behavior being observed, but the data are less likely to be distorted by observer bias. Recording the stream of behavior from dawn to dusk may yield data that are tedious to collect, difficult to interpret, and subjective but it is probably the only way to achieve a real "account" (Harré, 1977) of the phenomenon under investigation. In other words, whatever method is used will result in some form of compromise. Consequently, the choice of technique will depend on the nature of the research problem, and the personal preferences of the investigator.

7
CROSS-CULTURAL ASSESSMENT: FROM PRACTICE TO THEORY

SIDNEY H. IRVINE

BASICS IN TESTING

Those who decide to use tests across cultures come to grips with a technology that has been in place since the early years of the century. It has been in and out of fashion for decades; but has survived to find acceptance wherever decisions have to be made on who shall qualify for entry to schools or occupations. Consequently, there is a great deal to be learned about the *technicalities* of test use in other countries from books about test construction that are written for the student market in America or Europe. Such books often provide excellent practical advice on how to write items, how to standardize test procedures, how to treat data from scores to derive norms, and how to establish cut-off points for decision making. All of these skills come into play whenever and wherever one starts to put tests to applied use. They are invariant across cultures.

In my own library I have a few well-worn favorites that have long repaid the initial cost over the years. More recent texts are easily obtained and these references, in order of difficulty, are good investments of time and money (Kaplan & Sacuzzo, 1982; Guilford, 1965; Ghiselli, Campbell, & Zedeck, 1981). However, the most useful source for the newcomer, or the teacher who just wants to improve the quality of the weekly test, costs nothing. Educational Testing Service (ETS) has provided an information and advisory service on tests and testing for decades. The most helpful package (ETS, 1973) consists of four short pamphlets (Selecting an Achievement Test; Making the Classroom Test; Multiple-choice Questions; Short-cut

Statistics for Teacher-made Tests) that are readable, prescriptive, and accurate. They are the nearest thing available to a do-it-yourself handbook for the intelligent nonspecialist.

These sources are among the best in print, but simple common sense prompts one other reminder. The worker in other countries will find a wealth of experience in the government departments as well as colleges and universities that use assessment procedures for school selection and manpower training. No one who has worked overseas has been successful without the help and active cooperation of local officials, teachers, and university staff. They, above all, have models of what may be regarded locally as successful attempts to select and train promising candidates for school and work opportunities. It would be imprudent either to ignore them, to discuss them, or to offer uninvited criticism by implying that they might be improved.

This basic skill of testing in other cultures, that is, the explicit recognition of the years of work that have gone into local assessment systems, is the one that the newcomer has most need of, since our own advances in measurement since 1970 have been made possible by technological and theoretical shifts that have probably not come within the reach of the majority of overseas users. In fact, the testing industry in America has only recently begun to implement these changes.

Most of the effort in test development today is centered on machine- or computer-controlled tasks. This is a costly, high-technology venture. Paper-and-pencil tests are most likely to represent the cost-benefit limits imposed on the cross-cultural research worker. Any *labor-intensive* task or test will be equally acceptable; but the computer-based task is a theoretical, rather than a practical instrument. Hence much of what is presented in the next section takes account of the fact that tests across cultures are going to be practical workhorses (and rather old ones at that) and not theoretical thoroughbreds.

A *commentary* on the problems of using tests as workhorses is offered now, but not as a prescription for their survival as a breed. Their survival as theoretical instruments is highly unlikely, but tests will persevere for decades in developing countries until they are replaced by the will of those who live there. If one doubts the wisdom of this, one should consult Silvey (1983) for case studies in the communal politics of selection systems. In short, this methods chapter is about the salient issues that surround test use today, since so much of what seems to pass for acceptable method in test use is to me mistaken and is, in fact, systematically misleading. At the end some explicit prescriptions are given, but only with all the qualifications of the intervening pages in mind. The next section of the chapter provides warnings and cautions on what to avoid at all costs, since a concept is learned just as much by finding out what it is not, as by discovering what it is.

IMPLICIT INSTRUCTIONS FROM
PAST SUCCESS AND FAILURE

The controversies about psychological measurement across cultures have been about what the results of test scores or task latencies or responses to structured interviews mean for individuals, groups, and populations. The literature reveals (Irvine & Carroll, 1980) that it has been comparatively easy to collect data from subjects anywhere in the world. Such widespread empiricism has provided psychology with a rich legacy of inferences and speculation about human performance. Constant theoretical revisions in the field of cognitive abilities, however, deny certainty about what the data base portends about the subjects, their culture, or the discipline that inspires the inquiry in the first place. These three traditional goals of enquiry — mapping the dimensions of individual differences in ability (Irvine & Berry, 1983), accounting for the effects of cultural factors on thought (Cole & Scribner, 1974), and defining the limits of the discipline (Malpass, 1977b) — have all been attempted from a cognitive test or task position.

Moreover, the enterprise has been operating for so long that the ways of going about collecting data have had to be rediscovered for every generation of psychologists, contexts, and subjects. From the basic similarity of the practices evolved, often in isolation, by each new wave of field workers during data collection, a theory-based approach to cognitive measurement may be constructed. This chapter presents an account of the several and different schools of psychologists working in contexts that are not "Euramerican."[1] It provides traditional testing, Piagetian, experimental, and information-processing case studies. From these, methods are defined in a framework that is consistent with current knowledge about cognition. References have been kept to a minimum, and extended descriptions of materials that are not readily available have been included.

Ability Testing

Each approach to human assessment has its conventions and rules. The conventions increase with the degree of theoretical uncertainty, and often include the very tests and procedures that may be used for data collection. The rules, generally quite strict, affect the way that data are analyzed once they are collected. This distinction between conventions and rules is nowhere more clearly understood than in the field of mental testing. Scarcely a study has been carried out with the same tests used over and over again. Nevertheless the same families of tests are apparent in a meta-analysis of testing studies carried out by Irvine (1979). While risking test idiosyncracy within limits, the users of tests have generally been consistent in the ways that they have treated the results of their investigations. They have either sought predictive validity for the measures in school or work situations, attempted domain studies of construct validity, or employed environmental and dispositional variables as correlates or quasi-independent variables to estimate the effect of such influences on test performance. There seems to be little, so far, to distinguish cross-cultural use of tests and their results from practices in Euramerican psychology.

Some conventions in test practice were well established in Euramerican countries by World War I. Subjects had to be assessed as fit to train for military service in the United States. Coping with the insecure language-comprehension skills of a large immigrant, and an even larger semi-literate native-born population, mass testing demanded two parallel forms of assessment. One was verbal (the Army Alpha), the other figural (the Army Beta). The assumption was that both tested the same cognitive capacities and processes, in spite of stimulus differences. This early cross-cultural enterprise has been subjected to political scrutiny, but the scientific importance of the decision to abandon stimulus identity in the quest for predictive, if not construct, validity has gone unnoticed. In contrast, the history of cross-cultural testing, and indeed inter-ethnic testing in Western societies, has been marked by efforts to keep stimuli identical rather than by attempts to define constructs exactly. The reports of the prescriptions for field trials attempting to keep stimuli constant have told us more about human cognition, perhaps, than the means, variances, and correlations derived from the stimuli themselves.

The classic studies of test use in what I wish to define as exotic [2] contexts include two from Africa (Macdonald, 1945; Biesheuvel, 1952, 1954); one from India (Bhatia, 1955); and one from Papua New Guinea (Ord, 1971). While these addressed the problems of testing illiterates individually or in small groups, many test users took advantage of growing literacy in official languages, including English, to test ever-increasing numbers in group contexts. The most widely publicized of them include Schwarz, (1964); Irvine, (1965, 1969); and Vernon (1969).

All of these enterprises have common features, but the most salient is the attempt to predict suitability for schooling or work where the criterion demands are well understood. This applied aspect of exotic test use should not be minimized. The acknowledged success of test application must be taken as evidence of a robust and predictable interaction between classes of stimuli and their purposive processing in the brain. Without that foundation, the test families would fail to predict performance in similar contexts with any recognizable consistency. As far as can be determined from literature review, these test families define dimensions of individual differences in reasoning, spatial, verbal, perceptual, numerical, and memory tasks.

The first major exercise in exotic application of traditional testing procedures was carried out by a British army testing unit towards the end of World War II. This was led by the late Alan Macdonald (1945). African male recruits to the British war effort had been sent from East Africa, specifically from Kenya, Tanzania, and Uganda. Macdonald stated that 209,000 Africans were in service at the war end. His unit tested 1,855 men and produced seventeen standardization tests for use as a vocational aptitude battery.[3] The list of tests reveals a close application of British psychometric theory, conventions, and rules. Tests that had been used to select British soldiers had been adopted with minimum change (dexterity tasks); adapted through restandardization (matrices); or, rarely but significantly, recast in local context (mechanical comprehension) with entirely new stimuli. A strong general factor was uncovered in the tests: but this was to prove the rule in studies of illiterates that ensued. Not too much should be read into this finding, since there are many possible explanations for it (Irvine & Carroll, 1980). A much more important issue concerns how Macdonald produced the results he did.

He concluded that it was possible to apply selection tests to Africans; that their response to test situations was immediate and spontaneous; that their test results showed a wide range of performances; and that criterion correlations were positive and reasonably high (Macdonald, 1945, p. 65). The reasons for Macdonald's success can be credited to three prescriptions for test use;. *the detailed sets of instructions for each test; motivation of subjects in communicating the instructions; and the careful control exerted over the initial attempts* of the recruits to perform the tasks so that errors were minimized.

These three guidelines are seen in action in Macdonald's report. They are as sound now as they were then. The instructions are printed in English and Swahili. They are meant to be given to the men either singly or in small groups. Demonstrations of item types and strategies were standard. Practice items were prescribed and supervised in a generous tester-subject ratio. As most of the tests were performance task batteries, requiring apparatus, external stimuli were identical for Africans, once determined empirically. They were often quite different from the English parent tests after field try-out, and yet they seemed to be testing the same processes, albeit crudely, in African as in British recruits.

With the benefit of hindsight, one realizes that the instructions and training were designed to ensure that the correct control processes operated on the task through information about it that was deliberately put into working memory by the instructor. In short, the subjects had to *learn* how to treat a nonstandard task (exotic to their experience), just as the test constructors had to learn how to adapt a standard test of mechanical principles to East African rural life, which they clearly regarded as exotic. Both sets of adaptations were aimed at modifying the stimulus percept internally by the subject, so that stimuli that were no longer identical with those of the original test were nevertheless internally represented in an equivalent fashion. Given an approximation to such equivalence, meaning could be assigned to the test task by the subject and to the test score by the experimenter.

The same conclusions can be drawn about the development of the General Adaptability Battery (GAB) by Biesheuvel.[4] In direct line from the Macdonald Askari Battery, it concerned itself with selecting recruits for work in mining jobs. Although less comprehensive in its coverage, it achieved remarkable acceptance as a valid and reliable means of selecting recruits to heavy industry throughout Southern and Central Africa. Significantly, the adminstration of the battery required an equivalent of Swahili, since the mine recruits were drawn from a wide range of tribes and language families. The mine-language Fanakalo, a pidgin derivative, sufficed. Relying on mime, film, demonstration, practice, and rapport for its methods of stimulus internalization, it proved to be a major contributor to the acceptability of large numbers of African workers for initial and advanced training.

The fullest account of test construction, adaptation, and use in exotic contexts is provided in Ord's detailed description of the New Guinea Performance Scales (Ord, 1971, pp. 20–21 and 90ff.) for preliterates. First, he sets out broad criteria of test acceptability. The tasks had to be readily understood following simple explanation and practice. They had to be demonstrable by manipulating "concrete material with the barest instructions" (p. 20). These manipulations had to be uncomplicated, so that item difficulty was a function of cognitive, and not manual, dexterity. Explicit cultural content of the materials used was to be minimal. Information about task solutions could not be easily passed on orally in small communities. These general requirements were operationalized in the tasks finally adopted for aptitude testing among the tribes of Papua New Guinea. Ord's verbal instructions to subjects performing these tasks are by far the most laconic of any encountered in the literature. On the other hand, his descriptions of the tasks and of how to administer them are the fullest of any. It is quite easy to reconstruct Ord's measures from the written descriptions. This is not true of most tests. Moreover, the experimenter has two clear functions: the first to *teach* the subject by observation, planned repetition, and performance on the test materials; the second to assess his competence. Like the earlier efforts of Macdonald and Biesheuvel, it is characteristically different from the traditional Euramerican test of intelligence *in the amount of initial information it provides and the insistence that the tester be clinically satisfied about the confidence of the subject to perform the task prior to embarking on the actual items to be regarded as scoring trials*. It is the fullest written record of the systematic attempts by cross-cultural testers to represent the external stimuli in such a way that operations can be carried out on them by attentional and control processes inside the subject's brain.

One of the most important, but also one of the least noticed case studies of test transfer from a parent to a host culture is Bhatia's (1955) account of the adaptation of performance tests for use in India with literates *and* nonliterates. Bhatia's work was not influenced by either Macdonald's or Biesheuvel's material, simply because he had no access to it. While Bhatia discovered for himself the basic problems of test use in exotic contexts, and found solutions that were remarkably close to those adopted by his contemporaries in Africa, his contribution to our awareness of the manifold difficulties of test score definition is unique. Of particular note is his adaptation of an aural, or listening, digit span test to a syllable span test for illiterate subjects, and his reasoning for the adaptation:

> When we gave this test to illiterate boys in the initial stage ... we were struck by the unusual difficulty these boys felt in repeating the digits or reversing them .... Whereas the sound of a number, such as seven or five constitutes a unit perceptual experience for a literate boy, it is not so for an illiterate boy. The sound seven, for example, is almost a set of nonsense syllables for him, and constitutes, ... for the purpose of understanding and memorisation, as many units as there are unit sounds in the word ... the names of digits would have to be replaced by something more unitary in the experience of the illiterate boys in order to achieve some sort of equivalence of the test for the literate and illiterate groups. The sounds of the Hindi consonants were selected for this purpose ... and ... are built on the scientific principle of one consonant for each unit sound.

Bhatia had found out that the short-term memory capacity of the illiterate boys was being exceeded by the percept of the spoken number as a series of separate sounds. The Hindi consonants offered no such encoding and storage problem. This adaptation is probably the first in the literature to address a specific problem of "equivalence" in a functional sense. Different stimuli were needed to produce the same internal representations and operations in subjects. The maintenance of stimulus constancy would have produced responses that were not strictly comparable for the two groups being studied. A much more recent acknowledgment of this same problem in digit span work can be seen in Ellis and Hennelly (1980). This ingenious experiment clarifies the initial observation of apparently poor performance of Welsh speakers in digit span. When vowel length was controlled, the difference disappeared.

Bhatia's answer, thirty years ago, was to give monosyllable span tasks to illiterates and digit span tasks to literates. This satisfied him and Godfrey Thomson, his supervisor. When Bhatia analyzed the correlations between the tasks, his memory span tasks behaved predictably. They seemed to test in illiterates what they tested in literates, although the stimuli were no longer identical. However, the average score of literates on digit span was *always* superior to that of illiterates on syllable span. In fact literates outperformed illiterates on every intellective task, whether or not the stimuli were identical or different. If readers have a *déjà vu* experience here when recalling much more recent accounts of ethnic differences in North America, that is as it should be. But read on.

From a strictly experimental point of view, the comparison of average scores between literates and illiterates is logically impossible if the stimuli change between groups, even if the correlation coefficients suggest that the different stimuli are in fact testing the same set of processes in both groups. Moreover, one can imagine the *political* outcry that would attend the use of two quite different sets of stimuli for two different ethnic groups if their job or educational placements depended on the results. By finding a plausible, and theoretically coherent, substitute for one of his groups, Bhatia could have been assailed both by scientists and politicians had he used the new test for placement. Illiterates might well have argued that the new test was the *cause* of their poor showing.

Workers in the field of cross-cultural testing would bring out one more point. Bhatia's knowledge of Hindi provided an alternative. An outsider could not have found that answer. In fact, an insider's view of a testing context is probably a prerequisite to successful assessment, as the next paradigm so eloquently shows, and as the hints at the end of the chapter prescribe. But before we progress to that, the testing principles of the decade of large-scale data collection in school and college contexts outside "Euramerica" provide a point of comparison with the lessons learned by those who faced groups of preliterates.

The Decade of Paper-and-Pencil Tests

The years between 1960 and 1970 proved to be a decade of large-scale administration of paper-and-pencil tests in exotic contexts.

Much of it took place in Africa, as Brislin (1983) has pointed out. The decolonization of that continent depended on the provision of a well-educated cadre of workers to take over the administration and business enterprises of Ghana, Kenya, Nigeria, Tanzania, Zambia, Zimbabwe, to be specific. In those countries, most of the test activity took place as part of surveys of manpower potential. The availability of large numbers of subjects who could comprehend verbal instructions, who were familiar with the contexts of group administration procedures in schoolrooms and workplaces, and who were capable of learning from demonstration and practice how to record their answers by themselves on paper, was a historical accident that psychologists working outside Euramerican laboratories were able to adapt to. Their efforts were directed to problems of manpower allocation and selection that arose as a consequence of political change. Invariably, the response to requests for help in selection and training produced studies in predictive validity and some *post hoc* attempts to relate the empirical results of large-scale testing to expatriate theories of abilities and achievement. The utilitarian parallel between this enterprise and the goals of preliterate testing is exact. There was no grand design for psychometric research in Africa, filed in the laboratories of Euramerican universities. The effort was diffuse, uncoordinated, idiosyncratic, exciting, and creative. It has been ignored by mainstream psychology ever since.

The important legacies of the paper-and-pencil testing (PPT) decade are handed on in the conventions of testing that emerged, and the rules of evidence for validity that were enforced. Successful use of tests on a large scale may be observed in the work of Schwarz (1964), MacArthur, Irvine, and Brimble (1964), Vernon (1969), and Irvine, (1965, 1966, 1969). From these quite widely separated studies in West, East, and Central Africa substantial agreement on how to carry out large-scale PPT surveys emerges. Irvine (1973) summarized seven principles of test use that were common ground for all African work at the time. Nothing has been published since that challenges their claim to be a series of conventions that meet the need for an interim industrial standard.

The seven principles begin with a general prescription. This cautions against the assumption that a subject necessarily understands each link in the chain of conventions in testing. The very instructions, that are arguably the weakest links, must be forged before the subject is tested. In short, every test response must be learned.

From that insistence, several heuristics, or hints for beginners, emerge. Avoid test booklets, where confusions about going on or turning back to previous tests can arise; put each test on a separate, preferably single, sheet of paper; give instructions orally, and teach the subjects what is needed by visual aids and demonstrations; allow generous, and ensure supervised, practice; where possible present familiar material first, in order to minimize the amount of learning in the early stages; use dramatic and convivial strategies of presentation, with a script that allows some "ad libbing" as necessary in the idiom of the testing language; train and employ native speakers who are lively and bright in demeanour. The aim throughout is to make sure that the external, written or spoken, test items are capable of being processed correctly by the subject following precise internal representation.

The most instructive account of these group testing procedures in action is provided by Schwarz (1964). With great ingenuity, Schwarz and his team put a variety of tests to use. Each test had its separate instructions, practice items, and illustrations; and each was exactly two sides of a quarto page in length. The subjects, after listening to the tester read out each item in turn, checked the correct answer on the test itself. The items were represented figurally, pictorially, or verbally. All were hand-scored by stencil. Their survival value is witnessed in Akeju's (1983) account of their continuous use in Nigeria since 1964. Moreover, MacArthur, Irvine, and Brimble (1964) were able to use these tests in Zambia with no changes. The testing principles are ideally demonstrated in this unique series.

It is one thing to collect data using such methods, quite another to produce proof that the conventions of test administration have yielded scientific findings that are worthwhile. The advent of large-scale PPT use provided the means to check results in three contexts by using some rules of data analysis that are strictly observed by psychologists, or should be. Were the tests predictors of concurrent and future success and failure? Did they relate to each other in logical and consistent fashion? When dispositional qualities (such as gender) or environmental variables (social background, tribal affinity, school quality) were correlated with test scores, did they confirm in exotic contexts what one had come to expect in Euramerican studies?

The answers to these questions may not all be definite and reassuring, but there is a grudging consensus, even among the severest critics of the testing approach to cognition. The inclusive reference source to PPT results during the twenty years from 1960 to 1980 is Irvine's (1979) tabulation and analysis of the body of test literature that addresses the issues of test validity. There is no doubt that tests administered with care and consistency predict concurrent status at school and work, whatever the culture.

Moreover, when analyzed, the correlations among tests show the broad dimensions of human ability referred to earlier. Only when dispositional and environmental variables are correlated with test results do we find disagreement with Euramerican results. Two brief examples are as follows. First, several studies independently confirm that males outperform females in the elementary schools of Africa in almost every subject, but particularly in second-language acquisition; next, there are strong environmental influences on test performance owing more to widespread variation in school quality than social status as measured by parental income. These results are contrary to Euramerican experience. They confirm that ability theory has to be revised before the influence of culture on thinking can be precisely formulated. One must be alert to the simplistic conclusion. Performance on tests is affected by cultural contexts in distinctly different ways. Too often, that emerges as hindsight.

The Testing Inheritance

All of the case material presented is coherent in the perspective it offers. As each generation of testers confronted the problems of administering tests to exotic groups, the crucial questions were not *what items* constituted the stuff of testing but *how to present the items* to the subjects in ways that were meaningful to them. Once that breakthrough was achieved, psychologists found that they could put their constructions on the results with confidence. Above all, they found that the conventions of testing in Euramerican contexts needed revision to enable the rules of psychometric analysis to take place. When these rules were eventually applied, some of the limitations of the discipline in determining theories of ability were uncovered.

With the advantage of hindsight, it seems clear that identical test items do not guarantee equal percepts or processes in humans, either for individuals within cultures, or for groups classified by some cultural or ethnic label. The quest has been to approximate to a cognitive core of meaning within individuals. This accomplished, their subsequent behavior yields constructs that psychology can use to interpret mental life. The reports of exotic test construction and use from 1940 onwards refute any paradigm in human cognition that assumes S-R (stimulus-response) as the baseline. The S-O-R (adding organism) formulation is marginally better, but O-S-O-R is consistent with the empirical findings of test use with preliterates and literates. Otherwise, the preoccupation with test instructions and stimulus modification through these instructions that identifies the psychometric approach would not only have been misplaced, but it would also have proved unnecessary.

Piagetian Assessment

The essence of the "piagetian,"[5] or even the modified or "quasipiagetian" approacn to measurement is a clinical interview structured by a small number of tasks. In that respect it is different from an individually administered intelligence test only in degree. Intelligence tests usually have far more items available than piagetian tasks (PGTs). Moreover the subtests have external reference in the very strict statistical rules for items acceptance that are employed. The PGTs available to the field worker have been arrived at conventionally but empirically; and they constitute an absolute scale of progression in the development of thinking. At the end of the interview the experimenter decides, on the basis of performance and verbal explanation, what stage of mental operations has been reached by the subject. That decision, and how it best may be arrived at, is the focus of enquiry now.

There has grown up round the set of tasks that were developed by Piaget to uncover the nature of thought in young children a large literature of cross-cultural findings. The standard reference is Dasen and Heron (1981). While these studies claim some quite dramatic cultural differences, they have come under strong attack from Cole and Scribner (1983) and Irvine (1983a). The main points raised by these critics can be summarized in the phrase "domain inconsistency." By this, Cole and Scribner mean that the tasks show little sign of invariably testing what the field workers think that they test; and Irvine's reanalysis of conservation study material supports that judgment. Moreover, Judith Irvine (1979) has added an anthropological veto to the debate by demonstrating the frailty of inferences by expatriate psychologists relying on data provided by interpreters in clinical interviews.[6]

Finally, a recently released bibliography of African cognitive research contains abstracts of piagetian work carried out by indigenous psychologists (Andor, 1983). My preliminary reading of this material determines that the indigenous scholars' results generally reveal normal development of African children, while those of expatriates tend to show lag or failure to reach Western norms, with some rare exceptions. If psychology is as exact a science as we would like, this kind of result ought not to emerge. If it persists, it means that the claims advanced for results using this approach have to be scrutinized most carefully for method and inference.

There are, as before, two questions to answer. First, what tasks may be used? Second, how are they to be used? The standard framework for PGTs is still that provided by Dasen in his many bouts of field work. These are Genevan PGTs that have been used in diverse contexts. However, no longer is there agreement that these are the only tasks that may be used, or that they should always be used. Neopiagetian, or new wave revisions of traditional tasks and methods are upon us, and have been for some time. For example, Bryant (1974) in an experimental series of elegance and rigor, advances an alternative set of tasks, along with some sharp theoretical divergences from standard piagetian wisdom about tasks and what they tell us about child development. A useful case study of this uncertainty is contained in Chung (1983), and Dasen's (1983) criticisms of her work. While Bryant poses a general threat to the theoretical position advanced by Piaget, Chung challenges the whole corpus of conservation studies claiming lag in development of children in exotic contexts. She does this by a radical departure from presenting Genevan PGTs alone. She echoes the early Price-Williams (1961) principle of adaptation of tasks to context. Like him, Chung finds little support for lag; and none of that failure to conserve in almost half the population that Heron and Dasen term "asymptote." By offering three parallel forms of PGTs in a Korean context she takes the correct step of including both PGTs and her alternates in the same experiment. Dasen (1983) denies that Chung's revisions are "true" conservation tasks, and asserts that the experiment is flawed through failure to observe order effects, in spite of Chung's report that a check on order effects was included (p. 125). The dependence of the meaning of the tasks on the instructions to subjects and the sequencing of tasks should now be a familiar precept for the reader.

What to use is by no means settled. How to use the tasks may be no simple matter either. In fact, it should be clear by now that what is used is not independent of how it is used. By definition, Dasen and others provide mandatory instructions about procedures, but the procedures count for nought in a clinical context if they do not arrive at a correct decision about the status of the subjects on an absolute scale of thought development. It might even be argued, on the other hand, that in a clinical context it matters not what is used as long as the message is exact. Nevertheless, rapport, clear and unequivocal directions, and, above all, a standard form of question to the subject are all emphasized by Dasen. It would be reasonable not to worry about the physical stimulus, but about its meaning to the subject. Stimulus equivalence in the form of the question posed is sought as the basis for initial classification.

The emphasis on the form of the question may seem to be admirable in its aim. The difficulties of realizing that goal are nowhere more adequately expressed than in Judith Irvine's (1979) account of her failure to replicate Greenfield's (1966) study of so-called magical thinking among the Wolof. Greenfield equated short laconic answers as ambiguous, and classified silence thereafter as failure to conserve. She was, of course, working with an interpreter. Judith Irvine's adopted role was that of a language learner seeking linguistic certainty. She conducted no experiments until the villagers had found a good reason to answer more than once to a question involving equivalence. This exact context was the explanation of the Wolof terms *same, equal to, more than, less than*, using water levels in beakers of different diameters as a prop for a rather slow language learner. When asked to elaborate on the customary "You poured it" response as a reason for an apparent change in water level on transfer to a new beaker, the villages waxed eloquent to the slow language learner who was one with them if not of them. They conserved admirably, answered supplementaries, and the fifty percent failure rate observed by Greenfield in 1966 was never replicated.

The results of Greenfield's much-publicized work are seriously challenged by failure to use the Wolof difficulty in distinguishing "equal to" from "same as" in the design of the work; or if that was initially unknown, to compensate for it during the experiment when it became obvious. And, Greenfield became aware of the difficulty (1966, p. 232); but her attempt at its solution produced responses at the chance level, as Irvine (1983a, p. 54) points out. Furthermore, she failed to understand the significance of silence. Magic action was suggested by Greenfield as the reason given in the laconic response: "You poured it." This explanation now seems more like an ethnocentric attribute by the experimenter than the only possible explanation from the data.

Judith Irvine's case study is, in fact, the best of all the prescriptions for obtaining good interview data from exotic contexts. But it counts for more than that. It carries with it a much more important prescription for neo-piagetian research than any so far encountered. *Her very approach depends on a prior knowledge of the structure of the language of the subject as a prerequisite for any kind of explanation of an inference. Second, it shows that social conventions prescribe answers to spoken questions.* Piaget (1966) himself made the case for disentangling competence from its possibly confounding linguistic context twenty years ago. In spite of this early warning, a serious weakness of much published piagetian work is the failure to specify any structural language attribute, or social convention, that might be used to predict enhanced or depressed performance. Some are exempt from this criticism. As a counsel to perfection, one should note that Price (1978, p. 17) confirms that languages in Papua New Guinea *vary* in their capability to offer explanations for conservation judgments. One must, it seems, know that the language is a particularly good or bad vehicle for putting the question and/or explaining one's beliefs about the question before answers can be evaluated. Given that a clinical method has to arrive at the truth, it follows that truth is mediated by what the experimenter knows. It is also inhibited by what he is ignorant or unaware of.

The prescriptions that emerge from the use of PGTs across cultures are few, but salutary. Reliance on a small number of conventional PGT tasks does not fairly encompass the serious challenges that have been issued to the theory that underpins their use. As alternatives to Piaget's view of the world of the child emerge, so the need grows to put one set of tasks against the other, especially if the developmental status of societies is compared as a result. Second, there seems little justification for using the results of exotic task presentation if an interpreter has been used to assist in the interview. Such an expedient, I maintain, probably admits in the experimenter the absence of social knowledge that is essential to carrying out the interview with flexibility born of fluency and social acceptability. Last, a prior study of the structural properties of the vernacular has to be a part of the rationale for the investigation. To dramatize the point, consider this question. Given a language without a conditional (if ... then) structure, how could PGT conservation tasks be meaningfully conveyed, assuming common-sense observation of conservation in domestic tasks?

One other aspect of PGT data collection seems central. Data collection based on lengthy interviews is time-consuming. A consequence has been the extremely small samples of children (typically ten per age group) that define a proportion in calculations of developmental "graphs" said to represent major cultural effects. It is perhaps worth stating that in a sample of ten children, each replying at random to two questions requiring a yes-or-no answer, 25 percent of them would get both right, within the confidence limits of the sample size. The confidence limits of that sample estimate of 25 percent are, for ten children, zero and six. Any value between zero and six has to be regarded as chance-generated, as a single data point. If there were four age groups of ten, and the conserving responses were 0, 2, 4, 4, could these nonsignificant frequencies be said to represent a trend? A full account of the problems inherited by the interpretation of quasi-random data in neopiagetian work is available in Irvine (1983a). While the protest from those who have produced the data has been loud, it fails to answer the charge that too much has been claimed for too few items administered to too few subjects by interpreters. Answers will require much more than ten children per group.

Experimental Routes to Cognitive Processes

If tests are concerned with individual standings in relation to group means, and PGTs with individual progress along a maturing continuum of thinking, experimental approaches are primarily concerned with the verification and observation of strong effects in human cognition that are evident in all of us. For example, Segall,

Campbell, and Herskovits (1966) had no doubt that mankind is susceptible to illusions of line length. Their concern was the effect of the presence or absence of "carpentered" environments on the habits of perception responsible for degrees of susceptibility. Similarly, the work of Scribner (1974) never assumed for one moment that the Kpelle subjects she worked with would fail to cluster everyday household objects to aid free recall. She was determined to observe the effects of literacy on the networks of recall available to her subjects. Finally, Berry's (1969b) paper on the effects of different habitats in the attribution of meaning to ambiguous line drawings assumed that human nature would supply meaning. Exactly what meaning, he correctly guessed, would be a function of ecological press. In these three classic studies of human assessment, little doubt existed about the phenomenon under investigation, the method of investigating it, or the interpretation of findings. Such confidence is rare in cross-cultural research. Is there a moral somewhere for would-be test users?

Perhaps there are no morals to be drawn from cross-cultural stories about psychology, but the examples just quoted provide some sharp contrasts that are instructive. Attention should first be given to the phenomenon of stimulus identity preserved consistently in the line drawings that represented tests of illusion susceptibility. These were never altered. Nor could they be, because alteration would have changed the degree of illusion susceptibility. Again, Berry's ambiguous line drawings remained constant. Only the subjects differed in their percepts of them. These two examples demonstrate the logical necessity for stimulus identity, since the line is the medium by which the subject's percept is captured. Stimulus substitution can be fostered in illusion and percept experiments, as Brislin's (1974) garden version of the Ponzo quaintly illustrates. Subject, not stimulus change, is the normal procedure, however. And Pollnac's (1977) investigation of the seaworthiness of the size of the Horizontal–Vertical illusion is a neat, but very small-sample, case in point.

The abandonment of identical stimuli presents acute scientific problems for which there exist none but judgmental and common-sense answers. Bhatia's problem is not confined to tests. Scribner's work on free recall depended not on preserving the same objects as were used in Euramerican laboratories, but in deliberately altering them. After observation in the community, Scribner chose those that were culture consonant. They then became elements in concept formation for Kpelle subjects so that the clustering effect could not be destroyed by objects that did not form associative groupings. What would cluster in Euramerican experience would not necessarily do so in the Kpelle village.

Scribner's success in demonstrating the clustering phenomenon vindicated her judgment about what were valid objects for Kpelle villages and school children. The Bhatia digit span adaptation previously described is in the same league as the Scribner work on clustering. Chung's adaptations can not be judged tendentious, or as unscientific, as would changes in line length in illusion experiments. Scribner, Bhatia, and Chung find support in Mitchell's (1959) early adaptation of the Bogardus social distance scale in studies in tribal affinity in Zambia. The scale was freely adapted, but there was no doubt that it measured social distance among Zambian tribes. One would then have been foolish to compare Zambians and Americans on their respective degree of ethnocentrism by averaging scores and conducting analyses of variance. The construct of social distance was not invalidated by the research methods used, but there the inferences stop, or ought to. This approach has to be contrasted with the confusion that results from the comparison of test scores, and the comparison of frequencies attaining developmental status in exotic groups according to PGTs or their analogs.

Finally, the experimental search for ways of thinking that identify cultures has proof positive of the successful use of language as a prior consideration in research design. The early work by Gay and Cole (1967, pp. 67–68) on disjunctive reasoning among the Kpelle shows that the Kpelle language is well suited to problems involving "and not". The language handles "if … then" implications very poorly, and finds equivalence almost impossible. It takes no great stretch of the imagination to *predict* the outcome of a question such as "If I pour the water in here, then will I have more, less, or will the amount be the same?" on observed performance. But confidence about the outcome might well be misplaced, when Zepp's (1983) failure to replicate the Kpelle findings with a highly similar West African language is considered relevant. These apparent contrasts are part of the same underlying phenomenon. The object itself is only a means to an end. What is perceived is the only datum available to us. While this is a truism, the verification of these perceptions must begin somewhere. Description is one thing; prediction quite another matter. In many ways, cognitive research across cultures is aptly characterized as anthropological cognition, since an adequate description of the subject matter had to be the first aim.

Information-Processing Trends

The everyday business of human assessment continues in more sophisticated fashion these days. The advent of computers and microcomputers is making apparatus redundant, and PPTs are being supplanted by CCTs (computer-controlled tasks). It would be imprudent to embrace the computer if all that happens is the translation of old tasks into a machine. That will undoubtedly happen, or already has happened, and group differences in times to complete tasks are being compared instead of standardized test scores. Nevertheless, there are signs that lessons from all the previous errors and false trails of cross-cultural assessment are slowly being applied. In an attempt to demonstrate how, three series of results are reported here: Poortinga (1971), Irvine and Reuning (1981), and Verster (1983).

Information-processing approaches to cognition attempt to reconcile what is known about the *limits* of human capacity to process amounts of information with *performance* on tasks whose demands on that capacity can be estimated. It is well known that the time to respond to a question about the presence or absence of a signal depends on the number of possible alternatives that have to be considered before an answer can be arrived at. It takes less time to react to a single tone than to decide which of two tones is the higher or lower, and react to one or the other. If we increase the number of tones to three, recognizing the highest of three when it is presented will take longer than recognizing one of two. In fact, we know that the time to recognize one from a set of possible alternatives increases linearly with set size.

One could take this general rule as a starting point for inquiry about how people in different cultures process information. In fact, Poortinga (1971) did just that in the pioneering study of auditory and visual choice reaction times in Africans, black and white. He identified female and male subjects for each ethnic group. He found that reaction time increased with set size irrespective of ethnic group. African times were observably slower, but sex differences within ethnic groups and overall were not. Yet he was unwilling to concede that the group average times were interpretable because he was not satisfied that the results he obtained were exactly equivalent for the two samples. He submitted the data to rigorous tests of the assumption of "bias-free" stimuli, but the results did not support the comparison of group averages thereafter. The visual stimuli were lights of different colors. The pattern of response times for the different colors was not identical for whites and blacks. Nor were they identical for sounds of different quality.

That account demonstrates that even the "simplest" stimuli can conceal inferential traps for the unwary. Poortinga revealed the complexity of everyday visual and auditory signals by applying what he already knew about techniques for uncovering group differences in item difficulty to latencies. The results pressed caution on the interpretation of average latencies from seemingly everyday and simple information-processing tasks.

Irvine and Reuning (1981) adopted a similarly conservative approach. They began by reviving a letter-checking task that had considerable use as a measure of individual differences in work rate (Reuning, 1983). While its empirical strength had been observed, the problem of fitting a theory to the data was not satisfactorily overcome until the work of Posner and Keele (1967) and Clark and Chase (1972) was applied to the task to produce an additive model of two encoding stages as identifiable sources of individual differences. The fit for the model has proved consistent in over a dozen replications, half of them cross-cultural. This work helps us understand why the psychometric test "factor" of perceptual speed has been identified in every part of the world (Irvine, 1979). It also underlines the crudity of the assumptions of those who compare group averages in even the most overlearned stimuli materials, like numbers and letters, without first understanding what the model behind performance implies for such a comparison. Since the publication of that experimental series, the task has been computerized and the principles behind that decision round off this section.

The fullest account of cross-cultural information processing under computerized conditions is obtained in Verster's study of speed and accuracy performance in black and white South Africans. Like the other casework in this section, a theoretical model was first postulated. The tasks were devised to test its robustness, and the groups identified to extend the range of cultural and dispositional (males were compared with females) variation available to the experimenter. Verster found good fits for models of performance in conditions of speed and accuracy. He also found the same scientific evidence for uncertainty about inferences from black-white average performance that is characteristic of Poortinga's work.

Each of these studies has some precepts for modern assessment of individual differences. They are identified as first seeking robust and well-researched dimensions of individual differences. Then, a performance model, or hypothesis for such a model, is framed. Tasks are defined to account for human variation within and across cultures. The first step is to fit the model. The subsequent cross-cultural studies serve to test the working limits of the model itself. They are not concerned with between-culture variance in initial proving of the assumptions that determine the construction and use of the task. If variation between gender or cultural groups persistently occurs, one has to determine if it is a difference that requires a modification to general theories that account for performance, or to some rather more trivial concern, such as experimental artefact.

There is, finally, no point in transferring traditional tasks to machines unless there are good reasons for doing so. Somewhat alarmed by the lack of rationale for CCT use in human assessment in Euramerican contexts, Irvine and his colleagues (Brooks, Dann, & Irvine, 1984) prescribe the following principles. First, any CCT must be anchored in theory so that it can be generated from first principles. Next, analogs of the basic task should be easily constructed. Then, a performance model should be generated and verified. Between-group and within-group validity for the model must be demonstrated. Above all, the machine version must provide a form of verification that pencil-and-paper versions prevent. This additional information is the central argument for introducing machine-controlled tasks.

SOME CONSIDERED ADVICE

At the beginning of the chapter were listed some sources for acquiring basic skills in test use and application. Since then, there has been a commentary on the difficulties of learning how to apply this basic knowledge in the different contexts of testing. I have taken this approach because prior knowledge about these enduring difficulties is a logical prerequisite to their solution. Perhaps the fundamental criticism of test use is that too many researchers have discovered what these are after the fact. Much of that *post hoc* wisdom had been forced on field workers by theoretical gaps and patches. Throughout, I have hesitated to prescribe actions that did not seem to me to be theory-based. If so-called practical hints fail to resolve the problems of stimulus identity or equivalence, or even if they do but provide no rationale that is consistent with what we know about human performance, then they are given in hope rather than in certainty. There is small comfort in a science that can offer little in the way of predictions for the outcome of its prescriptions.

Nevertheless, there is an obligation to tell what one knows, even if one cannot swear to tell the truth. This knowledge is consistent with performance models of testing, and pursues consonance with theory as we understand it today. The advice offered now attempts to help the experimenter produce stimuli that the subject can process. It also aims to preserve the experimenter from some of the gross errors of comparison, within and between cultures, that have characterized much empirical work using cognitive tasks.

The dangers of misattribution, characteristic of all the schools of measurement reviewed thus far, are essentially of two types, which are here called Type A and Type B. Those of attributing to subjects in an exotic culture abilities that they may not have is a Type A error. Greenfield's ascription of magic action belief to illiterate villagers is probably the easiest to categorize in this way. Or, more common, not giving them credit for skills that are obvious only in contexts that the experimenter has not witnessed is a Type B error. Judith Irvine saw conservation among Greenfield's villagers only when the social climate allowed it. The standard experimental setting was a poor context for witnessing conservation. Applying the same criticism to psychometric tests, one realizes that there is no point in using multiple-choice formats to test subjects for whom custom has dictated only one correct answer (Type A), unless one first trains the subjects in that particular test mode. Reasoning and spatial skills have been said by Berry (1971, p. 332) and other cognitive style proponents to be weakly realized in nonhunting, subsistence farming communities such as the Temne and Telefomin: but they are evident in traditional games, in house and toy construction, in wood and stone carvings among the supreme nonhunters, and excellent farmers, the Shona of Zimbabwe (Type B). Among farmers with communal grazing, spatial memory for the location of animals is acute, since social custom dictates no offence to neighbors, as any herd-boy knows. Most of them remember their mistakes because of the harsh physical punishment received for failure to remember. Spatial skills of all kinds exist at the village level. It is pointless to assert that they are poorly represented in a subsistence farming community because subjects may perform badly in standardized tests (Type B). To check assumptions or hearsay about what skills are generally present in any community, *the test user should collect school syllabuses to discover what is taught in school at what age; must observe the games played in the school playground and at home. In the village one should examine closely the home-made toys most favored by children.* These elementary prophylactics will guard against the disease of misattribution.

Once tests are constructed, the major problem is to motivate subjects to perform well. Test administration in a group context requires good demonstration and supervised, preferably error-free, practice. Written instructions should be avoided, and subjects should be able to attempt each item once the test has begun. Vernacular presentation is preferable, and testers should be known to the subjects and respected by them. Cheerless and dull presenters will demotivate the subjects faster than giving them the most difficult items in a test to practice on. A simple motivating source is the promise of a reward. For example, pencils are valued much more highly in rural Africa than in urban "Euramerica"; and the hope of retaining the one issued for recording answers has been known to work wonders. It also is seen as a gift for services volunteered by students and staff alike. Some post-test interviews with students and teachers will reveal strategies, difficulties, and misunderstandings. Be brave: try some.

Once data are collected, then one has to decide whether it has been worth the effort. This evaluation will depend on what the test scores mean, or more accurately, what the experimenter says they mean. Meaning will also be a function of aim. If the aim is to find some objectively-scored, convenient test that will predict future performance, it may not really matter what it means, as long as it is politically defensible and has claim to technical soundness. Such operational definitions are not unusual, but they lead to trouble when *comparisons* are made among various groups who have taken the test. The simplest estimate of approximate comparability is based on item difficulties. The proportions passing each item in the various groups taking the test are recorded. The items will each have as many difficulty values as there are groups. These item difficulties may then be intercorrelated, If the correlations are very high (0.9 or thereabouts) averages can probably be compared for that test. On the other hand, the correlations among the tests themselves may tell a different story. As a general rule, unless the intercorrelations among all the pairs of tests used are within sampling error of each other, it is unwise to compare average scores across groups.

So important is the manner of presenting a test or task to the subject that an index of the test's sensitivity to experimenter differences is well worth acquiring. This can be done by analysis of variance techniques, where testers are between subjects' main effects. The proportion of variance attributable to tester effects is the index. If one goes this far, it is worth considering giving the test twice or more, to find out how strong the tester effect is against the far more likely effect of improvement with practice that is a frequent result in exotic environments. If strong practice effects are shown, then some interest in the intercorrelations of the trials will yield first estimates of reliability. Sophisticated readers will realize that the intercorrelations of groups of tests on the first trial and on subsequent trials are indices of structural stability overall. If one gives a test more than once, is its meaning the same on subsequent occasions as it was on the first? If intercorrelation of tests suggests that it is, and practice effects are observed, how does one know what the "correct" score is? First attempt? Second or subsequent attempts? Once again, the "correct" score for prediction is the one that reduces the errors of prediction most effectively. But for comparing levels of accomplishment on a cultural continuum, we need more than the single test or task given by a foreigner through an interpreter. All too often, that is exactly what cross-cultural test results amount to. For a full discussion of practice effects in exotic cultures, see Irvine (1983b).

The meaning of a test or task is strengthened when more than one type of measure tests the same thing. If comparisons are to be made, then standard tests of abilities and skills, properly and sympathetically administered, will just have to be there. Nevertheless, Irvine and Carroll (1980) recommend that local versions of each type of test be used alongside the "standards." If these local versions correlate as strongly with the standards as they do with each other, for each test family, then perhaps some use might come out of making comparisons. When the cross-correlations between standard and local versions are weak, then comparisons based on average on the standards probably lie in the region between the standard horse and the local wagon. Not much imagination is needed to locate that scientific area.

Moving now to an even more sophisticated level of analysis, one encounters attempts to reduce the amount of data in tests by factoring. That is, by subjecting the correlation matrices from test scores to techniques of factor analysis. If the reader does not understand what that last sentence means, or possibly could mean, then the rest of this section should be disregarded. For those who think they understand it, here are a few hints. I am well aware that I am passing on biases here, but they are the best I can think of.

The mistakes most commonly made in factor analysis of cross-cultural data are generic to the technique as a whole. Cross-cultural psychologists are, in fact, a bit better at factor analysis than most. First, remember that the standard error of a correlation is roughly equivalent to $1/N$, or the reciprocal of the square root of the number of subjects in the sample. This means that even for a sample of 100 subjects, any observed correlation has a single standard error of 0.1, and 95 percent confidence limits of ±0.2. As factor analysis reduces matrices by extracting variance, small samples increase the chances of adding factors that are simply due to the odd fluctuations in correlations generated by chance.

Next, because the technique of factor analysis *must* take out the largest amount of variance possible in the first pass at the matrix, the first principal component or factor is an artefact of the technique itself. It is unwise to interpret first factors as if they were psychological truths chiseled on stone. First factors are no more interpretable, in their unrotated state, than a score on a test manufactured in one country and applied in another. The score is an artefact of the technique, and is uninterpretable without a lot of further analysis.

Finally, if one must factor-analyze data, there can be no prior relationship among the variables. Part-whole scores, and family size *and* position data, to take only two common examples, are already related to each other before they are correlated, so that they produce spurious factors or artefactors. There are many more variables like them, for example, latencies on the same task at different phases in the experiment.

There are so many pitfalls in factor analysis that it is better left to the experts. If I want to use it nowadays, I seek broad dimensions of ability to use within cultures, so that I can then use the factor scores as classification variables for scrutinizing the processes that underpin the broad dimension. I believe it to be a useful tool as a prerequisite to sound research in individual differences, but it is not an end in itself, and should never be used as such.

CONCLUSIONS

Those who seek to use ability tests as aids to decision making within cultures are probably doing the right thing, since there are technically worse ways of allocating training opportunities. Those who use them for trait comparisons across cultures are perceived by critics as creating more scientific problems than they are able to solve. When that happens, the credibility of science itself is put at risk. Much current theorizing about abilities, styles, stages of mental development, and information processing has been derived from data whose theoretical origins and operational assumptions have proved debatable if not implausible. Because of theoretical and operational flaws in tests that are customarily advocated, the methods described here are not perfect, and it would be irresponsible to assert that they are. In many ways, those who use tests across cultures today are closer to Macdonald, Biesheuvel, Bhatia, Ord, and Schwarz than these pioneers could ever have imagined possible, given a belief in the progress of the discipline. The sober acceptance of that position is the recipe for learning that may follow.

Because the practices of testing in the earlier decades of the century became a crude technology reinforced by a potent belief system, they encountered no significant scientific challenge. The practice of administering tests in exotic contexts itself precipitated confrontation, and continues to do so. Fortunately, the grounds of the debate are increasingly scientific. By scrutinizing the accumulated wisdom of the results of the enterprise, a theory of sorts is emerging. The theory of cross-cultural testing begins with the axiom that no true-score variance is measurable until the stimulus is represented in operational form within the subject. Hence, only proof of transfer from practice to actual test items provides the rationale for modeling test performance. That model accomplished, item construction may proceed on an *a priori* basis. Thereafter, validity studies may be pursued. The need for techniques of data analysis is subservient to the prime aim of providing an operational definition of the construct to be measured. Nevertheless, when theoretical rigor is not feasible, for reasons that are beyond scientific control, the observance of the seven principles (see above) should minimize gross errors of measurement. They will never, of course, provide a prophylactic against errors of interpretation. These are experimenter-dependent, as the whole history of the enterprise reveals, and as the passions aroused in debates about ethnic group performance dramatize more forcibly than any scientific appraisal.

NOTES

1. By the technical term "Euramerican" is meant the type of society that provides universal secondary education, has a manufacturing economy, urban as well as rural environments, and claims significant space-age technology provision. In such societies the discipline of psychology has had its formal specification and growth.

2. From the Greek, exotikos, meaning foreign, or alien, and in contrast to Euramerican. I have decided to use this word in a technical sense to cover all test use that is a specimen, and therefore worthy of study, without necessarily having a theoretical specification for its operation.

3. The list, in its printed order, is as follows: African Matrix Test (adaptation of Raven's Matrices); Pegboard Manual Dexterity; Reversible Blocks Manual Dexterity; Screwboard Manual Dexterity; English Comprehension (Elementary); Physical Agility Test; Mechanical Assembly A; Mechanical Assembly B; Mechanical Comprehension; Cube Construction; Fourth Corner Test; Block Design Test; Picture Completion Test; Arithmetic Attainment; Formboard (circular insets); Formboard (square insets); Isihara Color Vision.

4. In a conversation with Biesheuvel in 1982, I established that he had access to the Macdonald material when the GAB was being constructed. There are generic similarities in methods of testing illiterates and in some of the tasks. Nevertheless, Biesheuvel's battery introduced several tasks that have no counterpart in the Askari Battery.

5. The word is spelt piagetian, avoiding a capital letter, to draw attention to the widespread modification of standard Piagetian tasks that has defined their cross-cultural use. The exact word quasipiagetian is altogether too much for any patient reader, but it does convey my own qualifications about the enterprise.

6. Judith Irvine is neither related to nor known by the present author.

8

ASSESSMENT OF PERSONALITY AND PSYCHOPATHOLOGY

GEORGE M. GUTHRIE
WALTER J. LONNER

Anyone who wishes to study or to assess personality or psychopathology across cultures must be reminded that the obstacles are many in this very broad and diffuse area. That "personality" exists and that "psychopathology" also exists is obvious. Everyone in every country has some unique, more or less predictable pattern of behavior that can be referred to as one's personality. Likewise, everyone is a candidate for mild to severe forms of psychopathology, principally because the stresses and strains of living, as well as the vicissitudes of body chemistry, are essentially part of the human situation. The problem, however, is how these abstract concepts are to be studied, assessed and understood.

Many scholars throughout the history of Psychology and Anthropology have attempted to explain and predict personality, as well as its disintegration, which takes shape as psychopathology. It is not our intent in this chapter to review the many efforts in these areas; one needs only to read any modern textbook summarizing these fields to see how varied and diffuse the different efforts have been and continue to be. Rather, in the introductory part of this chapter we wish to make the relatively uninitiated reader aware of what we believe are four basic realities that face the researcher who wants to understand the interface between culture, personality, and pathology.

Reality 1: The first reality is that no one yet has developed a theory of personality and /or psychopathology that will serve all researchers, all the time, in all cultures. While some believe that the Freudian perspective is basically sound and essentially correct, others denounce it as a scientific fairy tale. And the Jungians, or the Adlerians, or the Frommians may be ignored by the radical behaviorists (there is no personality, only observable behavior) who may in turn be criticized as superficial by the existentialists. And so it goes. A corollary to this reality is the fact that nearly everthing that a student learns about human personality is from a decidedly Western orientation. The linear, scientifically oriented Western minds that have molded most of our thoughts about personality and pathology may, after all, be wrong despite their brilliance. Or, if any one of them is correct, then that correctness may only be able to account for a very small aspect of behavior, behavior that is often specific to one culture.

Reality 2: The second reality is that dealing with personality and/or psychopathology in broad, sweeping, abstract terms has proven unsatisfactory. We advocate the avoidance of such terms as "national character" or "modal personality" to describe the core characteristics of people from one culture or country (e.g. the self-effacing Chinese, the emotional Spaniard, or the independent American). All cultures will have a wide range of "personalities" and perhaps an equally wide range of situations and conditions that may lead to psychopathology. Furthermore, unknown antecedent "ambient" factors (see Chapter 2) may be playing as large a role in affecting behavior as those we think we have "controlled." It seems essential, therefore, for researchers to be as specific as possible when studying or assessing personality or pathology from a cross-cultural perspective. While it is common to do so, and often very colorful, we suggest that cross-cultural psychologists may make better headway if they avoid phenomenological or existential viewpoints (for example, Carl Rogers' or Abraham Maslow's) when examining culture, personality, and pathology. However, by making this suggestion we are not saying that phenomenological or existential approaches and/or evidence are to be discarded as trivial or a scientific bore. To the contrary, we acknowledge these perspectives as serious and genuine, and well worth reading for insights into the behavior of individuals from specific cultures. What we strongly advocate is the use of *testable* hypotheses.

To qualify as a scientifically credible guideline, many believe that a theory of personality or psychopathology should be *falsifiable*. That is, through methodological and epistemological guidelines such as those outlined in Chapters 1 and 2, a theory-generated hypothesis should be stated in terms specific enough to allow it either to be confirmed or refuted unequivocally. If, for example, it is hypothesized that certain conditions in culture A should lead to a certain level of aggression, then we have a statement that can be falsified (or confirmed). Through the careful selection of subjects, the detailing of both independent and dependent variables, and the use of appropriate statistical analyses, a *point prediction* can be made. For instance, if the value on the dependent variable reaches a certain level (scores on a test of frustration, to take a common example), the statement concerning a predicted relationship will or will not receive support. If it does not receive the support as predicted, the theory (or that aspect of the theory) has been falsified, at least on that occasion.

It is on the matter of making *point predictions* (nearly always done in the "hard" sciences) as opposed to testing for probable differences through variations of the t-test that "soft" psychology has received deserved criticism (see Meehl [1978] for a detailed essay on the topic). Because cross-cultural psychology — at least that part which deals with personality and psychopathology — can be called "soft," Meehl's laments warrant serious attention. Meehl says that we can usually find t-test and/or statistical support for our pet theory simply by increasing sample size and therefore lowering the hurdle that must be jumped if we are to make a statement that is statistically justified. Furthermore, if lowering the hurdle doesn't work, we might fall victim to hedging or explaining away negative findings through *ad hoc* commentary.

Freudian theory, existential theory, humanistic theory, and other broad-banded abstract, complex theories do not lend themselvs to falsifiability. It is difficult to imagine a specific hypothesis, or series of testable hypotheses, which would either confirm or refute such comprehensive viewpoints about the nature of human personality and psychopathology. One usually has to accept these theories on faith alone. If this is not acceptable, then one has to depend upon guidance from perspectives that are more verifiable.

Reality 3: In cross-cultural research concerning personality/pathology, there is no substitute for a fairly detailed knowledge of the culture(s) being studied. It is a mistake to assume that library research alone (for example, through the use of the Human Relations Area Files — see Chapter 3) or a brief period in a certain culture will create an adequate background for research. One should develop a "feel" for the culture through relatively long-term immersion and/or prolonged contact with colleagues and other informants who are native to the culture or country in question. Cross-cultural psychology has received valid criticism for "airport research," a criticism that is best countered through cultural immersion and other types of meaningful contact with the culture(s) being used as research sites.

Reality 4: A fourth reality is that those who serve as "subjects" in cross-cultural research projects may be unable or unwilling to accommodate to the research plans of some scientific interloper who usually enters some "other cultural" setting with an array of perhaps unwarranted assumptions. Consider, for example, the following:

1. Most psychological research and testing has been done in the West, most frequently with college students or at least with individuals who have had experience with tests, instructions, the imposition of time limitations, and other routines surrounding psychological research.
2. It is often assumed that people everywhere can rank stimuli along a linearly constructed continuum (e.g. on a seven-point scale can make distinctions between "good" and "bad"). Perhaps some individuals, and/or some languages, can make distinctions only between good – not good, and that intermediate positions are meaningless.
3. Another assumption is that all people are somehow automatically equipped to make judgments about social and psychological stimuli through the use of complex cognitions that require prior exposure to such stimuli.
4. It is also frequently assumed that all people are capable of, and equally adept at, self-reflection and self-assessment. This common methodological requirement, which surely has its roots in the self-oriented West, may simply not be true of some groups. Or, if some people are capable of self-assessment, perhaps they will not be willing to disclose themselves on some self-report inventory.

We want to repeat that researchers who attempt to study "national character" or "culture and personality" or "modal personality" are inviting difficulties and confusion. A few noteworthy projects are exceptions, however, such as the work of McClelland (1961) and others on achievement motivation and the Whitings' famous six cultures project (Whiting & Whiting, 1975). But most time-limited, personnel-limited, and method-bound studies that have tried to explain culture and personality have failed to yield convincing results. Serpell (1976) explains the major difficulties as follows:

... the failure of most studies to yield convincing results may well be due in part to a rather simple conceptual flaw in the notion of a

personality test. Although its objective is to gauge enduring dispositions, the test itself collects information over a very limited timespan
and in a limited situation. Thus the dispositions expressed by an
individual, whether openly or implicitly, in the context of a one-hour
interview, with an unfamiliar doctor, in a clinic or a classroom, form
the basis of the test's assessment of how that individual is likely to
behave in a whole variety of different situations in which he has not
been observed, and on future occasions when his mood may be greatly
altered (pp. 27–28).

Collapsing individual responses among a sample of individuals is no
panacea, either, for the same sources of variance and their complex
interactions will affect the group as easily as the individual.

What we have been emphasizing in this introductory statement is
the simple fact the the study of personality and psychopathology in
and across cultures other than one's own is fraught with conceptual,
epistemological, and methodological difficulties. While the tone of
these cautionary remarks may be discouraging to many, we do not
want to throw a wet blanket on the entire enterprise. Rather, we
encourage forging ahead, but with the full knowledge that our tools
and conceptualizations may not yet be ready to meet the test
demanded of them.

In most of the remainder of this chapter we intend to give a
sampling of many of the frameworks that have been used in the
cross-cultural study of personality and pathology.

A MAJOR PURPOSE OF CROSS-CULTURAL RESEARCH

Cross-cultural research has been characterized as a natural
experiment in which different societies bring about variations in
antecedent conditions, variations that one cannot bring about in a
more usual experiment. The classical example is Malinowski's (1927)
study of conflicts between fathers and sons in the Trobriands where
uncles rather than fathers were responsible for the sons' training and
discipline thus unconfounding important variables that were con-
founded in Freud's Vienna. His findings that boys' resentment was
directed toward the uncle disciplinarians rather than the fathers,
sexual partners of their mothers, cast doubt on Freud's theory of the
Oedipus complex. Malinowski's work was rejected by Freudians
because he had not gone through a personal analysis (Jones, 1928). In
short, he was not able to assess the fundamental variables in the

theory of oedipal conflicts, according to the Freudians.

Regardless of its lack of impact on theories, the Malinowski design remains a prototype of the contribution that cross-cultural research might make to theories developed in a single society. Unfortunately, for a number of reasons, there have been few instances where theories have actually been tested in second societies, using the natural laboratory of cultural differences.

In the sixty years since the Malinowski–Jones debate there has been a disappointing failure of cross-cultural research to influence theories of human behavior, normal or abnormal. If one examines the indexes of books in psychiatry, abnormal psychology, or personality theory, one finds few entries under such terms as culture, society, ethos, etc. There are several reasons for this state of affairs. Many psychological theories are not stated in terms that lend themselves to testing in one's own society, let alone in another. This is especially true of psychodynamic theories that invoke unconscious processes to account for a wide variety of behavioral manifestations but do not suggest steps that would enable an experimenter to modify those experiences. The variables are defined in terms of responses rather than in terms of stimuli. At the same time more behaviorally-oriented thinkers have been insensitive to cultural differences in the reinforcement contingencies and models that confront people in different societies. Most significant of all, however, has been a strong predilection of theorists and researchers to emphasize *inner* determinants of behavior or dispositions and to pay scant attention to the *situational* determinants of behavior. This tendency is epitomized in the psychoanalytic emphasis on the universality of their dynamic processes such as the psychosexual stages, oedipal strivings, and the whole panoply of repressed and instinctual drives.

In any cross-cultural study of personality or behavior, normal or abnormal, there is a need for assessment or measurement of variables in which one is interested. Case studies are an exception to this requirement, but case studies by their very nature usually illustrate rather than prove a point and should be considered as hypothesis-raising rather than testing. In case studies and in other designs there is need a for a theoretical framework within which to formulate relationships between conditions and results. Data by themselves are not very useful.

RELATIONSHIP OF ASSESSMENT TO THEORY

At first glance many measurement techniques would appear to be atheoretical. A variable such as intelligence, dominance, or paranoia is assessed by steps that follow logically from the definition. Reliability is assessed by retesting or the application of Kuder–Richardson Formula 20 and validity is assumed from the content of the scale.

In a review of research on alienation, Guthrie and Tanco (1980) found that in many cases researchers defined alienation carefully, established reasons that a sample should be alienated, and then proceeded to measure alienation with a scale whose items were heterogeneous in content and whose items bore little relationship to the alienation that the researcher had described. Giving a set of items a certain label or title is insufficient grounds for assuming that they will be a valid measure of a trait. In their review the authors found that frequently there was only a tenuous relationship between alienation as defined and alienation as measured.

Research on achievement is another area in which there is a danger that an investigator, who is interested in raising the level of performance of school children or of some category of workers, may use a measure of need for achievement without determining whether the researcher's definition of achievement bears a satisfactory relationship to the definition of the test builder. If someone has offered a test for a given personality trait it does not follow that the test will measure what an investigator wants to measure even though test maker and researcher are using the same label for a personality trait.

At a deeper level there is the question of whether one should think in terms of situational or dispositional determinants of behavior, of states or traits. The notion that our behavior is determined by traits, or underlying characteristics that exercise a pervasive influence over a wide range of activities, has been called into question by Mischel (1968) and others. It has been argued that people do not show similar behavior patterns across a wide variety of situations. One may be dominant in one situation but not in another, aggressive in some circumstances and passive in others. Behavior is much more a function of the situation than of inner dispositions. Our everyday language, however, predisposes us to think of people doing things because they have certain traits. For instance, in his research on attribution processes, Jones (1976) concluded that American subjects are situationists when it comes to explaining their own actions but dispositionists in explaining the actions of others. "I did it because the situation called for it; they acted as they did because that's the kind of people they are." With Philippine subjects, Guthrie, Jackson, Astilla, and Elwood (1983) found a strong tendency for situational explanations of behavior to be used. Respondents found it difficult to rate acquaintances on traits without a specification of the situation in which the trait might be expressed. This suggests that there may be marked differences from one society to another in the degree to which trait explanations are invoked to account for behavior. This would, in turn, affect assessment of personality factors.

There is a parallel set of problems when one attempts to measure psychopathology. The same diagnostic terms may have different meanings in different societies. For instance, it was found during diagnosis that American psychiatrists tended to attach a quite different meaning to the term schizophrenia from that used by British psychiatrists when all were examining the same set of histories (Cooper, Kendall, Garland, Sharpe, Copeland, & Simon, 1972).

HOW TO SELECT A MEASUREMENT PROCEDURE

Anyone who undertakes to assess personality or psychopathology in his or her own culture faces a number of problems; difficulties and hazards are compounded as one carries that activity to an alien setting. At the beginning we want to remind readers that measurement is a means to an end and not an end in itself. The purposes and methods of measurement activities must be determined by the theory being used or tested or the questions the researcher has in mind. Choice of measurement technique would be among the last decisions to be made in planning research on personological variables. When such a sequence is followed one's measurement strategies flow from one's conceptualization of the problem. Consequently, the results are more likely to bear unambiguously on the questions that prompted the research. The converse is the situation in which one uses a familiar measuring device such as the Rorschach or MMPI and then is forced to try to make some connection between the results and purposes of the research.

There may be many reasons guiding cross-cultural research, but most generally stated, the standard reason is that the researcher is interested in the relationships among specific variables under conditions where these variables have been modified extensively by cultural conditions. For instance, we might be concerned with differences in specific abilities between males and females. To determine whether cultural factors make a difference we could examine differences in a Western setting, where sexes receive approximately equal treatment during their formative years, and in a Middle Eastern or Southwest Asian setting where males are expected to develop many skills to a greater degree than females. A more frequent question that might be examined would have to do with the effects of a given pattern of child rearing on adult entrepreneurial behavior. In this case we would cast the problems in some theoretical context and then measure entrepreneurial outlooks by some method congenial with our theory.

As explained in Chapters 1 and 2, cross-cultural research designs are complicated by the fact that it is difficult to equate measures of both antecedent and consequent variables in two or more societies. Nor can it be assumed that all other conditions are constant to the same degree that one can when research is being carried out within one's own society. Because pairs of societies differ on many dimensions one cannot assert that a specific antecedent is the cause of a specified and measured adult behavior pattern. This is probably the reason that studies of childrearing in non-Western societies proved disappointing; they did not make it possible to rule out alternative explanations. This problem could be reduced by carrying out parallel studies in several societies, but such a strategy is extremely costly.

Finally, it must be remembered that almost all cross-cultural research is descriptive in method rather than experimental. Following the conceptualization of Cronbach (1957), cross-cultural research takes conditions as they exist and looks for relationships. Although we speak of cultures as "experimental conditions" we rarely design our research as true experiments (see Chapter 2). In the first place, subjects are not assigned randomly to societies and, secondly, we usually do not impose a second experimental condition on subjects, However, an experimental design is, in a sense, possible. Suppose that we want to determine whether praise has more effect on boys in Society A than in B. We can assign boys in A to high and low praise treatments and similarly boys from B. Then we have a 2 × 2 table with levels of praise on the ordinate and societies A and B on the abscissa. The interaction term then becomes the measure of culture. The more common approach is to measure an aspect of personality or psychopathology in two or more societies and then to interpret the outcome in terms of cultural patterns.

Let us suppose then that one has formulated a problem and developed a design in which one needs to measure aspects of personality. One would then choose or develop a measure that is congenial with the theoretical formulation of the questions posed by the researcher. If one is working within the psychoanalytic framework, for instance, one might be led to use the Rorschach or the Thematic Apperception Test. A problem formulated in behavioral terms might suggest a behavioral assessment with a checklist. Most pencil-and-paper inventories are based on common-sense trait theory or on typologies. The MMPI and CPI were designed to identify types — that is people who have certain characteristics — although many current interpreting practices treat the scales as traits. The EPPS, 16 PF, Eysenck's inventories, and Jackson's PRF and JPI (see below) were designed in various ways to measure traits. Each of the above measures has been used with English-speaking samples in alien societies. Most have been translated and demonstrated to have satisfactory reliability in translation, but there have been virtually no assessments of validity in nonWestern societies. Demonstrations of validity have also proven to be infrequent in their home societies, with the possible exception of the Minnesota Multiphasic Personality Inventory (see below) where there are occasional reports that the test differentiates a clinical from a normal group.

Those who construct tests offer different evidences of validity that vary with methods of construction. Those who use factor analysis rely on evidence that the translated items yield similar factors, as in the research in Sri Lanka by Perera and Eysenck (1984) who were able to achieve similar factor structures in a translated version of the Eysenck Personality Questionnaire. But that still leaves unanswered the question whether people high on neuroticism in Sri Lanka, for instance, are like those high on the same scale in the United Kingdom.

There is a broad split within the ranks of personality theorists. There are many who emphasize dispositional variables, or factors within people such as traits, needs, and drives, and there are also many who see the determinants of behavior as lying within the situation that a person faces. The former tend to be individual, clinical, and descriptive in orientation, while the latter are experimental in their preferred method of research. The whole base of operation of the personality measurement enterprise is in the former camp. Guthrie et al. (1983) encountered this problem in a study of the validity of Jackson's PRF (1974) with Philippine subjects. Their criteria were peer ratings of the traits that the PRF was designed to measure. This method of assessing validity, earlier shown to be quite workable in North America, turned out to be unsatisfactory with Philippine subjects because they did not think of their peers as having more or less fixed traits, but rather as responding to the social situation as the situation demanded. They were situationists to the core. At a fundamental level we were trying to measure something (traits) that did not exist for them.

Reliability and validity are affected by other factors as well. To varying degrees people have habits of responding that distort the results of self-report inventories. These response biases include the tendency to say *yes* or to agree with statements and the tendency to respond so as to place oneself in a favorable light. Asking respondents to choose between two equally desirable alternatives, as is done in the EPPS, is one way of reducing the effects of these tendencies. Balancing the number of *yes* and *no* answers and selecting items that are not related to scores on a *desirability* scale are other methods used with the PRF. But many older inventories and many special purpose symptom lists are most vulnerable to these sources of error. Although used widely, the California F scale is an example of a device where answering true frequently leads to a markedly elevated score. One should always scrutinize any potential measuring procedure to determine whether a majority of items tend to be scored plus for agreement and whether the content is so transparent that one can readily create a high or low score. These considerations are especially important where the respondent has an interest in creating a favorable impression on the one who is administering the instrument.

Similar considerations apply to the measurement of psychopathology. The authors of the MMPI have tried to cope with these problems with a variety of validity scales, including the K scale that was designed to correct clinical scales both for tendencies to minimize symptoms and for tendencies to exaggerate difficulties. It is also the case that different types of patients, in North America at least, demonstrate differing degrees of defensiveness. Depressed people and most schizophrenic patients admit their difficulties while suspicious paranoids and sociopaths often deny symptoms. Measurement problems thus vary depending on the cultural background of patients and probably with the disorder, if any, that a respondent may be experiencing.

Finally, there are other problems that may arise if one finds it necessary to develop a special purpose measuring procedure. In a review of alienation research, for instance, Guthrie and Tanco (1980) report that some investigators used scales of three to five items which must inevitably be of low reliability. Others selected the best items for a variety of scales and combined them into a new instrument without giving sufficient attention to whether the parts could justifiably be added. As a result the total score could be ambiguous.

In summary, then, there is a great danger that data on personality or psychopathology may be artefactual for a variety of reasons. These sources of measurement error can be reduced if the investigator examines his or her instruments carefully, scrutinizes authors' test manuals, and examines each data collection method in the light of reports in the literature. One can usually benefit also by seeking the advice of someone expert in the construction and interpretation of inventories.

Levels of Sophistication in Measurement

When gathering data on abstract personological variables, the data should be analyzable, permitting the researcher to make statements confidently about possible relationships between the variables (see Chapters 1 and 2 for more detailed discussion). Because there is often a strong tendency for cross-cultural data to be "messy" or otherwise difficult to prepare for proper analysis, researchers should take care in gathering data and preparing them for analysis.

Tseng and Tseng (1982) assert that in attempting to measure abstract concepts of personality, the *applicability* of specific techniques to a set of empirical data should be a "necessary precondition for further analysis." They list four levels of sophistication in technique, arranged in order of importance. The first three are (1) *mechanical computability* (can statistical formulas and/or computing instructions be adapted and applied to the data?), (2) *statistical adaptability* (can statistical models or equations be used with the anticipation of reasonable outcome?), (3) measurement suitability (is there compatibility between the measurement properties of the data and the analytic strategies to be used?). The fourth and highest level of sophistication is what they call *nomological operationalization*. Tseng and Tseng describe this as having the properties of integrated assessment of the "three-way nomological relations among the theoretical rationale of person perception and human cognition [e.g. how we evaluate and think about others], the psychological properties of measurement procedures and data, and the intrinsic characteristics of statistical techniques" (p. 234). The characteristics of a research program of this type would be stringent, but if followed the Tsengs feel that they will guarantee that the empirical results from data gathering and analysis are generalizable and impartial.

This notion of *nomological operationalization* can be considered in the same breath with Campbell and Fiske's (1959) well-known advocation of the process of convergent and discriminant validation using a multi-trait, multi-method matrix of correlations. Although this sounds like it involves a complicated procedure, it is rather straightforward, and has often been used to determine the validity of scales or tests that purport to measure some construct of personality or psychopathology.

For example, suppose that a bank president wants us to design a scale to measure honesty so that dishonest bank applicants could be identified. Although we might balk at this task because we cannot conceive of honesty being measurable (or to be "nomologically operationalized" sufficiently well to provide us with analyzable data), we might nevertheless try to measure honesty and come up with a useful scale. Perhaps a multi-item scale could contain a number of "true–false" items such as "I have never stolen anything." We could balance the number of items answered true for honesty with those answered false. We could then compute item-by-item and total scale correlations with an independent measure of social desirability (or attempts to be considered in a favorable light), eliminating or rewriting items on our "honesty" scale that are highly correlated with desirability. Independently, we could develop one or two other measures of honesty, such as manager's ratings, employment records that lend themselves to quantification, or judgments made by co-workers of the person being assessed. In addition, we could administer some scales designed to measure traits that might be confused with honesty, such as conservatism, conformity, and

244

responsibility. In this way, one develops several different methods to measure several traits. This procedure can lead to a table of multi-traits, multi-method correlations, and one can examine it for evidence that our honesty scale is doing its intended job.

This scale will pass the test insofar as scores on it correlate well with other measures of honesty based on other methods (like interviews and peer ratings); this would be the convergent validation aspect of the procedure. But the scale should correlate at low levels with measures of traits that might be confused with honesty, and measured by using the same kinds of methods, but which in fact measure *other* "operational" personological variables; this is the discriminant validation part of the procedure.

An Overview of Viable Cross-Cultural Measures of Personality/Pathology

In their book on cross-cultural research methods, Brislin, Lonner, and Thorndike (1973) gave brief summaries of several tests that at that time appeared to be well suited for cross-cultural research, theoretically and empirically, on a more or less continuing experimental basis. The list was not presented as definitive, and it was noted that the decided American and British flavor of nearly all the items on the list merely reflected the general one-sidedness of test construction and validation. Moreover, the list did not contain projectives, which were dealt with in another section of the book. The items in the "Personality–Interest" domain, in alphabetical order, were: Adjective Check List, California Psychological Inventory, Eysenck Personality Inventory, Minnesota Multiphasic Personality Inventory, Rotter's I–E (Locus of Control) Scale, Semantic Differential Technique, Sixteen PF Test, Strong Vocational Interest Blank, Study of Values Survey of Personal Values, and the Ways to Live Questionnaire. Only the first seven of these seem to have retained some cross-cultural visibility and interest since the list appeared; in hindsight, the State–Trait Anxiety Inventory should have been included in that list. The same could be said for a few other standard, multi-scale personality tests, such as the Edwards Personal Preference Schedule or the Personality Research Form. On the following pages we will give a brief, contemporary overview of these measures, presented alphabetically.

The inclusion of these tests does not necessarily imply our endorsement of any one or more of them over others that are not mentioned. Moreover, we realize that the field researcher may have limited access to the tests or inventories themselves, or — perhaps more importantly — may not have computer and scoring facilities at his or her disposal. Among the more important things that these summaries may provide are the rationale used in the development of these data-gathering devices, and the assumptions made about the range of variation in personality or psychopathology among human beings as well as the sociocultural factors that contribute to such variations. Furthermore, some of the methods, because of their popularity or overall potential usefulness, are discussed in somewhat more detail because of the issues that are involved.

Adjective Check List (ACL). The ACL (Gough & Heilbrun, 1980) consists of 300 self- or other-descriptive adjectives that are to be endorsed ("checked") if they are deemed descriptive of self or some specified other person. The list has its historical roots in the work of Allport and Odbert (1936) and others who can be identified with trait theories of personality. The assumption is that the traits included on the ACL represent the broad spectrum of personality types or dispositions, and therefore can be adapted for numerous uses. The ACL has been translated into many languages. For complete information on the available translations and recommendations for research, consult the Revised Adjective Check List Manual (Gough & Heilbrun, 1984). A most extensive use of the ACL is the ongoing multinational project of measuring sex-trait stereotypes (Williams & Best, 1982).

California Psychological Inventory (CPI). In the United States, the CPI is the second most frequently used objective personality measure (after the MMPI). Its 18 basic scales are focussed on interpersonal behavior or social interaction. Constructs such as Dominance, Tolerance, and Responsibility are termed "folk concepts," which Gough (1968) defines as "aspects and attributes of interpersonal behavior that are to be found in all cultures and societies, and that possess a direct and integral relationship to all forms of social interaction." These folk concepts make the CPI relatively easy to translate (there are currently about thirty translations in use), and also make the scales more meaningful and comprehensible than, for example, an inventory that might be based on esoteric theoretical concepts. The 480-item, self-report, and criterion-keyed inventory is not based on any personality theory, nor does it purport to measure personality traits. Rather, the purpose of each scale is *"to predict what an individual will do in a specified context,* and/or *to identify individuals who will be described in a certain way"* (Gough, 1968).

The most recent CPI manual (Gough, 1975) will be updated in 1986, and will reflect some changes in the inventory and in its interpretation. These include reducing the number of items, shortening some scales while lengthening others, and adding two new full scales. Other modifications will also be introduced, few of which at present have any noteworthy cross-cultural validity.

Edwards Personal Preference Schedule (EPPS). The EPPS (Edwards, 1959) is a self-report inventory that purports to measure 15 of approximately 28 needs that are an important aspect of Murray's (1938) personological system. These needs (*n* Affiliation, *n* Dominance, and *n* Order, for example) have been incorporated into much of contemporary psychological theory and research.

Eysenck Personality Questionnaire (EPQ). This paper-and-pencil measure, like its predecessors the Maudsley Personality Inventory and the Eysenck Personality Inventory, is a standard self-report device. It has been used extensively in a wide range of psychological studies, mainly in England, but also cross-culturally. The evolution of the EPQ (Eysenck & Eysenck, 1975) parallels the evolution of Eysenck's theory of personality, a summary of which can be found in most broad-banded textbooks on personality theories or abnormal psychology. Variously called neurophysiological, genetically-based, neo-Pavlovian, complex, and reductionistic, Eysenck's personality theory asserts that there are three continua or dimensions that constitute the human personality: Extraversion-Introversion, Neuroticism (high to low), and Psychoticism (high to low). It is purported that all individuals can be placed within this scheme. Recently, a Lie scale has been added to these factors, and it may measure another personality dimension, called conformity. Yet another factor may be intelligence.

Described as a "rifle" (few specific factors) approach rather than a "shotgun" (multidimensional) approach, this perspective, if valid, has a simplicity about it that is attractive to any cross-cultural researcher who is in search of a few basic, panculturally meaningful dimensions on which to compare people. Those who work with the EPQ cross-culturally have a few common goals. One of them is to determine if people from different cultures have the same personality factors. In the words of the Eysencks, the major purpose is to "validate a fundamental theory of human nature involving the definition and measurement of the major dimensions of personality" (Eysenck & Eysenck, 1982, p. 302). If it is ascertained that those few personality factors are culturally generalizable, then other goals can be pursued. These would include the construction of scoring keys for each country and the quantification and interpretation of mean scores and profiles achieved by people from different countries (Eysenck & Eysenck, 1983; S.B.G. Eysenck & Opolot, 1983; Perera & S.B.G. Eysenck, 1984).

Locus of Control (I–E Scale). The social learning theory-generated notion of locus of control refers to expectancies about who controls reinforcement. Also referred to as internal–external control of reinforcement, the concept refers to the degree to which one accepts personal responsibility for what happens to him or her (internal control) as opposed to attributing responsibility to factors that are beyond one's personal control, such as luck, fate, or chance (external control).

The concept was first systematically outlined by Rotter (1966), and has generated a staggering amount of research and interest. Two books (Lefcourt, 1982; Phares, 1976) are standard resources, and nearly every contemporary textbook on personality theory or personality research and assessment includes reviews or evaluations of locus of control (e.g. Corsini and Marsella, 1982; Feshbach & Weiner, 1982). Different "locus of control" scales have appeared. Because of their relative (and perhaps incorrectly alleged) simplicity, assumed ease of administration, and obvious relatedness to a likely universal process (expectations about life events, and the extent to which these expectations are reinforced or confirmed by one's own actions), they have drawn considerable interest. The concept of locus of control cuts across social, clinical, and political realms, and has direct relevance to experiences such as social alienation, learned helplessness, and a fairly common desire to achieve the Western ideal of self-determination and personal autonomy. Unsurprisingly, this simple device has attracted considerable attention cross-culturally (e.g. Jones & Zoppel, 1979; Munro, 1979; Niles, 1981; Trimble & Richardson, 1982).

The generic form is known as the I–E Scale. It consists of 23 items (plus six filler items which disguise the purpose of the test), each containing two statements such as the following:

1. a. Most people are victims of circumstances.
   b. What happens to a person is pretty much of his or her own making.
2. a. No matter how hard you study, the grade you get has already been more or less determined by the teacher.
   b. The only way to get good grades is to study hard so that you can earn them.

In both examples, alternative "a" is the "external" option.

While it is easy to use the terms *internals* and *externals*, I–E is actually a continuum and not a typology. A person can fall anywhere along that continuum, with end points labeled external and internal. As in most typologies, most people are clustered somewhere in the middle. The terms internals and externals are semantic conveniences. A host of variables have been studied by using this scale and its various offspring, and, not surprisingly, numerous findings have been reported. A sampling:

1. In social influence, externals are likely to be compliant and conforming.
2. Internals tend more than externals to seek knowledge about their environment.
3. Externals attribute the responsibility of their own behavior to factors which lie beyond their control.
4. Internals are more achievement-oriented, work harder, and delay gratification.
5. Easterners are typically more external than Westerners.
6. People from industrial nations are more internal than people from developing nations.
7. Men tend to be internal, woman external.
8. Internals are more socially active.
9. Internals are better adjusted, less anxious, and less likely to be burdened with psychiatric labels.

In his review of the literature, Phares (1984) suggests that the origins of I–E beliefs fall into three general categories. The first is in the area of *family antecedents*, wherein child-rearing practices that are "warm, protective, positive, and nurturant seem to be related to the subsequent development of internal locus of control." The second is the *consistency of experience* dimension. Inconsistent parental discipline may foster the perception that the world is capricious and unpredictable. The third antecedent is *social*, whereby individuals who enjoy little access to power, social mobility, opportunities for personal or financial growth, or material advantages would be predisposed toward an external belief system. It is easy to see how the concept of locus of control, based upon the nature of these origins, and learned helplessness (Seligman, 1975) are highly related. It is similarly simple to make the connection between locus of control and two other research orientations that have enjoyed considerable cross-cultural success — McClelland's (1961) need for achievement and Witkin's cognitive style framework (Witkin & Berry, 1975; Witkin & Goodenough, 1981). It is also easy to understand the attraction that this concept has had to many individuals who have studied personality variations across cultures and within multicultural societies.

Although it is not our intent to review the voluminous cross-cultural publications that have dealt with the I–E Scale, we will present a brief overview of some of the major cross-cultural findings. In the process, we will underscore the fact that if locus of control, or I–E, has any meaning at all, it usually comes by way of factor structures that appear to vary across different cultural groups.

A factor analysis of the response of 170 Brazilian women who took the Portuguese version of the I–E Scale uncovered two factors (Nagelschmidt & Jakob, 1977). One factor, they said, was close to the original internal versus external control, while the other was termed "fatalism," which linked items on that factor to a sense of "definiteness" of things; the world is seen as ruled by powerful others.

Jones and Zoppel (1979) administered the scale to 159 subjects from three different populations — two samples of Black Americans from different backgrounds and one sample of Black Jamaicans. Through factor analysis emerged what the authors called a striking finding — that for each group there was a substantially different factor structure, and that those structures did not resemble those found by other researchers. Niles (1981) found two factors — fatalism and powerlessness — in Sri Lanka, again supporting the multi-dimensionality of the construct.

Further support for the multidimensionality of the concept comes from a study by Trimble and Richardson (1982). Their large (N = 740) sample of American Indians came from five different sites. Nine factors emerged, and through the technique of hierarchical clustering, five clusters emerged.

Finally, Munro (1979) demonstrated in Africa that the standard I–E Scale can be cross-validated with locally constructed scales or questionnaires that are designed to be sensitive to culture-specific interpretations of events and causality.

This simple scale and its variations will no doubt continue to be used to help contribute to an understanding of some major differences between groups with different cultural orientations. Moreover, refinements or extensions of the construct of control will certainly continue to be popular in cross-cultural research. Recently, for instance, a distinction has been made between primary control and secondary control (Weisz, Rothbaum, & Blackburn, 1984). The general strategy in primary control is to influence existing realities, while accommodating to existing realities is the goal of secondary control (in which four different forms have been postulated). Weisz et al. (1984) contrasted the United States with Japan, perhaps two of the better examples of primary and secondary control cultures, respectively, in the areas of childrearing, socialization, religion and philosophy, work, and psychotherapy. This two-process model of control is at least an interesting heuristic; developing a device which is simple to use and to translate in order to measure these dimensions will be challenging.

We have devoted more attention to the notion of control and its cross-cultural measurement than to others because the concept of being able to do something about one's circumstances—efficacy (Inkeles & Smith, 1974), is very useful in the study and promotion of socioeconomic development. In addition, the I–E Scale has been subject to a good deal of evaluation by factor analysis in a number of countries yielding results indicating important differences in the structure of the concept. Similar country-to-country differences occur with respect to symptoms of schizophrenia and of depression. But very similar structures appear on the EPQ (Perera & S.B.G. Eysenck, 1984) and on the PRF (Jackson et al., 1983). The implication is that we cannot assume similarity of concepts without checking for it.

Minnesota Multiphasic Personality Inventory. In the assessment of psychopathology, both in the United States and in cross-cultural research, certainly the most widely used psychological test is the 556-item, self-report Minnesota Multiphasic Personality Inventory (MMPI). There have been many summaries of the applications of the MMPI in US Settings, including Dahlstrom and Welsh (1960) and Rannigan (1985), while Butcher (1979), Butcher and Pancheri (1979), and Butcher and Clark (1979) have reviewed research in other societies. A number of short forms of the MMPI are available (Faschingbauer & Newmark, 1978), which have drawn both cautionary notes (Butcher, Kendall, & Hoffman, 1980) and concerns about their reliability (McLaughlin, Helms, & Howe, 1983).

Anyone considering using the MMPI should be aware of the purposes of the original authors, the theory of psychopathology they held and the methods of scale construction they used. Each of these factors has important implications. The MMPI was developed in the early 1940s in Minnesota with the stated purpose of providing the user with an assessment of some of the major dimensions of psychopathology that a physician might encounter in general practice. It was designed to answer a series of questions: Is this patient a hypochondriac? Is he/she depressed? Is he/she an hysteric? and so on for the nine syndromes implied by the nine clinical scales. After they began giving the test it became apparent to early users that the scales were not independent of one another and that an interpreter had to pay attention to the *pattern* of scores rather than to each score by itself. The interpretations of the scales shifted from types to traits.

The test authors worked within the framework of descriptive psychiatry, an orientation that avoided a dogmatic emphasis on genetic or learned or unconscious determinants of symptoms. The MMPI can probably best be characterized as having an atheoretical basis. The treatment implications of various configurations of scale scores were developed from clinical experience rather than deduced from theoretical formulations.

The authors' orientation is most clearly seen in their methods of scale construction. Following the method used to derive the Strong Vocational Interest Blank, they used empirical item selection strategies in which the responses of a defined sample of patients are compared item by item with a normal or general group and then items on which the sample differs significantly are used to form a new scale. In the case of the MMPI, using psychiatry texts, earlier tests, patients' statements during interviews and their own clinical experiences, the authors assembled a pool of 550 statements which gave a broad coverage of symptoms that various disturbed persons might make in an evaluation setting.

Each subject was asked to read each statement and indicate whether it was true or mostly true or false or mostly false as it applied to him/her. The authors asked, "How do hypochondriacs, depressed people, or hysterics, etc. differ from normals of similar age and background?" A sample of 541 normals was obtained from persons visiting patients at the University of Minnesota Hospital, visitors who were not themselves under a physician's care nor were they visiting the psychiatric wards. The samples of patients carrying various diagnoses were assembled from those seen on the psychiatric wards and as referrals.

For each scale the MMPI authors collected responses from approximately 50 patients who presented relatively unmixed pictures of one of the nine syndromes in which the authors were interested — 50 hypochondriacs, 50 depressed patients, 50 paranoids, etc. The hypochondriasis scale (H_s) was made up of those items which the 50 or so people diagnosed as hypochondriac answered differently, either more frequently true or more often false, to a significant degree than did the normals. Item 125, *I have a great deal of stomach trouble*, appears on the H_s scale. More hypochondriac patients answered the statement true than did the 10 to 15 percent of normals who responded true. Not all items, however, are so obvious. Item 231, *I like to talk about sex*, on the psychopathic deviate (P_d) scale is keyed false so that those who deny the statement get one plus for psychopathic deviate. The individual scales were assembled from the 550-item pool, purely on the basis that each item differentiated a clinical group from normals and that this item stood up on cross-validation with a new sample of the same diagnosis. The method of empirical item selection is blind to the content of the items and entails no theory that patients of a given diagnosis should say specific things about themselves. The method also selects all items on which the clinical sample differs from normals, including cultural differences. The role of cultural factors is most apparent in the case of the M_f (masculinity–femininity) scale. The clinical population had a representation of middle class, urban, male homosexuals with the result that urban, educated males tend to score very high on M_f because they share many views with the clinical group as opposed to the less educated, rural males of the normal group.

Anyone who considers using the MMPI in cross-cultural research should keep in mind that the scales were developed in a specific cultural setting some years ago and that the scales are still made up of those items that were answered differently by certain rural patient groups when compared with a sample of mostly rural nonpatients. The *rural* comes about because the University of Minnesota hospitals served Minnesotans outside of Minneapolis and St Paul. The latter were served by city public hospitals. These circumstances of sampling and of item selection, however, reduced rather than augmented the cultural bias of the scales. If the normal sample had been representative of the whole country, cultural differences would have been much more prominent in the clinical scales. Recall that the method of empirical item selection is blind to the content of items, and to the extraneous factors on which the clinical sample and the normal group may also differ. For instance, if a clinical sample of schizophrenics has less education on the average than the normal group the two groups may differ on items reflective of schizophrenia.

The implication of all this for the researcher who wants to use the MMPI in various cultures is that the scales may or may not measure the syndromes implied by the names of the scales. An inspection of the items in the scale by someone who understands the culture of the research area is not satisfactory by itself because the MMPI scales contain many items whose psychiatric implications are by no means obvious. Empirical item selection was used to improve measurement over scales developed by selection of items on face validity only. Items whose implication are clear to judges are also clear to most subjects. What we have then is a series of scales that have been developed by a procedure that identifies all differences, clinical and social, between a group of patients and a group of socially similar nonpatients within, of course, the limitations of the coverage of the item pool.

The implications of the foregoing are compounded by translation (see Chapter 5). The items of most inventories are in the idiom of the authors. Consider Item 110: *Someone has it in for me*. How does one render such an item in a Philippine language version, or even in a French language version? A word-by-word literal translation would probably meet the criterion of back-translation to English but it might not give the same emotional meaning in the second language. It is our opinion that re-standardization is necessary if one translates an inventory. Evidence of test–retest reliability is not sufficient; a scale may be reliable but of unsatisfactory validity.

In their review of the applications of the MMPI in other societies, Butcher and Clark (1979) report for the most part clinical applications of the test. As a rule, the items are translated and the same scales are used, often with the same norms. There are virtually no re-standardizations or checks on the validity of the translated form. The authors counsel against revisions because a revised test cannot be interpreted in the light of the vast body of research and clinical experience that has grown up around the current version.

Of all groups outside the United States it would appear that the Japanese have attempted to adapt the test more than researchers from other countries. New scales have been added and sets of items for current diagnostic categories have been freshly derived from groups of Japanese patients contrasted with groups of Japanese normals. Some of their findings are very interesting to those concerned with cross-cultural differences. Hidano (1967) began by modifying and adding items. Empirical item selection techniques, as with the development of the test, were used to develop new scales and norms were derived. The important question now is whether the same items appeared on the scales because, if different items are found to discriminate, use of the original test even in translation does not seem warranted. Overlap with original MMPI scales ranged from 3 items for P_a to 23 items for the F scale, a scale that has 64 items. This means that at best fewer than one-third of the items on MMPI scales have cross-cultural validity in the case of Japan. We do not know what the situation is for other non-English-speaking countries because little attention has been paid to the question. If an investigator merely checks the mean and test-retest reliability of an MMPI scale in a second culture he/she will not know whether the scale is measuring the same thing as it measured in Minnesota. Indeed, no one will know if it is measuring anything at all. With the advent of lower cost, small computers it is hoped that others will follow the example of Hidano in other societies. Data reduction that once proved a formidable deterrent is no longer so. The principal difficulty now is getting enough patients of various diagnoses and selecting and getting data from a normal group. Of course, the same facilities are even more accessible to American researchers but no one has brought out a revised version of the MMPI or constructed a new test that might capitalize on what has been learned from the development and use of the MMPI.

Personality Research Form (PRF). This is one of a series of tests prepared by Jackson using a different approach to item selection. He begins by carefully defining the traits he plans to measure and then writes and edits items for each trait selected. The items are given to more than 100 subjects and tentative scores are derived by scoring each scale using an *a priori* key. Correlations are then computed between each item and the total score of its scale, the other total scale scores, and a measure of desirability. Items are then selected for each scale that have highest correlations with scale score and low correlations with scores on other scales and with desirability. The procedure is very simple and inexpensive with computers. The product is a scale that is usually quite independent of other scales and one that is not distorted by the respondent's tendency to place himself in a favorable light. Guthrie et al. (1983) and Jackson et al. (1983) repeated the standardization of the PRF in the Philippines, finding that items stayed with the same scales, and that scales were reliable. But validity as assessed against peer ratings was disappointing. It was found also that some scales had different meanings in the Philippines from that which the test author had in mind when he constructed them.

Sixteen Personality Factor Test (16 PF). The 16 PF is a paper-and-pencil inventory that purports to measure the 16 "primary" and several "second-order" dimensions of personality that Cattell claims to have found through factor analysis. Influenced by Allport and Odbert's (1936) psycholexical study of trait-labels in the English language, Cattell took 171 of these common, nonorthogonal (relatively unrelated) adjectives, developed a huge item-by-item correlation matrix after preliminary try-out, and named the clusters that factor analysis identified. The names of the dimensions include Reserved versus Outgoing (Factor A), Shy versus Venturesome (Factor H), and Relaxed versus Tense (Factor Q4). These and the other 13 factors are more or less standard personality dimensions. Cattell, however, had a penchant for giving these dimensions their own identities. Thus, Reserved is "sizothymia," Shy is "threctia," and Relaxed is "low ergic tension." The four principal second-order factors are anxiety, extraversion versus introversion, tough poise versus responsive emotionality, and independence versus dependence.

Those who extend the 16 PF to other countries have the same goals as those who use other inventories: Translate it and determine if the same personality structure exists elsewhere. Tsujioka and Cattell (1965) claimed that marked progress had been made cross-culturally at the primary source trait level, but that little was known about cultural variations at the secondary source trait level. Brislin, Lonner, and Thorndike (1973) reported that the 16 PF at that time was among the most popular psychological tests in use cross-culturally. The same statement cannot be made today, however.

State–Trait Anxiety Inventory (STAI). Numerous tests and inventories have been developed to measure anxiety, a construct which any theory of personality or pathology with or without cross-cultural aspirations must attempt to explain or define. Among the most widely used measures of anxiety is the STAI (Spielberger, Gorsuch, & Lushene, 1970). This inventory has enjoyed extensive international use, both for the measurement of anxiety within specific countries and for culture-comparative analysis (Spielberger & Diaz-Guerrero, 1976, 1983).

The distinction between state and trait anxiety was first made by Cattell (Cattell & Scheier, 1961), and has more recently been elaborated by Spielberger and his colleagues and a growing list of individuals who have used the STAI in various countries. Spielberger defines state anxiety (A-State) as a "transitory emotional state or condition of the organism that varies in intensity and fluctuates over time," whereas trait anxiety (A-Trait) is considered to be a "relatively stable disposition to perceive a wide range of stimulus situations as dangerous or threatening, and to respond to such threats with A-State reactions" (see Spielberger & Diaz-Guerrero, 1976, pp. 90–91).

The A-State scale of the STAI consists of 20 statements that describe feelings as they are currently being experienced, such as "I am worried," "I feel happy," or "I am jittery." The 20 items on the A-Trait scale are more generally descriptive, such as "I lack self-confidence" and "I try to avoid facing a crisis or difficulty." A subject's score is simply the weighted sum of response on a 4-point scale. As reported by Cronbach (1984), the trait scale correlates nearly 0.8 with other anxiety scales and its test-retest reliability over three months is at that level.

The many attempts to translate and use the STAI in diverse cultures have generally been successful, and the inventory at least has proven to be an important heuristic device. However, since there is neither one completely accepted definition of anxiety nor one totally endorsed paper-and-pencil measure of it in North America, it should come as no surprise if attempts to use the STAI in other cultures run afoul. Because anxiety may take on different meanings and have different antecedents elsewhere, the problems of linguistic, functional, and conceptual equivalence will be of continued concern. This is not to fault the STAI or its authors' intent, for their contributions merit praise. One may indeed measure "anxiety" elsewhere, in accordance with the authors' definition; one may also, however, be missing something important in another culture because the STAI may not be equipped to measure it. A thermometer can measure heat uniformly, but it cannot be expected to measure simultaneously other important environmental factors such as humidity, quality of the air, and wind velocity.

The interpretation given by Eysenck and Eysenck (1982) of cross-cultural research with the STAI, compared with cross-cultural research using two other paper-and-pencil tests, is instructive. The Eysencks claim that Spielberger and his colleagues:

> ... are not concerned either with a psychiatric system of nosology (as are the MMPI authors) or with a fundamental system of personality description (as are the Eysencks). The aim of Spielberger and his colleagues is a relatively simple one (that being the adaptation of the state or trait scales for use in other countries). Success cannot be gainsaid, although from the point of view of transcultural comparison of mean values, the evidence is not sufficient to enable us to attribute much meaning to such comparisons.

Yet, despite that critical observation, the STAI represents the best contemporary paper-and-pencil approach to the measurement of anxiety which, however (and if ever) it may finally be defined to everyone's satisfaction, is certainly one of the more fundamental human emotions.

Projective Techniques

Holtzman (1980) began his chapter on the cross-cultural use of projective techniques with the following sentence: "Prophets, sooth-sayers, and personologists for centuries have searched for the hidden meaning in what an individual reports seeing in clouds, inkblots, and other ambiguous stimuli" (p. 246). He might well have added, and in fact implies in his review, that most cross-cultural methodologists have searched for good, solid reasons to include projectives among their data-gathering techniques, and have more often than not come up short. Projectives are, however, in continued use, and often are the preferred instrument. Projective methodology and its rationale has been among the more controversial areas in the behavioral sciences; cross-culturally, the divisiveness is even more pronounced.

The cross-cultural field worker who either anticipates using projectives or wishes to consider them would be wise to review the issues and the arguments surrounding their use in other cultures or for culture-comparative projects. Space limitations do not permit us to cover the advantages and disadvantages of using projective tests cross-culturally. The interested field worker should study this topic independently and intensively. In addition to Holtzman's (1980) extensive treatment of projectives, one would benefit from a perusal of the first comprehensive evaluation of the cross-cultural evidence surrounding their use (Lindzey, 1961). Sandwiched between these reviews are variable-length treatments of projectives by Abel (1973), Spain (1972), Molish (1972), Manaster and Havighurst (1972), and Brislin, Lonner, and Thorndike (1973). More recent and brief synopses of projectives and their use cross-culturally can be found in Lonner (1981), Sundberg and Gonzales (1981), and Draguns (1984).

ASSESSMENT OF PSYCHOPATHOLOGY

Research workers with many different purposes and orientations have reasons to be interested in data on the incidence, prevalence, course, treatment, and symptom pictures of various behavioral disorders in different societies. To the psychoanalytically inclined, data on early childhood experiences and on adult behavior patterns provide an opportunity to apply or evaluate psychoanalytic theories that place much emphasis on the significance of the first few years of life. Other societies provide variations in childhood experiences that cannot be found in or imposed on one's society. Socially- or interpersonally oriented therapists can find in alien societies patterns of parent–child and sibling–sibling relationships that cannot be found in their own society. For instance, throughout much of Polynesia there is a pattern of fosterage in which babies and children are informally adopted by other couples who raise them as their own. Children may pass through several sets of parents in the course of a decade. What little evidence there is suggests that the adoptees are not adversely affected. This poorly documented conclusion calls into question our emphasis on the importance of the stability of parental models and of parent–child relationships.

Even someone interested in genetics can find much of interest in societies with different gene pools. Much light could be shed on the heritability of disorders by considering data in other societies. The larger nuclear and extended families of traditional societies also provide excellent opportunities for pedigree studies of schizophrenia, depression, or paranoia. Whereas the modal schizophrenic may have two siblings in the United States, he may have six in the Philippines. Numbers of other blood relatives are similarly larger.

The opportunities outlined above have, however, not been exploited. Such research would be difficult because few psychiatrically disturbed have been identified because they are kept at home, and fewer still have received careful study and diagnosis. In addition, symptom pictures vary from those in standard Western practice. Clinical syndromes may be distorted by concurrent disease processes such as tuberculosis or malaria, by local herbal medicines, and by indigenous brief systems about the role of ancestral spirits and other forces that usually do not figure in the illness of patients in North America. A major problem, therefore, in cross-cultural research on mental illness is that of making sure of the equivalence of diagnoses. When we make comparisons and find differences we must be sure that the differences do not simply reflect differences in diagnostic practices.

But what if there are differences in the incidence and symptom pictures of paranoid schizophrenia between two societies? Let us imagine that the belief system in one culture emphasizes sorcery so that the members spend time and effort protecting themselves from the ill-will of others. Such a social climate would exacerbate paranoid patterns of thought but might lead indigenous diagnosticians to label fewer disturbed persons as paranoid. Both symptom formation and diagnostic formulation go on within a social context; belief systems have the potential to modify both symptom formation and diagnostic practices.

Some may argue that the search for cross-cultural agreement on diagnosis is an inappropriate application of the medical model to disorders of behavior. Certainly major diseases such as tuberculosis, malaria, and leprosy can be diagnosed with considerable accuracy in different settings with the aid of standard laboratory procedures. It is because there are no comparable laboratory techniques for schizophrenia, depression, or sociopathy that comparability of diagnosis is a problem.

There is also a paradox because if cultural factors modify symptom formation, as has been assumed by those interested in this area of research, one would not expect the major symptom syndromes to be constant across societies. Within the United States it has been found that the treatment milieu of crowded wards, before the advent of policies that reduced the use of hospitals, produced or made worse many of the symptoms that had been considered the inevitable result of a chronic deteriorative schizophrenic process. In other societies, as in the United States, for example, reactions to psychopathology by those who are not disordered have a profound influence on the course of a psychiatric disorder.

In addition to the interaction of culture and behavior disorder that we have just described there are syndromes that are unique to certain societies. These *culture bound* syndromes include such disorders as *latah*, an exaggerated startle response found in older Malay women, *koro*, a fear among some Chinese males that their penis is being drawn into their abdominal cavity, and *bulimia*, a binge and purge eating pattern among young, American, middle-class women. The facts that these disorders seem to be confined to specific sociocultural groups, and do not have plausible organic bases suggest strongly that they are learned and are without unique organic etiology.

Comments on the Study of Schizophrenia across Cultures

In an extensive attempt to deal with the problem of variations in diagnoses and the associated difficulties in cross-cultural comparisons, the World Health Organization has sponsored an International Pilot Study of Schizophrenia (IPSS) (Sartorius, Shapiro, & Jablensky 1974). Designed to develop standardized research instruments and procedures, this project involved collaboration of psychiatrists and mental health workers from nine countries: Colombia, Czechoslovakia, Denmark, India, Nigeria, Taiwan, USSR, United Kingdom and United States. The study was designed to cope with frequent problems, including (1) differing diagnostic criteria, (2) variations in methods of assessment, (3) variations in definitions of outcome criteria, (4) variations in methods of follow-up, and (5) insufficient consideration of intervening factors that affect course and outcome. This was a tall order entailing almost a decade of work. Anyone considering cross-cultural research in psychopathology should study the IPSS reports carefully; they confront many of the problems one might encounter as well as many of which one might be unaware.

As summarized by Sartorius et al. (1974), the project involved designing and planning, selection of field research centers, training of participants, identification of patients, selection and standardization of instruments (various rating forms for the most part), and finally, collection and analysis of data. The study was designed to answer such major questions as: (1) In what sense can it be said that schizophrenic disorders exist in different parts of the world? (2) Are there groups of patients with similar symptoms in each country? (3) Are there groups that can be considered unique to one or more countries? (4) Does the course of the disorder vary? (5) How do patients called schizophrenic differ from other categories of patients in various countries, i.e. are there unique problems of differential diagnosis in some countries? For data collection, they relied primarily on the Present State Examination (PSE) (Wing, Cooper, & Sartorius, 1974), and also on the Psychiatric History Schedule and the Social Description Schedule.

The PSE (Sartorius et al., 1974, pp. 76–79) is based on an extended 60- to 90-minute interview in which the interviewer rates both observations and the patient's responses to questions. For example, the interviewer rates whether or not the patient shows a bland, expressionless face, and tabulates yes or no to the patient's response to, "Do you think people want to harm you?" The ratings and questions deal with explicit matters so that the interviewer does not have to draw inferences. We can contrast this approach with a more holistic assessment such as that offered by Grinker and Holtzman (1973). They offered five distinguishing features of schizophrenia: (1) presence of a thought disorder, (2) reduced capacity for pleasure, (3) characterological dependency, (4) significant impairment of social competence, and (5) exquisitely vulnerable sense of self-regard. Such a tabulation of schizophrenia characteristics may give one the sense that he is getting at the essence of the schizophrenic process, but it would be virtually unusable in cross-cultural research even if the raters were all members of the same society as the people being rated. These criteria would not be useful to an outside investigator who was working through an interpreter.

Another, less cumbersome evaluating scheme is that of Schneider (1971) who offered 11 first-ranked symptoms (FRS) which he felt were discriminating and pathognomonic, or strongly indicative of schizophrenia. The FRS included audible thoughts, voices commenting on the patients' activity, and thought insertion.

With the aid of computers, Carpenter, Strauss, and Bartko (1974) and Bartko, Strauss, and Carpenter (1974) applied clustering and other multivariate techniques to the PSE data. Anyone considering cross-cultural research in psychopathology should study carefully the IPSS reports. The problems are formidable but they must be faced, because failure to do so will likely lead to results that have many alternative explanations.

But schizophrenia is not the only disorder that should be examined from a cultural perspective. Recent evidence that a neurochemical defect, a disorder of neurotransmitters, may be a major factor in symptom formation and maintenance would suggest that cultural factors may not play a major, direct, causal role. If we want to learn about the contribution of culture to psychopathology we should direct our attention to functional disorders where interpersonal behavior and beliefs may play a larger role. But, in contrast to IPPS, there are no extensive studies of neuroses, psycho-physiological disorders, or sociopathic behavior across two or more societies. There are, however, very interesting studies of depression.

Comments on the Study of Depression across Cultures

Marsella (1985) has provided a very useful review of the problems one can and should encounter in studying depression in different societies. He notes that:

> Cross-cultural studies (of depression) have posed particular difficulties for comparison purposes because of several factors including cultural variations in the definitions of depression, differences in case finding and sampling procedures, diagnostic reliability problems, and failure to consider indigenous definitions.

Psychopathological conditions are usually defined in terms of syndromes or clusters of symptoms. Problems develop when presenting symptoms vary from culture to culture. For instance, in Nigeria depressed patients complain of heaviness or heat in the head, crawling sensations in the head or the legs, burning sensations in the body, and the feeling that the belly is bloated with water (Ebigno, 1982). These symptoms are infrequent among North American depressed patients who are likely to complain of feelings of worthlessness, inability to get anything started or finished, loss of interest in usual activities, and thoughts of suicide. In the same vein,

Kleinman (1982) found that in China depressed patients did not in the majority of cases show the loss of ability to experience pleasure, the helplessness, hopelessness, guilt, and suicidal thoughts so characteristic of depressives in North America.

In light of these important differences from one society to another, someone interested in a cross-cultural study will be grossly misled if he/she relies on a Depression scale developed in North America and applied to a sample of patients called depressed by North American trained clinicians. As a minimum a researcher must determine the indigenous definitions of depression, take cognizance of different syndromes of depressive behavior, be aware of biased samples due to case-finding procedures and examine the meanings of various symptoms within the shared belief systems of the population under study.

Concluding Comments

Throughout this chaper we have emphasized that great caution should be used when studying personality or pathology across cultures. Most of the concepts in personality and pathology are ill-defined or vague at best; to study them across cultures automatically compounds definitional and methodological problems. The concepts that must be used in attempting to study human personality or pathology are essentially real, and of course essential in the behavioral sciences; their characteristic vagueness need not totally inhibit research into cultural variations.

The field worker has perhaps three options from which to choose in the study of personological or psychopathological variables and their meanings and variations in other cultures:

1. By using some well-known test or technique such as the MMPI or the I–E Scale, the researcher can benefit from a readily available device with its good characteristics as well as its blemishes. The resulting data can be compared and contrasted with a wealth of existing data, norms, and interpretations. The major disadvantages with this option are that tailor-made approaches developed in one culture may not be appropriate for use elsewhere; moreover, by resorting only to ready-made procedures, the researcher may be overlooking something quite valuable in another culture.

2. The researcher may want to construct his/her own device to measure some aspect of personality or some facet of psychopath-

ology. A person so inclined would normally be familiar with the central issues and problems of test and scale construction, perhaps even to a point of sophistication where major psychometric and other methodological errors can be avoided. The advantage here is that one can shape the device to the specific concept and cultures being studied. The major disadvantage is the amount of time this would take, and the potential for error that would be evident.

3. A third option would be to study personality/pathology through procedures other than tests, scales, or related devices, to which subjects must respond, or by which they must be rated according to some prearranged scheme. Systematic observation, unobtrusive methodology, clever experiments, the interaction between acculturation and personality/pathology, and other perspectives outlined in this book can be quite useful in the creation of methodologies that would be constructive alternatives to the standard and limited test and scale orientation.

We have avoided writing this chapter in such a way that it would have looked like a cookbook, or an approach that would have said, for example, "This is how to proceed in studying depression in other cultures." The chapter is mainly designed to acquaint researchers with recurring problems and issues in studying personality and psychopathology across cultures. Perhaps the best recommendation that we can give to the field worker is this: before field work takes place, be as fully prepared as possible, and then keep things simple. Finally, it goes without saying that this chapter will reach its most beneficial level only when integrated with all the other chapters in this book.

9
ASSESSMENT OF SOCIAL BEHAVIOR

MARSHALL H. SEGALL

INTRODUCTION

Since humans are social animals, nearly all human behavior is social behavior. That is, nearly everything everyone does in the course of a lifetime is influenced by other people, by the behavior of other people, and by various products of the earlier behavior of other people. Even when alone and merely thinking, a person is usually in a place designed, constructed, and furnished by someone else (or, if not, assembled according to cultural practices invented by someone else), and the lone person's private thinking at least occurs in a language that was created and modified by many other persons. Indeed, even the contents of the private thoughts are influenced by cultural concerns; one normally thinks about what there is to think about and what that is, most likely, is part of one's own culture. So, it is very difficult to point to any human act that is not social, in the broad sense of the term.

Nevertheless, for purposes of this chapter, we limit our concern to those behaviors which are social in a more constrained sense; here we will focus on behaviors that are overtly interactional — behaviors displayed by people when they are actively relating to other people or to representations of other people. Even this sub-set of social behaviors is large and its study complicated. It includes all behaviors (attitudes, values, and other ideas governing those behaviors) performed by persons when other people are the objects or targets of the behavior.

Those other people may be nearly constant companions, like close relatives (parents and children, spouse and spouse, sibling and sibling, etc.) or frequently encountered age-mates, playmates, classmates, or workmates, or occasionally encountered strangers like traders, customers, visitors, performers, or fellow audience-members at a public spectacle, or even seldom or never seen, but often thought about, members of faraway societies, including persons who live no more and the as-yet-unborn. About all such "other people" we each possess ways of thinking and acting. We hold attitudes toward them and beliefs about them. And we have expectations regarding their behavior toward us.

For this sub-set of social behavior — these attitudes, beliefs, expectations, and overt acts relating to other people — social scientists have developed methods of study. These methods can be used within cultural groups or across them. When used within cultures they are complicated enough; they are even more complicated when applied cross-culturally. By complicated, I mean that we have to go to some length to try to ensure that the methods are reliable and valid (see Chapters 1 and 2), which is to say that they yield information consistently and in a fashion that is not misleading.

It is the purpose of this chapter to review some of the methods that have been developed to try to secure reliable and valid information about the social behavior of human beings in any cultural group, with a particular emphasis on the application of these methods, often by "outsiders," in settings different from the ones in which the methods were originally designed. Since most of them originated in Western, technologically developed societies, our emphasis will be on their use in nonWestern, nontechnically developed societies — the kinds of societies which Western social scientists usually have in mind when they say that they are doing research "in the field."

We will *not* cover all such methods in this chapter, since several are admirably covered in other chapters in this volume (see especially Bochner's chapter.) We *will* cover techniques of measuring attitudes by questionnaires, interviews, and other more structured observational techniques that are rather like "tests"; we thus include methods involving standard sets of stimuli or test items designed to yield individual scores and distributions of such scores for groups of individuals, with the scores intended to serve as a summary description of behavioral tendencies which might then be used to predict actual behavior. We will be especially interested in those questionnaire, interview, and test procedures that reveal interactional dispositions, enabling us to predict how given individuals are likely to respond to other people under specified circumstances.

In the course of doing this, we will see how to measure interpersonal and intergroup attraction, and how to assess the potential for acceptance or rejection of social events, both unplanned encounters and planned interventions, like social programs. We shall also see how the same kinds of methods may be used after the fact, to evaluate a social event or to discover how individuals reacted to it or were even changed by it. Throughout this review of assessment methods, we will consider both the promises and pitfalls inherent in them, thereby both initiating the would-be, first-time field worker into their "mysteries" and reminding seasoned researchers that even "old hands" need to review the basics on occasion. Our objective, of course, is to transform the mysterious into something commonplace, permitting the initiate to apply these methods to practical as well as scientific ends.

SURVEYS, QUESTIONNAIRES, AND INTERVIEWS

We often need to know what people think about some particular, specific, concrete phenomenon, like an event that has taken place or is about to, or a group of persons they have encountered or are about to. To find out, we have to ask them. That's simple enough. But, we have to decide whom to ask, what to ask, and how to ask it. That's a bit more complicated.

The first complication has to do with *whom to ask*. That is an issue of sampling, and is so complicated that a whole chapter in this volume has been devoted to it (see Chapter 3). A reading of that chapter should convince you that whenever you can't direct your questions to everybody whose views interest you, you must select people whose views represent well the views of *all* those persons. In this way, you will have a *sample* that represents the *population* of interest to you.

Assuming that the sampling problem has been solved, we can turn to the problem of questionnaire construction. The objective is a set of questions that will efficiently yield the information you need from a survey of your sample. *Efficiency* is a concern because conducting a survey is expensive. It takes time. One wants not to waste time asking irrelevant questions. And it is not only the questioner's time that is valuable, so is the respondent's. People don't like to have their time wasted answering questions; there is no reason why they should. So, the questions contained on a survey instrument (a questionnaire or interview schedule) should all serve a purpose. And they should appear to the respondent to be worth asking and worth answering.

They should also yield reliable and valid information. In other words, the answers people give should be the same answers they would give if someone else asked the questions, or if the questions were asked on another occasion (unless, of course, from occasion to occasion, what the questions refer to has actually changed). That is reliability. Validity refers to the accuracy, honesty, and meaningfulness of the answers. If we are asking to discover what people really believe about something, we don't want our questions to elicit from them only what they think will please us. If they happen to think that their true beliefs might displease us, we must find a way to frame our questions so that our respondents will be willing to take the risk of displeasing us. Of course, as scientific surveyors of social behavior, *no* answer displeases us if we have reason to believe it is the truth. But our respondent might not know that we are disinterested scientists, with no axe to grind, and only interested in obtaining the facts, so we have to guard against his or her fears, anxieties, and misperceptions of our intent and purpose.

Accordingly, the most important phase of conducting a survey by questionnaire or interview is the construction of the set of questions. Incidentally, the distinction between a questionnaire and an interview is not very important, but since we use both terms here, let us deal now with the differences between them. A questionnaire is usually a printed (or otherwise written down) set of questions, which the respondent reads and to which he provides written answers. An interview is usually conducted in a face-to-face situation, with the interviewer reading the questions aloud to the respondent and then recording the respondent's orally-presented answers. With regard to this distinction, the interview technique is obviously to be preferred over the questionnaire technique with nonliterate respondents, and there are other circumstances when one might prefer an interview. For example, if one expects that it would be useful to be able to insert additional questions, thereby probing for more elaboration of answers already given, an interview situation facilitates doing that. If cultural traditions are such that more reliable and valid responding occurs in face-to-face situations, then, again, interviews are preferred. In an early phase of a survey, before one is absolutely sure of the usefulness of one's questions, preliminary sets might be tried out in an interview. On the other hand, advantages of questionnaires include the ability of administering them to many people at once, thereby increasing the efficiency of the survey. A questionnaire, once duplicated, ensures that every respondent has been asked exactly the same set of questions, a feature which is often desirable. But despite these distinctions, different features, and preferences for question- naires under some circumstances and interviews under others, the techniques of construction that we are about to review pertain to both.

Questionnaire (or Interview) Construction

Assuming that we know what it is that we wish to learn, it would be very nice if we simply had to ask our respondents to tell us. Unfortunately, that is seldom possible. We must distinguish between what we want to know (which is usually something rather abstract, like whether a parent is more apt to favor birth control if the parents' existing children are relatively well-nourished and healthy) and what we must ask the respondent to tell us (which should be something concrete, like what the children are normally fed, what illnesses they suffer from, and whether birth control is practiced). In other words, we cannot ask the respondent to answer our research question directly but, instead, to provide us with the kind of data that we can use to test our hypothesis. This distinction is very important. It is often missed by neophyte questionnaire designers, who confuse their research question with the questions to be included in the question- naire.

Thus, the very first step in questionnaire construction is to decide what kind of information one needs and can collect from our sample of respondents that will be of use to us in our efforts to learn what we wish to learn. Pursuing the present example, we would *not* ask "Do parents favor birth control when they have healthy children?" We ask a series of questions that can be answered on the basis of each person's own circumstances and experiences.

For example, here is a series of questions we might ask a mother about, say, her oldest child:

What is the most serious illness this child ever had?
What other illness has this child had?
Does the child have any illnesses now?

Over the child's lifetime so far, is this child very healthy,
of average health, or sickly? What do you think?

Such questions would provide us with data about the child's health. To learn about that child's nutritional status, we could ask, for example, the following questions:

Would you tell me all about the foods that this child has been given to eat today?

How many meals did the child eat yesterday?

What did the child eat at the first meal? (repeat for each meal)

What does the child *usually* eat?

How often does the child eat meat/fish/eggs/etc.?

To learn about parental attitudes, beliefs, and practices regarding birth control, another series of questions would have to be asked, such as:

How many more children would you like to have?

Are you or your spouse now doing anything to delay or prevent the birth of another child?

Have you ever done anything to prevent or delay a pregnancy?

What methods of preventing pregnancy do you know about?

Do you approve or disapprove of using this method? (repeat for each)

From three sets of questions, of which those listed above are examples, we would emerge with three sets of answers and it would be up to us to search for the relationships among those sets of answers, using the data provided by all of the respondents in our sample. In other words, the researcher would eventually analyze the data in order to answer the research question. The questions built into the questionnaire are there because their answers can later be used in the analysis of the research question.

A most important characteristic of questions like those just provided here as examples is concreteness. For the most part, these questions ask for specific factual information that the respondent is likely to be able to provide. Even when we ask for matters of opinion, it is the respondent's own opinion that we seek.

A second consideration is question wording. Questions should be as unambiguous as possible, so that the respondent understands the question as it was meant to be understood. All words should be familiar, and word arrangements (phrasing, sentence structure, etc.) should communicate what was intended to be communicated. At the same time, care must be taken to avoid giving the impression that there is a preferred answer. Thus, the questions must be structured enough that their meaning is clear, but open-ended enough that the respondent feels free to give whatever answer seems right to him or her. Achieving these goals may require pre-testing of the questions. In fact, pre-testing should always be done, because one can never be sure that the questions one writes actually work the way they are meant to. Pre-testing will reveal which ones do and which ones don't, and will enable one to rewrite those that need modification.

Ordering the questions is the next consideration. It is nearly always preferable to begin with the most specific questions relating to a particular topic and then move on to the more general ones. Thus, "What did the child eat today?" should precede "What does the child usually eat?"

A special consideration that often pertains to cross-cultural research has to do with the language in which the questions are asked. Obviously, a questionnaire or interview should be in the respondent's own language if she is monolingual and in her language of choice if she speaks more than one. But once again we are dealing with a simple idea that is somewhat complex in its realization. Problems of translation are many and difficult and their solution calls for some special techniques. Straightforward one-way translation is usually not good enough, especially when the questionnaire's original author does not know the language of his respondents. Can the author simply rely on a single bilingual translator to transform the questionnaire into an equivalent set of questions? Probably not, simply because many concepts and ideas have multiple translations, each with a somewhat different connotation. Among the special techniques that must be used, a technique called "back-translation" is highly recommended (see Chapter 5). Starting with, say, an English-language form that is potentially translatable, an English-speaking researcher would employ two native speakers of the target language who are themselves bilingual. One translates from English to the target language and the result is then translated by the second bilingual speaker back to English. If identical English versions result, the target version is likely to be of satisfactory equivalence. Until identical versions are produced, the two translators would have to confer to try to iron out their differences. And unless procedures like this are employed, one can never be sure that the answers one gets from two different cultural groups are really answers to the same questions. The problem is obviously serious, especially when one gets different answers. Are the answers different because the two groups are different or only because they were asked different questions? To avoid that critical ambiguity, techniques like "back-translation" must be used (Chapter 5 outlines additional techniques).

Analysis of Questionnaire or Interview Answers

Coding: As we have seen, when questionnaires and interviews are used, respondents are encouraged to respond freely. Consequently, with a large number of respondents, there will usually be many different answers given to each question. In some respects, each answer will be unique. Typically, then, a survey researcher will be confronted by a large number of answers that in effect comprise an embarrassment of riches. What is the researcher to do with a given set of answers? Aiming ultimately at some comprehensible summary of all the different answers obtained, the researcher's first job of analysis is likely to be *coding*. By coding, we mean placing each answer into a category in some manner such that the end number of categories is smaller than the total number of answers. Coding is a scientific process, but it involves some artistry. That is to say, the coder must make judgments about how many categories adequately cover the range of answers and judgments about which answers belong in which categories. The process is artistic in the sense that it must begin with guesses and must continue with flexible rearrangements. One starts with what appears to be a plausible category system, but one must gradually discover the most meaningful way to emerge with a final version that does justice to the material being categorized (or coded). That final version should involve the least number of categories that maintains meaningful differences represented by the total set of answers.

Suppose, for example, one of the questions asked was "For how long did you breast feed your first child?" Answers might have included the following: "sixteen weeks" and "I always used a bottled formula" and "until I was pregnant again" and "until she was about a year and a half old" and so on. Suppose, further, that we have a few hundred such answers. What we would try to do with them is code them into a small set of categories that might resemble the following:

0 = didn't breast feed, or only for a few days
1 = less than 3 months

2 = 3–6 months

3 = more than 6 months but less than 1 year

4 = 1–2 years

5 = longer than 2 years

6 = unspecified or don't know

With this coding system, the response "sixteen weeks" would be coded 2, "I always used a bottled formula" would be coded 0, "until she was about a year and a half old" would be coded 4, and, at first, we wouldn't know how to code "until I was pregnant again." To code it we might have to seek information from that respondent's answers to other questions; if we learned elsewhere in her interview that she became aware of being pregnant with her second child when her first child was 16 months old, then we could code her response 4.

Once having applied this coding system, we might discover, for example, that many responses (say 74 percent of all of them) were coded 4, but that the range covered by that code category (12 full months) was fully represented by those answers, with many answers falling between 12 and 18 months, and many others between 19 and 24 months. We might then find it reasonable to revise our code so that what was originally a single, large category is broken down into two smaller categories. The reason for this, of course, is that weaning before eighteen months and weaning after eighteen months might represent a meaningful difference that we don't want to lose sight of.

When coding answers, the code categories can be labeled by numbers, as in the preceding example, or simply by words, like *never*, *very early*, *moderately early*, and *late*. However, numbers are preferable for a number of reasons, including convenience of storage and retrieval of the information, particularly if one is storing the data on some kind of computer. Also, if the numbers used in the coding system comprise a *scale* (that is, a set of numbers in which the numbers are not merely arbitrary labels but one in which some of the properties of numbers matter, such as *order*, such that 3 is less than 5 and not merely different), then those numbers may be used in a later phase of the analysis. A bit later in this chapter, we will deal with *scaling*, but first we must consider what to do with our responses once we have coded them, whether or not the coding system we are using is a scale.

Tabulating: Having developed a code, which we have just seen is simply a set of categories into which we have placed all the answers obtained to a particular question, the next step is to count the number of answers in each category. That's all there is to tabulation. We can then display the answers in a table. It might look like Table 9.1.

TABLE 9.1
Duration of Breast Feeding, 1st Child

Code	Responses	N	%	cum. %
0	none at all	6	12	12
1	less than 3 months	14	28	40
2	from 3 to 6 months	4	8	48
3	from 7 to 12 months	2	4	52
4	from 13 to 18 months	12	24	76
5	from 19 to 24 months	12	24	100

As constructed here, the table shows how fifty answers were placed in six categories, ranging from never through two years. The table also displays those numbers as percentages; thus it is possible to tell at a glance that 24 percent of the respondents reported breast feeding for a period of 13 to 18 months. Since it might be of interest, with a set of categories like these that do comprise an ordinal scale (that is, the higher the category, the longer the duration) to identify the cumulative proportion of respondents who reach each category, that statistic is also shown in this table in the right-most column. There one can see, again at a glance, that 52 percent of the sample stop breast feeding by the time the baby reaches one year of age, if they haven't stopped earlier.

What we have in this kind of table, then, is a summary of a great deal of information, in this case answers given by fifty different people, arranged, classified, and tabulated so as to be easily communicated. Such tabulation can be done for the answers to every question in the interview or questionnaire.

Cross-tabulating: When all answers have been coded and tabulated, any pair of tables (or more) can be cross-tabulated. To do this, one classifies the answers given to one question across the categories of answers given to another. For example, if on the basis of a question dealing with child health, we obtained answers that were meaningfully classifiable as follows:

very healthy   14
moderately healthy   16
sickly   20

and wondered whether there was a statistical relationship between the reported state of the child's health and duration of breast feeding, we could cross-tabulate the data provided by the pair of relevant questions. A resultant array of cross-tabulated data might look like Table 9.2.

TABLE 9.2

	Very Healthy	Health Mod. Healthy	Sickly
Breast feeding			
never or less than 3 months	2	4	14
up to 12 months	6	6	6
more than 18 months	6	6	0

This table would then tell us something of considerable interest, namely that the sickly children of mothers in this sample were most likely never to be breast fed and that healthier kids were more apt to have been breast fed and for longer durations. In short, this cross-tabulation would reveal that there is some relationship between child health and duration of breast feeding.

The numbers in the table do not tell us, of course, what the relationship really means; we cannot conclude that health is a consequence of breast feeding, but that is one possible explanation for the relationship displayed in this cross-tabulation table. Another plausible interpretation is that both health and breast feeding are consequences of some other variable, like economic well-being. We would need additional research to evaluate such competing alternative interpretations.

It should now be clear that when one uses a set of questions, coding, tabulation, and cross-tabulation are the steps the researcher takes after the questions have been answered by the respondents to extract from their answers the answers the researcher has been searching for. Earlier, the distinction was drawn between the questions that the respondents answer and the "research question." Now it should be clear that a cross-tabulation results in an answer to a research question. In the example just given, the research question concerns the relationship between child health and breast feeding, and the answer is, "there is one!"

Whether the obtained relationship that emerged from the cross-tabulation is best thought of as a real linkage between the two phenomena — breast feeding and child health — or as a misleading outcome of the interplay of chance factors is a question that would have to be addressed by the use of certain statistical tests of association. Various techniques are appropriate and one or another is essential. They include correlation, chi-square, and others, coupled with assessment of the statistical significance of obtained values of those measures. However, discussion of statistical techniques is beyond the bounds of the present chapter. It must suffice to note that the field researcher has the responsibility of subjecting his findings to these techniques, the details of which may be found in any number of statistics textbooks.

Since we must omit discussion of statistical analyses, we can now summarize the procedures involved in using questionnaires or interviews to survey persons about social behavior. We have seen that the procedures include (1) deciding on the population of interest, (2) selecting a sample from that population, (3) constructing the questionnaire or interview schedule, (4) administering it to the sample, (5) tabulating answers, (6) doing cross-tabulations to determine relationships, and (7) applying tests to determine the statistical significance of the obtained relationships. These steps are common to all kinds of survey research, whether done intraculturally or across cultures. When doing survey research cross-culturally, some special steps need be taken, particularly with regard to translation problems and modes of presentation of the questions to respondents for whom such interviewing comprises a novel, possibly even frightening, experience.

The kinds of questionnaires and interviews that we have discussed here are frequently employed in cross-cultural research. They are very useful when we are working among people about whom we initially know very little. They are an excellent device for learning a great deal about such people in a relatively short time. Their main virtue is that they can be used to study almost any conceivable topic. But with some topics, we can use other techniques that are somewhat more structured and quantitative than simple questionnaires and interviews, and it is to one such technique that we now turn.

ATTITUDE SCALES

Students of social behavior, particularly social psychologists, have long been interested in people's "attitudes" and have devised and refined methods for measuring them. An attitude is best thought of as a behavioral disposition; that is, a tendency to behave in one way or another. In the end, we usually seek to be able to predict how certain people will behave under certain circumstances, and knowing their relevant attitudes (or behavioral dispositions) should enhance our ability to make such predictions. Attitudes may be assessed in a variety of ways, but many of those ways (and the ones on which we will concentrate here) involve obtaining a sample of people's verbalizations about some object about which they might possess an attitude. Objects can include any social stimulus, such as another person, a whole group of people, a social institution, a program or policy, or a contemporary social issue. Examples of such objects and of attitudes relating to them might include attitudes toward a proposed new health program in a rural community, attitudes toward a neighboring group, attitudes toward three alternative candidates for public office, and so on. It has been suggested by many social psychologists that attitudes have several components, including cognitive, affective, and behavioral components, which is simply a way of saying that people can express their attitudes by stating beliefs about the object's characteristics (cognitive), the quality of their own emotional reaction to it (affective), or their own leanings, for or against, with regard to the object, (behavioral). In any case, these components are all contained within verbal expressions of opinion (see Chapter 6 for a discussion of the complex relationship between verbal expression of attitude and other behaviors). Hence, expressions of opinion are what we usually elicit from our respondents when we set out to measure their attitudes.

Here, for example, are some expressions of opinion about a neighboring group, expressed by a resident of the United States, for whom the neighboring group is composed of residents of Canada. (a) Canadians are warm and friendly people. (b) I would feel pleased if my daughter chose to marry a Canadian. (c) Canadians should be permitted free and open access to the United States. From these three statements of opinion, which are respectively cognitive, affective, and behavioral, it probably seems reasonable to infer that the person who expressed them holds a positive attitude toward

Canadians, and if given an opportunity to display that attitude in some meaningful behavior, such as taking advantage of an opportunity to interact with Canadians in a friendly manner, would do so.

From this example we can now derive a basic principle of attitude measurement: *Attitudes are inferred from a pattern of expressed opinions*. From this principle, we should expect to discover that attitude scaling consists of methods to elicit opinions and techniques for discerning the pattern inherent in them. We will now examine those methods and techniques in some detail.

Attitude Scale Construction

The most common and useful procedure for eliciting opinions is to provide respondents with expressed opinions and ask them to indicate agreement or disagreement with them. This means that the researcher will initially have to write a series of opinion statements about the object of concern. These will be statements that express beliefs and feelings regarding that object and they will be statements with which all persons might either agree or disagree. Since any given statement might be agreed with or disagreed with to some extent, we usually present statements in a format that allows expression of degrees of agreement or disagreement; for example, *Canadians are warm and friendly people. Do you agree strongly, agree somewhat, disagree somewhat, or disagree strongly?* Since any single statement has characteristics of its own, we usually employ many statements, each with its own characteristics, but all presumably referring to the same object. Thus, a second item we might use in an effort to assess "attitudes toward Canadians" could be: *Whenever Canadians deal with outsiders, they are likely to cheat them. Agree strongly, agree somewhat, disagree somewhat, or disagree strongly?*

Although these two sample items both refer to Canadians, in several ways the two items are unique. In one obvious way, they are very different from each other; one of them is worded in a positive direction (i.e. is pro-Canadian) and the other negative (i.e. is anti-Canadian). It is common practice in attitude measurement to employ many items (because each is unique) and among them about as many worded in a positive direction as in a negative direction. This latter technique is meant to guard against certain response biases leading to invalid attitude scores. To pursue this particular point, consider the possibility that some respondents tend to agree with whatever they hear or read (such persons are sometimes referred to as yea-saying). If all the items on our attitude scale were worded in, say, a pro-Canadian direction, then yea-sayers would appear to be pro-Canadian, even if they weren't. By balancing the numbers of items in both directions, neither of those response tendencies would have that invalidating impact.

This principle of attitude scale construction is potentially of major significance for field research. Samples of people who perceive themselves to be of inferior status in some respect (e.g. not as well educated as the field worker) might well be prone to agree with whatever the field worker says. They might then express agreement with every item he presents. Or the reverse might be the case if people feel threatened by the field worker and express what is in fact a negative attitude toward him or her by disagreeing with each item, regardless of their content. So, especially in field work conditions, it is important to construct the set of items in a way that takes into account the possibility of these response biases.

The point we have just covered will now be expanded into a more general one. We must assume that any response anyone makes to an item on the scale has multiple determinants. That is, a given response may be made for a variety of reasons. But we are interested in only one determinant, the presumed-to-exist underlying attitude. Hence, our entire effort of scale construction and, as we shall see in a moment, of scale analysis, must be dedicated to assuring that the responses we obtain do in fact reveal that attitude.

Attitude Scale Analysis

Scale construction and scale analysis, although conceptually separate parts of the process of attitude measurement, are intimately related to each other. They are in fact intertwined. An initial set of items, written because they seem, *a priori*, to relate to a particular attitude object, are *only* an initial set. That set must be administered to a sample of persons like those whose attitude we wish to measure, and then their responses must be subjected to an analysis, the object of which is to determine whether the items really do what we expected them to do, which is, of course, to measure an attitude.

Over the years, many different psychologists have contributed important ideas and techniques for such an analysis. Here, we will consider only one, known as the Guttman Scaling Technique, because, in the opinion of this writer, it captures the essence of what we are trying to do when we construct an attitude scale, and because its use requires no sophisticated mathematics (even though it is most rigorously described in mathematical terms).

The technique is based on an assumption that the attitude we wish to measure is unidimensional. That is to say, all persons who hold an attitude toward a particular object can all be placed on a single dimension, ranging from extremely negative to extremely positive. While it may be the case that some attitudes we can conceive of are more complicated (and, hence, best thought of as multidimensional) for all practical purposes nearly all attitudes we might wish to measure can be treated as unidimensional.

How we actually do this is probably best communicated by an example. The one we will use is a real example. While doing field work among rural populations in Kenya some years ago, I was interested in assessing attitudes toward family planning. To do so, I began with a set of fifteen statements, all of which, on an *a priori* basis, seemed to relate to family planning, either directly or indirectly, either obviously or in a more subtle way. All items were declarative sentences to which five responses were possible, ranging from *agree strongly* through *don't know* to *disagree strongly*. The items, in the order in which they appeared on a questionnaire, are as follows:

1. These days it is wise to space and limit the number of children.
2. A woman should bear as many children as possible.
3. Children represent wealth for the future.
4. A few healthy children are better to have than many children some of whom may not be very healthy.
5. Men are too bossy and women should become more powerful.
6. Life in the city would be better than life on the farm.
7. The government should reward people who have small families.
8. Schools should teach about family planning.
9. It is immoral to use contraceptives.
10. If an unmarried girl becomes pregnant, she should have an abortion.
11. The husband, not the wife, should decide whether to have children, and how many.
12. Many people have so many children that some of the children they have are unwanted.

13. When a parent loses a child through death, that child should be replaced by another.
14. Condoms should not be used by decent people; they are used with prostitutes.
15. Family planning will never be popular in this country.

These fifteen items were administered to a sample of rural women. The first thing to notice about these items is that some are worded in an obvious pro-family planning direction (#s 1, 4, 7, 8, 10, and 12), and some in an anti-family planning direction (#s 2, 3, 9, 13, 14, and 15), while for the rest (#s 5, 6, and 11) the direction of wording is somewhat ambiguous. This reflects the necessary effort to produce a balanced set of items in order to avoid score contamination from response bias, as we discussed a bit earlier. Given that we have items worded in both directions, the first step in our analysis is to assign numerical scores in a manner that takes into account this bi-directionality. Thus, agreeing strongly with a pro-family planning item would be functionally equivalent to disagreeing strongly with an anti-family planning item, and our scoring system must reflect that.

If, following Likert, a pioneer student of attitude measurement, we call *agree strongly* to a *pro* item a 1, we must also call *disagree strongly* to an *anti* item a 1, and so on. Doing that, each person's fifteen responses are coded on a 1 to 5 dimension, with a 1 reflecting the maximally *pro* response to any item and a 5 the maximally *anti* response to any item. Thus, a person who makes such responses consistently over all items would earn a score of 15 (fifteen times one); this is the most pro-family planning score possible. At the other extreme, a person who responds in the most anti-family planning manner consistently over all items would earn a score of 75 (fifteen times five). So, all scores would range from 15 to 75, with the lower numbers indicating favorable attitudes toward family planning. Whether or not that is what the scores really mean is what we must determine by our Guttman analysis.

Steps in Guttman analysis: The analysis can begin once we have assigned to each person a numerical score based on the procedure just described. Assuming that the persons with the lowest numerical scores have the most pro-family planning attitudes, we arrange the persons in order. Thus, we start with those whose score is 15, follow with those whose score is 16, then 17, and so on. Now we are ready to shift our attention to what each person did by way of response to each item.

When we focus on the items, we perform a small transformation of each person's response to each item. The transformation involves calling certain responses a "pass" and others a "nonpass." Although there is some arbitrariness in this procedure, it is logical and systematic. It is done as follows: For positively worded items, define "agree strongly" and "agree" responses as "pass" and all other responses as "nonpass." For negatively worded items, do the opposite. (For ambiguously worded items, we must make a tentative decision as to their direction, positive or negative, and define "passing" accordingly.) Then, assign to each item a score that indicates the number of passes, and arrange them in order from highest to lowest number of passes. What we achieve by this step is an ordering of items that reflects their relative "ease of being passed" at least by this sample of respondents. In other words, an item with many passes is an item that we can assume requires minimal amount of favorable pro-family planning attitude to be passed.

To better understand this logic, consider a simplified example involving only five items and ten respondents. To follow the example, consult Table 9.3, where the respondents and the items are simultaneously ordered according to the rules we have just articulated. (Note that with only five items, respondents' scores can range from 5 to 25.)

In Table 9.3 plus signs indicate passes. As we see, John and Walt passed all five items, Wally earned nonpasses on all five. The other respondents passed some items and responded in a nonpass fashion on other items. Looking down the columns, we see that item #2 was the easiest to pass (eight out of our ten respondents passed it) and #4 the hardest (only three passed it).

Now we must recall that via this procedure, we are attempting to calibrate our instrument by comparing it with an *ideal model*, one that describes what the table we have prepared *would* look like, if the five items constituted a unidimensional measure of attitude toward family planning and if the responses made by our ten respondents were completely determined by their own attitudes toward family planning. If that *were* the case, there would be no plus signs following a minus sign in any row. Why not? Because once a respondent had passed the hardest item for him to pass (as a result, as it were, of running out of attitude), he should not be able to pass a harder item. Thus, in no row should there be a plus sign after a minus sign. However, as in the example we are using here, that happened several times; what we obtained fell short of what the ideal model demanded.

TABLE 9.3

		Items (arranged in order of ease of passing)				
		#2	#5	#3	#1	#4
Respondents (arranged in order of descending pro-ness)	Score					
John	5	+	+	+	+	+
Walt	5	+	+	+	+	+
Sid	8	+	+	+	+	−
Herb	10	+	+	−	+	−
Joe	13	+	+	−	−	+
Alan	17	+	−	+	−	−
Dick	19	+	−	−	−	−
Tom	21	+	−	−	−	−
Harry	23	−	+	−	−	−
Wally	25	−	−	−	−	−

Let's look at some of these events more closely. Herb, for example, passed item #1 after not passing item #3. According to the ideal model, he should either have passed both or not passed both. One or another of his responses is a kind of "error." But his "error" could be corrected in any one of three ways. (1) We could assume that he passed item #3; then his row would appear as + + + + −. (2) We could assume that he did not pass item #1; then his row would appear as + + − − −. (3) Finally, we could assume that the items require some rearrangement, with #1 preceding #3 (a not unreasonable assumption, since the two items have the same number of pass responses, and just as reasonably could be ordered 1 3 as 3 1); then Herb's row would appear as + + + − −. Now, notice that each of those three different assumptions result in different scores for Herb, since the first results in 4 passes, the second 2 passes, and the third 3 passes. Given that the third assumption results in the least possible change of Herb's original score, it might be the preferred option, especially since it is arrived at simply by transforming the order of two items that were ambiguously ordered anyway.

Without going into the laborious detail that would be entailed if we did for Joe, Alan, and the others, what we just did for Herb, I will simply state that in actual practice, one must continue rearranging items and rescoring respondents until one arrives at the array of pluses and minuses that is the closest possible to a perfect array, that is, one with no reversals. Usually, in order to achieve this, we actually have to drop an item because for some reason or another (usually unknown to us) that item contributes a disproportionately large amount of disorder to the array. When we have such an item, the rationale for dropping it is that it must not be measuring the same thing as the other items. In other words, it is not on the same dimension, and since our goal is to emerge with an instrument that is as unidimensional as possible, an item like that must be dropped.

Typically, when this procedure is followed, one ends up with a refined attitude scale that contains fewer items than one started with, but it is, of course, a better scale than one started with. If it is a better scale, then it is giving us a purer measure of the attitude we are seeking to assess.

In the study done in Kenya, that was referred to earlier, the original fifteen item scale that appeared in the questionnaire was reduced to an eight item scale for purposes of final scoring. That eight item scale was a very pure measure of family planning attitudes, one for which considerable confidence could be placed in the validity of the scores. With the refined scale, the one composed of the eight best items, over 90 percent of every respondent's responses to each item were pluses when they should have been or minuses when they should have been. Rarely did a plus follow a minus.

What this lengthy description of attitude scaling procedure attempted to achieve is an understanding of how one can with precision define an attitude and measure it for a given population. To summarize the procedure: Create an *a priori* set of items, worded in both directions, administer them to a sample of respondents, arrange respondents in order and items in order, eliminate those items which persistently contribute disorder to the array, and, finally, live with the reduced set of items as the best possible scale. Respondents are then re-scored on that best possible scale and the new scores constitute the best possible estimate of the respondents' attitudes.

APPLICATIONS OF SURVEYS, QUESTIONNAIRES, INTERVIEWS, AND ATTITUDE SCALES

In the previous sections of this chapter, we attended almost exclusively to methods of constructing and analyzing instruments that may be used to acquire information from human beings about their behavioral dispositions with regard to other people, the behavior of other people, or any product of the behavior of other people, like an institution or a program. We emphasized *methods* because research must be done methodically if it is to be done well. We emphasized *construction* of instruments because under field conditions it is usually preferable for a researcher to construct his own instrument rather than to use one that was constructed by someone else originally for use somewhere else. Now, our emphasis shifts away from methods (even though we merely skimmed the surface of what is known about methods for the assessment of social behavior) to a consideration of some practical, straightforward ideas about applying research methods in field settings.

The Scope of Application

Anything that persons believe or feel about any social stimulus is potentially measurable by methods like those considered earlier in this chapter. Whatever a person might have an attitude about can be measured. One can assess intergroup attitudes by employing items about known groups. Such procedures have been employed in various parts of the world where persons in certain societies have been queried about their views regarding persons in other societies. Among the particular techniques that are employed in such studies are measures of social distance, wherein respondents indicate the social situations in which they would gladly participate (or not) with persons from other groups. Scoring responses to such items involves precisely the kind of procedure we examined when we considered the Guttman analysis technique.

The methods reviewed here can also be used to assess all kinds of values people hold. Measuring attitudes toward family planning, to recall an example that was developed in some detail in this chapter, can be viewed as a means for assessing the values held by a group of people regarding having children. By *value* is meant an attitude that is more or less shared by a large proportion of persons who are members of a particular cultural group, usually because that value is rooted in the culture and transmitted intergenerationally via the socialization and enculturation process.

It is also possible to study change in attitudes and values. In fact, of course, no culture is static; all cultures are undergoing changes of one kind or another; sometimes slowly, sometimes rapidly, and as they change, values and attitudes change. The changing values and attitudes can be measured by re-applying the techniques we have learned about in this chapter, using them several times over a period of time.

Similarly, techniques like those discussed here can be used to assess either the receptivity of a group to an impending event (say, the introduction of a new program or policy) or the impact of the event after the fact. These two related kinds of assessment techniques can play a critical role in the design and evaluation of social programs. Since in so many settings that are of concern to field workers social programs are regularly being designed and implemented, and since, as the record clearly shows, so many of them fail to achieve their goals, the assessment of social receptivity or reaction may comprise a very valuable contribution that field workers can make to that mysterious and elusive objective—development.

The Manner of Application

If, as has been asserted here, social behavior of a wide variety of forms can be measured by the use of various kinds of survey techniques, there is virtually no limit to what we could find out about peoples' attitudes, beliefs, and values. However, it is essential to remember that social behavior is often, ironically, very personal behavior. Assessing it, therefore, must be done with considerable sensitivity. People are not guinea pigs and should not be treated as such. People are not there to serve the researcher; the researcher is there to serve the people. Particularly in field settings, we must have a very good reason for assessing social behavior. The best reason is that such assessment can directly or indirectly serve the interests of the people themselves. They should be the ultimate beneficiaries of the assessment. When they contribute to our research, they are incurring a cost; such cost must, for moral and ethical reasons, be matched or exceeded by benefit.

In the end, the best judges of whether benefits are accruing to participants in a research project are the participants themselves. Accordingly, to the maximum extent possible, field research should involve its participants as consultants in design and interpretation.

Researchers should think of the participants as colleagues and not merely as respondents.

Care must be taken not to ask embarrassing or upsetting questions, especially when it is not absolutely necessary to deal with certain sensitive issues. Care must be taken to protect respondents from unhappy experiences, such as perceiving that they have somehow "failed" by not making a particular response to an item in an interview.

In short, field workers must appreciate that they have, potentially, considerable power *vis à vis* their respondents. At least, the researcher is likely to be perceived as powerful and he must not abuse or exploit that perception.

The considerations which we are addressing in this section may be summarized as follows: the process of assessment of social behavior is itself an example of social behavior. It comprises an interaction between unequals, with most of the advantages residing with the researcher. It is his ethical responsibility to engage in this interaction in a manner which makes it more equal.

What we have seen in this chapter is that we can indeed assess social behavior. We have the techniques for constructing instruments that may do so reliably and validly. We should use them whenever there are good reasons for doing so, but only then, and in a manner that upholds the dignity of our respondents. The assessment of social behavior is, thus, not an end in itself. It is a means to an end, and that end must be the attainment or refinement of information, the possession of which can enhance the likelihood of improving the quality of life enjoyed by our collaborators, those who permit us to assess their social behavior.

CONCLUDING REMARKS

In this chapter, we have been interested in people, members of any social group, whose distribution of attitudes, values, aspirations, or expectations are of legitimate, practical concern to a field worker, a person who conducts research, not in specially designed laboratories but in real-world settings. The focus in this chapter has been *how* field workers may achieve accurate, meaningful measures of these socially relevant psychological characteristics.

Here, "field worker" was thought of as an agent of a social service organization, engaged in planning, implementing, or evaluating programs intended to assist a social group. So defined, a field worker must acknowledge the need to take into account the felt needs, wants, and other relevant dispositions of the community for whom the program is designed. I assumed that such field workers are not highly trained in psychological measurement techniques but need to know how to obtain reliable and valid assessments of the socially relevant behavioral dispositions of the groups they are serving. Thus, the chapter consisted primarily of material designed to instruct field workers in the means available for practical application of socio-assessment methods in nonlaboratory settings.

Most of the chapter dealt with the use, cross-culturally, of structured questionnaires. We saw that such instruments are composed of sets of questions or statements to be endorsed or rejected, that they are employed to assess attitudes, beliefs, and values, and sometimes to elicit self-reports of behavioral tendencies. We saw, too, that they may be tailor-made to fit particular situations; their content can reflect the characteristics of concern to the field worker while their format remains fairly standard. The flexibility of content is a virtue, since the methods discussed in this chapter can be applied anywhere to almost any psychological construct (like particular attitude) for which the field worker is ingenious enough to construct appropriate items. But this virtue implies also a problem. It is difficult to interpret responses obtained with what are, in terms of content, unique instruments. To discern what in fact is being measured by such instruments requires careful analysis. The discussion of the Guttman technique for attitude scaling was meant to illustrate the logical underpinnings of steps that must be taken in order to properly interpret responses made to attitude questionnaires.

There are limitations to what we discussed, and some omissions. Structured assessment techniques, of the kind emphasized here, are extremely obtrusive. Indeed, a strong case can be made for the encouragement, particularly under field conditions, of assessment techniques that are less trait-related, more observational, more naturalistic, and less obtrusive. Numerous prototype examples could be mentioned (some are found elsewhere in this volume, especially in Chapter 6).

One of these alternative techniques is the "revealed preferences" approach, often used by economists to assess differential values attached by persons or communities to competing goods or alternative services, by observing what persons do, or give up doing, in order to avail themselves of those goods or services. Measures of effort expended are then used as proxies of measures of value. Another technique, dubbed "archival" is the use of data that already exist and that, therefore, do not require intrusions by the field worker. The strengths inherent in collecting existing reports or of making casual observations (systematically recorded) of ongoing behaviors in real-world settings without disturbing those settings, reside primarily in the nonartificial, "natural" quality of the behaviors observed. When behaviors are unobtrusively observed, the observation *per se* has no chance of distorting the behavior. It must be noted, then, that the measurement techniques featured in this chapter are extremely obtrusive. This is one of their inherent weaknesses.

Moreover, the techniques covered in this chapter, when competently employed, may tell us a lot about how things really are, but they can tell us nothing about how they got that way. Causes of behavior are very difficult to discern. Experimental or quasi-experimental research designs, involving presentation of a program to some people but not to others, are required for causal analysis. To design research to reveal behavioral causes involves decisions about *who* to measure, and *where* and *when*. We did not deal at all in this chapter with such considerations, primarily because they are the focus of Chapters 1 and 2. Instead, we dealt only with why a field worker might wish to assess social behavior and, in the largest portion of the chapter, *how* to do this in a rigorous fashion.

Since no research project can be better than the quality of the measurements attained therein, the skills dealt with in this chapter, while clearly limited, are essential to all field workers who would understand better the people they are trying to serve.

NOTE

This chapter contains no references to previously published works. These omissions are deliberate. It is the case, of course, that the material in this chapter derives from earlier work by many students of social behavior. But who they are is, I assume, of little concern to the audience that I am addressing, neophyte field workers who need to know how to assess social behavior not for academic reasons, but for practical purposes. Hence, to emphasize the nonacademic objective of the present enterprise, the academic practice of citation of published work was abandoned. However, wherever it is useful for readers of this chapter to refer to other chapters in the present volume, sign-posts indicating this have been judiciously placed by the volume's editors. Those readers who seek additional details pertaining to assessment techniques discussed in this chapter should consult Fishbein (1967), Brislin, Lonner, and Thorndike (1973), and Pareek and Rao (1980).

10

ASSESSMENT OF ACCULTURATION

JOHN W. BERRY
JOSEPH E. TRIMBLE
ESTEBAN L. OLMEDO

INTRODUCTION

The assessment of individual behavior across cultures is plagued by numerous problems, as we have seen over and over again in this volume. The one addressed in this chapter is that behavior is not only influenced by the culture in which one develops (by enculturation), but also possibly by other cultures impinging from outside (by acculturation). Unless the researcher can gauge this acculturative influence, and its impact on the individual, inappropriate conclusions could be drawn about the sources of cross-cultural variation in behavior.

The purpose of this chapter is to provide the field worker with a grasp of the concepts and measurement techniques which relate to conducting acculturation research. Appropriate background reading prior to field work would be Berry (1980c), Olmedo (1979), Padilla (1980a), and Taft (1977). While work on acculturation was initially carried out almost entirely within the discipline of anthropology, it is now an important concept in the field of ethnic studies, social psychiatry, and cross-cultural psychology. It is our intention to present materials which are both conceptually and empirically relevant to all these disciplines.

Definition

The two classic statements about acculturation were made years ago:

> Acculturation comprehends those phenomena which result when groups of individuals having different cultures come into continuous first-hand contact, with subsequent changes in the original culture patterns of either or both groups ... under this definition acculturation is to be distinguished from culture change, of which it is but one aspect, and assimilation, which is at times a phase of acculturation. It is also to be differentiated from diffusion which while occurring in all instances of acculturation, is not only a phenomenon which frequently takes place without the occurrence of the types of contact between peoples specified in the definition above, but also constitutes only one aspect of the process of acculturation (Redfield, Linton, and Herskovits, 1936, pp. 149–152).

In a later formulation acculturation was defined as:

> ... culture change that is initiated by the conjunction of two or more autonomous cultural systems. Acculturative change may be the consequence of direct cultural transmission; it may be derived from noncultural causes, such as ecological or demographic modification induced by an impinging culture; it may be delayed, as with internal adjustments following upon the acceptance of alien traits or patterns; or it may be a reactive adaptation of traditional modes of life. Its dynamics can be seen as the selective adaptation of value systems, the processes of integration and differentiation, the generation of developmental sequences, and the operation of role determinants and personality factors (Social Science Research Council, 1954, p. 974).

To these early formulations (which are concerned mainly with cultural phenomena) has been added a psychological component — the changes which individuals undergo during the acculturation of their group; this has been referred to as *psychological acculturation* by Graves (1967). In this chapter we will be concerned with both the group (cultural) level and the individual (psychological) level of acculturation phenomena.

Framework

From these definitions we may identify some key elements. First there needs to be *contact* or interaction between cultures which is continuous and first hand; this rules out short-term, accidental contact, and it rules out diffusion of single cultural practices over long distances. Second, the result is some *change* in the cultural or psychological phenomena among the people in contact. Third, taking these first two aspects together, we can distinguish between a *process* and a *state*: there is activity during and after contact which is dynamic, and there is a result of the process which may be relatively stable, but which may also continue to change in an ongoing process.

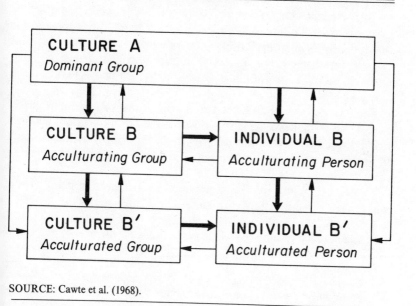

SOURCE: Cawte et al. (1968).

Figure 10.1   Framework for Identifying Variables and Relationships in Acculturation Research

Considering these distinctions as part of a general system of acculturation, the framework in Figure 10.1 can be proposed (cf. Berry 1980c; Berry et al., 1982). It depicts two cultures (A and B) in contact. In principle each could influence the other equally, but in practice, one tends to dominate the other; in this framework the "dominant group" (or "donor") is Culture A and the "acculturating group" (or "receptor") is Culture B. For completeness, mutual influence is depicted by the two arrows between Cultures A and B, as is the influence of Culture A directly on individuals in Culture B. However, the consequences for Culture A are not represented and for the balance of this exposition we will focus on a single culture (B), the one receiving the greater influence.

One result of the contact and influence is that aspects of group B become transformed so that cultural features of the acculturated group (B^1) are not identical to those in the original group at the time of first contact. Of course, if contact is still maintained, further influence from Culture A is experienced. A parallel phenomenon is that individuals in group B undergo psychological changes (as a result of both influences from their own group and from group A), and again, if there is continuing contact, further psychological changes may take place.

The point of presenting this framework is not to develop a grand model, but to make as explicit as possible the kinds of variables which may be assessed in acculturation research. We simply list these here; in the next section we will present examples of procedures for their assessment.

Culture A: What are the characteristics of the dominant group which need research attention? The essential ones are:

1. *Purpose:* Why is the contact taking place; what are its goals? Clearly acculturation phenomena will vary according to whether the purpose is colonization, enslavement, trade, military control, evangelization, education, etc.
2. *Length:* For how long has the contact been taking place, and does it occur daily, seasonally or annually? Once again variations in acculturation may be present due to the history, phase, and persistence of contact.
3. *Permanence:* Is the dominant group here to stay; have they settled in, or is it a passing venture?
4. *Population:* How many are there; do they form a majority, or are there only a few?
5. *Policy:* What are the policies being exercised toward acculturating

groups? Is it assimilation, eventual extermination, indirect rule, ghettoization, dispersion, etc.?

6. *Cultural Qualities:* Are there cultural qualities possessed by the dominant group which can meet specific needs, or improve the quality of life of the acculturating group? Potentially desirable cultural traits such as medicines, guns and traps (for hunter population), seeds, ploughs, and irrigation techniques (for agricultural populations) will obviously lead to acculturative changes more than will unwanted or nonfunctional culture traits.

This is not an exhaustive list, but only serves as an example of the kinds of cultural variables which may contribute to the ways in which acculturation takes place. Without some indication of the nature of these variables, no account of acculturation would be complete.

Culture B: A parallel account is needed of the characteristics of Culture B.

1. *Purpose:* Is the group in contact voluntarily (e.g. immigrants) or under duress (e.g. native peoples)?

2. *Location:* Is the group in its traditional location, with its land and other resources available, or are they displaced to some new environment (e.g. reservation, refugee camp)?

3. *Length and Permanence:* These variables are much the same as for the description of Culture A. In particular, the phase of acculturation needs to be specified: Has contact only begun; have acculturative pressures been building up; has a conflict or crisis appeared?

4. *Population:* How many are there; are they a majority or minority; is the population vital (sustaining or increasing in number) or declining?

5. *Policy:* To what extent does the group have an organized response to acculturation? If there is a policy orientation, is it one of resistance or exclusion (get rid of acculturative influence), of inclusion (accepting the influence), or of control (selective inclusion according to some scale of acceptability)?

6. *Cultural Qualities:* Are there certain aspects of the traditional culture which affect the acculturative process? For example hunter-gatherers are susceptible to habitat destruction due to war, forest reduction, or mineral exploration, while agricultural peoples may be dispossessed of their land by permanent settlers from Culture A. More complex societies may be able to organize better politically and militarily than less complex societies in order to alter the course of acculturation, while nomads may be in a position to disperse to avoid major acculturative influences.

Individual B: While there are individual differences in any acculturating group (a point we will be emphasizing later), it is likely that there will be characteristic psychological phenomena in a particular group which will affect the acculturation process. These have not been widely studied, but one example in the literature (Berry, 1979a; Hallowell, 1955) is that of the independence of individuals in hunter-gatherer societies; it has been argued that the values of independence and egalitarianism make it difficult for such persons to accept the new authority which often arrives with acculturation, and as a consequence the process of acculturation tends to be much more uneven among nomads than among sedentary groups.

In addition to these specific psychological characteristics which may be discerned in particular groups, it is also important to consider how the set of cultural-level phenomena listed above for Culture B is distributed across individuals in the group: do they vary according to the person's age, sex, family position, personal abilities, etc.? *The crucial point is that not every person in the acculturating group will necessarily enter into the acculturation process in the same way or to the same degree.* Hence, assessment of individual acculturation is an important aspect of acculturation research.

Culture B^1: At this point we turn our attention to the changes which have actually taken place as a result of the acculturation process (recognizing, of course, that in many cases the acculturative influences continue to affect the group). These global consequences of acculturation have received considerable attention in the literature (see Berry, 1980c, for a review of some general trends), and include such global descriptors as Westernization, Modernization, Industrialization, Americanization, Russification, Sinofication, Sanskritization, Toyotafication, Cocacolonization, etc. For the purposes of this chapter such broad characterizations are considered to be too general. Instead, we will attempt to look more closely at some specific phenomena which can be organized according to a number of headings.

1. *Political:* Have there been changes in political characteristics as a result of acculturation? For example, has independence been lost, have previously unrelated (even warring) groups been placed within a common framework, have new authority systems (e.g. chiefs, mayors, governor) been added, have people with regional similarities been "upgraded" to "tribes" or "provinces"?

2. *Economic:* Has the subsistence base been changed, or the distribution of wealth been altered? For example, have hunter-

gatherers been converted into herders or farmers, others into industrial or wage workers? Have previous concentrations of wealth in certain families or regions been eliminated, or conversely, has a new wealthy class emerged from a previously uniform system? Have new economic activities been introduced, such as mining, forestry, game management, tourism, manufacturing?

3. *Demographic:* Has there been a change in the population size, its urban/rural distribution, its age or sex profile, or in regional dispersion?

4. *Cultural:* To what extent are there new languages, religions, modes of dress, schooling, transportation, housing, and forms of social organization and social relations in the acculturated group? How do these relate to the previous norms; do they conflict with them, partially displace them, or merge (as in some forms of Creole, or of African Christian churches)?

All of these, and possibly many more depending on one's particular field site, are important markers of the extent to which acculturation has taken place in the group.

Individual B[1]: Here we pick up on two points made previously: there are very likely to be individual differences in the psychological characteristics which a person brings to the acculturation process; and not every person will necessarily participate to the same extent in the process. Taken together, this means that we need to shift our focus away from general characterizations and assessments of acculturation phenomena to a concern for individual variation in a sample (see Chapter 3) of persons who are taken to represent the group undergoing acculturation.

We also need to be aware that individual acculturation (as well as group-level phenomena) does not cohere as a nice neat package. Not only will groups and individuals vary in their participation and response to acculturative influences, some domains of culture and behavior may become altered without comparable changes in other domains. For example, attitudes toward the value of traditional technology may change without a parallel change in beliefs and behaviors associated with it. That is, the process of acculturation is an uneven one, and does not affect all cultural and psychological phenomena in a uniform manner.

Research Designs

As we have noted, acculturation is a process which takes place over time, and results in changes both in the culture and in the individual. The measurement of change, between two or more points in time, is a topic which has a considerable literature in developmental and educational psychology, but not much in anthropology or in cross-cultural psychology. This lack has recently been highlighted for anthropology by a volume devoted to conducting long-term, even continuous, field work (Foster, Scudder, Colson, and Kemper, 1978), but no similar treatment exists for cross-cultural psychology

Culture change *per se* can only be noted and assessed when two sets of data (from Cultures B and B^1) are compared. While this is ideal, in practice such a two point contrast is not possible except with longitudinal research. Instead, a more usual practice is that many of the features of Culture B are identified from other sources (e.g. earlier ethnographic accounts) or partially reconstructed from reports of the older and/or the less acculturated members of the community. Similarly, individual change can ideally be assessed by longitudinal research, and this is often plagued with problems of loss through death or out-migration, and by problems of the continuing relevance of research instruments.

A common alternative to longitudinal research is cross-sectional research in which a time-related variable, such as length of residence or generational status, is employed. For example, among immigrants, those who have resided longer in Culture A may experience more acculturation than those residing for a shorter period (usually controlling for present age and age of arrival). Similarly, it is common to classify group members by their generation (first generation are themselves immigrants, second generation are their offspring, etc.). An assumption here is that acculturation is a linear process over time, an assumption which we will consider later.

One longitudinal study (Berry, Wintrob, Sindell, & Mawhinney, 1982) which employed both a longitudinal and cross-sectional design, was concerned with how the Cree communities and individuals of James Bay (northern Quebec) would respond to a large-scale hydroelectric project constructed in their midst. Initial field work with adults and teenagers was carried out before construction began. Eight years later (after construction), about half the original sample was studied again, supplemented by an equal number of new individuals who were the same ages as the original sample was eight years earlier. This provided a longitudinal analysis for one group (who were compared at two points in time), and a cross-sectional analysis to maintain an age control.

Other designs may be needed in other acculturation arenas. For example, among a settled population where longitudinal work is not done, length of residence, and generational status are not appropriate variables. Here a respondent's age may be a suitable surrogate, since the younger are usually more exposed to acculturative influences, while the older have a longer history of enculturation in culture B and hence may be more resistive. The essential issue, though, is to ensure that both the design and the measures match as well as possible the local acculturation phenomena, rather than emulating more precise but irrelevant or impossible designs which are standard in other domains of research.

SPECIFIC VARIABLES AND THEIR MEASUREMENT

To work our way through these individual psychological phenomena, we present them in three categories: individual contact or participation variables; attitudes toward the acculturation process; and psychological consequences of acculturation.

Contact and Participation

The central issue here is the extent to which a particular individual has engaged in the acculturation process. Numerous indicators may be sought, and from a variety of sources (the individual, an informant, or by direct observation). Precisely because others may be the source of information, as well as the individual, we may obtain some objective cross-validation in many cases.

We approach the topic in two ways: first we list (and briefly comment on) many of the variables which appear in the literature; and second we present illustrative measures to show how the variables have actually been employed in field work. The list includes:

1. *Education:* How far has an individual gone in the formal schooling which has been introduced from outside? If there is one single indicator of individual contact and participation to be taken in the field, previous research suggests that this is likely to be the most fruitful one.

2. *Wage employment:* To what extent has an individual entered the work force for wages, as opposed to remaining with traditional economic activity?

3. *Urbanization:* In predominantly rural societies, to what extent has the individual migrated to, and lived in, a new urban agglomeration; to what extent has he traveled to or visited these urban areas?

4. *Media:* To what extent does the individual listen to radio, watch television, and read newspapers and magazines which introduce him to Culture A?

5. *Political participation:* To what extent does the individual involve himself in the new political structures, including voting, running for office, or volunteering for Boards, etc.?

6. *Religion:* Has the individual changed his religion to one introduced by Culture A, and to what extent does he practice it?

7. *Language:* What is the extent of knowledge and use of the language(s) introduced by Culture A?

8. *Daily practices:* To what extent is there a change in personal dress, housing and furniture styles, food habits, etc.?

9. *Social relations:* To what extent does the individual relate to (marry, play with, work with, reside with) those of Culture A as opposed to those of his own group?

These numerous variables are likely to be interrelated; thus we find in the literature attempts to develop scales or indices of contact and participation which sum across these various experiences. Some examples of these are:

Contact Indices. An Index of Contact (de Lacey, 1970) was developed as a general contact index for Australian Aboriginal children with white Australian society. It contains two sections: *exposure variables* (which include some cultural-level as well as individual-level variables) and *adaptation variables.* Exposure was assessed by proportion of school population and of community which is Euro-Australian, visits to Euro-Australian houses, shopping experiences of children, travel to Euro-Australian centers, use of English, access to mass media and to Euro-Australian artifacts. Adaptation was assessed by ratings of persistence of Aboriginal culture, use of Euro-Australian games and hobbies, use of Euro-Australian food, the home physical environment (Euro-Australian versus Aboriginal), and community organization (primarily tribal versus virtually Euro-Australian). Total scores were then calculated for each child. This index illustrates how acculturation may be assessed at the individual level, but of course, the actual items will vary depending on population and research goals.

Another contact scale (Berry et al., 1985) was developed for use in Central Africa with Biaka Pygmy and Bangandu Villagers. It consists of eight variables: number of local languages spoken; knowledge of French; knowledge of Sango (the national *lingua franca*); ownership (cf. below, with items for knives, pottery, ornaments, outside goods); employment and technology (transitional hunter or farmer, through to wage earner); religion (animism through to Islam); adoption of clothing (in European style), and travel (to towns and cities). All these variables were positively and (in most cases) significantly correlated, and were used to create a single standardized index for each person.

Ownership Index. This was developed (by Berry & Annis, 1974) for use among the James Bay Cree as a Guttman-type scale such that participation at the "high end" of the scale usually included activities at the "low end," but not vice versa. The items in the scale (low to high) were ownership of: radio, outboard motor, snowmobile, washer, freezer, bank account, and life insurance. The scale may be used either in a Guttman form or simply by summing across items owned. The intention is to obtain objective evidence of the extent to which an individual has "bought into" Euro-Canadian society. Once again, this is illustrative of how to assess one aspect of acculturation, rather than a ready-made scale which can be used in all field settings.

Change Index. A measure of acculturation was developed to assess the degree of acculturation of Mexican-American adolescents living in California (Olmedo, Martinez, & Martinez, 1978). Questions related to sociocultural characteristics (e.g. language, nationality and occupational status) were included as well as ratings of concepts (e.g., "male") on potency scales which were thought to represent differences between Mexican and American cultures. Factor analysis revealed three factors: nationality and language, socioeconomic status, and the potency of "father" and "male." Validity was established by correlating acculturation scores with ethnic group membership (Mexican-American versus Anglo-American). A further validation study (Olmedo & Padilla, 1978) was conducted involving adults also in California. Samples were drawn from first and third generation Mexican-Americans and from the Anglo-American population. In this case, validity was established by a significant difference between generations, and between Mexican- and Anglo-Americans.

In addition to the use of these types of scales at the individual level (to predict such things as test performance, intergroup attitudes, or mental health status), the individual scores may also be aggregated to the sample level. This may permit comparison with more general characterizations of acculturation made, for example, by an ethnographer or government offical, yielding some cross-validation. It may also permit comparison across samples (for example, a rural and an urban sample) within the same culture.

It should be emphasized that these scales and indices are not universally valid, ready-made, or standard instruments which can be taken "as is" for use in any field setting. Some variables are clearly more relevant to Pygmies than to a community of Anglo-Americans (e.g. adoption of clothing), while others may be more relevant to an ethnic group undergoing acculturation (such as the language spoken in the family) than to a linguistically homogeneous community in Central Africa.

Attitudes Toward Acculturation

There are five distinct approaches to this topic which appear in the literature: intergroup relations, modernity, acculturation attitudes, opinion convergence, and ethnic loyalty research. Since the intergroup relations work is considered in Chapter 9, we will not deal with it further here, except to note the obvious fact that the attitude that an individual in Culture B has toward those in Culture A, and toward aspects of Culture A, will have some bearing on how an individual enters into the acculturation process. If own-group (B) attitudes are very positive, and out-group (A) attitudes are very negative (the classical ethnocentrism orientation), then acculturative influences are more likely to be screened out, resisted, rejected, or otherwise rendered less effective. On the other hand, if the reverse attitude pattern is prevalent among individuals in Culture B, then acculturative influences are more likely to be accepted.

Individual Modernity. The orientations individuals have toward changing their culture and adopting the ways of others have frequently been assessed on scales which range from "traditionalism" to "modernity" (see Berry 1980c, pp. 226-234 for a review, and Jones, 1977, for a criticism). Such a scale incorporates a number of theoretical assumptions, and these assumptions have implications for assessment. The three assumptions involve the *value*, the *universality*, and the *linearity* of this form of acculturation. Specifically, it is sometimes assumed that being "modern" ("Western," "industrialized," "civilized," etc.) is better than being "traditional;" that acculturation everywhere, among all peoples, is toward being "modern;" and that there is a single, linear path toward being "modern." An alternative set of assumptions is that there is no special or inherent value to being "traditional" or being "modern," or being something else; that groups and individuals can change during acculturation in a variety of ways (see later section) other than by becoming "modern;" and that there are many lines of change, some of which even backtrack, in the process of acculturation.

A number of scales have been designed to assess the individual modernity of persons who are experiencing acculturation and which exhibit the first set of assumptions. The Overall Modernity Scale of Inkeles and Smith (1974) is the best known of these, although those of Doob (1967) and Kahl (1968) are of the same type. In the Inkeles and Smith (1974) work, which was conducted in a number of countries (e.g. Chile, Bangladesh, Nigeria), a series of scales was developed around twenty-four themes which were considered to be indicative of modernity, (e.g. active public participation, occupational and educational aspirations, family size restrictions, kinship obligations, work commitment, women's rights). Statements were developed expressing an attitude to each theme, and response categories were provided. Individuals were then presented with the items and response alternatives, and then scored. Generally positive item correlations were found, leading them to amalgamate the items into a single "Overall Modernity" (OM) score. These scales, they claim (e.g. Inkeles, 1977), are suitable for assessing any individual's modernity.

We may ask, does it not matter where the individual is coming from, and where he aspires to go in terms of the acculturation process? The work of Dawson (1967, 1969, et al., 1972) provides a partial answer. While assuming that the end point of acculturation is generally that of "modernity" (as articulated by Inkeles), Dawson argues that individuals coming from differing cultures are on different tracks toward modernity, thus necessitating scales which are unique in content for each culture. In his empirical work Dawson has developed scales for West Africans, Australian Aborigines, and Hong Kong Chinese.

Dawson's approach is to identify a set of concepts which are important in the traditional culture (e.g. witchcraft, division of labor by sex, responsibility to kin), and then to construct four statements about each concept. One is designed to reflect the "traditional" point of view ("It is important that a man should fulfil his responsibilities by looking after his family and all his relations as well"), one a "semi-traditional" view ("It is important for a man to look after his family and close relations"), one a "semi-modern" view ("Although it is important for a man to help his cousins and uncles, he should look after his wife and children first"), and one a "modern" view ("It is important that a man should spend money mainly on his own wife and children, and not give it to all his uncles and cousins"). Each of the four statements is responded to on a standard five-point Likert scale (Strongly Agree, Agree, Not Sure, Disagree, Strongly Disagree). Four scale scores are then generated for each individual by adding up responses across concepts, one each for Traditional, Semi-Traditional, Semi-Modern, and Modern. The two advantages of this approach are first that the scales are culturally relative (in that the content is related to an issue of traditional importance in that group), and second that there can be an empirical examination of the degree to which there is linearity along the track from traditionalism to modernity. In fact Dawson has found considerable nonlinearity in his results: in one case high Traditionalism *and* high Modernity scores signal "attitudinal conflict" about the acculturation process, which he uses to predict certain stress reactions.

A third approach is not to assume even that there is a common "modern" end point to acculturation; rather it is to attempt to identify both a culture-specific starting point (the traditional concepts, as in Dawson's work), *and* culture-specific alternative end points. The work of Berry, Wintrob, Sindell, and Mawhinney (1982), illustrates this particular strategy. Among the James Bay Cree a number of alternative goals of change were being identified by the people, and these were classified by the researchers as Continuity (emphasizing a more characteristic Cree way of living), Change (an attempt to become more like Euro-Canadians in the region), and Synthesis (a position which attempts to select the best of both worlds). Note that Continuity does not represent a "traditional" Cree way (as it existed prior to contact). Change does not resemble the "modern" (industrial, urban) goals of other scales, and Synthesis is not a half-way house (cf. "semi-modern") but an attempt to forge a new life style.

A number of topics were chosen (e.g. technology, social relationships, medical practice) and a statement was developed to represent each of the three positions. Individuals were asked to select which of the three statements they most agreed with, and then which they least agreed with; the unchosen statement was assumed to be intermediate in acceptability. Scale scores were generated for each of the three options by summing across topics. The advantages of this approach are first that no universal "modern" end point is assumed; second, that the three positions are not assumed to fall on the same line or track; and third, the selection of response alternatives is rather easy and may prove to be more suitable for some populations who have little exposure to attitude assessment techniques using five- or seven-point scales.

In summary, these three approaches differ in assumptions and hence in assessment practices; they range from a largely *etic* approach (which may permit comparisons of attitudes across groups), through to a more *emic* one (which does not attempt comparison). The choice of approach will depend on the goals of the research, the nature of the group undergoing acculturation, and the direction in which acculturation seems to be heading.

Acculturation Attitudes. The valued goals of acculturation are not necessarily toward modernity or any other single alternative. Moreover, the goal as articulated by Culture A in their policy statements may not be the preferred course among the leaders of individuals in Culture B. In Australia (Sommerlad & Berry, 1970) an attempt was made to discover what the attitudes of Aborigines were to their future in Australia; the Commonwealth Government proposed assimilation, but others were not so sure. Since then (Berry, 1980b) the argument has been made that acculturation can be viewed as a multilinear phenomenon, as a set of alternatives, rather than a single dimension ending in absorption into a "modern" society.

The ways in which an individual (or a group) of Culture B wishes to relate to Culture A have been termed "Acculturation Attitudes" (see Berry et al. 1984, for a review of the reliability, validity, and correlations of these attitudes). In a sense, they are conceptually the result of an interaction between ideas deriving from the modernity literature and the intergroup relations literature. In the former, the central issue is the degree to which one wishes to remain culturally as one has been (e.g. in terms of identity, language, way of life) as opposed to giving it all up to become part of a "modern" society; in the latter, the central issue is the extent one wishes to have day-to-day interactions with those of other groups, as opposed to turning away from other groups, and relating only to those of one's own group.

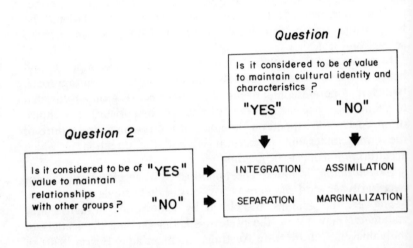

Figure 10.2 Four Varieties of Acculturation Defined by Position with Respect to Two Issues: 1. Modernity (value placed on maintaining cultural identity and traditions); and 2. Intergroup Relations (value placed on maintaining relations with other groups in the society).

When these two central issues are posed simultaneously, a conceptual framework (Figure 10.2) is generated which posits four varieties of acculturation. It is, of course, recognized that each issue can be responded to on an attitudinal dimension, but for purposes of conceptual presentation, a dichotomous response ("yes" or "no") is shown. When an individual in Culture B does not wish to maintain his identity (etc.) and seeks daily interaction with Culture A, then the Assimilation path or mode is defined. In contrast, when there is a value placed on holding onto one's original culture, and at the same time a wish to avoid interaction with others, then the Separation alternative is defined. When there is an interest in both maintaining one's original culture, and in daily interactions with others, Integration is the option; here, there is some degree of cultural integrity maintained, while moving to participate as an integral part of the larger social network. Finally, when there is little possibility or interest in cultural maintenance (often for reasons of enforced cultural loss), and little interest in relations with others (often for reasons of exclusion or discrimination) then Marginalization is defined.

Each of these four conceptual alternatives has been assessed with individuals in a variety of groups which are experiencing acculturation. The original study (Sommerlad & Berry, 1970) primarily sought to measure attitudes to Assimilation and Integration; other studies (e.g. Berry et al., 1982) assessed all four attitudes among James Bay Cree, while work with other groups (such as French-, Portuguese-, and Korean-Canadians) has demonstrated the usefulness of the approach not only with native peoples, but also with acculturating ethnic groups.

The four scales are developed by selecting a number of topics (e.g. endogamy, ethnic media) which are relevant to acculturation in the particular group. Then four statements (one for each alternative) are generated with the help of informants. Usually it is possible to establish face validity for the statements by asking judges who are familiar with the model (Figure 10.2) to sort them into the four alternatives; those statements with good inter-rater agreement are then kept. Administration involves either a Likert scale response to each statement, or a statement of preference for one of the four statements within a topic. Four scores are then calculated for each person by summing across topics within each alternative. Reliability (Cronbach's alpha) is enhanced by item selection, and validity is checked against behavioral measures (e.g. high Separation scorers read only ethnic newspapers, high Assimilation read only English, high Integration read both).

308   FIELD METHODS IN CROSS-CULTURAL RESEARCH

Opinion Convergence. Working with a variety of European immigrant groups in Australia, Taft (1966, 1976b) has developed an "Australianism Scale" which assesses the degree to which opinions on a variety of social topics converge with those held by Australians. An item is in the form "The clergy should keep completely out of politics," and degree of agreement is requested. Validation studies have been carried out with over twenty samples (about 1,200 persons), and indicate the first generation samples are significantly lower than Australian groups, with second generation scores generally falling in between.

Ethnic Loyalty. Another approach combines the attitudinal dimension of this section with the contact/participation dimension of the previous section. In this work, Padilla (1980a, b) employs the concepts of "ethnic loyalty" to refer to the former, and "cultural awareness" to refer to the latter. Working with Hispanics in the United States, Padilla has employed eleven dimensions to operationalize ethnic loyalty (e.g. language preference, name preference for children, food preference), and fifteen dimensions to operationalize cultural awareness (e.g. knowledge of Spanish, contact, endogamy, parental contacts). When the ethnic loyalty dimensions are factor analyzed four factors emerge: "language preference and use," "cultural pride and affiliation," "cultural identification and preference," and "social behavior orientation" (i.e. preference for things Mexican). Similarly, there were four factors among the cultural awareness dimensions: "respondent's cultural heritage," "spouse's cultural heritage," "parents' cultural heritage," and "perceived discrimination." Working further with these data, eight scales were developed (one for each factor), and these were again factor analyzed (after standardization). Two factors emerged: Factor one loaded six of the eight scores (three from the loyalty and three from the awareness domains) while factor two loaded three dimensions (perceived discrimination, cultural pride and affiliation, and social behavior orientation, the latter being shared by both factors). Padilla concluded that "cultural awareness is the more general component of acculturation" ... while "ethnic loyalty is the more tenuous component" (1980b, p. 65).

Further work will be necessary to bring the various measures reviewed here together conceptually and empirically. In particular, the political and cultural context in which acculturation is taking place (usually determined by the power of Culture A) will almost certainly affect the topics chosen, the options or alternatives which are conceivable, and the factor structure of the results. Thus, in widely differing acculturation arenas, such conceptual and empirical convergence may be impossible, while in more similar contexts, it may be that common dimensions to acculturation phenomena will be found. However, for the field worker, in any specific setting, the most important decision is whether the scales developed are modeled in the appropriate way so that they match the actual situation in which the research is being conducted. Put in terms of methodology (Trimble, Lonner, & Boucher, 1983) we are a long way from achieving any *etic* constructs; so make sure your *emic* characteristics are right!

Consequences of Acculturation

In this section we want to focus on the assessment of what happens to individuals as a result of acculturation. As we saw in the last section, it is not always possible to maintain a clear separation between contact measures and attitude measures when we examine a particular acculturation study. Similarly, we will see in this section that not all changes actually result directly from acculturation; some may be delayed in time, and some may even bring about acculturation in a continuing antecedent-consequent chain. For example, more contact often results in a more positive attitude to assimilation; thus the attitude could be classified as a "consequence of acculturation." Conversely, an initially positive attitude toward assimilation may result in a person seeking out more contact; here, the contact could just as well be classified as a consequence. Despite these qualifications, a number of studies have attempted to comprehend the results of acculturation, and have developed instruments specifically to measure them.

Another distinction can be found in the literature between two kinds of consequences (Berry, 1976, 1980c). One refers to the relatively conflict-free changes in behavior, such as an individual gradually taking on wage employment and giving up another economic role; these have been termed *behavioral shifts*, and are characterized by a continuity in quality, but a change in quantity (e.g. from a pattern of 20 percent wage employment/80 percent farming at time 1 to 90 percent wage employment/10 percent farming at time 2). The other refers to new behaviors which often accompany acculturation, which appear to result from psychological conflict and social disintegration, such as an increase in homicide, spouse abuse, or a decline in mental health status; this type of consequence has been termed *acculturative stress*, and is characterized by a qualitative change in the life of an individual or community. Once again it is possible to challenge the distinction; after all, homicide, aggression, and neglect are present in most societies prior to acculturation, but we frequently encounter new forms as well as new rates, such that rather than being regarded as deviant (in Culture B) they become the norm in some cases in Culture B[1].

As the definitions of acculturation presented earlier suggested, there can also be novel phenomena, those stimulated or even created by the process of acculturation. These are not just shifts in previous behaviors or problematic stress phenomena; they are new cultural and behavioral phenomena which arise by way of social and political movements, themselves stimulated by acculturative contact. We turn now to a consideration of all three sets of phenomena: shifts, stress, and some novel features of acculturation.

Behavioral Shifts. Virtually any behavior studied by psychology is a candidate for a shift during acculturation. Of course, this challenges the basic notions of personality trait and behavioral stability, which posit continuity over time and across situations. However, the field of cross-cultural psychology has established some fairly solid linkages between how an individual acts (including thoughts, feelings, and motives) and the culture which nurtured him; it should not be difficult to accept, then, that when the culture changes the individual may change as well. What may be stable over time is the culture-behavior linkage, but not the behavior itself.

Among the many behaviors which could be included here, only a few can be presented. We will begin with identity, move to aspects of cognition, then to personality, and finally (to come full circle) consider attitudes and contact as psychological characteristics which themselves shift as a result of acculturation.

Identity (or how one usually thinks of oneself) can be in terms of cultural (including ethnic and racial) or other (e.g. age, sex, location) factors (Aboud, 1981). Here we are primarily interested in cultural identity, and how it may change over the course of acculturation. There is widespread evidence that cultural identities do change. At the beginning of contact, there is usually little question: one thinks of oneself as a member of the group into which one was enculturated, be it small in scale (a village or a band), or large (a state or country). As contact continues, identity changes may be monitored by a variety of techniques which can provide evidence for simple shifts, and for identity conflict and confusion (related to acculturative stress).

The three most common methods to assess cultural identity are by observations, by interviewing, and by testing. Direct observation of whom one commonly associates with may indicate one's identity; clothing, hobbies, and language use may also be observed. However, opportunity or factors other than personal preference may affect actual behaviors, and hence these direct observations should be supplemented by more subjective techniques. Moreover, these overt behaviors may already have been employed as objective indices of contact/participation, and hence should not be duplicated.

Interviewing has been employed often in large-scale survey or community studies. Among immigrants and their descendants, a typical approach is to ask for one's ancestral country of origin, on both the father's (F) and mother's (M) side, and then to pose the question: "How do you usually think of yourself?" The options can be: as an "F"; as an "M"; as an "F-Australian"; as an "M-Australian"; as an "Australian"; or some other identity. Work in this mode (e.g. O'Bryan et al., 1976; and Berry et al., 1977, in Canada) has usually found a significant change over time or over generations: immigrants themselves often identify as "F" or "M", second and third generations as "F-C" or "M-C", and third and subsequent generations as "Canadian." Identity shifts are also common among native peoples undergoing acculturation, but tend to be more resistant to change toward an identification with the dominant society (Sommerlad & Berry, 1970; Berry & Annis, 1974).

In new nation states, identity shifts tend to be away from small-scale or local cultural identities toward larger nation-wide identities. In one study (Segall, Doornbos, & Davis, 1976), Munyankore men in Uganda were interviewed before a new national constitution was enacted, and again three years later. When asked "What are you?", the local cultural identity predominated over the national (Ugandan) identity. However, when asked "How should the Banyankore think of themselves?", the majority responded with a Ugandan identity. Segall et al. (1976) concluded that while the typical Munyankore man knew it was appropriate to identify with the new nation state, few had yet come to do so.

Among native peoples in the United States, Trimble & Richardson (1983) have studied "tribal identity" with a sample of close to 14,000 Indian youth, aged nine to nineteen. Rather than posing a single question, a set of seven questions are asked, and respondents answer on a four-point scale (very much, somewhat, a little, not at all). Questions include: "How much would you like to go to a school where there are mostly Indians?", "How proud are you to be a member of your tribe?", and "How much would you like your tribal language to be taught in school?" Here, the research question is broader than ethnic identity *per se*, and approaches the concept of ethnic attachment and ethnic loyalty.

Testing, using a variety of techniques, has also been employed (see Brand, Ruiz, & Padilla, 1974, and Akoodie, 1983 for reviews). The most common form of test has been the doll-choice technique among children, where a range of dolls of different skin color, or in different cultural costumes are presented; the child is asked to select the one which is "like you" (or some other question thought to elicit preference and identity). Unfortunately this technique has been fraught with so many methodological problems that it is no longer recommended.

An alternative technique (Berry et al., 1982) uses a card-sorting task in which a number of ethnic group names (say 25 to 30) are each printed on a card, and on one card is printed "myself." The respondent is asked to sort the cards into piles on the basis of perceived similarity; there is no limitation on the number of piles, and there is no request to name the piles after completion, with the exception of identifying a "miscellaneous" pile if there is one. Multidimensional scaling analyses are then used to organize the card-sorts for the sample as a whole. Usually interpretable clusters emerge, and the location of "myself" can be assessed relative to the location of the clusters. For example, among the James Bay Cree, there was a cluster formed by all the bands who belong to the Grand Council of the Crees of Quebec, another cluster formed by adjacent but non-Cree groups, and another by non-native groups (mainly Euro-Canadian). The location of "myself" was right in the center of the Cree cluster indicating that in general for this group there is little identity shift, uncertainty, or conflict. A second possible measure is at the individual level, where the placement of the "myself" card by any particular individual can be examined both in relation to the individual's own pile arrangement, and in relation to those which emerged collectively from the sample as a whole.

Cognitive shifts are also frequently observed in studies of acculturation. Indeed cognitive shifts are often the very goal of acculturation, as in the case of educational or religious missions in many parts of the world. Here we are primarily interested in the intellectual changes which may occur with acculturation. A major focus (e.g. Scribner & Cole, 1973, and Rogoff, 1981) has been on the cognitive consequences of formal education, with an associated interest in the consequences of literacy (Scribner & Cole, 1981). Cognitive qualities which have been assessed are general intelligence (e.g. Vernon, 1969), cognitive style (e.g. Berry, 1976), memory (e.g. Wagner, 1981), classification (e.g. Scribner & Cole, 1981), as well as some of the more overt consequences such as success at school.

Perhaps the most common (and ambiguous) finding is that performance on cognitive tests becomes "better" (i.e. more like the test maker, or test administrator) as the test taker becomes more acculturated to the society of origin of the tests. Phrased in this way, the finding is obvious and perhaps meaningless. The use of such tests among cultural groups in various parts of the world, and among ethnic groups in plural societies continues, and continues to be criticized (e.g. Samuda, 1983), and the results continue to be open to numerous interpretations. One point of view about such results is that there is no substantive shift in cognitive functioning, only a superficial change in performance due to learning some "test taking tricks" (e.g. familiarity with the language of the test, with test-like situations, etc.). Another point of view is that there may indeed be new cognitive qualities or operations that develop with acculturation influences such as literacy or industrialization. While this view is held by many who work in the field of modernization research (e.g. Inkeles & Smith, 1974), and in literacy (e.g. Goody, 1968), the evidence for such fundamental changes is rather sparse. For example, the study by Scribner & Cole (1981) revealed very little in the way of general cognitive consequences of literacy, only a few changes which are more specific to skills directly related to the practice of literacy.

The evident conclusion to be drawn is that the search for cognitive consequences of acculturation is methodologically very difficult to carry out if one wants unambiguous results. If the point is to demonstrate that over time or over generations beliefs, abilities, or even general intelligence (as defined and measured in Culture A) change in Culture B in the direction of the norms in Culture A, then the task is rather easy. But the meaning (or "depth") of these changes is much more difficult to specify.

Personality shifts have also been observed during acculturation (which may appear to be a contradiction in terms). In one classical study by Hallowell (1955), three groups of Ojibwa Indians were administered the Rorschach test. One sample was located close to Euro-Canadian influence, one was in the remote hinterland, and the third was geographically in between with an intermediate degree of contact. Hallowell interpreted his results as showing a continuity of a model Ojibwa personality, but with differences from one sample to another such that the most remote was most intact, the higher contact sample had shifted more toward Euro-Canadian personality, and the mid-community was in between. However, such a "linear gradient" may not always be evident. Peck et al. (1976) have found that some individuals may show this pattern, but others may not change at all, or indeed may reverse the process. One way of interpreting these variations is to argue that those who are in the "assimilation mode" may show a linear gradient, while those who are separating or integrating may not exhibit the pattern.

Louise and George Spindler (1958) are responsible for conducting an extensive study of the Menomini Indians of Wisconsin. In an effort to study the "levels of acculturation" existing among the North American Indian group the two anthropologists used a Rorschach protocol to measure perceptual structure — the way people tend to organize the world around them. A sociocultural interview schedule containing some 23 indexes and 180 coded items also was developed to tap life-style activities including such demographics as house type, income, use of medical facilities, education level, and items about belief systems.

The Spindlers, however, did not rely exclusively on the data provided by the Rorschach and the interview schedule. They skilfully developed an expressive autobiographic interview technique. Essentially, in the technique informants are asked to tell the story of their life; at critical moments the interviewer breaks in and seeks, through probing questions, to obtain clarity and meaning. The data served to supplement and substantiate Rorschach and interview schedule findings.

In a comparable research effort among the Blood, another North American Indian tribe, the Spindlers developed another projective technique they referred to as the Instrumental Activities Inventory (Spindler & Spindler, 1963); this is a step-child version of the TAT. It consists of 24 drawings of Indians engaged in numerous daily activities. The activities coincide with those things one must do to adapt to the pressures of the outside world. These broad categories were developed and included: traditional Blood activities, particularly those having little or no influence from outside sources; those which were more contemporary and reflected strong influences of modern, rural cultures; and those which directly reflected the influence of contemporary society. The three categories closely followed those developed for study among the Menomini: native-oriented, peyote cult, and transitional.

Attitudes, as we have seen, may predispose contact and hence lead to acculturative change. To come full circle, then, we should remind ourselves that the consequences of acculturation can be changes in attitudes (modernity, acculturation attitudes, etc.) and changes in contact itself. Evidence does indeed show that there is a complex of interrelationships among many variables; for example, both modernity and a preference for assimilation have often been observed to increase as a result of acculturation by individuals of Culture B in the life of Culture A. However, lest there be left the impression that there is a continuous linear skid towards assimilation and cultural and psychological homogeneity, we may remind ourselves that conflict, reaction, and other resistive strategies also frequently occur during acculturation. These are important factors in acculturative stress phenomena, to which we now turn.

Acculturative Stress. One of the most obvious and frequently reported consequences of acculturation is that of societal disintegration and personal crisis (see Berry & Kim, 1986, for a review). The old social order and cultural norms often disappear, and individuals may be lost in the change. At the group level, previous patterns of authority, of civility, and of welfare no longer operate, and at the individual level, hostility, uncertainty, and depression may set in.

Taken together these changes constitute the negative side of acculturation, changes which are frequently, but not inevitably, present.

Archival, observational, and interview methods have been employed to assess these phenomena. Archival approaches can provide collective data for the society or community as a whole: rates of suicide, homicide, family and substance abuse (etc.) can provide important information about the acculturation context in which an individual is operating. In particular, rates of psychiatric attention have been employed often in the literature. However, all of these archival records require an organized social system, which may itself be suffering from disintegration; thus such macro-indicators may not always be available, or if available they may not be reliable.

Observational studies have typically employed third-party sources of information about, or direct observations of, more specific research subjects. For example, counting court appearances, alcohol consumption, or work and school absenteeism for specific individuals or target communities can provide, over time, a reasonable indicator of problem behaviors during acculturation.

Interviewing samples of individuals in acculturating communities has been a particularly important source of evidence about stress both in Western urban groups undergoing change (e.g. Srole et al., 1962) and in specific cultural groups experiencing acculturation (e.g. Wintrob & Sindell, 1972). Because of the popularity of this approach, some fairly concise interview measures have been developed, of which we will consider three.

The 22-item Langner (1962) scale has been widely used to assess mental health status. It contains statements about psychological, and psychosomatic disorders, such as "Do you have personal worries that get you down physically?" Respondents are asked to indicate with a "yes" or "no," and the total score is simply the number of problems claimed. While there are no absolute criteria, Langner (1962) considers that a score of four or above indicates psychiatric impairment.

A similar scale has been developed in a number of versions from the Cornell Medical Index (Brodman et al., 1952). The full scale consists of 195 items concerned with somatic functioning, and 51 items concerned with psychological life, arranged into six subscales (Inadequacy, Depression, Anxiety, Sensitivity, Anger, and Tension). Work in Alaska by Chance (1965) revealed somewhat heightened levels of psychological problems among acculturating Inuit. A twenty-item version was developed by Cawte et al. (1968) containing ten somatic items and ten psychological items. This version was employed with an Australian Aborigine group which had experienced both relocation and acculturation. Later use was made of the scale by Berry (1976) with various acculturating Canadian Indian groups, and Blue and Blue (1983) have employed it with Canadian Indian university students. The full 51-item psychological scales have also been employed with various groups, including Vietnamese refugees (Masuda et al., 1980; Berry & Blondel, 1982). Because of its wide usage, and its good psychometric properties (internal consistency usually high, and cross-group validation usually significant), the Cawte short form of the scale is reproduced in full in Table 10.1. As in the case of the Langner scale, the total score is simply the total of those problems claimed by the respondent.

TABLE 10.1

Twenty-Item Stress Scale

1. Do you have pains in the heart or chest?
2. Do you usually belch a lot after eating?
3. Do you constantly suffer from bad constipation?
4. Do your muscles and joints constantly feel stiff?
5. Is your skin very sensitive or tender?
6. Do you suffer badly from frequent severe headaches?
7. Do you often have spells of severe dizziness?
8. Do you usually get up tired and exhausted in the morning?
9. Do you wear yourself out worrying about your health?
10. Do you usually have great difficulty in falling asleep or staying asleep?
11. Do strange people or places make you afraid?
12. Do you wish you always had someone at your side to advise you?
13. Do you usually feel unhappy and depressed?
14. Do you often wish you were dead and away from it all?
15. Does worrying continually get you down?
16. Are you extremely shy or sensitive?
17. Does it make you angry to have anyone tell you what to do?
18. Do people often annoy or irritate you?
19. Do you often shake or tremble?
20. Do you often break out in a cold sweat?

A third scale has been devised to assess the concept of Marginality by Mann (1958). The essence of being marginal is being "poised in psychological uncertainty between two worlds" (Stonequist, 1935), being unable to participate fully in either culture. The scale consists of 14 items, such as "I feel that I don't belong anywhere" and "I feel that nobody really understands me." Respondents indicate those statements with which they agree, and the total score is the number of items agreed with.

A major problem with these three scales is that all the items are phrased in a positive direction; thus, those with a tendency to agree will score higher than others. Another problem is that self report of these disorders may not bear any relationship to their actual presence. While these are important problems to be aware of, in practice they seem not to have created much difficulty: cross-validation with other tests (as we shall see in the next section), and with observational data, tend to support their continued use in studies of acculturation as indicators of the stresses and strains being experienced by individuals.

Novel Phenomena. Acculturation can be a creative, as well as a reactive process. Novel cultural and behavioral phenomena can appear, stimulated by contact, and/or in reaction to contact. One area of research which has examined these issues has been that of *social movements* (Spindler, 1978).

In preparing and organizing research on the acculturation process the researcher must partial out those characteristics that can be attributed to participation in a social movement. Change can occur within a culture without any direct and overt contact with another culture; these days most (of not all) tribes, communities, and settlements are not immune from some sort of indirect social contact with outside groups. Hence, intralocal versus interlocal change is really a matter of degree contingent on the presence and pressure imposed by Culture A. For example, was Margaret Mead's (1956) classic study of change among the Manus of the Admiralty Islands a study of acculturative influences or of social change? Some would say it's a question of whether or not one is talking to an anthropologist or a sociologist.

In addition to being a result of acculturation, a social movement may be a precursor to the acculturative process. If the elements indicative of a social movement are identified early on and the group in question is accessible, the researcher is in a unique position to collect seminal data that could lead to a long-term acculturation study.

Social movements actually involve a series of episodes stimulated by the increased involvement of participants, fluctuations in the roles and responsibilities of leaders, formation of protagonistic and antagonistic factions, and the pressure placed on the group by dominant outside forces. While there are numerous attempts to define what a social movement is we prefer the one offered by the social psychologists Muzafer and Carolyn Sherif:

> A social movement consists of a pattern of attempts over time — prompted by a state of common unrest, discontent, or aspiration shared by a large number of individuals — to bring about change in, to establish, to maintain, or to suppress a definite scheme of human relations and values through pronouncements, literature, meetings, and direct collective action (1969, p. 543).

The latter part of the Sherifs' definition actually targets rich research areas. Pronouncements and quotations from literature are often cast as slogans and woven into the fabric of posters, bulletins, and leaflets and distributed accordingly. The content of the propaganda makes an excellent source for content analysis. In short, the text, photos, drawings, and cartoons often found in early social movement propaganda can be a valuable data source; in fact, a researcher could easily track the changes of a movement by following and closely monitoring the flow of the literature.

Meetings and collective action form another valuable data source for investigating social movements. The occasions typically come about because concerned participants are seeking to solve, through collective action, a social, political, economic, or any mutually agreed upon problem which they share in common. Political revolutions, religious cults, and civil-rights groups are just a few that seem to be occurring more and more frequently in different parts of the world, and all of them involve some collective action on the part of a disenfranchised or dissatisfied segment of a culture.

Research methods developed for the study of collective actions and crowd behavior are well known in the field of social psychology (Katz, 1974). Milgram and Toch (1969), along with providing an elegant, sophisticated treatment of the subject, nonetheless remind us "of the difficulties that the field presents for scientific study" (p.

577). Collective behavior is often very unpredictable; occasionally it can be quite dangerous, and certainly not manageable. It never seems to occur at a convenient time and place. As a consequence the researcher often must obtain the data from secondary sources such as newspapers, anecdotal accounts from observers and participants, and from police and military files if they are accessible and available.

Milgram and Toch (1969) recommend the use of objective survey research techniques and projective techniques to document the various effects generated by crowd behavior. Survey techniques, with the aid of proper sampling procedures, can assist the researcher in verifying rumor and journalistic accounts. Projective techniques, particularly photos of crowd events, can be used to elicit various attitudes towards a collective event. Participants, bystanders, or a sample of the general population can be shown the photos and asked in traditional projective technique fashion to tell a story about the picture in question. In addition, photos could serve as an unobtrusive measure of self-identity; respondents would be asked to pick out those in the photos with whom they might agree, be opposed, or might identify.

Social movements can generate long-term effects on attitudes, values, and individual identity. Changes brought about by the social movement could benefit some, restrict others, and for still others create hardships well beyond their imagination. Out of collective action changes will influence the acculturative process since the elements comprising a culture will undergo dramatic change. More to the point, careful study of the factors which contribute to social movements can aid in our understandings of the full range of factors which contribute to sociocultural change in general.

RELEVANCE TO INDIVIDUAL ASSESSMENT
IN OTHER DOMAINS

As we indicated earlier in this chapter, a common finding in cross-cultural research is that performance on cognitive tests becomes "better" as the test taker becomes more acculturated to Culture A (within which the tests were originally developed). This is but one example of the relevance of assessment of acculturation to other individual assessment. Because of psychologists' extensive reliance on culture-bound norm-referenced measurement instruments, this issue is an important one from a variety of perspectives.

First of all, the *external validity* of cross-cultural studies is at stake. Differences between Cultures A and B (or B[1]) on test x may represent real differences in the attribute being measured, or they may simply reflect a measurement artifact due to the lack of cross-cultural transportability of test x. In other words, the test is not measuring the same phenomenon in Cultures A and B. Thus, assessing the degree of acculturation to A of the members of Culture B provides information that is relevant to any cross-cultural comparison based on measurement instruments that are "culture-loaded." Should members of Culture B turn out to be relatively unacculturated (or exhibit substantial variability in acculturation), then other procedures such as confirmatory factor analysis across cultural groups are recommended to determine the degree of cross-cultural equivalence of test x (Brislin, Lonner, & Thorndike, 1973; Olmedo, 1979).

Assessment of acculturation is also relevant to the *replicability* of cross-cultural research findings. When conducting cross-cultural studies involving groups that may be undergoing cultural change it is important to ascertain the acculturation status of the samples involved. Particularly in cross-sectional studies it is possible that different samples of the "same" cultural population may differ in acculturation levels, often yielding conflicting findings when attempts are made to replicate a given study. Thus similar studies may show differences between groups in one direction, show differences in the opposite direction, or show no differences at all. This has been the case, for example, in a number of cross-cultural studies of ethnic groups in the United States involving variables such as prosocial and competitive behavior, field independence, locus of control, and self esteem (Olmedo, 1979).

At a more individual level, assessment of acculturation is relevant to the identification of appropriate or inappropriate uses of assessment instruments with individuals from different groups in plural societies. These are issues of more than academic interest, because in many instances the relative allocation of a variety of benefits and opportunities is at stake (Olmedo, 1981). Usually most of the research (and debate) tends to focus on the "fairness" of tests and test-based selection procedures for various ethnic or cultural *groups* (see, for example, Wigdor & Gardner, 1982). Although the reduction of culture to group membership may be expeditious for political and/or legal reasons, it is not congruent with what is known about within-group differences in acculturation. A more appropriate approach involves identification of the acculturation status of the individual, which, in turn, is used to modify interpretation of performance in other assessment instruments.

Within the foregoing framework it is possible that assessment instruments may be more or less appropriate for individuals of a cultural group depending on the similarity of the individual's cultural background to that of the normative group (usually Culture A) for the instrument in question (Mercer, 1976, 1977). The implications of this line of reasoning are fairly complex, because acculturation is

TABLE 10.2
Factor Analysis of Variables in Study
of James Bay Cree Acculturation (loadings 0.30 and above)

Variable	Factor		
	I	II	III
CONTACT			
Education	0.91		
Employment	(0.28)	0.30	
Ownership	0.39		
Language Use	0.76		
Literacy	0.51		
Media Use	0.38		
Age	0.78		
ATTITUDES			
Assimilation	0.47		(−0.28)
Integration		0.38	
Separation	−0.59		(0.25)
Change			−0.73
Synthesis		0.45	
Continuity			0.82
COGNITIVE			
Kohs		0.34	
Ravens		0.39	
Vocabulary		0.38	
STRESS			
Cawte		−0.56	
Marginality		−0.54	

multidimensional in nature and most other psychological constructs measured by tests (e.g. cognitive and personality constructs) are also multidimensional in nature. Thus, ultimately, issues germane to the relevance of acculturation to other individual assessment are best addressed within a multivariate context.

Olmedo (1979) has proposed the use of a "full-measurement model" in acculturation research. The model provides a way to investigate relationships between multidimensional sets of quantitatively defined variables. In the model, there can be a set of acculturation scales or factors and a set of scales or factors of a cognitive or personality test. Within this framework it is possible to (a) determine the interdependence structure of acculturation variables; (b) determine the interdependence structure of cognitive or personality test variables; and (c) determine the structure of relationships between the two sets of variables. Thus it is possible to explore fully which, if any, acculturation variables are related to which, if any, test variables, and make some determinations as to the appropriateness of using the test (or some of its derived subscales) with the acculturating population being studied.

To summarize, we have highlighted in this section the fact that the assessment of acculturation is relevant to other aspects of cross-cultural research that go beyond the study of acculturation *per se*. Specifically, we have shown that, when the cultural groups under study are in "continuous first-hand contact" with each other, acculturation is relevant to the external validity and replicability of research findings. In addition, acculturation may be critical to the proper use and interpretation of cognitive and personality tests for different groups in plural societies.

CONCLUSION

It should be clear that while acculturation as a concept was originally proposed as a group-level phenomenon, it is also an important construct at the individual level. It should also be apparent that in cross-cultural psychology measurement of cultural variables *and* of acculturation (at *both* levels) are essential if the researcher is to be able to allocate relative contributions to development and behavioral variation to their various sources of influence. Armed with a knowledge of the concept of acculturation and with the variety of operationalizations presented in this chapter, field workers should be able to attend fully to this issue, and to draw appropriate conclusions from their cross-cultural data. Without such concerns and instruments, behavioral data collected across cultures would always remain open to alternative interpretations based upon uncontrolled acculturative influences.

References

Abel, T.M. (1973). *Psychological testing in cultural contexts*. New Haven, CT: College & University Press.

Aboud, F. (1981). Ethnic self identity. In R.C. Gardner & R. Kalin (Eds.), *A Canadian social psychology of ethnic relations*. Toronto: Methuen.

Adam, J. (1978). Sequential strategies and the separation of age, cohort, and time-of-measurement contributions to developmental data. *Psychological Bulletin, 85*, 1309–1316.

Ajzen, I., & Fishbein, M. (1977). Attitude-behavior relations: A theoretical analysis and review of empirical research. *Psychological Bulletin, 84*, 888–918.

Ajzen, I., & Fishbein, M. (1981). *Understanding attitudes and predicting social behavior*. Englewood Cliffs, NJ: Prentice-Hall.

Akeju, S.S.A. (1983). Large-scale assessment of educational aptitude in Nigeria. In S.H. Irvine & J.W. Berry (Eds.), *Human assessment and cultural factors*. New York: Plenum.

Akoodie, M. (1983). Identity and self concept in immigrant children. In R. Samuda, J.W. Berry, & M. Laferrière (Eds.), *Multiculturalism in Canada: Social and education perspectives*. Toronto: Allyn & Bacon.

Allport, G., & Odbert, H. (1936). Trait-names: A psycholexical study. *Psychological Monographs, 47*, 211.

American Anthropological Association (1973). *Professional ethics: Statements and procedures of the American Anthropological Association*. Washington, DC: Author.

American Anthropological Association (1984). *Guide to departments of anthropology 1984–85* (23rd ed.). Washington, DC: Author.

American Anthropological Association (1985). *Anthropology newsletter*. Washington, DC: Author.

American Psychological Association (1982). *Ethical principles in the conduct of research with human participants*. Washington, DC: Author.

American Sociological Association (1984). *Code of ethics*. Washington, DC: Author.

An impossible dream? The Child Development Research Units of Kenya and Nigeria (1979). *Carnegie Quarterly*, Fall, 1–7.

Andor, L.E. (1983). *Psychological and sociological studies of the black people of Africa, south of the Sahara*. Johannesburg: National Institute for Personnel Research.

Angoff, W.H., & Ford, S.F. (1973). Item–race interaction on a test of scholastic aptitude. *Journal of Educational Measurement, 10*, 95–105.

Appell, G.N. (1978). *Ethical dilemmas in anthropological inquiry: A case book*.

325

Waltham, MA: African Studies Association.

Argyle, M. (1979). *Bodily communication*. New York: International Universities Press.

Argyle, M., & Dean, J. (1965). Eye-contact, distance, and affiliation. *Sociometry, 28*, 289–304.

Argyle, M., Furnham, A., & Graham, J.A. (1981). *Social situations*. Cambridge: Cambridge University Press.

Argyle, M., Shimoda, K., & Little, B. (1978). Variance due to persons and situations in England and Japan. *British Journal of Social and Clinical Psychology, 17*, 335–337.

Aronson, E., & Carlsmith, J.M. (1968). Experimentation in social psychology. In G. Lindzey & E. Aronson (Eds.), *The handbook of social psychology* (Vol. 2) (2nd ed.) (pp. 1–79). Reading, MA: Addison-Wesley.

Aschenbrenner, J. (1975). *Lifelines: Black families in Chicago*. New York: Holt, Rinehart & Winston.

Ashmore, R. (1970). The problem of intergroup prejudice. In B. Collins, *Social psychology*. Reading, MA: Addison-Wesley.

Backstrom, C.H., & Hursh, G.D. (1963). *Survey research*. Evanston, IL: Northwestern University Press.

Barker, R.G. (1963). *The stream of behavior: Explorations of its structure and content*. New York: Meredith.

Barker, R.G. (1968). *Ecological psychology: Concepts and methods for studying the environment of human behavior*. Stanford, CA: Stanford University Press.

Barker, R.G. (Ed.) (1978). *Habitats, environments, and human behavior*. San Francisco: Jossey-Bass.

Barnes, J.A. (1984). Ethical and political compromises in social research. *Wisconsin Sociologist, 21*, 100–110.

Barry, H. (1980). Description and uses of the Human Relations Area Files. In H.C. Triandis & J.W. Berry (Eds.), *Handbook of cross-cultural psychology* (Vol. 2). *Methodology* (pp. 445–478). Boston: Allyn & Bacon.

Bartko, J.J., Strauss, J.S., & Carpenter, W.T. (1974). Expanded perspectives for describing and comparing schizophrenic patients. *Schizophrenia Bulletin, 11*, 50–60.

Berk, R.A. (Ed.) (1982). *Handbook of methods for detecting item bias*. Baltimore: Johns Hopkins University Press.

Berlin, B., & Kay, P. (1969). *Basic color terms: Their universality and evolution*. Berkeley, CA: University of California Press.

Berreman, G.D. (1968). Ethnography: Method and product. In J.A. Clifton (Ed.), *Introduction to cultural anthropology* (pp. 337–373). Boston: Houghton Mifflin.

Berry, J.W. (1966). Temne and Eskimo perceptual skills. *International Journal of Psychology, 1*, 207–229.

Berry, J.W. (1969a). On cross-cultural comparability. *International Journal of Psychology, 4*, 119–128.

Berry, J.W. (1969b). Ecology and socialization as factors in figural assimilation and the resolution of binocular rivalry. *International Journal of Psychology, 4*, 271–280.

Berry, J.W. (1972). Radical cultural relativism and the concept of intelligence. In L.J.

Cronbach & P.J.D. Drenth (Eds.), *Mental tests and cultural adaptation* (pp. 77–88). The Hague: Mouton.

Berry, J.W. (1976). *Human ecology and cognitive style: Comparative studies in cultural and psychological adaptation*. New York: Russell Sage/Halsted.

Berry, J.W. (1979a). A cultural ecology of social behavior. In L. Berkowitz (Ed.), *Advances in experimental social psychology* (Vol. 12). New York: Academic Press.

Berry J.W. (1979b). Unobtrusive measures in cross-cultural research. In L. Sechrest (Ed.), *Unobtrusive measurement today: New directions for methodology of behavioral sciences*. San Francisco: Jossey-Bass.

Berry, J.W. (1980). Ecological analyses for cross-cultural psychology. In N. Warren (Ed.), *Studies in cross-cultural psychology* (Vol. 2) (pp. 157–189). London: Academic Press.

Berry, J.W. (1980a). Introduction to methodology. In H. Triandis, & J. Berry (Eds.), *Handbook of cross-cultural psychology* (Vol. 2). *Methodology*. Boston: Allyn & Bacon.

Berry, J.W. (1980b). Acculturation as varieties of adaptation. In A. Padilla (Ed.), *Acculturation: Theory, models and some new findings*. Boulder: Westview Press.

Berry, J.W. (1980c). Social and cultural change. In H.C. Triandis & R. Brislin (Eds.), *Handbook of cross-cultural psychology* (Vol. 5). *Social psychology*. Boston: Allyn & Bacon.

Berry, J.W. (1981). Cultural systems and cognitive styles. In M.P. Friedman, J.P. Das, & N. O'Connor (Eds.), *Intelligence and learning*. New York: Plenum.

Berry, J.W. (1983). Textured contexts: Systems and situations in cross-cultural psychology. In S.H. Irvine & J.W. Berry (Eds.), *Human assessment and cultural factors* (pp. 117–126). New York: Plenum.

Berry, J.W., & Annis, R.C. (1974). Acculturative stress: The role of ecology, culture and differentiation. *Journal of Cross-Cultural Psychology*, *5*, 382–406.

Berry, J.W., & Blondel, T. (1982). Psychological adaptation of Vietnamese refugees in Canada. *Canadian Journal of Community Mental Health*, *1*, 81–88.

Berry, J.W., & Dasen, P. (Eds.) (1974). *Culture and cognition*. London: Methuen.

Berry, J.W., Kalin, R., & Taylor, D.M. (1977). *Multiculturalism and ethnic attitudes in Canada*. Ottawa: Supply and Services.

Berry, J.W., & Kim, U. (1986). Acculturation and mental health. In P. Dasen, J.W. Berry, & N. Sartorius (Eds.), *Applications of cross-cultural psychology to healthy human development*. Beverly Hills: Sage.

Berry, J.W., Kim, U., Power, S., & Young, M. (1974). *Acculturation attitudes in plural societies*. Paper presented at Society of Experimental Social Psychology, Utah, October.

Berry, J.W., van de Koppel, J., Sénéchal, C., Annis, R.C., Bahuchet, S., Cavalli-Sforza, L.L., & Witkin, H.A. (1985). *On the edge of the forest: Cultural adaptation and cognitive development in Central Africa*. Lisse: Swets & Zeitlinger.

Berry, J.W., Wintrob, R.M., Sindell, P.S., & Mawhinney, T.A. (1982). Psychological adaptation to culture change among the James Bay Cree. *Naturaliste Canadien*, *109*, 965–975.

Bhatia, C.M. (1955). *Performance tests of intelligence under Indian conditions*. London: Oxford University Press.

Bickman, L., & Henchy, T. (Eds.) (1972). *Beyond the laboratory: Field research in social psychology*. New York: McGraw-Hill.

Biesheuvel, S. (1952). Personnel selection tests for Africans. *South African Journal of Science, 49*, 5–12.

Biesheuvel, S. (1954). The measurement of occupational aptitudes in a multiracial society. *Occupational Psychology, 28*, 189–196.

Biesheuvel, S. (1972). Adaptability: Its measurement and determinants. In L.J. Cronbach & P.J.D. Drenth (Eds.), *Mental tests and cultural adaptation* (pp. 47–62). The Hague: Mouton.

Blue, A., & Blue, M. (1983). The trail of stress. In R. Samuda, J.W. Berry, & M. Laferrière (Eds.), *Multiculturalism in Canada: Social and educational perspectives*. Toronto: Allyn & Bacon.

Bochner, S. (1979). Designing unobtrusive field experiments in social psychology. In L. Sechrest (Ed.), *Unobtrusive measurement today: New directions for methodology of behavioral science*. San Francisco: Jossey-Bass.

Bochner, S. (1980). Unobtrusive methods in cross-cultural experimentation. In H.C. Triandis & J.W. Berry (Eds.), *Handbook of cross-cultural psychology* (Vol. 2). *Methodology*. Boston: Allyn & Bacon.

Bochner, S. (in press). Inter-cultural skills. In C.R. Hollin & P. Trower (Eds.), *Handbook of social skills training*. Oxford: Pergamon.

Bochner, S., Brislin, R.W., & Lonner, W.J. (1975). Introduction. In R.W. Brislin, S. Bochner, & W.J. Lonner (Eds.), *Cross-cultural perspectives on learning* (pp. 3–36). New York: Sage/Halsted.

Bogardus, E.S. (1925). Measuring social distance. *Journal of Applied Sociology, 9*, 299–308.

Bolton, R. (1973). Aggression and hypoglycemia among the Qolla: A study in psychobiological anthropology. *Ethnology, 12*, 227–257.

Brand, E.S., Ruiz, R.A., & Padilla, A. (1974). Ethnic identification and perference: A review. *Psychological Bulletin, 81*, 860–890.

Brandt, R.M. (1972). *Studying behavior in natural settings*. New York: Holt, Rinehart & Winston.

Brislin, R.W. (1970). Back-translation for cross-cultural research. *Journal of Cross-Cultural Psychology, 1*, 185–216.

Brislin, R.W. (1974). The Ponzo illusion: Additional cues, age, orientation, and culture. *Journal of Cross-Cultural Psychology, 5*, 139–161.

Brislin, R.W. (Ed.) (1976). *Translation: Applications and research*. New York: John Wiley/Halsted.

Brislin, R.W. (1977). Methodology of cognitive studies. In G. Kearney & D. McElwain (Eds.) *Aboriginal cognition*. Canberra: Australian Institute for Aboriginal Studies.

Brislin, R.W. (1979). The problems and prospects of cross-cultural studies as seen by experienced researchers. In L. Eckensberger, W. Lonner, & Y. Poortinga (Eds.), *Cross-cultural contributions to psychology*. Amsterdam: Swets & Zeitlinger.

Brislin, R.W. (1980). Translation and content analysis of oral and written material. In H.C. Triandis & J.W. Berry (Eds.), *Handbook of cross-cultural psychology* (Vol. 2). *Methodology* (pp.389–444). Boston: Allyn & Bacon.

Brislin, R.W. (1981). *Cross-cultural encounters: Face-to-face interaction.* Elmsford, NY: Pergamon.

Brislin, R.W. (1983). Cross-cultural psychology. *Annual Review of Psychology, 34,* 363–400.

Brislin, R.W., & Baumgardner, S.R. (1971). Non-random sampling of individuals in cross-cultural research. *Journal of Cross-Cultural Psychology, 2,* 397–400.

Brislin, R.W., & Holwill, R. (1977). Reactions of indigenous people to the writings of behavioral and social scientists. *International Journal of Intercultural Relations, 2,* 15–34.

Brislin, R.W., Lonner, W.J., & Thorndike, R.M. (1973). *Cross-cultural research methods.* New York: John Wiley.

Brodman, K., et al. (1952). The Cornell Medical Index health questionnaire, III. The evaluation of emotional disturbances. *Journal of Clinical Psychology, 8,* 119–124.

Brooks, P.G., Dann, P.L., & Irvine, S.H. (1984). Computerized testing: Exacting the levy. *Bulletin of the British Psychology Society, 37,* 372–374.

Brown, E.D., & Sechrest, L. (1980). Experiments in cross-cultural research. In H.C. Triandis & J.W. Berry (Eds.), *Handbook of cross-cultural psychology* (Vol. 2): *Methodology* (pp. 297–318). Boston: Allyn & Bacon.

Browne, M.W. (1978). The likelihood ratio test for the equality of correlation matrices. *British Journal of Mathematical and Statistical Psychology, 31,* 209–217.

Bryan, J.H., & Test, M.A. (1967). Models and helping: Naturalistic studies in aiding behavior. *Journal of Personality and Social Psychology, 6,* 400–407.

Bryant, P. (1974). *Perception and understanding in young children.* London: Methuen.

Buckley, T. (1982). Menstruation and the power of Yurok women: Methods in cultural reconstruction. *American Ethnologist, 9,* 47–60.

Bulmer, M., & Warwick, D.P. (1983). *Social research in developing countries: Surveys and censuses in the Third World.* Chichester: John Wiley.

Burisch, M. (1984). Approaches to personality inventory construction: A comparison of merits. *American Psychologist, 39,* 214–227.

Burling, R. (1984). *Learning a field language.* Ann Arbor: University of Michigan Press.

Buss, A.R., & Royce, J.R. (1975). Detecting cross-cultural commonalities and differences: Intergroup factor analysis. *Psychological Bulletin, 82,* 128–136.

Butcher, J.N. (Ed.) (1979). *New developments in the use of the MMPI.* Minneapolis: University of Minnesota Press.

Butcher, J.N. (1982). Cross-cultural research methods in clinical psychology. In P. Kendall & J. Butcher (Eds.), *Handbook of research methods in clinical psychology.* New York: John Wiley.

Butcher, J.N., & Clark, L.A. (1979). Recent trends in cross-cultural MMPI research and application. In J.N. Butcher (Ed.), *New developments in the use of the MMPI.* Minneapolis: University of Minnesota Press.

Butcher, J.N., & Garcia, R. (1978). Cross-national application of psychological tests. *Personnel and Guidance, 56,* 472–475.

Butcher, J.N., Kendall, P.C., & Hoffman, N. (1980). MMPI short forms: Caution. *Journal of Consulting and Clinical Psychology, 48,* 275–278.

Butcher, J.N., & Pancheri, P. (Eds.) (1976). *A handbook of cross-national MMPI research*. Minneapolis: University of Minnesota Press.

Byrne, D., & Nelson, D. (1965). Attraction as a linear function of proportion of positive reinforcements. *Journal of Personality and Social Psychology, 1*, 659–663.

Callan, V.J., Gallois, C., & Forbes, P.A. (1983). Evaluative reactions to accented English: Ethnicity, sex role, and context. *Journal of Cross-Cultural Psychology, 14*, 407–426.

Campbell, D.T. (1964). Distinguishing differences in perception from failures of communication in cross-cultural studies. In F. Northrop & H. Livingston (Eds.), *Cross-cultural understanding: Epistemology in anthropology*. New York: Harper & Row.

Campbell, D.T. (1968). A cooperative multinational opinion sample exchange. *Journal of Social Issues, 24* (2), 245–258.

Campbell, D.T., & Erlebacher, A. (1970). How regression artifacts in quasi-experimental evaluations can mistakenly make compensatory education look harmful. In J. Hellmuth (Ed.), *Compensatory education: A national debate*. New York: Brunner/Mazel.

Campbell, D.T., & Fiske, D.W. (1959). Convergent and discriminant validation by the multitrait-multimethod matrix. *Psychological Bulletin, 56*, 81–105.

Campbell, D.T., & LeVine, R.A. (1970). Field-manual anthropology. In R. Naroll & R. Cohen (Eds.), *Handbook of method in cultural anthropology*. New York: Natural History Press.

Campbell, D.T., & Naroll, R. (1972). The mutual methodological relevance of anthropology and psychology. In F.L.K. Hsu (Ed.), *Psychological anthropology* (2nd ed.) (pp. 435–463). Cambridge, MA: Schenkman.

Campbell, D.T., & Stanley, J. (1966). *Experimental and quasi-experimental designs for research*. Chicago: Rand-McNally.

Carpenter, W.T., Strauss, J.S., & Bartko, J.J. (1974). Use of signs and symptoms for identification of schizophrenic patients. *Schizophrenia Bulletin, 11*, 37–49.

Carter, W.E. (1972). Entering the world of the Aymara. In S.T. Kimball & J.B. Watson (Eds.), *Crossing cultural boundaries* (pp. 133–150). San Francisco: Chandler.

Cattell, R.B. (1970). The isopodic and equipotent principles for comparing factor scores across different populations. *The British Journal of Mathematical and Statistical Psychology, 23*, 23–41.

Cattell, R.B., & Scheier, I.H. (1961). *The meaning and measurement of neuroticism and anxiety*. New York: Ronald Press.

Cawte, J., Bianchi, G.N., & Kiloh, L.G. (1968). Personal discomfort in Australian Aborigines. *Australian and New Zealand Journal of Psychiatry, 2*, 69–79.

Ceci, S.J., & Bronfenbrenner, U. (1985). "Don't forget to take the cupcakes out of the oven": Prospective memory, strategic time-monitoring, and context. *Child Development, 56*, 152–164.

Chagnon, N.A. (1983). *Yanomamo*. New York: Holt, Rinehart & Winston.

Chambers, A.F., & Bolton, R. (1979). We all do it, but how? A survey of contemporary field note procedure. Paper presented at the meeting of the American Anthropological Association, Cincinnati, November 1979.

Chance, N.A. (1965). Acculturation, self-identification, and personality adjustment. *American Anthropologist, 67*, 372–393.

Chung, M.R. (1983). An examination of conservation performance by children from contrasting social and cultural backgrounds. In J.B. Deregowski, S. Dziurawiec, & R.C. Annis (Eds.), *Expiscations in cross-cultural psychology*. Lisse: Swets & Zeitlinger.

Cicourel, A.V. (1964). *Method and measurement in sociology*. New York: Free Press.

Clark, H.H., & Chase, W.H. (1972). On the process of comparing sentences against pictures. *Cognitive Psychology*, *3*, 472–517.

Cleary, T.A. (1968). Test bias: Prediction of grades of negro and white students in integrated colleges. *Journal of Educational Measurement*, *5*, 115–124.

Cleary, T.A., & Hilton, T.L. (1968). An investigation of item bias. *Educational and Psychological Measurement*, *28*, 61–75.

Cohen, J. (1977). *Statistical power analysis for the behavioral sciences* (rev. ed.). New York: Academic Press.

Cole, M., Gay, J., & Glick, J. (1968). Some experimental studies of Kpelle quantitative behavior. *Psychonomic Monograph Supplements*, *2* (10, whole of no. 26).

Cole, M., Gay, J., Glick, J.A., & Sharp, D.W. (1971). *The cultural context of learning and thinking*. New York: Basic Books.

Cole, M., Hood, L., & McDermott, R. (1982). Ecological niche picking: Ecological invalidity as an axiom of experimental cognitive psychology. In U. Neisser (Ed.), *Remembering in natural context* (pp. 336–341). San Francisco: W.H. Freeman.

Cole, M., & Scribner, S. (1974). *Culture and thought: A psychological introduction*. New York: John Wiley.

Cole, M., & Scribner, S. (1983). On the status of developmental theories in cross-cultural psychology. In L. Adler (Ed.), *Cross-cultural research at issue*. New York: Academic Press.

Cole, N.S. (1973). Bias in selection. *Journal of Educational Measurement*, *10*, 237–255.

Collett, P. (1982). Meetings and misunderstandings. In S. Bochner (Ed.), *Cultures in contact: Studies in cross-cultural interaction*. Oxford: Pergamon.

Colson, E. (1985). Ethics and codes of ethics. *Anthropology Newsletter*, *26*, (no. 3), 20; 13.

Cook, T.D., & Campbell, D.T. (1979). *Quasi-experimentation: Design and analysis issues for field settings*. Chicago: Rand-McNally.

Coombs, C.H., Dawes, R.M., & Tversky, A. (1970). *Mathematical psychology: An elementary introduction*. Englewood Cliffs, NJ: Prentice-Hall.

Cooper, J.E., Kendall, R.E., Garland, B.J., Sharpe, L., Copeland, J.R.M., & Simon, R. (1972). *Psychiatric diagnosis in New York and London*. London: Oxford University Press.

Corsini, R.J., and Marsella, A.J. (1983). *Personality theories, research and assessment*. Itasca, IL: Peacock.

Cronbach, L.J. (1957). The two disciplines of scientific psychology. *American Psychologist*, *12*, 671–684.

Cronbach, L.J. (1984). *Essentials of psychological testing* (4th ed.). New York: Harper & Row.

Cronbach, L.J., Gleser, G.C., Nanda, H., & Rajaratnam, N. (1972). *The dependability of behavioral measurements*. New York: John Wiley.

Crowne, D., & Marlowe, D. (1964). *The approval motive*. New York: John Wiley.

Cushing, F.H. (1882a). My adventures in Zuñi. *Century Magazine*, *25*, 191–207, 500–511.

Cushing, F.H. (1882b). My adventures in Zuñi. *Century Magazine, 26*, 28–47.

Cushing, F.H. (1884–85). Zuñi breadstuff. *The Millstone*. Reprinted in *Indian Notes and Monographs*, whole volume *8*, 1920.

Dahlstrom, W.G., & Welsh, G.S. (1960). *An MMPI handbook*. Minneapolis: University of Minnesota Press.

Darlington, R.B. (1971). Another look at cultural fairness. *Journal of Educational Measurement, 8*, 71–82.

Dasen, P.R. (1983). Commentary. In J.B. Deregowski, S. Dziurawiec, & R.C. Annis (Eds.), *Expiscations in cross-cultural psychology*. Lisse: Swets & Zeitlinger.

Dasen, P.R., & Heron, A. (1981). Cross-cultural tests of Piaget's theory. In H.C. Triandis & A. Heron (Eds.), *Handbook of cross-cultural psychology* (Vol. 4, Ch. 7). *Development*. Boston: Allyn & Bacon.

Davidson, A.R., Jaccard, J.J., Triandis, H.C., Morales, M.L., & Diaz-Guerrero, R.L. (1976). Cross-cultural model testing: Toward a solution of the etic-emic dilemma. *International Journal of Psychology, 11*, 1–14.

Dawson, J.L.M.B. (1967). Traditional versus Western attitudes in West Africa: The construction, validation, and application of a measuring device. *British Journal of Social and Clinical Psychology, 6*, 81–96.

Dawson, J.L.M.B. (1969). Attitude change and conflict among Australian Aborigines. *Australian Journal of Psychology, 21*, 101, 116.

Dawson, J.L.M.B., Whitney, R.E., & Law, R.T.-S. (1972). Attitude conflict, GSR and traditional-modern attitude change among Hong Kong Chinese. *Journal of Social Psychology, 88*, 163–176.

de Lacey, P.R. (1970). An index of contact. *Australian Journal of Social Issues, 5*, 219–223.

Deutscher, I. (1973). Asking questions cross-culturally: Some problems of linguistic comparability. In D.P. Warwick & S. Osheron (Eds.), *Comparative research methods*. Englewood Cliffs, NJ: Prentice-Hall.

Diamond, N. (1970). Fieldwork in a complex society: Taiwan. In G.D. Spindler (Ed.), *Being an anthropologist* (pp. 113–141). New York: Holt, Rinehart & Winston.

Doob, L.W. (1967). Scales for assaying psychological modernization. *Public Opinion Quarterly, 31*, 414–421.

Draguns, J. (1980). Psychological disorders of clinical severity. In H. Triandis, & J. Draguns (Eds.), *Handbook of cross-cultural psychology* (Vol. 6). *Psychopathology*. Boston: Allyn & Bacon.

Draguns, J. (1982). Methodology in cross-cultural psychopathology. In I. Al-Issa (Ed.), *Culture and psychopathology*. Baltimore: University Park Press.

Drasgow, F. (1982). Choice of test model for appropriateness measurement. *Applied Psychological Measurement, 6*, 297–308.

Ebigno, P. (1982). Development of a culture-specific screening scale of somatic complaints indicating psychiatric disturbance. *Culture, Medicine and Psychiatry, 6*, 29–43.

Eckensberger, L.H. (1979). A metamethodological evaluation of psychological theories from a cross-cultural perspective. In L. Eckensberger, W. Lonner, & Y.H. Poortinga (Eds.), *Cross-cultural contributions to psychology* (pp. 255–275). Lisse: Swets & Zeitlinger.

Eckensberger, L.H., & Burgard, P. (1983). The cross-cultural assessment of normative concepts: Some considerations of the affinity between methodological approaches and preferred theories. In S.H. Irvine & J.W. Berry (Eds.), *Human assessment and cultural factors* (pp. 459-480). New York: Plenum.

Edgerton, R.B. (1971). *The individual in cultural adaptation*. Berkeley, CA: University of California Press.

Edgerton, R.B., & Langness, L.L. (1974). *Methods and styles in the study of culture*. San Francisco: Chandler & Sharp.

Educational Testing Service (1973), *ETS makes a test*. Princeton, NJ: Advisory Service, ETS.

Edwards, A. (1959). *Edwards Personal Preference Schedule*. Psychological Corporation.

Eibl-Eibesfeldt, I. (1970). *Ethology: The biology of behavior*. New York: Holt, Rinehart & Winston.

Einhorn, H.J., & Bass, A.R. (1971). Methodological considerations relevant to discrimination in employment testing. *Psychological Bulletin, 75*, 261–269.

Ellis, N.C., & Hennelly, R.A. (1980). A bilingual word-length effect: Implications for intelligence testing and the relative ease of mental calculation in Welsh and English. *British Journal of Psychology, 71*, 43–51.

Ellsworth, P.C., Carlsmith, J.M., & Henson, A. (1972). The stare as a stimulus to flight in human subjects: A series of field experiments. *Journal of Personality and Social Psychology, 21*, 302–311.

Enriquez, V., & Marcelino, E. (1984). *Neo-colonial politics and language struggle in the Philippines: National consciousness and language in Philippine psychology, 1971–1983*. Quezon City, Philippines: Philippine Psychology Research and Training House.

Ervin-Tripp, S. (1964). Language and TAT content in French-English bilinguals. *Journal of Abnormal and Social Psychology, 68*, 500–507.

Eysenck, H.J., & Eysenck, S.B.G. (1975). *Manual of the Eysenck Personality Questionnaire*. London and San Diego, CA: Hodder & Stoughton.

Eysenck, H.J., & Eysenck, S.B.G. (1982). Culture and personality abnormalities. In I. Al-Issa (Ed.), *Culture and psychopathology*. Baltimore: University Park Press.

Eysenck, H.J., & Eysenck, S.B.G. (1983). Recent advances in the cross-cultural study of personality. In J.N. Butcher & C.D. Spielberger (Eds.), *Advances in personality assessment* (Vol. 2). London: Lawrence Erlbaum.

Eysenck, S.B.J., & Opolot, J.A. (1983). A comparative study of personality in Ugandan and English subjects. *Personality and Individual Differences, 4*, 583–589.

Faschingbauer, T.R., & Newmark, C.S. (1978). *Short forms of the MMPI*. Lexington, MA: Lexington Press.

Faucheux, C. (1976). Cross-cultural research on experimental social psychology. *European Journal of Social Psychology, 6*, 269–322.

Feshbach, A., & Weiner, B. (1982). *Personality*. Lexington, MA: D.C. Heath.

Finifter, B.M. (1977). The robustness of cross-cultural findings. In L.L. Adler (Ed.), Issues in cross-cultural research (pp. 151–184). *Annals of the New York Academy of Sciences* (Vol. 285).

Firth, R. (1972). From wife to anthropologist. In S.T. Kimball & J.B. Watson (Eds.), *Crossing cultural boundaries* (pp. 10–32). San Francisco: Chandler.

Fishbein, M. (Ed.) (1967). *Readings in attitude theory and measurement*. New York: John Wiley.

Fiske, D.W. (1971). *Measuring the concepts of personality*. Chicago: Aldine.

Foster, G.M., & Kemper, R.V. (Eds.) (1974). *Anthropologists in cities*. Boston: Little, Brown.

Foster, G.M., Scudder, T., Colson, E., & Kemper, R.V. (Eds.) (1978). *Long-term field research in social anthropology*. Orlando, FL: Academic Press.

Freeman, D. (1983). *Margaret Mead and Samoa: The making and unmaking of an anthropological myth*. Canberra: Australian National University Press.

Freilich, M. (Ed.) (1977). *Marginal natives at work*. Cambridge, MA: Schenkman.

Frey, F.W. (1963). Surveying peasant attitudes in Turkey. *Public Opinion Quarterly*, 27, 335–355.

Frey, F.W. (1970). Cross-cultural survey research in political science. In R. Holt & J. Turner (Eds.), *The methodology of comparative research*. New York: Free Press.

Frijda, N., & Jahoda, G. (1966). On the scope and methods of cross-cultural research. *International Journal of Psychology*, 1, 109–127.

Gaertner, S., & Bickman, L. (1971). Effects of race on the elicitation of helping behavior: The wrong number technique. *Journal of Personality and Social Psychology*, 20, 218–222.

Gallimore, R., Boggs, J.W., & Jordan, C. (1974). *Culture, behavior and education*. Beverly Hills, CA: Sage.

Gay, J., & Cole, M. (1967). *The new mathematics in an old culture*. New York: Holt, Rinehart & Winston.

Gewertz, D. (1981). A historical reconsideration of female dominance among the Chambri of Papua New Guinea. *American Ethnologist*, 8, 94–106.

Ghiselli, E., Campbell, J.P., & Zedeck, S. (1981). *Measurement theory for the behavioral sciences*. San Francisco: W.H. Freeman.

Gmelch, G., & Zenner, W.P. (Eds.) (1980). *Urban life: Readings in urban anthropology*. New York: St Martin's Press.

Goldberg, L.R. (1981). Language and individual differences: The search for universals in personality lexicons. In L. Wheeler (Ed.), *Review of personality and social psychology* (Vol. 2) (pp. 141–166). Beverly Hills, CA: Sage.

Golde, P. (Ed.) (1970). *Women in the field*. Chicago: Aldine.

Goodenough, F. (1936). The measurement of mental functions in primitive groups. *American Anthropologist*, 38, 1–11.

Goodenough, W.H. (1980). Ethnographic field techniques. In H.C. Triandis & J.W. Berry (Eds.), *Handbook of cross-cultural psychology* (Vol. 2). *Methodology* (pp. 29–55). Boston: Allyn & Bacon.

Goody, J. (1968). *Literacy in traditional societies*. New York: Cambridge University Press.

Gorsuch, R. (1984). Measurement: The boon and bane of investigating religion. *American Psychologist*, 39, 228–236.

Gough, H.G. (1969). *California Psychological Inventory*. Palo Alto, CA: Consulting Psychologists Press.

Gough, H.G., & Heilbrun, A.B. (1980). *The Adjective Check List Manual*. Palo Alto, CA: Consulting Psychologists Press.

Graves, T.D. (1967). Psychological acculturation in a tri-ethnic community. *Southwestern Journal of Anthropology*, 23, 337–350.

Greenfield, P.M. (1966). On culture and conservation. In J.S. Bruner, R.R. Olver, & P.M. Greenfield (Eds.), *Studies in cognitive growth*. New York: John Wiley.

Gregor, T. (1977). *Mehinaku: The drama of daily life in a Brazilian Indian village*. Chicago: University of Chicago Press.

Grinker, R.R., & Holzman, P.S. (1973). Schizophrenic pathology in young adults. *Archives of General Psychiatry*, *28*, 168–175.

Guilford, J.P. (1965). *Fundamental statistics in psychology and education*. New York: McGraw-Hill.

Guthrie, G.M., Jackson, D.N., Astilla, E., & Elwood, B. (1983). Personality measurement: Do the scales have similar meanings in another culture? In S.H. Irvine & J.W. Berry (Eds.), *Human assessment and cultural factors*. New York: Plenum.

Guthrie, G.M., & Tanco, P.P. (1980). Alienation. In H.C. Triandis & J.G. Draguns, *Handbook of cross-cultural psychology* (Vol. 6). *Psychopathology*. Boston: Allyn & Bacon.

Gynther, M. (1979). Ethnicity and personality: An update. In J.N. Butcher (Ed.), *New developments in the use of the MMPI*. Minneapolis: University of Minnesota Press.

Hall, E. (1959). *The silent language*. Garden City, NY: Doubleday.

Hallowell, A.I. (1955). Sociopsychological aspects of acculturation. In A.I. Hallowell, *Culture and experience*. Philadelphia: University of Pennsylvania Press.

Harré, R. (1977). The ethogenic approach: Theory and practice. In L. Berkowitz (Ed.), *Advances in experimental social psychology* (Vol. 10). New York: Academic Press.

Harris, M. (1964). *The nature of cultural things*. New York: Random House.

Harris, M. (1968). *The rise of anthropological theory*. New York: Thomas Y. Crowell.

Hays, W.L. (1973). *Statistics for the social sciences*. London: Holt, Rinehart & Winston.

Hidano, T. (1967). Personality test methods — MMPI. In T. Imura (Ed.), *Clinical psychology test methods* (2nd ed.). Tokyo: Igaku Shoin. Cited in J.N. Butcher (1979), *New developments in the use of the MMPI*. Minneapolis: University of Minnesota Press.

Hill, S. (1964). Cultural differences in mathematical concept learning. *American Anthropologist*, special publication, Vol. 66 (3), Part 2, 201–222.

Hofstede, G. (1980). *Culture's consequences: International differences in work-related values*. London: Sage.

Holt, R., & Turner, J. (1970). *The methodology of comparative research*. New York: Free Press.

Holtzman. W.H. (1980). Projective techniques. In H.C. Triandis & J.W. Berry (Eds.), *Handbook of cross-cultural psychology* (Vol. 2). *Methodology*. Boston: Allyn & Bacon.

Honigmann, J.J. (1970). Sampling in ethnographic field work. In R. Naroll & R. Cohen (Eds.), *Handbook of method in cultural anthropology*. New York: Natural History Press.

Howard, A. (1974). *Ain't no big thing*. Honolulu: University Press of Hawaii.

Hsu, F.L.K. (Ed.) (1972). *Psychological anthropology* (2nd ed.). Cambridge, MA: Schenkman.

Hudson, B.B., Barakat, M.K., & LaForge, R. (1959). Problems and methods of cross-cultural research. *Journal of Social Issues*, *15*, 5–19.

Hui, C.H. & Triandis, H.C. (1983). Multistratégy approach to cross-cultural research:

The case of locus of control. *Journal of Cross-Cultural Psychology, 14*, 65–84.

Hull, C.L. (1951). *Essentials of behavior*. New Haven, CN: Yale University Press.

Hursh-Cesar, G., & Roy, P. (Eds.) (1976). *Third World surveys*. Delhi: Macmillan of India.

Hutchins, E. (1980). *Culture and inference*. Cambridge, MA: Harvard University Press.

Immunizations and chemoprophylaxis for travelers (1983). *Medical Letter on Drugs and Therapeutics, 25* (issue 633), 37–40.

Inkeles, A. (1977). Understanding and misunderstanding individual modernity. *Journal of Cross-Cultural Psychology, 8*, 135–176.

Inkeles, A., & Smith, D. (1974). *Becoming modern*. Cambridge, MA: Harvard University Press.

Irvine, J. (1979). Wolof "magical thinking": Culture and conservation revisited. *Journal of Cross-Cultural Psychology, 9*, 300–310.

Irvine, S.H. (1965). Adapting tests to the cultural setting: A comment. *Occupational Psychology, 39*, 12–23.

Irvine, S.H. (1966). Towards a rationale for testing attainments and abilities in Africa. *British Journal of Educational Psychology, 36*, 24–32.

Irvine, S.H. (1968). Human behavior in Africa: Some research problems noted while compiling source materials. Paper presented to the East Africa Institute of Social Research Workshop in Social Psychology, New York City.

Irvine, S.H. (1969). The factor analysis of African abilities and attainments: Constructs across cultures. *Psychological Bulletin, 71*, 20–32.

Irvine, S.H. (1973). Tests as inadvertent sources of discrimination in personnel decisions. In P. Watson (Ed.), *Psychology and race*. Harmondsworth, Middx: Penguin.

Irvine, S.H. (1979). The place of factor analysis in cross-cultural methodology and its contribution to cognitive theory. In L.H. Eckensberger, W.H. Lonner, & Y.H. Poortinga, *Cross-cultural contributions to psychology*. Lisse: Swets & Zeitlinger.

Irvine, S.H. (1983a). Cross-cultural conservation studies at the asymptote: Striking out against the curve? In S. Modgil, C. Modgil, & G. Brown (Eds.), *Jean Piaget, an interdisciplinary critique*. London: Routledge & Kegan Paul.

Irvine, S.H. (1983b). Testing in Africa and America: The search for routes. In S.H. Irvine & J.W. Berry (Eds.), *Human assessment and cultural factors*. New York: Plenum.

Irvine, S.H. & J.W. Berry, (Eds.) (1983). *Human assessment and cultural factors*. New York: Plenum.

Irvine, S.H., & Carroll, W.K. (1980). Testing and assessment across cultures. In H.C. Triandis & J.W. Berry (Eds.), *Handbook of cross-cultural psychology* (Vol. 2). *Methodology*. Boston: Allyn & Bacon.

Irvine, S.H., & Reuning, H. (1981). Perceptual speed and cognitive controls. *Journal of Cross-Cultural Psychology, 12*, 425–444.

Istomina, Z.M. (1975). The development of voluntary memory in pre-school age children. *Soviet Psychology, 13*, 5–64.

Jackson, D.N. (1974). *Personality Research Form*. Port Huron, MI: Research Psychologists Press.

Jackson, D.N. (1975). The relative validity of scales prepared by naive item writers and those based on empirical methods of personality scale construction. *Educational and Psychological Measurement*, *35*, 361–370.

Jackson, D.N., Guthrie, G.M., Astilla, E., & Elwood, B. (1983). The cross-cultural generalizability of personality construct measures. In S.H. Irvine & J.W. Berry (Eds.), *Human assessment and cultural factors*. New York: Plenum.

Jacobson, D. (1973). *Itinerant townsmen: Friendship and social order in urban Uganda*. Menlo Park, CA: Cummings.

Jahoda, G. (1977). In pursuit of the emic-etic distinction: Can we ever capture it? In Y.H. Poortinga (Ed.), *Basic problems in cross-cultural psychology* (pp. 55–63). Lisse: Swets & Zeitlinger.

Jahoda, G. (1980). Cross-cultural comparisons. In M.H. Bornstein (Ed.), *Comparative methods in psychology* (pp. 105–148). Hillsdale, NJ: Lawrence Erlbaum.

Jahoda, G. (1982). *Psychology and anthropology: A psychological perspective*. London: Academic Press.

Jahoda, G. (1983). The cross-cultural emperor's conceptual clothes: The emic-etic issue revisited. In J.B. Deregowski, S. Dziurawiec, & R.C. Annis (Eds.), *Expiscations in cross-cultural psychology* (pp. 19–38). Lisse: Swets & Zeitlinger.

Jahoda, G., Cheyne, W.M., Deregowski, J.B. Sinha, D., & Collingbowne, R. (1976). Utilization of pictorial information in classroom learning: A cross-cultural study. *Communication Review*, *24*, 295–315.

Jensen, A.R. (1980). *Bias in mental testing*. New York: Free Press.

Jones, E. (1928). Sex and repression in savage society (book review). *International Journal of Psycho-Analysis*, *9*, 364–374.

Jones, E.E. (1976). How do people perceive the causes of behavior? *American Scientist*, *64*, 300–305.

Jones, E.E., & Zoppel, C.L. (1979). Personality differences among Blacks in Jamaica and the United States. *Journal of Cross-Cultural Psychology*, *10*, 435–456.

Jones, P. (1977). The validity of traditional-modern attitude measures. *Journal of Cross-Cultural Psychology*, *8*, 207–240.

Jöreskog, K.G. (1971). Simultaneous factor analysis in several populations. *Pyschometrika*, *36*, 409–426.

Kagitcibasi, C. (1982). Old-age security value of children and socio-economic development: cross-national evidence. *Journal of Cross-Cultural Psychology*, *13*, 29–42.

Kahl, J. (1968). *The measurement of modernism: A study of values in Brazil and Mexico*. Austin: University of Texas Press.

Kaiser, H.F., Hunka, S., & Bianchini, J.C. (1971). Relating factors between studies based upon different individuals. *Multivariate Behavioral Research*, *6*, 409–422.

Kalton, G. (1983). *Introduction to survey sampling*. No. 35 in the series, *Quantitative applications in the social sciences*. Beverly Hills, CA: Sage.

Kaplan, R.M., & Saccuzo, D.P. (1982). *Psychological Testing*. Monterey, CA: Brooks/Cole.

Katz, D. (1974). Factors affecting social change: A social-psychological interpretation. *Journal of Social Issues*, *39* (3), 159–180.

Keating, C.F., Mazur, A., Segall, M.H., Cysneiros, P.G., Kilbride, J.E., Leahy, P., Divale, W.T., Komin, S., Thurman, B., & Wirsing, R. (1981). Culture and the perception of social dominance from facial expression. *Journal of Personality and*

Social Psychology, *40*, 615–626.

Kimball, S.T., & Watson, J.B. (Eds.) (1972). *Crossing cultural boundaries*. San Francisco: Chandler.

Kleinman, A. (1982). Neurasthenia and depression: A study of somatization and culture in China. *Culture, Medicine and Psychiatry*, *6*, 117–190.

Krug, R.E. (1966). Some suggested approaches for test development and measurement. *Personnel Psychology*, *19*, 24–35.

Lagacé, R.O. (1974). *Nature and use of the HRAF files: A research and teaching guide*. New Haven, CT: Human Relations Area Files Inc.

Lagacé, R.O. (1979). The HRAF probability sample: Retrospect and prospect. *Behavior Science Research*, *14*, 211–229.

Lakatos, I. (1970). Falsification and the methodology of scientific research programmes. In I. Lakatos & A. Musgrave (Eds.), *Criticism and the growth of knowledge* (pp. 91-196). Cambridge: Cambridge University Press.

Langner, T.S. (1962). A twenty-two-item screening scale of psychiatric symptoms indicating impairment. *Journal of Health and Human Behavior*, *3*, 269–276.

Lee, D.D. (1949). Being and value in a primitive culture. *Journal of Philosophy*, *48*, 401–415.

Lefcourt, H.M. (1982). *Locus of control: Current trends in theory and research* (2nd ed.). Hillsdale, NJ: Lawrence Erlbaum.

Levine, M.V., & Drasgow, F. (1982). Appropriate measurement: Review, critique and validating studies. *British Journal of Mathematical and Statistical Psychology*, *35*, 42–56.

LeVine, R.A. (1970). Cross-cultural study in child psychology. In P. Mussen (Ed.), *Carmichael's manual of child psychology* (3rd ed.) (Vol. 2) (pp. 559–612). New York: John Wiley.

LeVine, R.A., & Campbell, D.T. (1965). *Ethnocentrism field manual*. The Cross-Cultural Study of Ethnocentrism. Supported by a grant from the Carnegie Corporation of New York to Northwestern University.

LeVine, R.A., Klein, N.H., & Owen, C.R. (1967). Father-child relationships and changing life-styles in Ibadan, Nigeria. In H. Miner (Ed.), *The city in modern Africa* (pp. 215–255). New York: Praeger.

Levine, R.V., & Bartlett, K. (1984). Pace of life, punctuality, and coronary heart disease in six countries. *Journal of Cross-Cultural Psychology*, *15*, 233–255.

Lewis, O. (1966). *La vida*. New York: Random House.

Lindenbaum, S. (1979). *Kuru sorcery*. Palo Alto, CA: Mayfield.

Lindzey, G. (1961). *Projective techniques and cross-cultural research*. New York: Appleton-Century-Crofts.

Liska, A.E. (1974). Emergent issues in the attitude-behavior consistency controversy. *American Sociological Review*, *39*, 261–272.

Longabaugh, R. (1980). The systematic observation of behavior in naturalistic settings. In H.C. Triandis & J.W. Berry (Eds.), *Handbook of cross-cultural psychology* (Vol. 2). *Methodology*. Boston: Allyn & Bacon.

Lonner, W.J. (1980a). A decade of cross-cultural psychology: JCCP, 1970–1979. *Journal of Cross-Cultural Psychology*, *11*, 7–34.

Lonner, W.J. (1980b). The search for psychological universals. In H.C. Triandis & W.W. Lambert (Eds.), *Handbook of cross-cultural psychology* (Vol. 1). *Perspectives* (pp. 143–204). Boston: Allyn & Bacon.

Lonner, W.J. (1981). Psychological tests and intercultural counseling. In P. Pedersen, J. Draguns, W. Lonner, & J. Trimble (Eds.), *Cross-cultural counseling* (2nd ed.). Honolulu: University of Hawaii Press.

Lord, F.M. (1977). A study of item bias, using item characteristics curve theory. In Y.H. Poortinga (Ed.), *Basic problems in cross-cultural psychology*. Amsterdam: Swets & Zeitlinger.

Lord, F.M. (1980). Applications of item response theory to practical testing problems. Hillsdale, NJ: Lawrence Erlbaum.

Lorenz, K. (1966). *On aggression*. New York: Harcourt Brace Jovanovich.

Lykken, D.T. (1968). Statistical significance in psychological research. *Psychological Bulletin, 70*, 151–159.

MacArthur, R.S., Irvine, S.H., & Brimble, A.R. (1964). *The Northern Rhodesia mental ability survey*. Lusaka, Zambia: Rhodes–Livingstone Institute.

Macdonald, A. (1945). *Selection of African personnel*. Report of the Personnel & Technical Research Unit, M.E.F. London: Ministry of Defence Archives.

Magnusson, D., & Stattin, H. (1978). A cross-cultural comparison of anxiety responses in an interactional frame of reference. *International Journal of Psychology, 13*, 317–322.

Malinowski, B. (1922). *Argonauts of the western Pacific*. London: Routledge & Kegan Paul.

Malinowski, B. (1927). *Sex and repression in savage society*. London: Kegan Paul.

Malinowski, B. (1929). *The sexual life of savages in northwestern Melanesia*. London: Kegan Paul.

Malinowski, B. (1935). *Coral gardens and their magic* (2 vols.). London: George Allen & Unwin.

Malpass, R. (1977a). On the theoretical basis of methodology: A return to basics. In Y.H. Poortinga (Ed.), *Basic problems in cross-cultural psychology*. Amsterdam: Swets & Zeitlinger.

Malpass, R. (1977b). Theory and method in cross-cultural psychology. *American Psychologist, 32*, 1069–1079.

Manaster, G.J., & Havighurst, R.J. (1972). *Cross-national research: Social psychological methods and problem*. Boston: Houghton Mifflin.

Mann, J. (1958). Group relations and the marginal man. *Human Relations, 11*, 77–92.

Marsella, A.J. (1985). The measurement of depressive experience and disorder across cultures. In A.J. Marsella, R. Hirschfield, & M. Katz (Eds.), *The measurement of depressive disorders: Biological, psychological, psychosocial and clinical perspectives*. New York: Guilford.

Masuda, M., Lin, K., & Tazuma, L. (1979–80). Adaptation problems of Vietnamese refugees. *Archives of General Psychiatry, 36–37*, 955–961, 447–450.

McClelland, D.C. (1961). *The achieving society*. Princeton, NJ: Van Nostrand.

McGuire, W.J. (1967). Some impending reorientations in social psychology: Some thoughts provoked by Kenneth Ring. *Journal of Experimental Social Psychology, 3*, 124–139.

McLaughlin, J.D., Helms, E., & Howe, M.G. (1983). Note on the reliability of three MMPI short forms. *Journal of Personality Assessment, 47*, 357–358.

Mead, M. (1956). *New lives for old*. New York: Morrow.

Meehl, P.E. (1978). Theoretical risks and tabular asterisks: Sir Karl, Sir Ronald, and the slow progress of soft psychology. *Journal of Consulting and Clinical*

Psychology, *46*, 806–834.

Mellenbergh, G.J. (1982). Contingency table models for assessing item bias. *Journal of Educational Statistics*, *7*, 105–118.

Mellenbergh, G.J. (1983). Conditional item bias methods. In S.H. Irvine & J.W. Berry (Eds.), *Human assessment and cultural factors* (pp. 293–302). New York: Plenum.

Mercer, J.R. (1976). Pluralistic diagnosis in the evaluation of Black and Chicano children: A procedure for taking sociocultural variables into account in clinical assessment. In C.A. Hernandez, M.J. Haug, & N.W. Wagner (Eds.), *Chicanos: Social and psychological perspectives* (2nd ed.). St Louis: C.V. Mosby.

Mercer, J.R. (1977). Identifying the gifted Chicano child. In J.L. Martinez, Jr (Ed.), *Chicano psychology*. New York: Academic Press.

Merck manual of diagnosis and therapy, The (1982) (14th ed.). Rahway, NJ: Merck, Sharp and Dohme Research Laboratories.

Milgram, S,. & Toch, H. (1969). Collective behavior: Crowds and social movements. In G. Lindzey & E. Aronson (Eds.), *The handbook of social psychology* (3rd ed.) (Vol. 4). *Group psychology and phenomena of interactions* (pp. 507–610). Reading MA: Addison-Wesley.

Miller, J., Slomczynski, K., & Schoenberg, R. (1981). Assessing comparability of measurement in cross-national research: Authoritarian-conservatism in different sociocultural settings. *Social Psychology Quarterly*, *44*, 173–191.

Mischel, W. (1968). *Personality and assessment*. New York: John Wiley.

Mitchell, J.C. (1959). *The Kalela dance*. Manchester: Manchester University Press for the Rhodes–Livingstone Institute, Lusaka.

Molish, B. (1972). Projective methodologies. *Annual Review of Psychology*, *23*, 577–614.

Moore, F.W. (1970). The Human Relations Area Files. In R. Naroll & R. Cohen (Eds.), *Handbook of method in cultural anthropology*. New York: Natural History Press.

Morris, D., Collett, P., Marsh, P., & O'Shaughnessy, M. (1979). *Gestures: Their origins and distribution*. London: Jonathan Cape.

Munro, D. (1979). Locus of control of attribution: Factors among Blacks and Whites in Africa. *Journal of Cross-Cultural Psychology*, *10*, 157–172.

Munroe, R.H., & Munroe, R.L. (1971). Household density and infant care in an East African society. *Journal of Social Psychology*, *83*, 3–13.

Munroe, R.H, & Munroe, R.L. (1978). Compliance socialization and short-term memory in an East African society. *Journal of Social Psychology*, *104*, 135–136.

Munroe, R.H., & Munroe, R.L. (1980). Infant experience and childhood affect among the Logoli: A longitudinal study. *Ethos*, *8*, 295–315.

Munroe, R.H., Munroe, R.L., Michelson, C., Koel, A., Bolton, R., & Bolton, C. (1983). Time allocation in four societies. *Ethnology*, *22*, 355–370.

Munroe, R.H., Munroe, R.L., & Shimmin, H.S. (1984). Children's work in four cultures: Determinants and consequences. *American Anthropologist*, *86*, 369–379.

Munroe, R.L. (1964). *Couvade practices of the Black Carib: A psychological study*. Unpublished doctoral dissertation, Harvard University, Cambridge, MA.

Munroe, R.L., Munroe, R.H., & Whiting, J.W.M. (1973). The couvade: A psychological analysis. *Ethos*, *1*, 30–74.

Murdock, G.P. (1967). *Ethnographic atlas*. Pittsburgh: University of Pittsburgh Press.

Murdock, G.P. (1971). *Outline of cultural materials* (4th rev. ed.). New Haven, CT: HRAF Press.

Murdock, G.P., (1975) *Outline of the world cultures* (5th ed.). New Haven, CT: HRAF Press.

Murdock, G.P., Ford, C.S., Hudson, A.E., Kennedy, R., Simmons, L.W., & Whiting, J.W.M. (1971). *Outline of cultural materials* (4th ed.). New Haven, CT: HRAF Press.

Murray, H.A. (1938). *Explorations in personality*. New York: Oxford University Press.

Nagelschmidt, A.M., & Jakob, R. (1977). Dimensionality of Rotter's I–E scale in a society in the process of modernization. *Journal of Cross-Cultural Psychology*, *8*, 101–112.

Naroll, R. (1970). Cross-cultural sampling. In R. Naroll & R. Cohen (Eds.), *Handbook of method in cultural anthropology*. New York: Natural History Press.

Naroll, R., & Cohen, R. (Eds.) (1970). *A handbook of method in cultural anthropology*. New York: Natural History Press.

Naroll, R., Michik, G., & Naroll, F. (1976). *Worldwide theory testing*. New Haven, CT: HRAF Press.

Naroll, R., Michik, G., & Naroll, F. (1980). Holocultural research methods. In H.C. Triandis & J.W. Berry (Eds.), *Handbook of cross-cultural psychology* (Vol. 2). *Methodology*. Boston: Allyn & Bacon.

Nerlove, S.B., Munroe, R.H., & Munroe, R.L. (1971). Effect of environmental experience on spatial ability: A replication. *Journal of Social Psychology*, *84*, 3–10.

Nerlove, S.B., Roberts, J.M., & Klein, R.E. (1975). Dimensions of listura ("smartness"): Community judgments of rural Guatemalan children. Paper presented at the meeting of the Society for Research in Child Development, Denver, CO.

Niles, F.S. (1981). Dimensionality of Rotter's I–E scale in Sri Lanka. *Journal of Cross-Cultural Psychology*, *12*, 473–479.

O'Bryan, K., Reitz, G., & Kuplowska, O. (1976). *Non-official languages study*. Ottawa: Supply and Services.

Oliver, R.A.C. (1932). The musical talents of natives in East Africa. *British Journal of Psychology*, *22*, 333–343.

Olmedo, E.L. (1978). Empirical and construct validation of a measure of acculturation for Mexican Americans. *Journal of Social Psychology*, *105*, 179–187.

Olmedo, E.L. (1979). Acculturation: A psychometric perspective. *American Psychologist*, *34*, 1061–1070.

Olmedo, E.L. (1981). Testing linguistic minorities. *American Psychologist*, *36*, 1078–1085.

Olmedo, E.L., Martinez, J.L., & Martinez, S.R. (1978). Measure of acculturation for Chicano adolescents. *Psychological Reports*, *42*, 159–170.

Olmedo, E.L., & Padilla, A.M. (1978). Empirical and construct validation of a measure of acculturation for Mexican Americans. *Journal of Social Psychology*, *105*, 179–187.

Ord, I.G. (1971). *Mental tests for preliterates*. London: Ginn.

Osgood, C. (1940). *Ingalik material culture*. New Haven, CT: Yale University Press (Yale University Publications in Anthropology no. 22).

Osgood, C.E., May, W.H., & Miron, M.S. (1975). *Cross-cultural universals of affective meaning*. Urbana, IL: University of Illinois Press.

Otterbein, K.F. (1972). *Comparative cultural analysis*. New York: Holt, Rinehart & Winston.

Padilla, A. (1980a). *Acculturation: Theory, models and some new findings*. Boulder, CO: Westview Press.

Padilla, A. (1980b). The role of cultural awareness and ethnic loyalty in acculturation. In A. Padilla (Ed.), *Acculturation: Theory, models and some new findings*. Boulder, CO: Westview Press.

Pareek, U., & Rao, T.V. (1980). Cross-cultural surveys and interviewing. In H.C. Triandis & J.W. Berry (Eds.), *Handbook of cross-cultural psychology* (Vol. 2). *Methodology* (pp. 127–179). Boston: Allyn & Bacon.

Pearlin, L. (1962). Alienation from work: A study of nursing personnel. *American Sociological Review, 27*, 314–326.

Peck, R., et al. (1976). A test of the universality of an acculturation gradient in three-culture triads. In K. Riegel & J. Meacham (Eds.), *The developing individual in a changing world*. The Hague: Mouton.

Pelto, P.J., & Pelto, G.H. (1973). Ethnography: The fieldwork enterprise. In J.J. Honigmann (Ed.), *Handbook of social and cultural anthropology* (pp. 241–288). Chicago: Rand-McNally.

Pelto, P.J., & Pelto, G.H. (1978). *Anthropological research* (2nd ed.). Cambridge: Cambridge University Press.

Perera, M., & Eysenck, S.B.G. (1984). A cross-cultural study of personality: Sri Lanka and England. *Journal of Cross-Cultural Psychology, 15*, 353–371.

Petersen, N.S., & Novick, M.R. (1976). An evaluation of some models for culture-fair selection. *Journal of Educational Measurement, 13*, 3–29.

Phares, E.J. (1976). *Locus of control in personality*. Morristown, NJ: General Learning Press.

Phares, E.J. (1984). *Introduction to personality*. Colombus, OH: Merrill.

Phillips, H. (1960). Problems of translation and meaning in field work. *Human Organization, 18*, 184–192.

Piaget, J. (1966). Nécessité et signification de recherches comparatives en psychologie génétique. *International Journal of Psychology, 1*, 3–13.

Piliavin, I.M., Rodin, J., & Piliavin, J.A. (1969). Good Samaritanism: An underground phenomenon? *Journal of Personality and Social Psychology, 13*, 289–299.

Pollack, R.H. (1970). Mueller-Lyer illusion: Effects of age, lightness contrast and hue. *Science, 170*, 93–94.

Pollnac, R.B. (1977). Illusion susceptibility and adaptation to the marine envrionment. *Journal of Cross-Cultural Psychology, 8*, 425–434.

Poortinga, Y.H. (1971). Cross-cultural comparison of maximum performance tests: Some methodological aspects and some experiments with simple auditory and visual stimuli. *Psychologia Africana*, Monograph Supplement No. 6.

Poortinga, Y.H. (1975a). Some implications of three different approaches to intercultural comparison. In J.W. Berry & W.J. Lonner (Eds.), *Applied cross-cultural psychology*. Amsterdam: Swets & Zeitlinger.

Poortinga, Y.H. (1975b). Limitations on intercultural comparison of psychological data. *Nederlands Tijdschrift voor de Psychologie, 30*, 23–39.

Poortinga, Y.H. (1982). Cross-culturele psychologie en minderhedenonderzoek

[Cross-cultural psychology and minority research]. *De Psycholoog, 17*, 708–720.

Poortinga, Y.H., & Foden, B.I.M. (1975). A comparative study of curiosity in black and white South African students. *Psychologia Africana Monographs, 8.*

Poortinga, Y.H., & Spies, E. (1972). An attempt to compare risk-taking in two culturally different groups. *Psychologica Africana, 14*, 186–199.

Posner, M., & Keele, S. (1967). Decay of visual information from a single letter. *Science, 158*, 137–139.

Pospisil, L. (1963). *Kapauku Papuan economy*. New Haven, CT: Yale University Press (Yale University Publications in Anthropology, 67).

Price, J.R. (1978). Conservation studies in Papua New Guinea: A review. *International Journal of Psychology, 13*, 1–24.

Price-Williams, D.R. (1961). A study concerning concepts of conservation among primitive children. *Acta Psychologica, 18*, 297–305.

Rannigan, R.L. (1985). *MMPI in testing, medicine and psychology*. Washington, DC: ABBE Publishers.

Redfield, R., Linton, R., & Herskovits, M.J. (1936). Memorandum on the study of acculturation. *American Anthropologist, 38*, 149–152.

Ring, K. (1967). Experimental social psychology: Some sober questions about some frivolous values. *Journal of Experimental Social Psychology, 3*, 113–123.

Rock, D.A., & Werts, C.E. (1979). *Construct validity of the SAT across populations. An empirical confirmatory study* (Report no. RR–79–2). Princeton, NJ: Educational Testing Service.

Rock, D.A., Werts, C., & Grandy, J. (1982). *Construct validity of the GRE aptitude test across populations. An empirical confirmatory study* (Research Report no. 81–57). Princeton, NJ: Educational Testing Service.

Rogoff, B. (1981). Schooling and the development of cognitive skills. In H.C. Triandis & A. Heron (Eds.), *Handbook of cross-cultural psychology* (Vol. 4). *Development*. Boston: Allyn & Bacon.

Rohner, R.P. (1975). Parental acceptance-rejection and personality development: A universalist approach to behavioral science. In R.W. Brislin, S. Bochner, & W.J. Lonner (Eds.), *Cross-cultural perspectives on learning*. New York: Sage/Halsted.

Rohner, R.P., DeWalt, B.R., & Ness, R.C. (1973). Ethnographer bias in cross-cultural research: An empirical study. *Behavior Science Notes, 8*, 275–317.

Rohner, R.P, Naroll, R., Barry, H., Divale, W.T., Erickson, E.E., Schaefer, J.M., & Sipes, R.G. (1978). Guidelines for holocultural research. *Current Anthropology, 19*, 128–129.

Rokeach, M., & Mezei, L. (1966). Race and shared belief as factors in social choice. *Science, 151*, 167–172.

Rokkan, S. (1968). *Comparative research across cultures and nations*. Paris: Mouton.

Romney, A.K. (1965). Kalmuk Mongol and the classification of linear kinship terminologies. *American Anthropologist, 67*, (no. 5, part 2, Special Publication), 127–141.

Romney, A.K., & D'Andrade, R.G. (1964). Cognitive aspects of English kin terms. *American Anthropologist, 66* (no. 3, part 2, Special Publication), 146–170.

Roskam, E.E. (1976). Multivariate analysis of change and growth: Critical review and perspectives. In D.N.M. de Gruyter & L.J.T. van der Kamp (Eds.), *Advances in psychological and educational measurement* (pp. 111–134). London: John Wiley.

Rotter, J.B. (1966). Generalized expectancies for internal versus external control of reinforcement. *Psychological Monographs, 80*, (whole no. 609).

Royal Anthropological Institute (1951). *Notes and queries on anthropology* (6th ed.). London: Routledge & Kegan Paul.

Rudner, L.M., Getson, P.M., & Knight, D.L. (1980). Biased item techniques. *Journal of Educational Statistics, 5*, 213–233.

Rynkiewich, M.A., & Spradley, J.P. (Eds.) (1976). *Ethics and anthropology: Dilemmas in field work*. New York: John Wiley.

Samuda, R. (1983). Cross-cultural testing within a multicultural society. In S.H. Irvine & J.W. Berry (Eds.), *Human assessment and cultural factors*. New York: Plenum.

Sartorius, N., Shapiro, R., & Jablensky, A. (1974). The international pilot study of schizophrenia. *Schizophrenia Bulletin, 11*, 21–34.

Saunders, D.R. (1956). Moderator variables in prediction. *Educational and Psychological Measurement, 16*, 209–222.

Schieffelin, E.L. (1976). *The sorrow of the lonely and the burning of the dancers*. New York: St Martin's Press.

Schneider, K. (1971). *Klinische Psychopathologie* (9th ed.). Stuttgart: Springer-Verlag.

Schuman, H. (1966). The random probe: A technique for evaluating the quality of closed questions. *American Sociological Review, 31*, 218–222.

Schwartz, P.A. (1964). Adapting tests to the cultural setting. *Educational and Psychological Measurement, 23*, 673–686.

Scribner, S. (1974). Developmental aspects of free recall in West African society. *Cognitive Psychology, 6*, 475–494.

Scribner, S., & Cole, M. (1973). Cognitive consequences of formal and informal education. *Science, 182*, 553–559.

Scribner, S., & Cole, M. (1981). *The psychology of literacy*. Cambridge, MA: Harvard University Press.

Sears, R.R. (1961). Transcultural variables and conceptual equivalence. In B. Kaplan (Ed.), *Studying personality cross-culturally* (pp. 445–455). Evanston, IL: Row & Peterson.

Sechrest, L., (1970). Experiments in the field. In R. Naroll & R. Cohen, *Handbook of method in cultural anthropology*. Garden City, NJ: Natural History Press.

Sechrest, L. (1975). Another look at unobtrusive measures: An alternative to what? In W. Sinaiko & L. Broedling (Eds.), *Perspectives on attitude assessment: Surveys and their alternatives*. Washington, DC: Smithsonian Institution.

Sechrest, L. (1977a). On the dearth of theory in cross-cultural psychology: There is madness in our method. In Y.H. Poortinga (Ed.), *Basic problems in cross-cultural psychology* (pp. 73–82). Amsterdam: Swets & Zeitlinger.

Sechrest, L. (1977b). On the need for experimentation in cross-cultural research. In L.L. Adler (Ed.), *Annals of the New York Academy of Sciences: Issues in cross-cultural research* (Vol. 285) (pp. 104–118). New York: New York Academy of Sciences.

Sechrest, L. (Ed.) (1979). *Unobtrusive measurement today: New directions for methodology of behavioral science*. San Francisco: Jossey-Bass.

Segall, M.H. (1981). Cross-cultural research on visual perception. In M.B. Brewer & C.B. Collins (Eds.), *Scientific inquiry and the social sciences* (pp. 361–384). San Francisco: Jossey-Bass.

Segall, M.H. (1983). On the search for the independent variable in cross-cultural psychology. In S.H. Irvine & J.W. Berry (Eds.), *Human assessment and cultural factors* (pp. 127–138). New York: Plenum.

Segall, M.H., Campbell, D.T., & Herskovits, M.J. (1966). *The influence of culture on visual perception.* Indianapolis: Bobbs-Merrill.

Segall, M.H., Doornbos, M., & Davis, C. (1976). *Political identity: A case study from Uganda.* Syracuse, NY: Maxwell Foreign and Comparative Studies/East Africa XXIV.

Seligman, M. (1975). *Helplessness.* San Francisco: W.H. Freeman.

Serpell, R. (1976). *Culture's influence on behavior.* London: Methuen.

Serpell, R. (1979). How specific are perceptual skills? *British Journal of Psychology, 70,* 365–380.

Serpell, R., & Deregowski, J.B. (1980). The skill of pictorial perception: An interpretation of cross-cultural evidence. *International Journal of Psychology, 15,* 145–180.

Seymour, S. (1980). Patterns of childbearing in a changing Indian town. In S. Seymour (Ed.), *The transformation of a sacred town: Bhubaneswar, India* (pp. 121–154). Boulder, CO: Westview.

Shaffer, L.S. (1977). The golden fleece: Anti-intellectualism and social science. *American Psychologist, 32,* 814–823.

Shepard, L., Camilli, G., & Averill, M. (1981). Comparison of six procedures for detecting test item bias using both internal and external ability criteria. *Journal of Educational Statistics, 6,* 317–375.

Sherif, M., & Sherif, C. (1969). *Social psychology.* New York: Harper & Row.

Silverman, M.G. (1972). Ambiguation and disambiguation in field work. In S.T. Kimball & J.B. Watson (Eds.), *Crossing cultural boundaries* (pp. 204–229). San Francisco: Chandler.

Silvey, J. (1983). Recent issues in educational selection in the Third World. In S.H. Irvine & J.W. Berry (Eds.), *Human assessment and cultural factors.* New York: Plenum.

Smith, L. (Ed.) (1981). *English for cross-cultural communication.* London: Macmillan.

Social Science Research Council (1954). Acculturation: An exploratory formulation. *American Anthropologist, 56,* 973–1002.

Sommerlad, E.A., & Berry J.W. (1970). The role of ethnic identification in distinguishing between attitudes towards assimilation and integration of a minority racial group. *Human Relations, 23,* 23–29.

Spain, D.H. (1972). On the use of projective techniques for psychological anthropology. In F.L.K. Hsu (Ed.), *Psychological anthropology* (new ed.). Cambridge, MA: Schenkman.

Spielberger, C.D., & Diaz-Guerrero, R. (1976). *Cross-cultural anxiety.* New York: John Wiley.

Spielberger, C.D., & Diaz-Guerrero, R. (1983). *Cross-cultural anxiety* (Vol. 2). New York: McGraw-Hill.

Spielberger, C.D., Gorsuch, R.L., & Lushene, R.E. (1970). *State–trait anxiety inventory.* Palo Alto, CA: Consulting Psychologists Press.

Spindler, G.D. (1968). Psychocultural adaptation. In E. Norbeck, D. Price-Williams, & W. McCord (Eds.), *The study of personality: An inter-disciplinary appraisal.* New York: Holt, Rinehart & Winston.

Spindler, G.D. (Ed.) (1970). *Being an anthropologist.* New York: Holt, Rinehart & Winston.

Spindler, G.D. (Ed.) (1978). *The making of psychological anthropology.* Berkeley,

CA: University of California Press.

Spindler, G.D., & Spindler, L. (1963). Psychology in anthropology: Applications to culture change. In S. Koch (Ed.), *Psychology: A study of a science*. New York: McGraw-Hill.

Spindler, L. (1978). Researching the psychology of cultural change and urbanization. In G.D. Spindler (Ed.), *The making of psychological anthropology* (pp. 176–200). Berkeley, CA: University of California Press.

Spindler, L., & Spindler, G. (1958). Male and female adaptation in culture change. *American Anthropologist, 60*, 217–233.

Spradley, J.P., & McCurdy, D.W. (1972). *The cultural experience: Ethnography in complex society*. Chicago: SRA.

Srole, L., Langner, T.S., & Michael, S.T. (1962). *Mental health in the metropolis*. New York: McGraw-Hill.

Stewart, M.V. (1973). Tests of the "carpentered world" hypothesis by race and environment in America and Zambia. *International Journal of Psychology, 8*, 83–94.

Stocking, G.W., Jr (1983). The ethnographer's magic: Fieldwork in British anthropology from Tylor to Malinowski. In G.W. Stocking, Jr (Ed.), *Observers observed: History of anthropology* (Vol. 1) (pp. 70–120). Madison, WI: University of Wisconsin Press.

Stonequist, E.V. (1935). The problem of the marginal man. *American Journal of Sociology, 41*, 1–12.

Strodtbeck. F.L. (1964). Considerations of metamethod in cross-cultural studies. *American Anthropologist* (Special publication), *66* (3, part 2), 223–229.

Sudman, S. (1976). *Applied sampling*. New York: Academic Press.

Sundberg, N.D., & Gonzales, L.R. (1981). Cross-cultural and cross-ethnic assessment: Overview and issues. In P. McReynolds (Ed.), *Advances in psychological assessment* (Vol. 5). San Francisco: Jossey-Bass.

Taft, R. (1966). *From stranger to citizen*. Perth: University of Western Australia Press.

Taft, R. (1976a). Cross-cultural psychology as a social science: Comments on Faucheux's paper. *European Journal of Social Psychology, 6*, 323–330.

Taft, R. (1976b). The Australianism scale re-visited: A review of recent data. *Australian Psychologist, 11*, 147–151.

Taft, R. (1977). Coping with unfamiliar cultures. In N. Warren (Ed.), *Studies in cross-cultural psychology* (Vol. 1). London: Academic Press.

Tapp, J.L., Kelman, H.C., Triandis, H.C., Wrightsman, L.S., & Coelho, G.V. (1974). Continuing concerns in cross-cultural ethics: A report. *International Journal of Psychology, 9*, 231–249.

Tatsuoka, K.K., & Tatsuoka, M.M. (1982). Detection of aberrant response patterns and their effect on dimensionality. *Journal of Educational Statistics, 7*, 215–231.

Thayer, S. (1973). Lend me your ears: Racial and sexual factors in helping the deaf. *Journal of Personality and Social Psychology, 28*, 8–11.

Thorndike, R.L. (1971). Concepts of culture-fairness. *Journal of Educational Measurement, 8*, 63–70.

Tinbergen, N. (1951). *The study of instinct*. Oxford: Clarendon Press.

Triandis, H.C. (1972). *The analysis of subjective culture*. New York: John Wiley.

Triandis, H.C. (1976). On the value of cross-cultural research in social psychology: Reactions to Faucheux's paper. *European Journal of Psychology, 6*, 331–341.

Triandis, H.C. (1977). *Interpersonal behavior*. Monterey, CA: Brooks/Cole.

Triandis, H.C. (1980a). Introduction. In H.C. Triandis & W.W. Lambert (Eds.), *Handbook of cross-cultural psychology* (Vol. 1). *Perspectives* (pp. 1–14). Boston: Allyn & Bacon.

Triandis, H.C. (1980b). Preface. In H.C. Triandis & W.W. Lambert (Eds.), *Handbook of cross-cultural psychology* (Vol. 1). *Perspectives* (pp. ix–xv). Boston: Allyn & Bacon.

Triandis, H.C. et al. (Eds.) (1980–81). *Handbook of cross-cultural psychology* (6 vols.). Boston: Allyn & Bacon.

Trimble, J.E. (1980). Forced migration: Its impact on shaping coping strategies. In G. Coelho & P. Ahmed (Eds.), *Uprooting and developing*. New York: Plenum.

Trimble, J.E., Lonner, W.J., & Boucher, J. (1983). Stalking the wily emic. In S.H. Irvine & J.W. Berry (Eds.), *Human assessment and cultural factors*. New York: Plenum.

Trimble, J.E., & Richardson, S.S. (1982). Locus of control measures among American Indians: Cluster structure analytic characteristics. *Journal of Cross-Cultural Psychology*, *13*, 228–238.

Trimble, J.E., & Richardson, S.S. (1983). American Indian and Alaskan Native student attitudes toward self and school. Unpublished research monograph, Western Washington University, Bellingham, WA.

Tseng, O.C.S. (1977). Differentiation of affective and denotative semantic subspaces. In L.L. Adler (Ed.), *Annals of the New York Academy of Sciences: Issues in cross-cultural research* (Vol. 285) (pp. 476–500). New York: New York Academy of Sciences.

Tseng, O.C.S., & Tseng, C. (1982). Implicit personality theory: Myth or fact? An illustration of how empirical research can miss. *Journal of Personality Theory*, *50*, 223–239.

Tsujioka, B., & Cattell, R.B. (1965). A cross-cultural comparison of second-stratum questionnaire factor structures—anxiety and extraversion—in America and Japan. *Journal of Social Psychology*, *65*, 205–219.

Uberoi, J.P.S. (1962). *Politics of the Kula Ring*. Manchester: Manchester University Press.

van de Koppel, J.M.H. (1983). *A developmental study of the Biaka Pygmies and the Bangandou*. Amsterdam: Swets & Zeitlinger.

Van der Flier, H. (1982). Deviant response patterns and comparability of test scores. *Journal of Cross-Cultural Psychology*, *13*, 267–298.

Van der Flier, H., Mellenbergh, G.J., Ader, J.H., & Wijn, M. (1984). An iterative item bias detection method. *Journal of Educational Measurement*, *21*, 131–145.

Van de Vijver, F.J.R., & Poortinga, Y.H. (1982). Cross-cultural generalization and universality. *Journal of Cross-Cultural Psychology*, *13*, 387–408.

Vernon, P.E. (1969). *Intelligence and cultural environment*. London: Methuen.

Vernon, P.E. (1979). *Intelligence: Heredity and Environment*. San Francisco: W.H. Freeman.

Verster, J.M. (1983). The structure, organization and correlates of cognitive speed and accuracy. In S.H. Irvine and J.W. Berry (Eds.), *Human assessment and cultural factors*. New York: Plenum.

Voegelin, C.F., & Voegelin, F.M. (1977). *Classification and index of the world's languages*. New York: Elsevier.

Wagner, D.A. (1981). Culture and memory development. In H.C. Triandis & A. Heron (Eds.), *Handbook of cross-cultural psychology* (Vol. 4). *Development*. Boston: Allyn & Bacon.

Wagner, D.A., Messick, B.M., & Spratt, J. (in press). Studying literacy in Morocco. In B.B. Schieffelin & P. Gilmore (Eds.), *The acquisition of literacy*. Norwood, NJ: Ablex.

Warren, N. (1980). Universality and plasticity, ontogeny and phylogeny: The resonance between culture and cognitive development. In J. Sants (Ed.), *Developmental psychology and society* (pp. 290–326). London: Macmillan.

Warwick. D.P. (1980). The politics and ethics of cross-cultural research. In H.C. Triandis & W.W. Lambert (Ed.), *Handbook of cross-cultural psychology* (Vol. 1). *Perspectives* (pp. 319–371). Boston: Allyn & Bacon.

Warwick, D.P., & Lininger, C. (1975). *The sample survey: Theory and practice*. New York: McGraw-Hill.

Warwick, D.P., & Osheron, S. (1973). *Comparative Research Methods*. Englewood Cliffs, NJ: Prentice-Hall.

Watrous, B., & Hsu, F.L.K. (1972). An experiment with TAT. In F.L.K. Hsu (Ed.), *Psychological Anthropology* (pp. 309–362). Cambridge, MA: Schenkman.

Watson, J.B. (1972). Talking to strangers. In S.T. Kimball & J.B. Watson (Eds.), *Crossing cultural boundaries* (pp. 172–181). San Francisco: Chandler.

Webb, E.J., Campbell, D.T., Schwartz, R.D., & Sechrest, L. (1966). *Unobtrusive measures: Nonreactive research in the social sciences*. Chicago: Rand-McNally.

Weiner, A.B. (1976). *Women of value, men of renown*. Austin: University of Texas Press.

Weisz, J.R., Rothbaum, F.M., & Blackburn, T.C. (1984). Standing out and standing in: The psychology of control in America and Japan. *American Psychologist, 39*, 955–969.

Werner, D. (1984). *Amazon journey*. New York: Simon and Schuster.

Werner, E.E., & Smith, R.S. (1982). *Vulnerable but invincible: A longitudinal study of resilient children and youth*. New York: McGraw-Hill.

Werner, O., & Campbell, D. (1970). Translating, working through interpreters, and the problem of decentering. In R. Naroll & R. Cohen (Eds.), *A handbook of method in cultural anthropology*. New York: Natural History Press (reprinted in 1973 by Columbia University Press).

Wesley, R., & Karr, C. (1966). Problems in establishing norms for cross-cultural comparison. *International Journal of Psychology*, 1, 257–262.

Whiting, B.B., & Whiting, J.W.M. (1975). *Children of six cultures: A psychocultural analysis*. Cambridge, MA: Harvard University Press.

Whiting, J.W.M. (1968). Methods and problems in cross-cultural research. In G. Lindzey & E. Aronson (Eds.), *The handbook of social psychology* (Vol. 2) (2nd ed.) (pp. 693–728). Reading, MA: Addison-Wesley.

Whiting, J.W.M. (1970). *Progress report*. Nairobi: Child Development Research Unit, University of Nairobi.

Whiting, J.W.M., Child, I.L., & Lambert, W.E. (1966). *Field guide for a study of socialization: Six cultures series* (Vol. 1). New York: John Wiley.

Whiting, J.W.M., & Whiting, B.B. (1978). A strategy for psychocultural research. In G.D. Spindler (Ed.), *The making of psychological anthropology*. Berkeley, CA: University of California Press.

Whyte, W.F. (1984). *Learning from the field*. Beverly Hills, CA: Sage.

Wicker, A.W. (1969). Attitudes versus actions: The relationship of verbal and behavioral responses to attitude objects. *Journal of Social Issues*, 25, (4), 41–78.

Wigdor, A.K., & Gardner, W.R. (1982). *Ability testing: Uses, consequences, and controversies*. Washington, DC: National Academy Press.

Wiggins, J.S. (1973). *Personality and prediction: Principles of personality assessment*. Reading, MA: Addison-Wesley.

Williams, J.E., & Best, D.L. (1982). *Measuring sex stereotypes*. Beverly Hills, CA: Sage.

Williams, T.R. (1967). *Field methods in the study of culture*. New York: Holt, Rinehart & Winston.

Wing, J.K., Cooper, J.E., & Sartorius, N. (1974). *The measurement and classification of psychiatric symptoms*. New York: Cambridge University Press.

Wintrob, R.M., & Sindell, P.S. (1972). Culture change and psychopathology: The case of Cree adolescent students in Quebec. In J.W. Berry & G.J.S. Wilde (Eds.), *Social psychology: The Canadian context*. Toronto: McClelland and Stewart.

Witkin, H.A., & Berry, J.W. (1975). Psychological differentiation in cross-cultural perspective. *Journal of Cross-Cultural Psychology*, 6, 4–87.

Witkin, H.A., & Goodenough, D.R. (1981). *Cognitive styles: Essence and origins*. New York: International Universities Press.

Wober, M. (1966). Sensotypes. *Journal of Social Psychology*, 70, 181–189.

Wober, M. (1969). Distinguishing centri-cultural from cross-cultural tests and research. *Perceptual and motor skills*, 28, 488.

Wolf, E.R. (1982). *Europe and the people without history*. Berkeley, CA: University of California Press.

World Health Organization. (1983). *Depressive disorders in different cultures*. Geneva: World Health Organization.

Zepp, R. (1983). A West African replication of the four-card problem. *Journal of Cross-Cultural Psychology*, 14, 323–327.

Author Index

Subject Index

About the Contributors

JOHN W. BERRY, whose Ph.D. is from the University of Edinburgh, is Professor of Psychology at Queen's University, Kingston, Ontario. A Canadian by birth, Berry has done extensive field work in several countries and for twenty years has been an influential contributor to the cross-cultural psychological literature. He is a past president of the International Association for Cross-Cultural Psychology.

RICHARD W. BRISLIN is a Research Associate at the East-West Center's Institute of Culture and Communication in Honolulu, Hawaii. His research interests include the preparation and training of individuals who anticipate foreign travel or work. Brislin is senior author of *Intercultural Interactions: A Practical Guide*, recently published by Sage Publications.

STEPHEN BOCHNER is Senior Lecturer in the School of Psychology, University of New South Wales, Kensington, NSW, Australia. A number of Bochner's publications concern adjustment problems encountered during various types of international travel. Among his newest books, written with Dr. Adrian Furnham of London, is *Culture Shock: Psychological Reactions to Unfamiliar Environments* (Methuen, 1986).

GEORGE M. GUTHRIE is a Professor in the Department of Psychology at The Pennsylvania State University, University Park, Pennsylvania. His cross-cultural research has primarily focused on the Philippines. A clinical psychologist, Guthrie has been concerned with the psychological consequences of modernization, the measurement of personality and psychopathology, and how people adapt to alien cultures.

SYDNEY H. IRVINE is Professor of Psychology at Plymouth Polytechnic University. Plymouth, England. He is widely known for his numerous pioneering cross-cultural research efforts, primarily in Africa and most notably in the area focusing on the factorial structure of human performance and abilities. He recently edited (with J.W. Berry) *Human Assessment and Cultural Factors* (Plenum, 1983).

WALTER J. LONNER lives in Bellingham, Washington where he is Professor of Psychology at Western Washington University. He is Founding Editor of the *Journal of Cross-Cultural Psychology*. His research efforts have taken him to Alaska, various

European countries, and Mexico. Lonner is President-elect of the International Association for Cross-Cultural Psychology, an office he will hold during 1986–88.

ROY S. MALPASS directs the Behavioural Science Program at the State University of New York, in Plattsburgh. Malpass has served as Editor of the *Journal of Cross-Cultural Psychology* for five years and earlier served as its Book Review Editor. In addition to his many contributions to cross-cultural psychology, he continues with a strong research program in the domain of eyewitness identification and testimony.

ROBERT L. MUNROE was trained b y John and Beatrice Whiting at Harvard University where he received his Ph.D. in Social Anthropology in 1964. He has conducted field work in Africa, Belize, North America, Asia, and the Pacific. With Ruth H. Munroe and Beatrice B. Whiting, he is co-editor of *The Handbook of Cross-Cultural Human Development*. He is Professor of Anthropology at Pitzer College, Claremont, California.

RUTH H. MUNROE, Professor of Psychology at Pitzer College and the Claremont Graduate School, received her Ed.D. from Harvard in 1964. She has done fieldwork in Belise, Kenya, American Samoa, and Nepal, emphasizing the study of cultural differences in socialization practices and the subsequent developmental differences in children. Her numerous publications include a special 1973 co-edited issue of *Ethos*, which contained essays in honor of J.W.M. Whiting.

ESTEBAN L. OLMEDO is currently Dean of Academic and Professional Affairs, California School of Professional Psychology in Los Angeles, California. Formerly, he was the Administrative Officer for the Office of Minority Affairs in the American Psychological Association. His major interests include the psychology of ethnic groups with a specific emphasis in acculturation, racial discrimination, and cross-cultural training issues.

YPE H. POORTINGA is a Professor in the Department of Psychology at Tilburg University, Tilburg, the Netherlands. His main cross-cultural research interests involve problems of methodology and research design. For several years he served as Secretary-General of the International Association for Cross-Cultural Psychology. Poortinga has done extensive field work in Africa and India, as well as in Europe.

MARSHALL H. SEGALL is a Professor of Social psychology at the Maxwell School, Syracuse University, Syracuse, New York. His text (with Donald Campbell and Melville Herskovits), *The Influence of Culture on Visual Perception*, has become a classic since its publication in 1966. He also edited (with A. Goldstein) *Aggression in Global Perspective* (Pergamon, 1983). His undergraduate text in cross-cultural psychology is currently being revised.

JOSEPH E. TRIMBLE is Professor of Psychology at Western Washington University, Bellingham, Washington. Currently he is Treasurer of the International Association for Cross-Cultural Psychology. Trimble's research interests include the study of adaptive strategies of culturally diverse groups to life-threatening and problematic life events, use of behavior/cognitive-mediated strategies in mental health, and substance abuse prevention and intervention.